D0909400

Notes from a
Wayfarer

Notes from a Wayfarer

THE AUTOBIOGRAPHY OF
HELMUT THIELICKE

Translated by David R. Law

PARAGON HOUSE

First U.S. edition, 1995

Published in the United States by

Paragon House
370 Lexington Avenue
New York, NY 10017

Copyright © 1995 by Paragon House

Originally published in German under the title . . . *Zu Gast auf einem schönen Stern.*
Copyright © 1984 by Hoffman und Campe Verlag

Library of Congress Cataloging-in-Publication Data

Thielicke, Helmut
[Zu Gast auf einem schönen Stern. English]
Notes from a wayfarer : the autobiography of Helmut Thielicke /
translated by David R. Law.-1st U.S. ed.
p.   cm.
Translation of: Zu Gast auf einem schönen Stern.
Bibliography of the author's works in English: p.
ISBN 1-55778-708-5
1. Thielicke, Helmut, 1908–1986.   2. Lutheran Church—Germany
(West)—Clergy—Biography.   3. Theologians—Germany (West)—
Biography.   I. Title.
BX8080.T475A38   1995
230'.41'092—dc20
[B]   94-36935
CIP

Manufactured in the United States of America

*For my wife, who even through dark valleys
kept me from becoming lost in the hospitality of this beautiful world.*

I have had the good fortune to be blessed in my old age with thoughts that would truly be worth a second lifetime to pursue. Therefore as long as it's still light, let us not busy ourselves with trivialities.
—JOHANN WOLFGANG VON GOETHE

Such lovely weather—and I'm here to enjoy it!
—WILHELM RAABE

My hosanna has passed through the purgatory of doubt.
—FYODOR MIKHAILOVICH DOSTOYEVSKY

It is not that our life is slowly and surely dismantled till Death has come but that our death is dismantled until Life has encompassed us completely.
—JOACHIM BRAUN

Contents

The Student Revolt in University and Church   377

Into the Final Rounds   400

Finale   415

Select List of Publications in English   421

Foreword

I N 1959, the translator of *The Waiting Father* invited readers to sample what he considered "the greatest preaching being carried on anywhere in the world today." For more than three decades thereafter, American readers agreed with that judgment by buying every book of sermons by Helmut Thielicke as translations became available in English. Thielicke was hailed as a model for preachers and as a celebrity in educated lay circles. Thirty-five titles, some of them written thirty years before, appeared almost annually between 1959 and 1990—a rate of better than one per year.

Thielicke's introduction to the general public came through one man. John W. Doberstein was Professor of Practical Theology at the Lutheran School of Theology in Philadelphia. He had translated Bonhoeffer's *Life Together* for Harper and Row in 1954, and the immense success of that book gave Doberstein a powerful voice at Harper. His familiarity with German theological literature had led him to Thielicke's work, and he recognized how pertinent Thielicke's sermons would be to the American scene. When Doberstein told his editor that Thielicke would fill a void in American religious life, the publisher took the risk—and realized the benefits.

The initial response to the *The Waiting Father* was so great that Doberstein had to translate additional material as fast as he could. Collections of sermons on the Lord's Prayer, the creation accounts in Genesis, the sermon on the mount and other passages appeared in rapid order. Doberstein produced thirteen translations in seven years. In addition to Doberstein's work for Harper, two other publishers began to cash in on the Thielicke boom by bringing out translations in 1962. In that year four new titles appeared, in addition to reprints of the earlier books.

Thielicke was pleased. He wrote to his friends that he was being translated by "the translator of Bonhoeffer," which bode well for his readership in America and for his standing in Germany. He considered the relationship a "special providence" and told his readers that he was "an author who had been elevated beyond himself by the translator" [*Ethics of Sex*, Harper, 1964, vii]. His relationship to Doberstein grew during the ensuing years through a constant correspondence over points of interpretation. Doberstein wanted to make Thielicke speak as relevantly to American audiences as he did to his fellow Germans, and that often meant that illustrations or references to current events had to be modified. The author and his translator became so well acquainted with one another's thought that, when *The Trouble with the Church* was being translated in 1965, Thielicke suggested that Doberstein revise it by leaving out parts and rewriting others so that it would speak more specifically to the American scene. He offered to share the title page with Doberstein as co-author.

Doberstein died suddenly in 1965, just after beginning another translation. After him, other Lutherans took up the work, and Fortress Press, a Lutheran publisher, continued to bring out translations on a nearly annual basis. At the same time, the noted translator of Karl Barth, Geoffrey W. Bromiley, was producing a steady flow of translations for Eerdmans, a more conservative press. These works included Thielicke's three volume systematics, *The Evangelical Faith*, which found a receptive readership among Eerdmans' constituency. By the late 1970s other publishers of the evangelical wing began to translate or reprint material. Seen as a whole, this publication history demonstrates a gradual drift toward the more conservative end of the religious spectrum.

Even though his popularity among the general public did not begin until 1959, Thielicke had been known in American theological circles throughout the post-war period. Some faculty members at North American seminaries had emigrated from pre-war Germany because of Hitler's efforts to eliminate opposing voices. These professors kept up with events in Germany after the war, including the latest theological discussions. For example, Paul Tillich of Union Seminary in New York, who had emigrated from Germany in 1933, reviewed Thielicke's *Theological Ethics* in 1953, shortly after its appearance in Germany. Furthermore, these professors began to send students to Europe for graduate study. When the students returned, they looked for opportunities to bring their European professors to the United States for lectures and visits. Thielicke accepted such an invitation from Drew University in 1956. He also visited Union Seminary, Princeton Seminary, and Washington, D.C. It is clear that his contacts were confined to the theological circles that knew about his scholarly work.

Although articles by Thielicke had appeared in American periodicals for a decade before the appearance of *The Waiting Father* in 1959, his earlier work received little attention. Just after the end of World War II he had written a brief and candid description of the religious situation in Germany for a special issue of the *Annals of The American Academy of Political and Social Science*. A few years later some Scottish and American theological journals translated essays in which he criticized the program of demythologization that had been introduced by Rudolf Bultmann. Beyond those brief glimpses, Americans had little opportunity to discover the growing body of theological work that Thielicke was producing. His multi-volume *Theological Ethics* has been described as the most extensive systematic work of the twentieth century, except for Karl Barth's monumental *Church Dogmatics*. Through the 1950s he wrote travel journals, essays and monographs that became a rich vein for American publishers to mine after Thielicke had become well-known on this side of the Atlantic.

It was Thielicke's sermons that brought him—and the rest of his theological work—to fame in America. His popularity stemmed from his ability to meet a spiritual hunger among well-educated people who found the typical sermonic fare of the 1950s less than satisfying. Billy Graham's enormous appeal to mass audiences did not extend to many church members and academics who found his basis too simple. He spoke to those looking for a beginning in Christian faith. Other preachers of the 50s, like Norman Vincent Peale, preferred "positive thinking" to the biblical struggle with a mysterious God. Their sermons were topical, focussing on personal crises rather than opening up the world of the Bible. Thielicke filled the void between revivalism and religious self-help. He aimed at the doubter, the marginal Christian. He then used a biblical text to explore some spiritual problem from a new perspective, frequently showing the larger social issues involved. Even when he preached on personal questions of faith and doubt, he grounded his exposition on a biblical passage—often a parable of Jesus. It was the same formula that had attracted audiences of up to three thousand Germans, from all segments of society, to the largest church in Hamburg whenever Professor Thielicke preached.

Unquestionably the power of Thielicke's preaching lay in his ability to take a biblical text, written thousands of years ago, and to show how that text could illuminate today's issues. That is not an easy task. It is complicated by the many differences that have arisen between the days of Abraham and Sarah and our own. Not only have the languages and cultures changed, but the concepts of earth and heaven, of weather and disease, politics and religion have changed as well. It is all very well to say the the basic "human situation" is always the same, but in fact almost every aspect of that situation's analysis, description and solution differs from the way it was treated in the Bible. The interpreter's task is to understand both the present and the Bible so well that the two worlds will be able to communicate with each other. The basic issue of preaching for Thielicke was to relate the "then and there" of biblical narrative with the "here and now" of contemporary society.

Thielicke had wrestled with that question during the difficult years of preaching to the shell-shocked citizens of Stuttgart during the war. In those same years German theologians were discussing the proposal of Rudolf Bultmann that the biblical message needed to be restated in contemporary thought-forms. Bultmann argued that there were vital truths hidden in the language of a three-story universe, but that those ideas needed to be freed from their ancient wrappings; they must be "demythologized." Then the timeless truths could be expressed in language more appropriate to modern society.

In a paper delivered at a pastors' conference in 1941, Thielicke agreed with Bultmann's analysis of the problem, but he strongly opposed Bultmann's solution. He argued that relying on contemporary philosophy would be a great mistake, because current philosophical systems, especially the existentialism that Bultmann employed, had lost the framework of transcendence; the universe was a closed system. To recast the biblical story in the contemporary worldview would be to lose the most important element of all: the action of God in history. The power of Nazi propaganda had been precisely its ability to bend the horizons of German intellectuals into a closed circle of thought. For the church to consider embracing a system that left no room for the judgment and historical action of God would be to risk further seduction.

The resurrection of Jesus, for example, remained absolutely essential as a basis for faith. It demonstrated the power of God to overcome every earthly system of oppression. It also showed that the crucified Jesus is an active power in history and not just an ancient example. To follow Bultmann's reinterpretation of the resurrection as no more than a faith response of the believer would be to rob the church's proclamation of its cutting edge against all human pretensions.

Because Thielicke was an early critic of Bultmann's program, he found sympathetic hearts among American conservatives. In the years following the war, Bultmann's ideas crossed the Atlantic and became the catalyst for intense religious debate in the United States. Thielicke's critique of Bultmann followed the discussion to these shores. The intensity of the debate left little room for shades of gray, so any opponent of Bultmann was considered a friend of the conservative camp. Furthermore, Thielicke had published a sympathetic study of the English Baptist preacher Charles Haddon Spurgeon (1834–1892), in which he commended Spurgeon for his direct and unapologetic presentation of biblical themes. These credentials gained him access to the ears of most American Protestants, who felt that Bultmann had indeed interpreted the heart out of the biblical message.

Thielicke realized that his early popularity in America rested on the fact that he was not well-known and that various theological camps judged him on the basis of meager evidence. He observed that

> The liberals probably thought: He speaks in modern style, so he must be one of us; the Baptists said: He has written a book on Spurgeon, so he is close to us; the fundamentalists noted that my sermons were expositions of biblical texts and often included me in their ranks; and the Lutherans said: After all, he comes from Hamburg.
>
> [*Between Heaven and Earth*, Harper's, 1965, xiv]

He liked the American conservative wing because he felt that its strong beliefs made it ready for serious discussion of basic religious issues. He did not agree with conservatives on all counts, but he conveyed his interest in continuing discussion rather than caricaturing or condemning them. They responded by coming to his lectures, inviting him to their seminaries, and publishing—and republishing—his books. His popularity among these fundamentalists and evangelicals lasted a decade longer than it did among more moderate and liberal theologians.

After his second visit to the United States in 1963 Thielicke published a book which re-created some of the dialogues he had held with American Christians. It is clear that his audiences wanted to press him further on his position regarding doctrines other than the resurrection, on which he had written so plainly. The tone of the questions was always polite—Thielicke remarked that, in contrast to German audiences, Americans always seemed ready to listen rather than being chronically skeptical. But the intent was to probe his views on matters like the inerrancy of the Bible, verbal inspiration, the Virgin Birth, and speaking in tongues. While complimenting his questioners on the directness of their inquiries, he carefully distinguished between doctrines that he considered essential, the resurrection for example, and doctrines he thought less central, such as the virgin birth of Jesus. He did not deny that Jesus could have been born of a virgin, but he pointed out what a slight role it played in the whole New Testament and suggested that it might have been a pious way to describe the "otherness" of Jesus. In this way he established a position which did not match fundamentalism, but which affirmed miracles and generally suited groups which later would bear the label "evangelical."

Fundamentalism remained a major concern of Thielicke's and in some respects it defined American Protestantism for him. He believed that the central issue facing the churches in the United States was how they would deal with the fundamentalists. He hoped that the strength of piety and conviction that the fundamentalists expressed would continue to infuse American religious life. He feared that those characteristics would be lost if fundamentalist voices were discredited or ignored. At the same time he urged the fundamentalists to realize that they were defending positions that were not central to faith—that in fact some of their rigidity might mask an inner mistrust of Christianity's ability to face the modern world.

In a sense, Thielicke brought the results of post-war German theology to America in an attractive package. For example, his greatest success, *The Waiting Father*, was basically an exposition of contemporary German biblical scholarship on the parables. Traditional preaching had found in the parable of the prodigal son a cautionary tale about the dangers of wasteful living, but German theologians were pointing out that the parables really focussed on God and the kingdom of God rather than on human nature. In the title sermon of *The Waiting Father* Thielicke begins with the traditional emphasis on the psychology of the young man who wanted to get away from parental authority, but then he turns his hearers' attention to the real point of the story: the patient love of the father who waited for the headstrong child to return. His use of examples from family life, business, contemporary authors and the youth culture led his audiences to feel that the parable really was describing their own situations. The fresh insight, however, came from the revelation that the parable was really about God's love rather than about our weaknesses.

Thielicke's personal appearances in America were a curious blend of disappointment and delight. Persons who had read his work in translation flocked to churches where he was preaching in order to hear more of his eloquence. However, he preferred to speak in German with an English translator at his side, or to read from a prepared translation. In either case it was difficult for him to build the rhetorical structures and cadences that propelled his preaching in his native language. The wit and content were still there, but following one of his sermons resembled a mountain hike more than a stroll through some forest cathedral.

Despite the barriers of language, Thielicke's personal gifts established immediate rapport with those who met him. He was a large, expansive man, ready to laugh and intensely curious about everything new. His taste in music covered the range from Gregorian chant to jazz. He told hilarious stories—of his student days, of fascinating places he had visited, and of the celebrities he had met. His comfortable childhood had given him the gift of ease in distinguished company. Whether on a steamer or at a formal dinner, he spoke easily with strangers.

Often a conversation that began on the most casual level would deepen and intensify as he explored issues that his partner had not allowed to come fully to light. Then at the end of the day, as he jotted down notes in his journal, Thielicke would reflect on the conversation and examine its implications for Christian faith and life. Sooner or later, those reflections would add reality and relevance to a sermon or an essay.

Thielicke's ability to speak directly to the inner needs of his hearers came from a life that had felt many of those doubts and pressures. His academic career was plagued by a progressive illness that rendered him weak at times and finally became life-threatening. Hopes for the completion of his graduate work grew dim; it was all he could do to cling to life itself. Then, at the moment of deepest despair, he took an overdose of an experimental drug. His condition began to improve. Thus death became a reality to him, as did the possibility of miracle.

His training as a theologian brought him into contact with the principal theological lights of the 1930s. He heard lectures from—and dared to differ with—Karl Barth, the leading figure of Reformed theology in the first half of this century. He went on to study at Erlangen, a Lutheran stronghold, where he worked with Paul Althaus. Although he felt more at home in the Lutheran context, he did not fully agree with his mentors and began to chart an independent course.

The rise of National Socialism forced him to think through the relation of Christianity to culture in a very concrete way. Hitler's campaign against Christianity was subtle and cautious, but every year that passed drew the lines more clearly. At first it was merely "Heil Hitler" and other patriotic acts, then the law required faculty members to participate in "seminars" that forced them to declare their political views. Thielicke spoke out in those sessions, and soon his resistance to the party line became known in academic—and party—circles. In the late 1930s, as he tried to find a teaching position in the German university system, he discovered that he had enemies in high places. He was faced with that most fundamental question:

personal advancement or personal principle. Should he bend to the political "realities" in order to find a job and support his new bride, or should he refuse to join the Nazis and risk losing any chance for a professorship? In retrospect the choice seems stark and clear, but as he describes the unfolding situation one realizes how ambiguous each decision really was. Those difficult days gave him personal experience of the way ethical decisions are made in everyday life.

When his refusal to bow to party demands resulted in his dismissal from academic life, he became a part of German society in a new way. After a year of military service he took a parish and began a ministry to his countrymen as they lived through war, bombing, loss of family members, and the ultimate chaos of defeat. It was in these years of parish work that he became known for his preaching. From his pulpit in Stuttgart he addressed the whole spectrum of human fears and sorrows; his sermons quoted persons to whom he had ministered during the week, at gun emplacements, in hospitals, and in bombed-out homes. Audiences swelled into the thousands as people from all walks of life found that he understood their lives and their problems. This period of ministry set him apart from the academics of his time. It gave him the voice of authenticity that continued to ring through his preaching in the post-war years.

After the end of the war, Thielicke resumed his university career, first at Tübingen and then at the newly-founded University of Hamburg. He also had the opportunity to continue his preaching ministry, and many of the sermons later published in the United States had their origin in Saturday evening services at the church of St. Michael in Hamburg.

Ultimately, Thielicke's success as a preacher brought about the confrontation that ended his sermon series. The student uprisings of the 1960s had their counterparts in Germany, where they took the form of attacks on the German university system. Thielicke did not approve of the radical agenda of the student reformers because it reminded him of the tactics used by the Nazis in his younger days. He publicly opposed the movement, just as he had opposed the Nazis. The students, in turn, targeted his preaching services as opportunities for gaining maximum attention from the media. In January of 1968 they attempted to disrupt a service and were thwarted when Thielicke led the congregation in lusty hymn-singing. Although Thielicke completed his 1968 preaching series, he did not continue the practice. Instead, he organized the Faith Information Project Group, an effort to use printed media as an outreach ministry to the unchurched.

In the United States, Thielicke's reputation as a preacher continued to fuel interest in almost everything he wrote. The "death of God" questions that were raised in the mid-60s stimulated concern for interpreting the core beliefs of Christianity to a secularized culture. Thielicke's work in Germany had taken that task very seriously, and so his writing continued to have appeal. As a result his books on theology, rather than his sermons, began to occupy the attention of American readers during the 1970s and 80s. Even his death in 1986 has not diminished the interest in his work and the flow of articles about him.

The following autobiography, written just two years before his death, will help American readers understand the powerful life experiences that shaped his understanding of God and of human society. It is a frank disclosure of the decisive events that molded him into one of the most noted of modern preachers, but at the same time it is an entertaining narrative of the small defeats and victories that make up the life of any human being.

H. George Anderson
Luther College
September, 1994

Childhood And Youth In Barmen

1908–1928

S TANDING ON TIPTOE, I managed with some difficulty to reach the door handle high above me. This feat enabled me to let myself in to the classroom where my grandfather, the headmaster of the Leibusch School at Wuppertal-Langerfeld, was teaching the big boys. There I saw the beloved patriarch sitting at a raised desk at the front. Before I noticed his smile, however, my eye was caught by the enormous desks on the left and right of the aisle along which I was toddling towards him. The big boys leant down towards me from these, bursting into laughter when I called out "Grandpa, Grandpa!" and flung myself into his arms.

That is probably one of my earliest memories. In these early memories both grandparents on my mother's side play an important role. I can still remember how it smelled in my grandmother's kitchen—of oilcloths, scouring powder, and coffee. On entering a house decades later, I would sometimes be reminded of my grandmother for no apparent reason. It took the collective experience of a lifetime to discover that this association had been triggered by a particular smell or aroma. Since then I have been aware that the nose is the organ for unconscious memories. In literature, I have learned to value particularly those poets who assign a role not only to the eye and the ear but also to the sensuous impressions provided by the nose. Such writers cultivate an appreciation for what lies between the lines of life and make the unutterable utterable. Among such authors are Joseph Conrad and Theodor Fontane. In the works of Marcel Proust, the sense of taste performs a similar function.

The death of my grandfather was also my very first experience of death. He died of a liver disorder at the beginning of the First World War. My mother sought to alleviate the pain I felt at his passing away by telling me how happy he now was and that he was now among God's angels and was quite certainly watching over me from heaven. At the same time, however, I was forbidden to enter the room in which he had died because his body was still sleeping there and he was not to be disturbed. To be with the angels and yet despite this to

1

continue to lie in his old, familiar bed at home was too much for my childish mind to cope with. This was something I had to investigate. So, disobeying my parent's instructions, I crept furtively into the bedroom. On this illegal venture I took my little three-year-old sister Elisabeth with me, holding her by the hand. In the semidarkness of the room I could see no sign of my grandfather at first, until I realized that the blanket covering him had also been pulled over his face. It now seemed to me that an oppressive secret haunted the room. It took me some time to summon up the courage to pull the blanket to one side. We started back, screaming at what we saw. Grandfather looked quite different, but then again not so different that I would not have recognized him. The most striking feature was that his complexion was an eerie and frightening yellow. Aghast and quite beside ourselves with fear, we rushed sobbing and crying to the grown-ups, who were only able to comfort us—or me at least—inadequately. Elisabeth was, of course, still too small to be more profoundly affected by this fright. She joined in the screaming mainly because her big brother was so beside himself.

The sight of my dead grandfather triggered a trauma from which I suffered for a long time. Sometimes, when my parents had gone out and I was supposed to look after my little sister, the paradoxical fascination of this frightening experience suddenly came over me and I would scream, "The yellow grandpa is coming!" Then my sister would join in the screaming until our panic-stricken bawling alerted the neighbors. When our parents returned home, they had to deal only with the last vestiges of our terror.

Calmly and affectionately, my father tried hard to explain to me that my dead grandfather's yellow complexion was natural and that I therefore ought not be frightened by it. But at best, this explanation made only a superficial impression upon my awakening intellect and did not penetrate into the deeper levels of my consciousness. My father was probably disappointed and hurt that my crying fits and terror of the yellow grandpa repeated themselves soon afterwards. But my mother hit upon a way of curing these panic-stricken fantasies in one fell swoop. The manner in which she did this seemed to me even in later life to be the right way of aiding panic-stricken children and even adults. She did not appeal to my understanding but addressed my feelings. She said, "You remember, Helmut, how fond your grandfather was of you, how he used to take you by the arm and tell you stories or make the wall clock chime for you. And in the evening he always visited you in bed until you fell asleep. Do you really think that he would now want to frighten you? He's sure to be very sad when he sees that you've suddenly become scared of him!" That helped; the ghosts departed.

That was my first dark encounter with death and finitude. I was soon to feel their coldness again, however, albeit in a different way. It cannot have been much later because I remember singing "Baby, you're my darling" in the street when the great event that caused this encounter occurred. This was a very popular song shortly before the outbreak of the First World War, so it must have taken place at around then. At that time it was my dearest wish to own a small cart I could steer with my feet and ride down the steep street in Barmen's Herzogplatz where we lived. My grandmother was the first to succumb to my heart-rending pleas and took me to the biggest toy shop in Barmen to buy the coveted vehicle. I was so happy I could hardly bear it and on our way home sang, "Baby, you're my darling."

When we arrived home, my father congratulated me. But as he was carrying the cart downstairs, my happiness evaporated and I burst into tears. Unable to make head or tail of this sudden transformation, my father bellowed somewhat indignantly at me, "What are you crying for, Helmut? You've just been given a lovely cart." I can still clearly recall that I replied, "Yes, but one day it's bound to get broken!"

In the midst of my greatest happiness, the terror of life's transience had come over me. This was a child's first foreboding that the happy moment does not last and that the cold breath of its demise sends a shiver through us at the very instant when our happiness is concentrated into a *single* and immeasurable point. This sense of the imminent end of all things has always accompanied me, even in sickness and when I was close to death, and it occupied my thoughts and many pages of my diary long before my later publications on the subject.

Idylls and Terrors

When I consider which experiences have had a decisive influence on my later life, mixed impressions come to mind. Of course, the idyll of early childhood was not absent from my first years, such as the image of my mother putting us to bed, making us say our prayers, and singing us to sleep. Whenever we were troubled or had hurt ourselves, she would take us in her arms and comfort us. From this memory, warmth flowed into the increasing coldness of later life.

I loved my crib, train set, and bench (which also contained a compartment for my toys) very much. I must have missed this inventory of the family nest terribly when I had to spend several weeks with my grandparents in

Hilchenbach because my mother was ill. My grandmother, a very affectionate woman, was also extremely superstitious and lived in constant fear of a
witch who lived a few houses from us. She was terrified that this witch, who
was nicknamed "Loony Lena," might put the evil eye on me. Before she took
me out, she would first convince herself that there were no egg shells stuck to
her chimney, for these were a sign, she believed, that "Loony Lena" was
plotting mischief against someone. But even when the coast was clear, she
would quick-march me past the witch's house. A tingle of fear always ran
down my spine despite the proximity of my grandmother. Interesting and
different though everything was in rural Hilchenbach, I never quite shook off
a feeling of foreignness. My parents told me later that I was overcome with joy
when I returned home. Apparently, I wanted to hug all the furniture and
actually kissed my toys.

And yet, the golden memories of our infant years deceive us if they blot out
the dark side of childhood and above all the secret fears suffered alone and
concealed even from one's mother. The verse, "O blessed, blessed, a child
still to be . . ." is just as much an example of false sentimentality as the
pseudoreligious nursery rhyme, "Always cheerful, always cheerful, every
day the sun does shine, for we are called the little children, of our Father so
divine."

The fear I suffered as the result of a dreadful experience of being blackmailed is still with me today. As a six-year-old, I had just begun to attend
primary school and was much taken by my charming teacher, Miss Scheib. A
bigger boy than I, who was jealous of my cart, persuaded me to disobey my
mother's instructions and to accompany him to a narrow footbridge which
crossed a railway line. The other boys, who had often been there, told
exciting stories about this bridge and said that a lot of military trains passed
under it on their way to the front. These trains were covered with garlands,
and from the open doors of the livestock trucks the soldiers waved and
shouted when children waved to them from the bridge.

My mother, however, was afraid I might fall through the wide gaps in the
railings. This was her reason for strictly forbidding me to accompany the
others boys there. But, because I was afraid of being jeered at as a mommy's
boy if I kept refusing to join in this fascinating adventure, Erwin, who was a
big boy, eventually succeeded in breaking down my resistance. So, with a
bad conscience I went with him, pulling my cart behind me. While we were
waiting on the bridge for a train, Erwin said, "The locomotive puffs out a lot
of steam. If you throw a stone from the bridge into its funnel, it flies through
the clouds straight into the sky. I've often done it. Here's a stone. Throw it

into the funnel when the locomotive is under the bridge. I'll tell you when: one, two, three—now."

This was indeed something I could not afford to miss. I was very nervous. At last the train came. Even from a distance I could see the soldiers waving when they caught sight of us children. The decisive moment was now rapidly approaching. When the locomotive was under the bridge, we were enveloped by the steam it puffed up at us, with the result that we could not see a thing. At that moment the boy shouted, "Now!" and I dropped the stone from the railings. My immediate thought was that it was highly unlikely that I would have hit the funnel in all that steam. Despite this, as soon as the view was clear again, I looked up to see if the stone was perhaps not actually hurtling into the sky. But the boy grabbed me by the arm and said, "My God! You missed the funnel and killed a soldier. I saw it all!" I was filled with a dreadful fear. Then Erwin added threateningly, "If I tell your Miss at school, you'll go to prison." I howled with despair. To complete my misery, he then took a little hammer out of his pocket, banged a nail into my cart and said, "The cart no longer belongs to you alone. The nail is my property." The dead soldier was bad enough, but this assassination attempt on my beloved cart dealt me a further blow.

From that day, the big boy blackmailed me for days and weeks on end. In return for keeping my atrocity a secret, I had to supply him with candy or buy pieces of sausage from the butcher for him. My protestation that I had no money made no impression upon him. "I'm sure you know," he said to me, "where your mother keeps her purse." Terrified by the thought of prison and tormented with shame, I stole money from my dear mother. Claiming "joint ownership," he also kept taking my cart away. He was much bigger and stronger than I was and blackmailed me with diabolical cunning and energy. I felt imprisoned in a dark hole of hopeless despair. I simply had no alternative but to keep my crime a secret, even from my mother. Deceiving my beloved mother was the worst of all. This whole problem had begun with my disobeying her strict instructions not to accompany the other boys to the bridge. And then I had gone and killed a soldier. I was not yet acquainted, of course, with Schiller's proverb about the evil deed which "must continue to give birth to evil." Nevertheless, a first premonition of this interrelationship was beginning to dawn. The big boy was always whispering with the other boys and giving me meaningful glances. I was certain that he had already told them of the atrocity I had committed. If only he would not say anything to my teacher! If he did, she would tell my parents, then my theft of money would be discovered, and finally the policeman who was responsible for our district and who was, of course, well-known to all of us, would come and take me away.

The lonely despair that was torturing me could not remain hidden indefinitely. When I cried myself to sleep at night, my mother stayed with me, spoke soothingly to me, and waited for a confession. Some sinister thing was oppressing her child. Then, one evening I confessed my secret in a dreadful outburst. That brought with it a wonderful sense of release. My parents were so happy to see the puzzling and frightening spell broken that they gladly forgave me the sin I had committed on the bridge. Of course, they did not deny themselves the opportunity of gently pointing out the moral lesson of what can happen when a child violates his parents' prohibitions. But I enjoyed being enveloped in a new and wonderful sense of security. What they did in addition to this, I do not know. Only from then on my blackmailer started to avoid me. And when my father then removed the nail from my cart with a pair of pliers, this story of terror was brought to a final conclusion.

A feeling of apprehensiveness has remained with me from these early childhood days. It kept reappearing—right up until the present day— whenever I met people whose motives and standards were strange or completely incomprehensible to me, as was the case in my childhood with my little blackmailer and his criminal energy. It manifested itself again in the following years when my parents moved to Eduard Street.

Eduard Street was a solidly middle-class area situated near a housing estate with a reputation for antisocial behavior. In our new neighborhood I made many friends and playmates with whom I am still in contact today. At the annual commemoration of the Battle of Sedan we held a procession with flags and Chinese lanterns. What then happened time and time again was that groups of boys from the neighboring estate would attack us and snatch the flags and lights away. We were simply no match for their violence. Because they were so different from us, we found them rather sinister. When we heard the cry, "The louts are coming," we found it difficult to appear calm. We middle-class boys also got into quite a few scraps with each other, but with us certain rules and codes of honor were in force. The louts, however, were a wild bunch who robbed, kicked, and were generally unscrupulous. What disturbed us far more than the loss of our toys and the bruises they gave us was the frightfulness and unpredictability of their attacks. When later, during the student unrest of the sixties, the extraparliamentary opposition undertook violent mass invasions of lectures and disturbed the services I conducted in the Church of St. Michael at Hamburg with their heckling and general rowdiness, I kept hearing inside me the cry, "The louts are here!" In all the years I had spent with my students I had not only worked with them but had also taken an intense personal interest in them. I always aimed at establishing a community of trust with them. Now, suddenly, there arose alarmingly and completely out of the blue a quite different and totally unfamiliar type of student—namely, students who formed violent raiding parties and took part in the mass picketing of professors. Some professors were so affected by this terror that they broke down and died. So the "louts," even when we do not include the Nazis in our reckoning, kept haunting me throughout my life. Sometimes the memory of my first encounter with the "louts" was of comfort to me, because I knew that I had survived them.

There were also other ways in which terror sometimes broke into the idyll of my childhood. Whenever my mother sent me to the butcher's to fetch meat for her, it was her policy never to give me a shopping list. This was because she wanted me to remember her instructions all by myself. So after I had repeated them several times for practice, I went on my way. But for some mysterious reason I kept bringing home half a pound of minced meat. It was very important to my mother—I'm sure out of love for me—to be rigorous in the way she brought me up, and so I had to keep taking back what I had brought home by mistake.

When I went back for the umpteenth time, the butcher, who had previously treated me with great patience, grew so angry that I could see the veins standing out on his forehead. He whetted his huge butcher's knife, waved it about in front of me, and threatened in a powerful voice to cut my ears off if I came back again. I fled screaming and, running most of the way, rushed to my grandparent's house in Langerfeld, which was quite some distance away. My frantic sobbing prevented me from telling my grandmother, who was very concerned and trying hard to comfort me, the reason for my distress. But she was furious when she learned what had happened to her little boy. I can still see how she put her bonnet on with a violent tug, tying the straps beneath her chin as if they were chin-straps on a helmet. She then took me by the hand and, while I stayed outside and followed the scene apprehensively through the shop window, she hauled the butcher over the coals with a variety of threatening gestures. My mother was also on the receiving end of a dressing-down, which upset me a great deal because I loved her more than anything in the world. It almost broke my heart to see this kindly woman get such telling-off.

Another early fear was much less harmful and was really no more than a childish worry. One day my mother said to me, "Well, Helmut, it's now time for you to go to kindergarten. Tomorrow morning I'll take you there!" From what my parents told me later, I must have cried quite a lot at this. I do not know if I told them the reason for my distress, but I do remember very well the worry this announcement caused me. I imagined that I was going to be planted in the earth by my feet and then watered constantly. But this worry very quickly disppeared and I had a great time there. My imagination had— for the first time?—played a trick on me. The imagination is not *always* a good thing.

When I started school, a new authority—or role model, as it is nowadays called—entered my life in the form of a teacher who was soon to become very dear to me. She had been taught by my father at the teacher-training college. I also got to know a few classmates from a very simple, proletarian milieu. Their crude expressions and curses made a considerable impression on me. Because of my well-to-do background, I felt inferior in their company and tried hard to match their coarseness. I must have been quite successful, for my parents were horrified by many of my new expressions and also by my determination not to wash my neck. So, at home, I had to turn back into a middle-class boy again. I had great admiration for those of my schoolfriends who were found by our teacher to have scabies or even lice. They were then given a printed note to take home to their parents. One day, my conspicuous scratching prompted my father to undertake a thorough examination of me. He actually found a few fleas, which he—half shocked, half proud of his successful hunt—showed me before crushing them with his nail. My self-esteem increased by several degrees since I felt myself now to belong to the higher circles of commonness.

When, shortly afterwards, I went shopping for my mother at the local shop, I beamed at the housewives who had gathered there and said, "We've got fleas too." These private family matters aroused considerable interest among the people in the shop, especially because my parents were well-known and respected in the neighborhood. Spurred on by their response, I blew the family's pest problem out of all proportion. The people in the shop enjoyed this so much that they asked me to continue with my story. My tendency to dramatize then led me to exaggerate what was really an innocuous tiff I had witnessed between my father and mother into an almost physical battle. I concluded my story (I can still remember this clearly!) with the melodramatic sentence, "Then my poor mother burst into tears." I simply got carried away by my audience. Even the shopkeeper stopped serving and listened spell-bound.

This event had, of course, a minor epilogue when my mother learned of my oratorical escapades via several different channels. She did not rightly know whether she should laugh or feel embarrassed. In my later career as a public speaker, it became clear to me that what had revealed itself in embryonic form as a dangerous trait of my personality on that occasion in the local shop was a problem which would force me to a critical assessment of myself.

Miss Scheib, the young and radiant teacher who taught us reading and writing, occupied my imagination a great deal. I admired her skill at drawing pictures on the blackboard with colored chalk, and found her voice captivating when she joined in with our singing. At that time I had not yet realized that I was unfortunately unmusical, so I must have gazed blankly at her when, on walking between the rows of benches, she kept saying to me, "Helmut, you're droning again." One day, with a smile on her face, she showed us her brand-new engagement ring and asked, "Who of you knows what 'engagement' means?" I felt myself to be an expert in this field because I had just experienced such a celebration at my aunt's, where I had also managed to get a very upset stomach. So I immediately put my hand up and said, "Engagement is when people kiss each other." To my surprise, Miss Scheib's face suddenly turned bright red. Without bestowing upon me the praise I had expected for my answer, she turned around and began to fiddle about with the blackboard. While she was doing this, I could see from the way her shoulders were twitching that she was laughing. But why? The relationship between cause and effect was at that time not yet familiar to me, and certainly not the variability of the causal process in matters of love.

One day, when I had already been a professor for a long time and Miss Scheib, or Mrs. Sassmann, as she was now called, was a grandmother of advanced years, my old teacher turned up at one of my lectures. Although she now had a wrinkled face, I recognized her immediately by her smile. "I can still remember," she said, "how a certain little blond boy explained the meaning of my engagement ring to me." And again, a soft crimson spread across her face as she recalled that happy occasion.

Is the coyness in which love was steeped in those days merely a symptom of the inhibitions which we have long since overcome through our objectification of sex? Or is it rather a sign of the sensitivity of our inner seismograph, which registers the most sublime expressions of the erotic and does not first need an orgasm before it records a reading? Have we not perhaps lost our awareness of the breadth of the erotic? Has it not been cheapened and distorted in a simplistic fashion? We think we are progressive, but. . . .

But these are thoughts that only come to mind when one has left one's childhood far behind. At that time, all that I noticed was that my teacher had blushed and for me that was something that only happened when I had been caught doing something wrong.

When, during the First World War, the church bells rang to celebrate a German victory—that soon stopped—on the following morning we used to go to school "in uniform." My uniform consisted of a hussar jacket decorated with numerous cords, which my mother tied around my back with string, a tall hussar's cap, and a little dagger. Dressed in such costumes, we would stage a military spectacle and thereby felt ourselves included in the events of the war. These events were, of course, a constant topic of conversation amongst the grown-ups. We were also shown pictures of the imperial family. The young princes were the same age as us. When, in 1951, I took part in my capacity as Rector of Tübingen University in the funeral service for the Crown Prince at Hohenzollern Castle, I immediately recognized the old Crown Princess from her hairstyle. This was familiar to me from my childhood and had not changed in the slightest.

Perhaps it was the Battle of Tannenberg that prompted us to perform our miniature military parade in the schoolyard once again. We must have already been able to count to a hundred, because I remember Miss Scheib telling us that Father Hindenburg had captured so many Russian prisoners that they would have filled a hundred schoolyards. I can still recall today how the hugeness of this figure petrified me. It was my first impression of the infinite. When, much later, I learned of the vastness of space, the effect on me was hardly more powerful than this first childhood experience.

In that same year, I felt death's cold breath once again. A classmate who sat near me and who often played with me and visited me at home, died of diphtheria. Because of the risk of infection, we were not allowed to accompany his coffin to the cemetery. The result of this was that his death had something oppressively unreal about it for us. When, shortly afterwards, Miss Scheib unpacked a suitcase in class and distributed some of the things he had left behind—shoes, suits, socks and his little uniform—to the poorer pupils, I was aghast but did not know why.

After my parents had moved to Eduard Street, I was transferred to a school in South Street (now German Street) for the remainder of my four years at primary school. To get a male teacher after having had such a wonderful female teacher filled me with apprehension, especially since Mr. Nelle had a reputation for great severity. I had already learned from my new classmates the rhyme: "Teacher Nelle makes life hell." He did indeed prove to be a man who made considerable use of the cane. At the same time, however, we sensed time and again that he was a good man and, above all, was fair.

Nevertheless, he was unable to become a tranfigured and mythical figure for me as Miss Scheib had been.

In 1917, famine broke out. Parts of our school were transformed into a soup kitchen, where at midday we collected meals for our families. Mass feedings obviously helped to save food. For the most part, we received pretty watery soup, which meant that we were always hungry. Our physical education teacher, an elderly and somewhat grumpy spinster, once took advantage of this in a rather unpleasant way to force us to produce better results. When we had lined up in front of the climbing poles in the gymnasium, she said to the first group, which I was in because of my height, "There's a sausage up there. Whoever gets to the top first can have it." With great effort I managed to arrive at the top first and found absolutely nothing. The disappointment at being cheated was boundless. I never forgave her and afterwards did my best to annoy her at every available opportunity.

My father had, in the meantime, been drafted into the army and was now fighting as an artilleryman in the Carpathians. My mother had great difficulty getting us enough to eat and kept giving us some of her own meager rations, although she only admitted this much later. On one occasion, I almost noticed this. She had just spread a slice of bread for herself and must then have sensed my covetous gaze. As she pushed it over to me I asked her, "Aren't *you* at all hungry then?" Smiling she replied, "I'm really full and couldn't eat another bite." That seemed odd to me but I *wanted* to believe it and so took the slice of bread from her. That was the first instance of many occasions on which I turned a blind eye to something I did not want to admit, a phenomenon which pervades all our lives. One day, my mother was suddenly overcome by a feeling of weakness. She turned pale and, grabbing onto me, lowered herself with some difficulty onto a chair. In tears, I shouted to a neighbor for help, who then told me that it was only hunger that had caused my mother to collapse. "She gives you too much of her own food," she said.

From then on, I went to Herzkamp in the country with my iron hoop, a common toy amongst little boys in those days, to forage milk from the farmers. This was by no means easy because the villagers who undertook such trips were not at all popular with the farmers. You only got something if you had something to exchange—which, of course, I didn't—or awoke their interest in some other way. That is what I tried to do. I told them goodness knows what stories, moved them with exaggerated reports of my starving mother and my distraught sister. By these means I was often able to bring home in my little rucksack a few bottles of milk and was, of course, greeted with great joy. On one of these trips, however, I had a very distressing experience, the pain of which I still feel today. As I was on my way home one day with an enormous haul of three bottles of milk in my rucksack, I got involved in a fight with several farm boys. I defended myself against their superior strength with all my might and eventually they left me alone. However, when I turned to continue my journey, they rained down upon me an unexpected hail of stones and smashed all three bottles to smithereens. In utter despair, I stood there in a pool of milk, eventually arriving home aghast, sobbing, and with empty hands. Without wasting any words on my painful loss, my mother comforted me and was concerned only about the cut on the head I had *also* received but had not noticed amongst all my other troubles.

When the war came to a catastrophic end, my parents' world collapsed. The Kaiser, whom they had idealized, had abdicated, and with the end of the monarchy the system of values that had been in force until then also disappeared. Military councils run by swaggering soldiers tore from the officers their epaulettes and medals, shots sounded in the town square, and a new type of person filled the streets with red flags. Although we children were not able to understand the changes that were taking place, our parents' anxiety spread to us and infected us with a feeling of dreadful foreboding. When I asked my father about some event or the other, he would dismiss my question with an air of resignation, saying, "You're still too young to understand, Helmut. I can only tell you that if you were able to comprehend what is happening, you would turn gray immediately, despite your youth." This spine-chilling picture encouraged me to all sorts of boyish reflections. These eventually condensed into my one day bombarding my mother with the question: "Father said that although I'm a boy my hair would turn gray if I understood everything that's happening now. But he doesn't understand it himself. How is it then that his hair hasn't turned gray, seeing that he's much older than I am?" Even my dear mother did not know how to respond to this question. I would like to have been a fly on the wall when my parents discussed this difficult problem with each other. I do not know what conclusion they reached.

This remark about gray hair was typical of my father. It betrayed his tendency to exaggerate and was evidence of an overactive imagination. Although this fascinated me during my childhood, as a sober adolescent it tended to repel me and in the course of time even led to my estrangement from him. This tendency to indulge in fantastic exaggeration had a particularly negative effect on me when my father noticed that I was approaching puberty and felt obliged to discuss the matter with me. I still have the most embarrassing memory of this conversation, not least because of the way in which it took place. When he asked me to "take a seat" next to him on the sofa, I sensed from his embarrassment and his unusually solemn gestures that something special was in store for me. He explained to me—at first fairly objectively—the physiological changes I was soon to undergo, before going on to warn me about older women and above all about the temptations of masturbation. During the conversation, he inflated the horror of the possible consequences of ignoring his warnings so fantastically that the frightening visions that resulted were to burden me for a long time afterwards. He informed me that sperm is the most precious substance of the brain and spinal cord, the loss of which not only reduces a young man's mental ability, but also ruins him and, yes, could even drive him insane. I can still remember the horror I felt when I ejaculated for the first time, believing that alongside my sperm, part of my brain had also been expelled. I came very close to panicking. My father was obviously of the naive opinion that the terror of this threat would strengthen my powers of resistance. The thought that the psychological burden might be incomparably worse than even the most excessive masturbation never crossed his mind. He was conditioned by the inhibitions of his own upbringing, which now combined to disastrous effect with an overheated imagination. As a result of this, the boyish sex games to which I was seduced by a somewhat older, otherwise very pleasant playmate whose voice had already broken, put me under severe psychological pressure. This was made all the worse by the fact that I had to keep this supposedly dreadful crime a secret from my parents. It was particularly traumatic for me whenever I felt my mother's love and trust. Then I was tortured by the thought: "If you only knew . . ."

In light of the removal of taboos that has taken place in recent years, and the uninhibited objectivity with which today's adolescents talk about sexual issues—even with adults—such complex-laden situations are scarcely comprehensible. Nevertheless, I think it is doubtful whether the change that has come about has had an *exclusively* liberating effect. The way in which my father explained the facts of life to me was, of course, in spite of his good intentions, wholly destructive and just about any alternative to it would count as progress. Nevertheless, negative experiences of this kind can prompt one to differentiate more precisely and to prevent one from thinking *exclusively* in black and white terms. My father's experiment in sex education was a perversion of what in many ways was a sensible procedure of making sexuality taboo. That sex contains secrets, possesses a certain degree of mystery, and that part of its essence is the polarity of *fascinosum* and *tremendum* is true of every sexual experience. For this reason, I sometimes have the heretical idea that even the prudishness of the Victorians contained an element of erotic artistry. Sex acquired a heightened sensitivity according to the degree in which it was taboo. Even the most modest revelation, such as a glimpse of a feminine ankle beneath the long dress of a lady going upstairs, could send a man's pulse racing. From this there resulted the rule of etiquette that a gentleman always let a lady precede him *except* when both were going upstairs! In those days there existed a wide range of erotic emotions. The game of love was a drama in many acts and one could hardly wish to argue that this caused the erotic to lose its fascination.

This observation raises the question of whether the modern objectification of sex does not entail a considerable impoverishment. Free of inhibitions we discuss sex in psychoanalytical terms over tea and reduce it to the physical act. In an age where nudity is a commonplace—one only has to think of the practices of the media—or is cleverly *accentuated* by dress, sexual arousal requires much more powerful stimulation than was the case when sex was taboo. Anyway, in my opinion, there is a need to put aside all moral or pseudo-moral criteria and consider sexuality exclusively from the perspective of the conditions that determine it as a rich or poor experience and that cause it to appear in sophisticated or crude forms. The distorted version of sex that I suffered at the hands of my father was that of sex as a taboo subject. But does not a sexuality that has been freed of taboos and reduced to the objective satisfaction of hormonal needs cast just as distorted a shadow over it?

Incidentally, I must add in my father's defense that in those days it was common in middle-class and Christian circles to place sex under a distorted and exaggerated taboo, although probably not quite so crassly as I had experienced it in my sex education. Thus I remember how in the summer camps provided for the school bible study groups, of which I myself was for many years an enthusiastic member, rainy days tended to be set aside for sex education. The first sentence of such lectures still resounds in my ears: "Dear boys, you have all heard of the organs that we males have between our legs. . . ."

But I really would like to say a little more about my father and mother. The excesses of my father's imagination, which sometimes led to a considerable degree of blindness to reality, had also a very positive aspect; or at least that is how I experienced it at first. He could tell gripping stories about how the police in Siegen just could not cope with the outrageous exploits of his youth; or how, as a young village schoolteacher in Grund, he appeared to have died from appendicitis and how the neighbors had with great lamentation made wreaths for his funeral. The adventures of Karl May were harmless in comparison to those my father had lived through. But when I later met one or another of the old friends with whom he had spent his wild days and mentioned some of these alleged exploits in the hope of learning of further sensations from them, they split their sides laughing; they could not remember anything about them. Despite this, I never met a single one of them who did not like him.

It would be unfair, however, if I were to create the impression that my father's *only occupation* was to tell stories about himself. He was *also* a first-rate historian and had amassed a library of over a thousand works. These he had studied thoroughly, underlining important passages and making many notes in the margin. He published essays of considerable profundity on many specialized issues in a variety of educational journals. He knew Dante's *Divine Comedy* inside out and was an acknowledged expert and interpreter of Wilhelm Raabe. His Bible, which I still treasure as a very special legacy, was extremely well thumbed and marked with the dates on which a passage had acquired particular importance for him. He was a shrewd lay theologian and whenever the vicar made a sloppy interpretation of a text in his sermon my father made use of his flawless knowledge to put him right.

Of course, many a time—not least because he was a Christian—he struggled to bring his rampant imagination under control. This clearly also made him somewhat unsure on how best to bring up his son. I was probably about seventeen years old before I was allowed to go to the theater for the first time. When previously I had pressed him with such a request, he would always reply, "First read the plays and try to imagine them being performed. If you get to see everything too early, your imagination will not develop." On the other hand, he forbade me to read the works of Karl May because he believed them to be permeated with an excessive imagination and this would have had a negative influence upon me.

How different in comparison was my mother! She was a sober woman who treated herself with puritanical strictness and demanded of herself complete fulfilment of her duties. She was an impressive personality who enjoyed universal respect and whose well-considered advice was sought by many, not least because of the goodness she radiated and her ability to empathize with people. High spirits were alien to her. Only in her loving care for her children, was she without restraint. She was our refuge in times of trouble and the comforting figure who banished our childish fears. Her piety was sincere and profound, though stamped with a Calvinistic sobriety. All forms of "religion" that made use of images and symbolic gestures and—as is the case with Roman Catholicism—loved a certain degree of self-portrayal were completely alien to her and in her eyes were the pitiful work of human beings. Her faith was personalistic and consisted of an I-Thou relationship with her Savior. To him she entrusted the care of her children, especially during the serious illness of my student days. She hardly ever expressed aloud what was going on inside her, not even in our closest moments. A strange shyness, which I have inherited from her, prevented her from doing so. But in her letters she poured out many of her feelings. She needed the indirect way of writing to reveal her inner thoughts. Although it was her dearest wish for me to become a theologian and my later career filled her with gratitude and happiness, she never exerted the slightest pressure on me and allowed me complete freedom to choose my profession. Clearly every mother hopes that her children will "become something" in life and dreams a little of a successful career for her children. Precisely for this reason it impressed me greatly that after the outbreak of the Third Reich my mother urged me to remain true to my convictions and to myself and not to give an inch to the Nazis. She shared my distress when I lost my beloved post at Heidelberg, but was at the same time happy that I had not succumbed to the temptation to conform. When somewhat banal acquaintances of ours told her that it was a great shame that her son, who with his supposedly considerable rhetorical ability and intelligence could have become a successful lawyer, continued to support that misguided rabble of the Confessing Church, her maternal instinct to defend her brood could reach Maccabean ferocity. Even later reports of such confrontations made her eyes flash.

Although my father loved my mother intensely, and looked to her to provide stability to his restless nature, I do not believe that my parents' marriage was in every respect happy. The difference in their personalities was certainly too stark. My father's inclination to overdo things and his tendency to abandon himself to uncontrolled emotions were so alien to my mother that it was a long time before she learned not to take all her husband's statements at face value. And certainly I played a sometimes dubious role in her growing disillusionment with him, for I encouraged her to be more sceptical and kept placing an ironical question mark over my father's dramatic reports. In her later years, my mother was increasingly repelled by this trait of her husband's character.

When my mother suffered severe and permanent loss of speech as a result of a stroke and needed constant care and attention, a reconciliation took place between her and my father. He was untiring in his attempts to teach her to speak again with the aid of children's primers and enveloped her in his devotion and love. He surrendered himself to the illusion that he could regenerate her damaged speech center through his efforts. But it was wishful thinking, born of his love for her, when he thought he could see progress, whereas it was really just a question of enduring the pain of her decline.

I have always fought those aspects of my nature which I realized I had inherited from my father. It must have hurt him that he increasingly became for me the symbol of that part of my personality I had to reject. The best cure for the feelings of vanity to which I was sometimes prone after some success or another was to hear the bombastic exaggeration with which my father described to our circle of acquaintances the admiration felt by my professors for my Ph.D. in philosophy. On the other hand, to receive praise from my mother was like being awarded a prize. I knew, after all, that she had wrung the praise from herself and had carefully considered beforehand whether it might not harm my character. Sometimes I have tried to elucidate what I have inherited from my parents by transforming a famous passage from Goethe into a rhyme and reversing its order:

> Stature to face all worldly woe,
> My blessed mother gave me,
> Fables to tell and a cheerful soul,
> I have, dear Father, from thee.

A Classical Education

My parents had decided that I should go to the grammar school in Barmen. This school, which later became the Wilhelm Dörpfeld Grammar School, had the reputation for being somewhat "élitist." In the first year, we wore green caps with silver cords. On being admitted into the exalted ranks of the sixth form, we then exchanged these for caps of white silk with golden cords. I was the only boy in the neighborhood who attended this grammar school, and my friends at various other secondary schools pitied me because I had to learn ancient and "unworldly" languages. In the first year, we wore green caps with silver cords. On being admitted into the exalted ranks of the sixth form, we then exchanged these for caps of white silk with golden cords. My school was indeed rather special and could boast a long tradition. When it celebrated its four-hundredth anniversary in 1979, I was invited to preach the commemorative sermon in the Church of Immanuel. Because our school had originated as the grammar school of the Reformed Parish of Gemarke*, and this origin had continued to leave its mark up until the present day, it seemed reasonable to bring to the fore in my sermon the problem of the relationship between Christianity and the classical ideal.

The entrance examination I sat in 1919 was, of course, an event of decisive importance for me. The candidates for this examination were taken by their parents to an imposing building in Bleicher Street. The solemnity of the occasion intimidated me at least as much as my fear of the examination. Shyly, I took stock of my companions in misfortune, who did the same back to me. Because of the importance of the occasion, my father had let me use his briefcase, which I now clutched firmly to me.

We waited in the great columned hall until our names were called, when we were then divided among the three first-form teachers who were to be our examiners. These teachers, who were to accompany us through the lower forms and further our writing and arithmetic, seemed like giants of the world of education to me. A shudder of awe seized me when I saw these powerful men march the first two groups of terrified candidates into the examination room. The first to stroll past us was Fey, the physical education teacher, a man with an enormous, fiery red beard. Although we soon discovered that he was a rather vulgar man—an impression strengthened by the way he rolled his "r's" in the Siegerland dialect—we were very afraid of him during our first years at school. We were frightened above all by the terrifying and brutal way he beat his own son. Even today, I can still hear the threatening and peremptory tone in which he bellowed at us whenever he wanted us to run faster, yelling, "Do you want me to grease your heels for you?"

The next teacher to go by was Mr. Pfeffer. With an air of indescribable gravity and with head held high, he slowly led his candidates past us and our parents, gracing us with a display of the privileged status accruing to the profession of schoolmaster. This performance commanded a silence which petrified me. Pfeffer was a tall man with a massive paunch and long curly hair. He had himself been a pupil at the school until the sixth form and had then become a primary school teacher. In the following years, he often had the opportunity to complain vociferously and extremely melodramatically to the class that he played what in his opinion was an inferior role to his university educated colleagues and was limited to teaching the lower forms. Such outbursts, which were accompanied by much wailing and gnashing of teeth, appealed to him, for although he had given up his acting career, it had

* A suburb of Barmen. *Translator's note.*

at least enabled him to take up recitation as a sideline, an art he also performed in public. With the exaggerated pathos customary in those days, he declaimed in the style of Ludwig Wüllner. When he recited epic poetry, a shiver would run down the spine of the audience. The declamation of poetry also played a major role in his German lessons. Whenever there was a bereavement, such as when our art teacher died, he would recite in the hall a suitable passage from the Psalms in a funereal and thunderous voice. I can still hear his enunciation of the sentence "As for man, his days are like grass." He went to town on the word "grass," building it into a sound picture of utter gloominess and positively groaning it out. It sounded like he was grinding a rusty can beneath his feet.

As chance would have it, I bumped into two other ex-pupils of my school a few years ago. Although ten years separated the dates on which we had taken our graduation examinations, one of the few teachers who had taught all three generations and was vividly remembered by each of us was none other than Ernst Pfeffer. The three of us took it in turns to declaim with exactly the same rhythm and intonation the *ErlKönig* (Elf King) and *Das Gewitter* (The Storm) by Gustav Schwab. Our training had been so precise and continuous that it had survived the passing of the decades. Even today, I could give such a performance, if requested.

Pfeffer's penchant for the more gruesome texts of the poetic canon was also sometimes capable of acquiring a sadistic streak. Instead of giving a pupil he hated an "F" for his essay—which was lowest mark possible—he gave him a whole side full of "Zs," adding that it would be impossible for the boy to cancel these out before the final examination, even if every piece of work he produced deserved an "A." Throughout my life I have never forgotten the horror I felt at the apparent finality of this cruel deed.

But I am already quite ahead of myself, and return now to the entrance examination. At last my name was called. Much to my embarrassment, my mother kissed me goodbye and placed me in the entourage of the third teacher responsible for the lower forms, namely our music teacher, Ernst Schnitzler. He was a small man with a goatee beard and a winning warmheartedness. His mere appearance was enough to alleviate my fear. He was already known to me as the organist of our church and enjoyed a high reputation both in the musical life of the school and as a choirmaster. It must have distressed him that even his most zealous efforts only succeeded in eliciting rather dubious sounds from me. (Although I loved music, it did not return my love.) On the other hand, my progress in his handwriting classes pleased him—which anyone who saw my present scrawl would hardly believe!—and I certainly did not mind attending his excellent religious studies classes. Well, I passed the examination, and when my parents congratulated me and threw their arms around me, my father pulled from a bag in which he had hidden the green and silver cap worn by first-year pupils and placed it without further ado upon my head.

On the Way to Life-Long Friendships

When school began, the class very soon developed a sense of community, the core of which has remained intact to this day.

One of my closest friends at school was Willi, who later became headmaster of the grammar school in Sedan Street, and who was also a highly capable classical philologist who was destined to die far too early. Willi was the son of a minor railroad official who was highly regarded for his reliability. As a young schoolboy, Willi had already developed such a strong personality and a mind of his own that he was also respected by the offspring of upper-class families, despite his modest social background. As early as the first days of our friendship, he impressed me with his linguistic ability. He would also often drag me off to a hidden corner of the schoolyard and read to me stories of a least a page long that he had written about Indians or criminals. What impressed me most about this was the virtuosity with which he employed the attributive participial phrase, which at that time was still unkown to me. In addition to this, I admired the resolutely formulated political position he had adopted from his father. "I am loyal to the Kaiser," he would confess with an intense and firm gaze. Although the Hohenzollerns also had the status of sacrosanct paragons for my parents, it would scarcely have occurred to me at the tender age of ten to regard myself as an autonomous subject capable of convictions of this kind. In our later school years, we became rivals in German composition. His linguistic talent, technical elegance, and deft turn of phrase reached perfect expression in his verse translations of ancient poets, above all Homer. Here his mastery elicited astonished admiration, even from the teachers themselves.

For many years, our star pupil was Hans, the son of the superintendent of Barmen. Despite being a good and loyal companion, we contemptuously called him a "swot." Although he continually passed himself off as an idler who had "done nothing," whenever he was asked a question in class, he would spout off everything by heart. He had the strange ambition to be accepted by the rougher elements of the class who lagged behind the rest of us. We took offense at this. In our eyes, he was a hypocrite, and because of this he became increasingly isolated. On one occasion, we hatched the diabolical plan of getting the whole class to give him a thrashing. In those days this was a rather barbaric custom occasionally practiced among boys. But then on the morning we were lying in wait for him, something happened that gave me cause for thought and, many years later, even found its way into my sermons. What then occurred appeared to me at a more mature age to be a symbol of the "strange dignity" (Luther) that makes a human being sacrosanct. This sacrosanctity is due not to the human being's nature or achievements, but to the fact that he is dear to God, indeed is "the apple of his eye" and may not be touched with impunity. What happened was that Hans' father, one of the most respected men in our town, had that morning by coincidence taken the same route as his little son took to school. When they took leave of each other in front of the school, we saw how he affectionately stroked his son's hair and patted his cheek. Then, as they parted, they both kept turning round to wave at each other for a long time afterwards. We were very touched by this scene. Whoever was loved by such a father stood under a protective taboo and could not be molested. This was certainly not a conscious thought at the time, but was rather a spontaneous and unacknowledged sense of awe. So Hans was spared and became one of us again.

Mind you, he always retained an element of the star pupil about him until his early death on the battlefield. After he had been made professor of history, a position he achieved when he was still very young, he said to me on one occasion, "Biebi (that was my nickname at school), you can ask me anything you want from the Middle Ages onwards. I know everything on the subject." This time he no longer disputed that he had "done something." We only learned later to appreciate his true personal qualities, particularly his loyalty, which, despite his one slight failing, he undoubtedly possessed.

I was also good friends with two classmates who at that tender age had already formed a life-long friendship with each other, namely Werner and Erich. It was Werner's flashing, sparkling eyes and his skill at drawing—a skill which expressed itself above all in a remarkable talent for caricature—that first drew my attention to him. His mother, who as a pastor's widow was forced to make great economies, had sewn together from pieces of a gray uniform a suit which did not quite fit his wiry body. But woe betide anyone who dared to make fun of him or insulted his mother because of it. From an early age, his upright character and resolute independence of mind became apparent.

Later, when we studied theology together, he continued resolutely to go his own way. He avoided the lectures of the star professors, whether it was Barth in Bonn or Bultmann in Marburg. He detested everything that was regarded as the "in" thing. Instead, he called on outsiders and those who had gone out of fashion. In this way, he constructed his own theological world. Werner was killed in the war.

Erich, who because of his somewhat girlish appearance was known in his youth as "Erica," had a very eventful adolescence, which none of us would have suspected when we were at school with him. At school, he was a gentle and endearing companion who was well liked by us all. But he had scarcely finished his high school examination when he was gripped by an unsuspected thirst for adventure. With no money and no knowledge of English, he set off for the United States with the intention of carrying out certain "sociological investigations." He visited every prison in the New World that was within reach and called on all their governors. He made such an impression on them—not least because, for some inexplicable reason, they held him to be a brilliant young professor—that more often than not they invited him to their homes. If no such invitation was forthcoming, then he requested to be allowed to spend a night in a cell for "study purposes." In this way and with a little money he had borrowed, he managed to travel through the whole continent, sending reports to German newspapers and paying off his debts with the fees he received. When I recall his eventful youth, it is almost impossible for me to believe that he later became a good, hard-working parish priest.

Of the schoolfriends that are still alive today I want to restrict myself to Herbert or "Skinny," as we affectionately called him because of his leptosome-asthenic figure. He began at a very tender age to charm us with his philosophizing and always had his head in the clouds. He grew up with his three sisters and one brother, all of whom were much older than he was and all unmarried. As long as his parents, who seemed ancient to me, were alive, I often stayed with his strange family. I found its sense of domestic contentment attractive and its relaxed atmosphere had something of a Spitzweg idyll about it. Herbert certainly suffered—and we with him—from the fact that, as the youngest, he was spoiled and pampered by his family. He was never allowed to go tobogganing with us or, when we were older, to accompany us on our hiking trips, because they envisaged a thousand perils lying in wait for their little brother. In the decades that followed he proved himself to be a loyal friend in all the changing circumstances of life and his friendship remains to this day a gift that I accept with gratitude.

There were two Jews in our class. The first, Rudi, came from an upper-class family and was the epitome of a Semite, as far as his phenotype was concerned. We could not help but notice that he belonged to another race, but in those harmless days, as yet uncontaminated by anti-Semitism, we all accepted him without reservation. He was a reliable friend whom we liked for his honesty in rejecting as alien to him everything associated with German Romanticism. When he reeled off a poem by Mörike or Eichendorff with complete incomprehension and the German teacher asked in despair whether he really did not feel something when he read it, he simply said, "No." With the arrival of the Third Reich he suddenly disappeared, and for decades we heard nothing more of him. Then a leading article about me in the German magazine *Der Spiegel* led to renewed contact. A copy had fallen into his hands in Israel, from where he got in touch with me. Uncomplainingly, he told me about his job as a bus driver (he had once been a law student!), merely hinted at his terrifying experiences under the Nazis, and asked for news of old friends. He was "an Israelite indeed, in whom is no guile" (John 1:47).

The other Jewish classmate was the opposite in every respect. He was blond and plump, obsequiously anxious to gain acceptance, calculating and opportunistic. Although he always remained an outsider, I cannot remember that he ever had to suffer any aggression. The worst we did was to despise him or laugh at him when his need to ingratiate himself had led to ridiculous escapades. Without doubt, the credit for our relative restraint belongs not to us but to the humanist and liberal spirit that reigned at our school and would not tolerate the oppression of the weak. That this did not cause any anti-Semitic resentment must have been due above all to the reputation Rudi enjoyed.

Remarkable Teachers

Of the teachers at Barmen, the first really great personality we met was Walter Holthöfer. He was our form teacher in the first year and, apart from a few brief interruptions, stayed with us until our graduation examination. At first he was our Latin teacher, but in the higher classes he was responsible for teaching us German.

From the first moment he entered the room, he was a figure of authority whom we treated with cautious respect. I will never forget the solemn way in which he commanded us to sit down after we had stood up in complete silence to greet him. His authority remained unaltered even when we had reached the sixth form, although by then he revealed his human and intellectual interest in us more clearly and treated us as mature conversational partners. Despite this, he was completely averse to all forms of precocious prattle about literature, such as a few enthusiasts of "modern" lyrical verse among us had begun to "indulge" in; rather, he wanted us to assess greatness on the basis of classical paradigms. However, he only allowed us to read material that he thought our minds could understand and intellectually digest. There seemed to him a great danger in the lack of synchronization between the immaturity of his pupils and the head start gained through their intellectual training—something that is commonly found in grammar school boys. His fear was that such training might alienate the intellect from life, thereby creating a mind which only functioned in a vacuum and never engaged with real life. This was the reason he refused our request to do Goethe's *Faust*; he believed that this work could only be understood by fully grown adults. But we would, he thought, certainly be capable of coping with *Iphigenia in Taurus*. Whether he was right or not, the fact remains that I will never forget the many lessons in which he elucidated the plot and characters of this work. It was my memory of these lessons which prompted me to dedicate my book on Goethe to him.

Holthöfer provided us with a remarkable initiation into the mysteries of tragedy by organizing large-scale performances at school of Sophocles' *Oedipus*, Aeschylus' *Orestia* and the *Medea* of Euripides for the parents and the general public. (Some of these productions attracted the attention of the press.) His stage directions and comments were essential in enabling us to understand the meaning of these powerful texts and immerse ourselves in the atmosphere of the Greek understanding of life. Occasionally, he gave some particularly talented sixth-formers—who by the time of the last performances were already at university—almost completely free rein to direct the plays themselves. For us young bit-part players, they were almost demigods.

For the moment, however, Walter Holthöfer was the little first-formers' first Latin teacher. He used to play incessantly with a long, silver watch chain he wore around his neck. This chain made a profound impression on my boyish mind. I also remember gazing in wonder at his high forehead, behind which was stored all the Latin vocabulary I did not yet know. In my imagination he became the mythical epitome of pure knowledge.

In his classes, he drummed the irregular verbs into us. We had to repeat them in unison, reciting them in a monotone plainsong until they sank in. While we were doing this, he would beat time by banging a penknife on the edge of his desk, which gradually acquired a deep notch. Even when we were in the sixth form we would occasionally gaze at that notch with a degree of nostalgia.

In the first year, we were not yet ready for the open discussions, brain-teasers, and problem analysis that were to make his lessons in the higher forms so fascinating. At that time, his task was simply to drum facts into us and train our minds. In this way, the material became firmly embedded in our memories, and we acquired the tools that would later enable us to handle classical authors with some degree of ease. His teaching method was planned on a long-term basis. Modern educationalists may shudder with horror at this because they prefer to introduce the serious side of life into their lessons through play. He, however, gave drills priority, aiming at establishing a solid foundation which would enable a playful development *later on.*

Nevertheless, we never found his teaching methods inhuman. His personality made such a conclusion impossible. Even as boys we did not fail to notice the little signs in which his humanity revealed itself. Once, when a pupil's mother had died, we were greatly moved by the way he spoke to him. He treated the boy with great lenience and for a long time afterwards was very gentle with him in class.

In the intermediate forms, he was responsible for teaching us essay writing. Like his Latin lessons, this consisted in the first place of hard, formal training. We learned how to formulate and arrange our thoughts clearly and coherently. At the same time, he inoculated us against all clichés and empty talk. I can still remember one of the rather dry topics we had to write on. The title was: "By what means does Homer succeed in portraying Polyphemus as a barbarian and what conclusions does this lead us to draw about the poet's ideal of civilized behavior?" Not only was this indeed a very dry subject, it was also very laborious and made our wrists ache. And yet, you can imagine the wealth of observations that Holthöfer stimulated in us by giving us such a topic, and how with the aid of his charming irony he enabled us to acquire an understanding of the heart of Greek culture.

Only in our last years at school were we allowed to write on our favorite subjects and undertake special studies. During this time, I sometimes composed essays that filled whole exercise books. Holthöfer went through our youthful productions sentence by sentence and left a trail of red ink behind him: No leap from one thought to another, no inelegance of style, and no distorted idea would escape him. Years later, when I was writing my first works for publication, I wondered what my old teacher would say about this or that phrase. I was pleased when I learned that he read these concoctions and held back neither with his criticisms nor with the occasional note of praise. We only gradually noticed how closely he followed the paths of those who had awoken his special interest. This interest in his pupils was not restricted to their time at school, but also continued into their later careers. He continued to radiate this interest even when he bumped into us decades later. Thus he never missed a lecture or sermon I gave when I was back in my old home town or nearby, and was always at hand with advice and helpful criticism.

His friendly guidance filled my final year before the high school examination with intellectual stimulation of particular richness. A new decree by the educational authorities had made it possible for some final year students in each class to write a so-called long essay as part of the high school examination. It was intended to be an additional test and was based on special studies conducted over a long period. I knew from reading the biography of Walter Flex, whose works had made a considerable impression on me in my youth, that Flex had written his doctoral thesis on the history of the Demetrius dramas. I conceived the bold plan (although I was not acquainted with Flex's dissertation) of choosing this same subject for my long essay. Whether Holthöfer permitted himself a little chuckle when he gave his permission for this project, I do not know. I then collected together the Demetrius dramas since Schiller and produced an opus of 120 large pages. When I spent a few weeks with the family at Lake Müritz, I even went so far as to take my materials with me—against the wish of my parents. I got up every morning at four o'clock and worked until ten o'clock. Mind you, I afterwards threw myself into the pleasures of lake-side life without a care in the world.

When Barmen was destroyed by a series of terrifying airraids—the magnificent school building thought by many a first-year pupil to be an impregnable fortress had also long since been reduced to rubble—the individual classes were evacuated to the country. This, however, did not prevent Holthöfer from making the risky journey to his pupils and to continue to look after them as their teacher. In the post-war years, he was appointed headmaster of the school, which had by now been merged with Elberfeld Grammar School, and had with unprecedented commitment built up a flourishing school from nothing. Since then, the school has traded under the name of the Wilhelm Dörpfeld Grammar School and continues to uphold the old tradition.

Walter Holthöfer was a great teacher. In the midst of the prosaic environment of day-to-day school life, to which he gave himself pedantically and untiringly, he always bore in mind the long-term goal of the education he was providing. The achievements of schoolmasters usually remain in a state of incubation for long periods of time, a fact that requires them to resist the threat of falling into weary resignation. His Christian faith, which he openly confessed even at inopportune moments (such as during the Nazi period), may have given him the strength to succeed in this.

Emil Christians, our mathematics teacher from the third year until our high school examination, occupied a position of similar importance in my life to that of Holthöfer. It took us a long time to discover the warmheartedness that lay hidden deep beneath his taciturn and austere nature. At first he seemed like a personified mathematical formula to us. He would tell us off with restrained severity and was extremely miserly with his praise. But in my youth there was hardly another human being to whom I wanted to prove myself as much as I did to him, despite the fact that I had little aptitude for his subject.

To me he was the epitome of manhood, and when he once said to me on some occasion or other, "That was well done," I was positively elated. But I was also more upset when, with a shake of his head, he threw a critical glance at me, than when other teachers had vociferously and verbosely told me off. This was the case, for example, when, as a fifteen-year-old fifth-former, I was one of the prizewinners in an essay competition organized by Barmen's local newspaper and had won a two week holiday in a hotel in Altenau, a little town in the Harz Mountains. My essay was entitled "The Most Beautiful View of Barmen" and was written in an imitation of the style of Walter Flex. On top of this, I had spiced up the essay by borrowing some of the language of the Romantics. But this self-criticism was far from my adolescent thoughts. On the contrary, I was extremely pompous when I saw myself in print for the first time, crowned with the laurels of "literary" success. When Christians entered the classroom I spotted immediately that he had a copy of the newspaper in his hand. My pulse began to race in anticipation of the eulogy I expected to hear from him. Everybody watched him keenly. But all he did was to hold the paper up and say, "Thielicke, your essay. . . ." And then, without a further word, he just shook his head and began immediately to write arithmetical formulae on the blackboard. That was one of the most severe and yet at the same time most healthy put-downs I have ever experienced.

A watershed in our relationship with him was reached when he held a commemorative speech in the hall on the death of an older pupil. It was as if the scales fell from our eyes. Despite the sober tone of his voice and his refusal to let it betray any emotion, we sensed that he was struggling hard to keep his composure. We were astonished at how sensitively he had understood this boy, how he sympathized with the boy's parents in their time of grief, and how he spoke his heart without indulging in any sentimentality. It suddenly dawned on us that behind the reserved facade there lived a human being who cared for us and with whom we were safe.

Right up until his death we remained in contact through letters and sporadic meetings. Not long before his death—he lived to well over eighty— he confided to me in our last conversation how frightened he was not of death itself but of dying, and asked me to pray for him. That this restrained man should request this of me shook me considerably.

It was 1946 and I had just been appointed to my chair at Tübingen when I had what was almost an occult experience with Christians. For some unaccountable reason he had became a formal member of the Nazi Party and because of this had now been removed from office by the occupying power. The shame and pain of this almost killed him. In a letter he hinted at his distress but did not ask for any assistance. Because I had got into trouble with the authorities during the Third Reich and for that reason had a clean slate, I now had to write many so-called clean bills of health for people who had in my opinion unfairly fallen victim to the process of denazification. (This was something I was happy to do because the punitive measures undertaken by the military government were often more than foolish and were more likely to give rise to renazification than to prevent it.) In the end, I was being asked for so many testimonials that I gave my secretary a standard letter in which she only had to fill in the individual details of the person concerned. In response to Christians' cry for help, I felt moved to write an individual testimonial for him. This was so important to me that I made a rough draft by hand, before making a final copy and posting it. My intense preoccupation with his person is probably the explanation of why I dreamed about him that night. In this dream, I saw myself giving a lecture in Düsseldorf, which was the center of local government. The president of the Rhine Province was himself present and during the lecture kept nodding his head in agreement. Afterwards, he made a few complimentary remarks on what I had said, took me back to his apartment, and to show his appreciation even promised to grant me any wish he was capable of fulfilling. So I said to him, "Help my old mathematics teacher!" I then described the case to him and obtained his pledge to do something about it.

About three months later, this strange dream actually came true. I had to give a speech in a newly built lecture room in Düsseldorf. I believe it was in the Collenbach Hall. Present at the proceedings was the president, Robert

Lehr, who was later to become secretary of the interior. It was only after he repeatedly nodded his head during my speech that my dream, which I had completely forgotten about until then, suddenly returned to me. After the speech, he kindly made a few appreciative remarks and asked me to spend the evening with him in his apartment. There he treated me to a good meal and excellent wines, which in those famine-stricken days was quite an event! The euphoria this produced gave me the frankness to blurt out an account of my dream. "You'll laugh, my dear Dr. Lehr," I said, "but I dreamed sometime ago of this evening at your home." Astonished, he replied, "Absolutely everything? Did you also see the pictures here? That would be really uncanny! Are you a visionary?" "No, certainly not," I replied. "I don't recall the details. But I really did dream that you would nod your head during my speech and afterwards invite me back to your house." Once again he was surprised and again followed up the theme with the question, "You really dreamed everything here?" To which I replied, "*Almost* everything. *One* detail was different." "Really? That's interesting. What was different, then?" "Well," I replied, "in my dream you promised to grant me a wish." I then told him the story of my mathematics teacher and his difficulties. "Then I think we should bring your dream to completion," he said. "What's the man called?" he asked, while taking a notebook from his breast pocket. "I also dreamed of you reaching into your breast pocket," I let slip. I think I was lying when I said that. At any rate, I'm no longer certain if I dreamed it or not. When I spoke the following evening in Wuppertal, and was afterwards approached by Christians, I told him what had happened. I can still see how his face lit up. A few weeks later he was indeed reinstated in his old job. Whether that evening in Düsseldorf played a role in this, I do not know.

I next met Christians under rather special circumstances in Tübingen. In 1951, it was my duty as rector to open a mathematics conference there, in which my old teacher was also taking part. I had to think quite hard about what sort of speech I should make in this delicate situation. In the end I drew a brief and rough portrait of my former mathematics teacher. In this way a "human" speech came about, in which I did not exactly go easy on myself in order all the more to sing the praises of my old teacher. I took advantage of this solemn occasion to express my gratitude to him. I include here a short passage from my old manuscript.

The return yielded from being taught mathematics at school certainly does not consist in the ability to look up logarithms or to celebrate the mysteries of differential calculus into ripe old age. No, this return, which has a creative result in the intellectual processes of later life, is of a completely different kind. Kerschensteiner once said that education is what is left when one has forgotten everything one has learned. If this is also applicable to the learning of mathematics, then we can say that its function in the education of the human being and consequently its continued influence in life consists of two things. First, it surely consists in the fact that even the individual with little aptitude for mathematics is confronted *once* in his life with the classical model of exactness. . . .

The second thing that remains is the impression made by the teacher whose intellectual honesty was molded by that law of exactness. Even what a teacher has said to a young person and has drawn on the blackboard for him may soon be forgotten. But it will not be forgotten that *he* said it. In the pupil's memory of a man for whom reality had passed into law and whose ethos was itself an example of mathematical exactitude and honesty, a permanent presence is given to the transcendent laws of mathematics.

So by saying a few words about my old mathematics teacher—I hope in his modesty he will be kind enough to forgive me—I would like to show my reverence for *all* teachers of this respectable discipline. I would like to tell them that precisely we untalented mathematics pupils have grasped a little of what they sought to teach us in their ill-fated labor of love and that their work was thus not completely in vain. Perhaps we even have special authority— possibly more so than our more gifted brethren—to join in discussions of the educational importance of mathematics. For we fulfill in a very special way every postulate laid down by Kerschensteiner in the passage I quoted earlier. Not only have we forgotten everything, but we never quite understood it in the first place. So what we have retained must really constitute a first-class proof of our education. . . .

At the dinner I gave afterwards for the leading personalities of the conference and a few of my colleagues from the university, I placed Emil Christians between the great Eduard Spranger and the Nobel Prize winner Adolf Butenandt. I wanted to honor him as much as I could.

In the higher forms, the dominant figure was Wilhelm Bohle. He was the last of our grammar school teachers to hold the title of professor (which he was in the literal meaning of the word). He was a figure who commanded great respect. We never actually saw him in "the lower corridor" where the lower years were taught. As adolescents, we only crossed his path when for some reason we had to enter the "hallowed sanctuary" of the upper corridor. That was where the sixth-formers lived, who in any case looked down upon us adolescents. The professor, who was always surrounded by an aura of lofty dignity, could be seen strolling in this upper corridor.

Even from behind, his authority was clearly visible. He had the habit of tilting his head forward by several degrees, which contrasted strangely with his upright posture. He compensated for the angle this created by constantly directing his gaze in a slightly upward direction. He never fixed his eyes on the floor but allowed them to flit back and forth incessantly and playfully. As a result, he never failed to notice everything that went on around him. When he later became our teacher, we discovered that it was impossible even for a moment to disengage one's mind, to let one's thoughts wander, or to doze off. You could be absolutely certain that he would notice the slightest nuance in a pupil's attentiveness, and would at that very moment call upon that pupil to answer a question. He kept watch over us with eagle eyes.

His clothes seemed unintentionally to underline his dignity. His suits gave the impression that he had commissioned a good tailor to save him from the banality of the common herd by designing clothes which spurned the latest fashions. The wide jackets, which he wore open, were draped around him like a robe. This manner of dress avoided every impression of snazzy chicness but never gave the impression of sloppiness.

If we had taken the trouble to bring this interrelation of attire, gait, and posture under a single concept, then we would have characterized him as "respectable middleclass." Only later did we notice that it was merely his pronounced consciousness of authority that was conservative and patriarchal in character. In every other area he held highly modern views, especially with regard to politics and education. His conservative appearance concealed an energetic man who kept abreast of the times and observed with great vigilance and sensitivity the way the world was moving.

We were already standing next to our benches when Wilhelm Bohle entered our classroom for the first time. You could have heard a pin drop. He walked towards his desk, and with an expressionless face fixed each of us with his lively eyes, before saying, "Take your seats, gentlemen."

That's right, in our nervousness we had completely forgotten that from now on we would be addressed formally. Bohle's formality was an appeal to our manhood that forbade us to show fear. His use of the term "gentlemen" was a brief straightforward entreaty to cooperate with him, to fulfill his not inconsiderable demands with loyalty, to behave as adults—and to keep our distance. A slight tinge of irony may have colored his words, a very thin, almost imperceptible descant containing the thought, "Right, you lot! I'm giving you the chance to become gentlemen!"

At the time, however, this passed us by unnoticed. We just understood instinctively that this man, who expected us to behave formally, would in turn also behave formally towards us. He was without doubt a real gentleman, and although we were only apprentices on the bottom rung of this hierarchy of gentlemen, we had at least been accepted into the order of adults.

And this did indeed turn out to be the way he acted. Of course, he saw us occasionally in the street with a girl, and of course he noticed the forbidden cigarette which we quickly hid behind our backs. But he overlooked such things; young gentlemen should not be made to lose face and stand there like stupid boys caught with their trousers down. To have treated us in such a manner would have forced him into the hated role of the teacher with the big stick, the "schoolmaster," and this was degrading to him. No, we associated with each other as gentlemen; we felt ourselves to be respected and we grew as a result of this respect.

It may be that we were a pretty talented class and that this pleased him. For this reason there awoke in us the passion to do well at Greek philology and to achieve technical accuracy in our translations. We were delighted by the historical perspectives he opened up to us and by his portrayal of great historical figures. For Wilhelm Bohle, history was not the summation of past epochs but the great model from which the driving forces and laws of human life could be read. He subjected history to close examination from a stand-point that was determined by the pressing problems of world, economic, and cultural policy. For this reason, we were constantly discussing the reports and editorials of the great daily newspapers. In this way, his history lessons pulsed with life and were filled with exciting topicality. In exchange, we accepted that we had to be exact and were not allowed to indulge in sloppy reasoning, for he was a stickler for numbers and names.

He was, by the way, a proper professor, for he "lectured" and did not simply ask us to regurgitate facts. And although his basic technique was the monologue, he had an extremely skillful way of compelling us to take an active part in his lessons by constantly breaking off his monologues to ask us questions. We were always partners and companions in his thought processes and never "pupils" to be talked at. He allowed us to give lengthy seminar papers and extracted from us in a genuinely Socratic manner whatever intellectual ability there was within us. And he was kind enough to let us know when our work stimulated his own thoughts. Anyway, after a short time a complete change had come over us and we began to love him. Perhaps his "young gentlemen" had seen through his stern appearance and broken through his reserve to a degree that he had not experienced in previous decades. He had always enjoyed respect, but love was something he first found with us. This came to expression in a touching scene.

It was his birthday and we wanted to serenade him and hold a torchlight procession in his honor. We had composed an extremely kitschy and cheeky song which we wanted to sing to the melody of "Gold and silver are my heart's desire." It concluded with the silly words that we wanted to get down on all fours to congratulate him and drink his wine-cellar dry. It was a truly adolescent creation. When the time came and we had assembled outside his apartment near North Park, we were extremely embarrassed at our childish song. But because we had now lit the torches we had no choice but to sing.

After the first verse the professor came outside and stood before his front door. From the emotional expression on his face, we saw that Apollo had only allowed him to hear the melody and not to understand the words. The tears ran slowly down his cheeks and we ourselves felt a lump in our throats—out of our love and gratitude for him as well as because of our embarrassment. Then we did indeed drink his cellar dry.

During the Second World War, he moved with his family to an isolated part of the Black Forest. Thanks to his wife's courage and prudence, he was able to spend the last days of his life in a little house of his own. The shadows of suffering now gradually descended upon his life and sometimes he was tortured by melancholy and loneliness.

One day I was informed by express letter that he was dying and that it would give him great joy if I would visit him one last time. When I approached his death-bed, he did not recognize me for quite some time. He was completely paralyzed and was seldom conscious. Eventually he recognized my voice and his features were transfigured by the glimmer of a last joy. I then read the twenty-third psalm to him, which he clearly was still able to take in, and spoke over him the words of the final benediction. Because I knew how fond he was of his home town, I referred to the names of a few streets in Barmen that he knew well and mentioned the names of a few friends and pupils whom he loved. "Good words," he said afterwards in a barely audible voice. A few days later he passed away almost unnoticed. His quiet, inconspicuous seeds bore fruit in many hearts. He lived a full life and over his way stands the promise that "the teachers shall shine like the glory of heaven."

No account of the teachers who were most important to me would be complete without at least mentioning Hans Stemler, Latin teacher for the upper forms at my school. He played the elegant dandy and not only wore clothes of the highest quality but in the swimming baths would pamper his body with a fragrant ointment in full view of everybody. He endeavored to impress the role model of the gentleman upon us and was constantly explaining to us that this was to be understood as "a fellow who is refined both inwardly and outwardly."

His Latin classes suffered from the reluctance with which he gave them. The formal linguistic refinement of the Romans did not appeal to his personality, which was aestheticistic and had a touch of oriental mysticism about it. I was the complete opposite; it was precisely the logical structure of Latin that appealed to me.

The result of his slipshod lessons was that our technical knowledge of the language deteriorated. Instead of parsing grammatical constructions, we preferred to encourage him to digressions on his favorite authors. These were first and foremost Leopold Ziegler and Leo Frobenius, but also theologians such as Rudolf Otto and Paul Tillich, who was a rising star at that time. These were all names we had heard nothing about elsewhere in the school. Stemler would react immediately to the relevant words, which we knew how to slip in with cunning and Socratic indirectness. With delight he would then slam shut Horace, Livy, and especially Cicero, whom he hated because of his "slickness." Unfortunately, I was also able to distinguish myself in this area, with the result that he came to regard me as a disciple and even once invited me for a cup of tea in his apartment, which was crammed full with souvenirs from his travels in the Far East and Africa. He invested a large part of his income in such expeditions. In his well-manicured, almost worshiping hands he showed me priceless pieces of porcelain and figures, and allowed me to examine them from every angle. His comments on them sounded like a liturgical celebration. A priest could not have held his monstrance with more care.

Hans Stemler's enthusiasm was so infectious that some of us, including myself, were prompted to read his favorite authors. So even at that tender age I immersed myself in the works of Leopold Ziegler and experienced a first hint of the enthusiasm that would bowl me over when I read his great work *Überlieferung* (Tradition) years later. I almost dislocated my brain trying to read Paul Tillich's book on the (then) *Religious Situation*, which Stemler had enthusiastically recommended to us. (Paul Tillich was quite moved when I told him decades later of my boyish efforts to scale the mighty edifice of his thought.) At his suggestion, I even had a go at Barth's *Epistle to the Romans*. Although Barth's paradoxes were far beyond me, I was at least able to sense the aura of something prophetically numinous.

Whenever there was a class reunion decades later, the memory of Stemler was always vivid. Each of us recognized that it was above all this "unschoollike" exception who provided our future lives with permanent stimuli. The gaps in our knowledge of Latin that he also bequeathed us did not upset too many of us.

High above the life of the school hovered the headmaster, Wolfgang Paeckelmann, who for us was the highest authority of all. He was an unusually affable and athletic man who was treated with respect by everyone, including his colleagues. This respect came as a matter of course and was by no means prompted by any affected headmasterly behavior.

During my time at school, I only came into contact with him once. This meeting took place when I was in the fifth form. The German teacher had rejected my essay on Bertrand de Born von Uhland and had written beneath it (I still have the manuscript): "A fifth-former does not write such essays, and no one expects him to. I cannot mark this work." I was in such despair over the injustice of his suspicion that I had not written the essay myself that I ran immediately to the holy of holies, the headmaster's office. I was sure that he would believe me and would most certainly help me. His goodwill and trust calmed me in a flash. He signed his name on the bottom of the essay and sorted everything out with my teacher.

He later became headmaster of a school in Kassel. After a lecture I gave there, I went with him and Bishop Wüstemann on a long walk. It was a hot summer's day, and before long we were tormented by hunger and thirst. As we were going past the fence of a large orchard, I commented, "A few apples would do us good now." But the Bishop, who was also tempted by this idea, fought against it, protesting, "We really shouldn't. . . ." But Paeckelmann, deploring what to him were ridiculous inhibitions, leapt elegantly over the fence and stole us some apples. He was still the same old Paeckelmann we knew of old and who had delighted our young hearts all those years ago.

Before taking our high school examination we had to state what career we intended to take up. When I replied that I wanted to become a theologian, Bohle, our professor, asked me if that meant that I wanted to enter the Church. "Not if I can help it," was my response. My school friends teased me about this reply at many class reunions in later years. And yet at the time this was precisely my intention. It is hard to imagine what little concern I had for the question of my later career. All I knew with reasonable certainty was what I did not want to be. For example, I did not want to become a priest because I was not in fact a Christian. Despite this I was attracted to theology. This was, in fact, for ideological reasons. I felt that this discipline was concerned with the eternal questions. This was admittedly also the case with philosophy, but I felt that philosophy was in essence a subject that was based on ingenious soloists, whereas behind theology there stood a community which was prepared to risk its life for what it believed in. That theology was also capable of intellectual fireworks became clear to me when I witnessed a blazing battle of words waged by the titanic Karl Barth at a church conference in Wuppertal. During this battle, he blew clouds of tobacco smoke at an aggressive Pietist. From out of this fog, he then brilliantly parried his opponent's arguments. With an indescribable charm which oscillated between good natured humor and irreverent irony, he swept away the sultry haze produced by this sanctimonious, servile person. He also gave the big names of my youth a rough time. This was when I totally lost my boyish heart to theology and applauded with such astonished enthusiasm that an elderly gentleman had to grab my knee to calm me down.

The high school examination—at least the celebration afterwards—went off rather differently than I had expected. Each year, I had watched with a pounding heart the ceremony in which the high school graduates marched into the hall and the assembly rose in their honor. I looked forward to the moment when it would be my turn. I have never forgiven Paeckelmann's successor—a respectable but somewhat introverted scholar—for spoiling this occasion for us. This happened in the following way.

For a few of us, the only examination we had still to take was the oral in our chosen subject. For us, the exams were practically already over. While we were waiting in a small hall for our names to be called, we were suddenly overcome by a postadolescent bout of high spirits. We began to rollick about and inadvertently smashed all the chairs. The teacher who then afterwards called us into the examination room took a look at the scene of the battle, shook his head, but said nothing. The disapprobation did not come until the ceremony in the hall. Before each of us was called to the rostrum to receive our certificates from the headmaster, he announced to the audience that a few graduates had behaved in a very immature fashion. Their destructive mania had caused considerable damage, as a result of which he was not prepared to give us our certificates until our fathers had paid for the damage. Although he then called us miscreants to the podium, instead of giving us our scrolls he just shook our hands. We left the podium feeling very humiliated, with the ironic applause and laughter of the younger members of the public surging around us.

That was the conclusion of those turbulent and eventful years.

Adolescent Religion

I grew up in the Reformed Parish of Barmen-Gemarke. This parish was later to be a light in the darkness during the Church's struggle with the Third Reich. In 1934 the "Barmen Theological Declaration," which was later to become so famous, was proclaimed in the church at Gemarke. This declaration acquired far and wide the status of a solemn document of confession and marked a sharp division between the Confessing Church and the ideological doctrine of salvation propounded by the Nazis and their "German-Christian"* accomplices.

The religious atmosphere of Gemarke was dominated by Calvinistic sobriety, but it also possessed a power and an aura which even a young person could not escape. The theology preached from the pulpits was a powerful, biblical Pietism which was characterized by a unique style that extended right down to phonetic details. That is, the true pastor was recognized by the crisp, throaty, and fervent tone in which he confessed his faith. "He spits it out well" was the congregation's usual comment. This comparison of the pastor's performance with sputum was considered to be one of the greatest spiritual praises that one could bestow upon on a shepherd of the parish. I only realized a long time afterward that style and form of language, atmospheric conditions, as well as the intimacy and communal spirit of the group were very often of greater influence than the contents of the Gospel itself. This may have been the reason why a considerable number of religious people were taken in by National Socialism, especially in the early days, for there were people among the Nazis who had spent their youth in this climate. They were thus able to imitate the style—with, of course, fraudulent intentions—with which these religious people were familiar. The boozy leader of the Labor Front, Robert Fey, was a prime example of this. He had the ability to speak about the Fuehrer in the ecstatic style common among the Pietists and also to employ the phonetic device of speaking in that emotive tremolo so loved in Pietist circles. By this means he was able to win over those with the appropriate background. Such people, believing that they recognized the voice of the "good shepherd," hardly paid any attention to the other contents of such speeches and so failed to notice the wolf lurking in the background.

Incidentally, Gemarke had a puritanical streak and even went so far as to

* A grouping within the German Protestant Church sympathetic to the Nazis. *Translator's note.*

condemn activities that from the legal perspective were completely legitimate. Dancing, visits to the theater and even to the cinema were frowned upon by the guardians on the walls of Zion. In my adolescence, this aroused an inner opposition within me and I found hardly anything in their language and conduct that had any relevance to my questions, desires, and fears.

It was only when I was a young assistant in Erlangen and experienced the honest and unwavering faith with which this parish and its pastors defied the ideological tyranny of the Nazis and their clerical supporters, the "German Christians,"* that I realized that there was a great deal more lurking behind the supposedly intellectual poverty of Gemarke. What had earlier been the boring routine of going to Church each Sunday with the family, now acquired a quite new explosive force when I visited my parents. Going to church became a confession of faith, especially as the sermons—in particular those of the by now widely known pastors Paul Humburg and Karl Immer—left nothing to be desired as far as explicitness was concerned. There references were made to the "whore of Babylon" in an unmistakable allusion to the Nazi regime and its misdeeds. In the prayers the routine formula ordered by the authorities, "May the Lord bless the Fuehrer," was not employed. Instead, the intercession consisted of the request that God might allow him to find the "right" path or even lead him to repent and change his ways. Both these messengers of the Gospel and the elders of the Church—several leading businessmen with emaciated Calvinistic faces and eminent knowledge of the Bible—demanded that their age confess their allegiance to the Word of God. If this was not forthcoming, they dared to refuse to move with the times and to throw the interloper out with militant courage. The inhabitants of Gemarke wanted to live "under the Word" (this was also the title of a journal they had played a major role in inspiring). Under no circumstances did they want to place themselves "above" the Word, to misuse it or allow it to be misused for the ideological embellishment of human machinations, as happened in the Third Reich and continues to happen today in different guises.

There was one other important religious experience that Gemarke gave me. One of its leading shepherds was a modest light, when measured according to the criteria of both worldly wisdom and theology. I can remember how during a controversy Gemarke had instigated with the "Chief Ideologist" of the anthroposophical Christian community, Friedrich Rittelmeyer, he was almost incapable of advancing a single argument other than to keep repeating the sentence "You should leave the Word as it is." He simply did not have a clue and had not read anything of any relevance. On another occasion, when the Gestapo had banned Karl Barth from speaking, he read Barth's manuscript out to the audience. Though with great courage he braved the danger that his defiance surely placed him in, he read the text falteringly and sometimes with an articulation that distorted its meaning. It was clear that he himself scarcely understood the paper he was delivering. Nevertheless, this man had something I would like to call the "instinct of the children of God." He could smell demons even upwind. He saw through every wolf in sheep's clothing and did not allow himself to be deceived by any chalk that the wolf had eaten. He had the charisma to distinguish between the genuine and the false. Thus it sometimes happened that he was able to win a whole synod over and bring them back onto the right path when their resistance was flagging and they were seeking to cover up their intended retreat with ever so clever theological arguments. On such occasions he would step in like an angry Jeremiah and tear to pieces the intellectual spider's webs with such authority than even much cleverer heads than his would capitulate before him and see their carefully concealed thoughts of escape brought to light. It became clear to me at that time what it means for the spirit of God to choose fragile earthen vessels for his work. I realized that he holds in contempt those who pass themselves off as great personages. Whenever I recalled this man, who let himself be dragged through the prisons, sang hymns of praise there, and in all his weakness was a pillar of the Confessing Church, I would think of Luther's saying about the God who rides even lame horses and creates sculptures from rotten wood.

It would be a delight to let the Gemarke pastors of that period pass before our eyes. Each one of them was a man of striking appearance and each was a character, God's handiwork, so to speak. They were anything but pale reflections of the spirit of the age. I will limit myself to sketching two of them who played a special role in my life.

I was confirmed by Adolf Lauffs, a black-haired man with a fresh complexion and a small goatee beard. He was also the father of my school friend Egbert and—first and foremost!—of the first love of my youth, the charming and idolized Minni. I cannot remember anything of his sermons or his lessons. Both must have been conventional and somewhat colorless. Nevertheless, his personality and his "quiet and self-effacing way of life" still continue to influence me. He placed the main emphasis of his work *outside* the pulpit. Every day he would walk his legs off calling on the houses of the sick, the poor, and the desperate. He never paid mere courtesy visits just to cultivate superficial contact or to demonstrate to people that "We from the church are also doing our bit." No, even at the bedside of the sick he remained true to his calling and came as a messenger of the Word of God.

The warm-heartedness that shone through his somewhat awkward nature prevented any embarrassment to those in his pastoral care. He lives on in me as an honest witness to his Lord.

The archetypal prophet complete with snow-white beard and powerful stentorian voice was old Hermann Kraft, the parish's highly revered patriarch. He loved apocalyptic texts and announced the approaching end of the world and the Second Coming of the Lord. The constantly new insights into the grave awaiting the world, in which all vices, rebels, and unrepentant sinners would sink, and his dramatic description of the birth pangs of the last days held a dreadful magic for us children. The adults flocked to the church in droves to hear him preach, so that one had to arrive early to be sure of a place. During his sermon, they would cower beneath the thunder of his prophetic word. This message was anything but modern. It was enough for him to speak of the "beast from the abyss." He reckoned with the relevant associations registering on the minds of his listeners as a matter of course. Without doubt, he knew his way round the heavenly Jerusalem better than he did the streets in uptown Barmen where he had his parish.

But he also had (which was a comfort!) some very human traits. His carnal desires were focused on all forms of cream gateau and on strong Berg coffee "with the works" (with additional dainties). My mother often told me the story of the vast quantity he had consumed at my christening. That was also the reason he liked to turn up at the birthday parties of old ladies, including those of my grandmother. The only difficulty was that the Creator had omitted to provide him with any talent for making light conversation. Because he could not simply fall silent or leave immediately after having at last eaten his fill, he resorted to the solution of testing the old ladies on the biblical texts used at their christenings, confirmations, and weddings. When this material was exhausted, he would go on to talk about the mottoes of sister parishes. As a consequence, my grandmother used to look forward to her birthday with trepidation and long before it arrived had already begun with a red face to memorize her collection of biblical texts.

Of all people, it was this old Kraft who exposed me to the first trace of what as a result of Bultmann's work was later to be known as "demythologization." One day there was a furious ringing at our glass door. When I opened it, the white beard of the venerable patriarch positively rushed in at me. Mumbling and in a peremptory tone, he said just two words: "The toilet!" At this my world collapsed. That a man who lived only in the higher sphere of the spirit should have the same needs as me was something I just could not grasp. If at that time I had had the intellectual wherewithal to explain why this event was such a shock to me, I would certainly have cited as my reason that such a man does not digest, but spiritualizes everything.

My religious life during my youth was determined for the most part by the "BG," the Bible Group for grammar school boys. We met every Saturday afternoon to practice throwing the javelin and afterward to take part in a prayer meeting led by an older pupil. It made a profound impression on me when sport heroes, who had distinguished themselves in school competitions and were idolized by us smaller boys, revealed themselves in simple words to be disciples of Jesus.

The highlight was a stay of several weeks at a summer camp at "Abbenroth," a holiday camp in a beautiful part of the countryside that was owned by the Bible Group. In retrospect, the semimilitary organization—we had to fall into pairs, call out our numbers, which were then reported to the chief—seems a little strange. But this paled into insignificance beside two other aspects of camp life which made a profound impression upon me. First, something took place there that was otherwise absent from my general school life, namely, a friendly cooperation between different age groups, which was heightened still further by our Christian brotherhood. Not only did the grown-up sixth-formers play games and sport with us adolescent fourth-formers, but we were also allowed to go on walks with them and discuss openly the lectures on the Bible we had heard, our difficulties at school, or our personal problems. As a result of this, we boys looked up to some of the older pupils with great enthusiasm. They became role models for us and we did our best to emulate them. Second, the dense and all-pervasive atmosphere of Pietism made a lasting impression upon me. Although in retrospect, this atmosphere seems pretty extravagant to me, when I experienced it, it aroused feelings of happiness that I had never known before. Its chief instigator was the leader of the camp, the Barmen bookseller, Emil Müller. He was a small, red-haired man—and for that reason was nicknamed "Blue Bonce"—with a walrus mustache. With his crooked legs and sloping shoulders, he cut a somewhat grotesque figure in the midst of our military rituals. The way his prayers were able to stimulate emotion, to lament over man's sinfulness, and to express from the heart the joy of redemption made a profound impression upon us in this enclosed spiritual milieu. They aroused in us the will to become disciples and kindled in us an ardent love for Jesus à la Zinzendorf. We experienced what amounted to a conversion. I was so carried away by this that when I was fourteen, I founded my own additional Bible group with a few classmates, in which we each took it in terms to present meditations on the Bible.

All of this was certainly due to the excessive and transient emotions of adolescence. Nevertheless, it would be dishonest of me if I were to conceal that one particular impression has remained with me from that time. What this is only became clear to me a long time afterwards when I was present at an African-American church service in the United States. In this service, in which I was the preacher, the congregation gradually worked itself into ecstasy. *I* too had *once* experienced the exuberance of a religiousness that was so elemental that it completely burst the heart and filled it with happiness. I later learnt that all this was more "psychological" than "spiritual," and that the mystery of faith has its home in a quite different dimension. Nevertheless, I would not like to have missed this effusive stage of my life. It has enabled me to understand many religious phenomena—including the disastrous youth sects of later decades—that would otherwise have remained incomprehensible to me.

Love's First Awakening

Another characteristic of the exuberance of adolescence is first love. The unusual prelude to my first experience of love gave it a special touch that distinguished it from the general cliché of adolescent love.

The drama began in our religious studies class, which (as I have already hinted at) bored me stiff. The tedium of these lessons provided the opportunity for all sorts of boyish dreams, and when you are only fifteen years old, such dreams ensnare you with shimmering webs. Was this odd feeling that seized my adolescent self with strange fascination really "love"? Was this what adults whispered about and what was described in novels?

It was strange, but a little, sandy-haired girl suddenly broke through the indifference with which I had usually treated these creatures with their satchels and plaits whenever our paths crossed on the way to school. A puzzling and previously unknown feeling began to stir within me. What was it that was prompting me all of a sudden to try my hand at poetry, and why did I feel the need to use red ink? What was it that suddenly moved me (when before it had merely been a prosaic sentence in one of our school books) when Hölderlin sang of the image of "his beloved" and how it overpowered him, causing him "solemnly to leave his boyish games?" What was this line that had now been drawn under my previous life?

The brother of my secret love, Egbert, was a good friend of mine. Was I not being disloyal to him by allowing something far more elemental to rise up within me and drive out the image which had previously adorned the altar of my heart? A first premonition began to dawn on me that conflicts of affection can be more painful than clashes of duty.

The monotonous words of the teacher continued to drip into the room, and the boredom of the lesson created an increasingly sharp contrast to the colorful and lively images that emerged from my suddenly active imagination. And behold! Almost in a trance, I had slipped a folded note to my friend sitting on the bench behind me. On it I had written "I love your sister. Can you arrange a meeting?" Two minutes later, the answer arrived by the same channel. "Sorry. Can't accept the responsibility." Did he really mean that, or was it jealousy? In our conversations with each other we never mentioned our exchange of notes.

About a fortnight later, a piece of an exercise book was passed to me from the bench behind me. On it were the words: "Father (he was the pastor who had confirmed me) is holding a lecture evening in the church hall. You can meet her there. If you want a ticket, it will cost you fifty pfennigs." After I had confirmed my acceptance of his suggestion in writing, he passed me the ticket. With great foresight, he had brought it with him. I handed over the money to him. These transactions too were passed over without a single word. During school breaks and when we visited each other at home, we talked naturally with each other as if nothing had happened.

I guarded my ticket as if it were treasure, although it was nothing more than a simple note stamped with the church hall's seal and with the date of the event written in by hand. Obviously, they wanted to save the cost of printing. What was to take place at that evening, the ticket did not say. But that did not matter. The main thing was that "she" would be there! Perhaps he had even tipped her off. That would make it easier for me to approach her. Strange, but until this moment it had never been a problem to establish contact with people of the same age. To use the slang employed by us boys, one simply spoke to such a "lass." Now, however, there was a distance to be overcome that was both puzzling and attractive at the same time.

When the evening arrived, I was very excited and could not make any progress with my school essay. The thoughts would not come and dissolved into clouds of mist out of which her image kept rising. The dialogue between Odysseus and Penelope that I was supposed to write about was replaced by imaginary conversations with her.

When later on I rubbed a perfumed haircream into my hair that I had bought specially for the occasion, and also ironed my trousers for the very first time by myself, I aroused the suspicion and the lewd mockery of my mother.

It may have been due to my confused analysis of myself, or to my having read some psychoanalytical literature—such literature was circulating in grammar school circles at that time—but at any rate, while I was on my way to that portentous hall, I reflected incessantly on myself. The extremely sharp creases and my spruced up hair may also have had something to do with the fact that I said to myself, "You'll now constantly think that everybody knows what you're up to. You'll have the feeling that your movements and looks, indeed your behavior as such, are different from usual and will betray you. But that's impossible. That would just be your imagination. Nobody can have the slightest idea of your intention." This was how I encouraged myself.

When I gave my ticket to the two young ladies standing at the door, I thought I saw them exchanging astonished glances and behaving a little like startled birds. But I disregarded this with a gesture of great resolution. Because I did not want to turn around under any circumstances, I was not able to check what I could feel was going on behind my back, namely, that they were whispering and that obviously a mass of people had gathered and were holding an agitated discussion. Then, although there was a considerable crush, the stream of people pouring into the hall stopped for a moment, so that I entered more or less on my own. "You're just imagining it," I said to myself again. And it could also only be due to self-deception, to the hypersensitivity of a young man in love, that it seemed to me as if the eyes of the assembled public were fixed upon my poor person and as if they were all whispering to each other. Or did they think that I perhaps looked all too spruced up for a fifteen-year-old? Oh, nonsense!

My gaze glided across the hall, which was already filled with people, and caught sight of her face. She sat quite far back where there was an almost empty bench. Was I seeing things or did she really start with fright and blush when she saw me? Then her brother must have spoken to her and she knew what was going on. I deliberately avoided her gaze. I was determined not to give myself away by showing any special interest.

Instead of complying with the law of least resistance and making for the seats at the back that were still empty, I spotted an empty chair in the middle of the packed audience and forced my way through the crowd. Again, people seemed to shrink back from me as if I were a poisonous insect. The people sitting on the left and right of me leaned away from me and began to whisper with their hands in front of their mouths. I myself just carried on staring at the podium. The people on the podium—a deaconess on the harmonium and a female doctor who was well known in the town—also seemed to look across at me. That was hardly surprising, for they both knew me. They had often seen me together with my father. Had there been or did there threaten to be a hitch in the proceedings? The reason I thought this was that both got together for a little conference and I saw how the doctor shrugged her shoulders and how the sister made a discreet gesture of helplessness. But why did they look furtively over at me while they were doing this? My impression that everybody seemed to know that I was courting was obviously well-founded.

At last it was time for the event to begin. The deaconess announced that we were all to sing a song, the text of which lay on our seats. After the prelude, I came in with my newly acquired bass and indeed—resolute as I was—at full volume. A few young things sitting in the rows in front of me immediately turned round in amazement and with a hint of horror at the phenomenon of my sonorous voice. At this I toned down the volume of my bass and for a moment stopped altogether. Something strange was going on, but what?

A few seconds later I knew what it was and froze with horror. The audience was without exception singing soprano. Apart from mine, not a single male voice was to be heard. This was confirmed when I allowed my gaze to wander furtively through the hall and spotted only young girls behind, next to, and in front of me. I was at a women's meeting. It was now no longer possible to leave the crowded rows without drawing attention to myself in the most embarrassing manner and really making a laughing-stock of myself. This fellow I called my friend—what had he done to me! What disgrace he had brought upon my head!

But there was even worse to come. The doctor now approached the lectern, and this time she looked steadfastly past me. She then gave a talk on sex education for girls. I thought the ground would open up and swallow me. In those days, fifteen-year-old boys were incomparably more stupid than they are today. Our biology lessons were considerably less advanced, and not as open as they are today. And *she* was sitting behind me and witnessing my shame! Was it her gaze that I could feel burning into the back of my neck? The lyre on which I had played my first love poetry broke into pieces in my sweating and clenched hands. I put up a smokescreen of thoughts around myself and manufactured empty spaces around me in order to survive this harrowing hour.

Afterwards I wanted to storm out into the night and imagined I was wearing a magic hat that would make me invisible. Then something extraordinary happened. Outside, in the semidarkness, the girl approached me and said quite without embarrassment, "Good evening, Biebi!" (She must have learned of my nickname from her brother.) "Will you take me home?" That was true greatness, that was class. We chatted without alluding to the dreadful evening and eventually she restored my uninhibitedness. Whenever we met afterwards not a word was said about that awful evening, but we also made no mention of our love for each other. Only a little note that I pressed into her hand now and again and to which she responded with a message of her own, hinted in dashes, little dots, and by reading between the lines what united us. (I also said nothing to my friend and spoke to him as innocently as before.) They were songs without words that we sang in secret duets. We were not able to cope with what filled us and felt we could almost burst with joy.

School Journeys

The energetic and imaginative headmaster of our school gave me and a few school friends the opportunity to go on journeys to what in those days in the early twenties were far-flung countries. We went twice to the Netherlands and once to Estonia. Paeckelmann sought rich pastures for tall, lanky, and undernourished lads, of which I was one, in order to fatten us up at the homes of hospitable foster parents there. These journeys probably saved me from suffering more serious damage to my health. I remember with gratitude the friendly and selfless people who took us under their wings.

One of the journeys began with an exciting adventure. When I was twelve, two classmates and I set out for the Netherlands. We were much envied by our class, for the Netherlands, as our teacher revealed to us, was a land flowing with milk and honey compared to our hunger-stricken country. What is more, we were spared the imminent mathematics assignment. My mother had lovingly packed my suitcase and my father had allowed his advice to me to culminate in the exhortation to represent my defeated Fatherland with dignity and modesty. Then, the last day at school arrived and I set off with great elation. It was, however, to be a disaster.

When we were called from our lessons into the headmaster's office, we did not suspect that something was wrong. We thought that he was going to hand us our travel documents. The Dutch foster-parents of the German children had to write their names and addresses on the upper part of a cardboard placard, which was then hung around our necks. We had to enter our personal details in the second column; everything possible was done to prevent us getting lost. We were of course very eager to learn where and to whom our identity placards would direct us. But the headmaster, who was normally a very cheerful man, received us with unusual gravity and revealed to us that our trip had fallen through. The acceptance we had hoped for from the foster parents had not arrived. With this news, it seemed as if the ground had opened up beneath our feet: we began to sob. Paeckelmann watched us full of pity and fell silent. But suddenly he laughed and said, "Boys, I've got an idea. I'll get you the placards and bring them to you at the station concourse in Rittershausen." Our tears dried in a flash, and when we pushed off back to class, one of us said, "Paecki would never leave us in the lurch."

On the following morning, the station concourse was filled with children with placards for the journey around their necks—all except us. When we reported to the official responsible for transportation, he curtly turned us away. Nor did our assurance that our headmaster would bring our passes bear fruit, for our names were not on his list. At this new disappointment our eyes once again filled with tears. Nearly all the other children had gone through the barriers and it looked like we were going to be the only ones left behind. Then, at the last moment, the headmaster arrived, waving our placards from a long way off. The curt official, however, did not want to accept them. They could not possibly be right, he argued, because we were not on his list. But our Paecki gave him such a going-over that in the end he made several humble bows and let us board the train.

We needed two days for the journey and had to spend the night in rather primitive conditions. This was because we had to travel around the whole of the occupied territory. We had hardly arrived in our carriage when we began to study our placards eagerly. Utrecht was to be our destination. When we then went on to read the names and addresses of our foster parents, our hearts almost stopped beating. They were all nobility living in castles and manor houses—a count, a baron, a lord van something or other. This was going to be some life! We would surely be able to go riding, travel in elegant coaches, and go hunting with them. And we would be waited on by liveried butlers!

On the second evening of the journey, we arrived dead tired at Utrecht railway station, where many foster parents were waiting for the train that was carrying the children. In dreadful confusion and with much yelling and shouting, everybody sought to find the unknown person they had come to meet. We also held our placards up. But while all around us children were being embraced and kissed, nobody seemed to be on the lookout for us. In the end, we were left alone and deserted on the empty platform and sat down exhausted and overtired on our suitcases with homesickness gnawing away at us.

The stationmaster must have noticed the three lonely boys on the platform. At any rate, a man wearing a red cap approached us. Although we did not understand what he was saying, we noticed that he wanted to solve the riddle of our presence in his station. He read our placards and shook his head. When he took us into his office and looked up the names of our foster parents in the address and telephone books there, he frightened us by constantly shaking his head. Eventually, without concerning himself any further with us, he picked up the telephone. This increased our despair still further. Sometime later, there arrived a young German-speaking lady by the name of Miss Kraft. She inquired warm-heartedly and compassionately why we had been abandoned. When we showed her our aristocratic addresses, she too began to shake her head in that by now very familiar way. Later she explained what had befallen us.

Paecki had simply been unable to bear our disappointment at our rejection and so simply made up some imaginary names for our placards. He probably said to himself: Once the boys have got across the border in this way, they will not be sent back and are sure to be put up somewhere.

At any rate, the buck had now stopped with Miss Kraft. She was not able to conceal completely the embarrassing difficulty that our existence caused her when she confessed helplessly to us that she only lived in lodgings and could not possibly put us up. Nevertheless, she took us for the time being to her landlady so that we could still our ravenous hunger to some degree. The landlady, however, was less than delighted to see us and treated us—the only case I ever experienced in the Netherlands—in a surly and prickly manner. All the same, we enjoyed our soup and blancmange as if they were ambrosia and nectar. However, now no longer distracted by hunger and with the abatement of our nervous tension, our dismal situation and the displeasure with which we had been received seemed very black indeed; I could feel a crying fit coming on. In order not to lose face—I thought of my father's exhortations—I crept off to the toilet and had a good cry. Because I had not locked the door, the maid came in unsuspectingly, starting back when she saw me. Because a German boy does not cry, which was a common maxim in those days, and I was abroad where I had to represent my fatherland, I pretended to feel sick: that, after all, could not compromise my country! This dear lady then instructed me on what to do. She put her finger down her throat and asked me to copy her. For the sake of my country's honor, I bravely played out to the end the role I had begun and so brought up my first Dutch meal.

After many telephone calls, Miss Kraft found a place for our first night in a home for fallen women. Before I fell into a sleep of exhaustion, I heard the chimes of the cathedral ring out "Jesu, my joy. . . ," which softly led me in to the world of dreams. We never found out how it was done, but on the next day, word of our situation was put around town and, eventually, we found wonderful foster parents. They lived in an upper-class area on the Kromme Nieuwe Canal. We spent several fabulous weeks there and had many boyish adventures. I have only related the first of these, namely, our experience of being abandoned in Utrecht railway station. This experience retained a certain arechtypal significance for me even in later situations in my life.

For Barmen grammar school boys of almost every age group to set off in 1923 for a stay of several weeks in Estonia was, at that time, a sensation. Nobody we knew had ever been to this far-flung place. Most of them did not even know where this distant land lay, and my grandmother was horrified that my parents were prepared to let me go with the others to this distant "jungle," where there might still be wolves. That our innocuous journey was regarded as a great adventure is hardly conceivable today where adolescents jet in large numbers to other countries and even to other continents.

For most of my friends, and also for me, it was marvelous to make our first sea voyage from Stettin to Reval on the double-propeller-driven, high-speed steamer *Rügen*. Merely the description of this ship was overpowering! This was followed by a bone-shaking journey to Weissenstein, where we were put up in a boarding school run by a former lady-in-waiting to the Czarina of Russia. In conversation with the diverse inhabitants and visitors, she switched effortlessly from Russian into French and German.

We were invited to many of the manors of the Baltic aristocracy. Although I was only a fourth-former, I gained an impression of the human greatness of these figures. For the most part, they had lost their possessions and now sat around in wretched conditions in dark little rooms or in converted stables. Despite this, however, they still extended their hospitality to us. They invited us to glittering parties, took us with them to catch crabs at night by torchlight, and took us on long boat trips over the flooded land. In my memory, I can still see the countryside before me like an impressionistic painting. There were floods right up to the horizon, so that a giant lake appeared to stretch out before us, and in the distance lay unending forests.

Only from afar, as if they came from a different world, did the letters of our parents about inflation and the misery caused by the occupation touch us in this rapture. But there was one occasion when the outside world did indeed impinge on me quite closely. This occurred in a conversation with a

Weissenstein civil servant whose unworldliness annoyed me. He could not understand, he said, why we did not simply throw the French out of the country if they were causing us such bother. "How are we supposed to do that?" I replied. "We've been defeated and have no weapons." "Alright," the civil servant said, "then you just have to resort to cunning. You have to attack them from behind when they are not at all prepared for it." Such naiveté silenced even my boyish enthusiasm for discussion.

I have never forgotten the moving farewell at the end of the trip. Both those who were returning and those who were staying behind faced an uncertain, but at all events, dark fate. Hopelessness weighed heavily on everyone. The brief contact of these two so different worlds had illuminated the past weeks and had allowed a piece of vanishing Baltic history to light up once more before us. As far as anyone could judge, we would never see each other again. So we waved back at them from our narrow-gauge express train for a long time, until we closed the windows and were alone with our emotions.

Our time at school ended with the traditional "Weimar trip," which our teachers Holthöfer and Bohle were in charge of. I will resist the temptation to relate how this trip breathed life into what we had learned at school, the awe we felt when we entered Goethe's house in Frauenplan and visited his mausoleum. Nor will I relate how our hearts stood still when the great Ludwig Wüllner forgot his lines while reciting in the national theater and was helped along by a shout from his young audience. (He answered with a furious "thank you!") Many others have experienced and described similar events. I will limit myself to two personal memories.

In the evenings, we used to chat and drink with each other, especially after we had been to the theater to see one of the classics. On one of these evenings we met a former student of our school by the name of Ebbinghaus. He was a senior civil servant resident in Weimar and was a brilliant storyteller. He told us that as a young man he had been close to the philosopher Friedrich Nietzsche in the last days of his life, when the darkness of insanity enveloped him. He spoke very movingly of how he acted as a sort of servant to Nietzsche and Nietzsche's mother.

His title alone, "senior civil servant," was enough to fill me with respect, because in my childish innocence I thought it meant something like a ruling statesman. This delusion had a disastrous result when I was chosen to deliver an after-dinner speech, in which I was supposed to extend a special welcome to our guest of honor. It was the first speech I had ever made in my young life, and I was filled with an indescribable stage fright, especially when I thought of this venerable person. I had taken the precaution of discreetly jotting down my notes on a beer mat. And, to give myself an air of casualness, I put one hand in my pocket and wrapped my fingers around the huge keys of the room I was staying at. These formed a triangle in my pocket because the bit of one was stuck in the handle of the other. When Bohle at last gave me the signal, I rose and began by addressing Ebbinghaus as "Prime Minister." At this everybody burst into laughter and Ebbinghaus interjected, "That might yet really happen!" While I was struggling with my confusion, I watched with horror how my "rival," who also would have liked to have held this speech, picked up the beer mat on which my notes were written and apparently innocently put it under his glass. I not only bit my teeth together at this, but pressed the keys in my trouser pocket together so abruptly that the bit broke off. This meant that I was later unable to get into my room and had to make do with shacking up with a friend.

That evening, I realized for the first time what Morgenstern has expressed in verse in his gallows song on "Greaseproof Paper"—namely, that fear can be creative and can produce quick-wittedness, for, you see, in a way that was quite mysterious to me, I somehow managed to find the appropriate words, the cheerful and amusing nature of which won me my audience's appreciation. This, too, was yet another archetypal experience that was later confirmed time and again; namely, that I was at my most successful when I was in dire straits and did not have my manuscript with me. Not only enthusiasm, but also fear can be a source of inspiration.

The other memory goes much deeper. In my class, there were quite a few of us who enjoyed writing essays and who were also pretty good at it. So we hit on the idea of making a particularly successful essay we had written in class about our visit to Weimar into a little book. Then, together with a few of our own photos and a foreword by our German teacher, we published it as a booklet. I myself had contributed a much–too–lyrical, verbose, and effusive essay describing the view from the Wartburg. In this essay, there was a sentence that was repeatedly quoted in newspaper reviews. I spoke there of the miserable, soulless present, which we would only be able to rise above if we immersed ourselves in the greatness of our past. I then formulated the rather powerful aphorism: "This is the tragedy of our century: We do not mature by moving forwards, we mature by looking backwards. Greatness lies in the womb of the past." Journalists were fond of adding the remark that this aphorism betrayed the inner condition of "modern" youth.

Attitude to the Weimar Republic

Reading this passage again today, I really believe that this rather precocious formulation was an accurate description of our attitude to the present as it was then. For us, the Weimar Republic had no future. It awoke no political interest in us whatsoever. If any interest was shown, it was, at best, negative in character. We despised it. Even men like Friedrich Ebert, whose greatness is clear to us today, seemed to us to be ridiculous in those days. I can still remember seeing in a magazine a sick and disparaging photograph of him and Gustav Noske in their swimming costumes.

Compared with the splendor of the Kaiser's reign, this "journeyman saddler" seemed a dull figure to us. Of course, this distortion of perspective did not originate in our youthful mentality. It was only the reflection and crude expression of our encounter with the collective opinion of middle-class adults. On one occasion, this contempt reached such proportions that our sporting heroes tore the black-red-and-gold ribbons from their victor's laurels and trampled them into the dirt. This had an unpleasant sequel. Paecki gave us an unparalleled telling-off in the hall and punished us severely. But I do not recall that this made any great impression upon us. We just thought that his position as a state employee forced him to react in this way.

In this respect, contemporary political history was irrelevant and uninteresting to us. Even the obligatory discussions of newspaper articles in our lessons with Bohle, our history teacher, were scarcely able to change this attitude, at least not as far as domestic politics was concerned. And because politics was a vacuum for us, political objectives, let alone utopian dreams, held no fascination for us. That we were not motivated by any ideologies— unless one saw ideological motives at work in our disownment of the Weimar Republic—was founded not on our immunity, but our indifference. This was one of the reasons why half a decade later Nazism was able to sweep everything before it like a torrential river, encountering almost no resistance. This political indifference on the part of the middle class and its offspring had created a vacuum which the Nazis were able to fill with their ideology.

Today, my essay's odd aphorism seems to me to be the confession that the meaning of history had reached fulfillment in the past and, for us boys at least, there were no new tasks in store worth living for. We withdrew from history into a small, private circle of friends, into the romance of rambling, into hobbies and—at emotional moments—into the admiration for what Nietzsche called "monumental history," that is, that realization of the human being's utmost possibilities as they presented themselves to us in the greatest moments of humanity's past.

The classical grammar school may have contributed towards this attitude. Despite all the respect I have for the principle that lies behind this type of school, I have not failed to notice the danger that can lurk within it, namely, that in being saturated with a sense of history, one may be led to lose one's own history. It was indeed precisely this danger that Nietzsche wanted to draw attention to. Nevertheless, this can never become an argument against the classical grammar school itself, for what its loss means to us—and today we are indeed confronted with the disaster of its liquidation—will only gradually become clear to us. What I described as its possible danger, namely, a predominance of historical consciousness replacing concrete life, is only relevant in historical epochs in which appreciation for antiquity and *eo ipso* for past history in general clashes with a deficit of consciously experienced contemporary history. The youth of the Weimar Republic actually saw themselves handed over to this deficit.

Student and Assistant Days

1928–1936

MY STUDENT DAYS BEGAN IN GREIFSWALD, where I was lured primarily by the Baltic Sea. I studied there for only one and a half semesters and I have only vague memories of my last days there because I spent them seriously ill in hospital. That first semester lies shrouded in a strange twilight for me. I felt unhappy for a number of reasons and was approaching a personal crisis about which I will say more later. But I also have many positive memories of that time. I made some good friends in the fraternity Sedinia, and am still in contact with many of them today.

My fraternity was molded by the romantic tradition of the German Youth Movement. At night, we sang songs around a camp fire, went sailing in our own boat on the Bodden, and once went on a fabulous ramble on the Isle of Rügen, where I heard the sound of nightingales singing for the first time. Two professors, whose books I have kept with me to the present day, also had an important influence on my life.

Rudolf Hermann, the systematic theologian—as a freshman I was not actually supposed to attend his lectures—was a penetrating thinker of almost masochistic intensity, the epitome of a seeker of the truth. He even went so far as to make his audience participants in his thought processes. They were witnesses to the genesis of his reflections, to his constant critical examination of these reflections, and to the sublime way in which he groped towards preliminary results. All this was accompanied by much moaning and groaning, and by periods of silence in which he stared out of the window into the distance. His muted voice and urgent gestures revealed his struggle to find the correct formulation of a thought. There was nobody in his day who had so plumbed the theological depths of the young Luther as he had. His greatest pupil, whose research on Luther he decisively influenced, is Hans Iwand.

Rudolf Hermann often used to invite his students to his home in Wolgaster Lane, where we enjoyed the hospitality of his motherly wife. Even at home,

54

however, this serious man was unable to free himself completely from whatever problem was occupying his thoughts at the time. As a young man, I learned from him what it means to have a passion for theology. This, however, confronted me for the first time with the question of whether it was right for such a passion to consume the life it was actually intended to serve. Should the redemption that was the subject of such intellectual passion not also bring with it both freedom and the playful acceptance and use of the gifts of creation? Only later did the conflicts these questions touched upon become clear to me.

Nevertheless, Hermann did not live solely in the rarified atmosphere of pure thought. If he had, he would certainly have been quite alien to a twenty-year-old. We could sense that warm-hearted human qualities lay behind his intellectual inexorability. When I was in the hospital, he visited me every week. Although I was too ill to talk to him, he would sit for hours at my bedside, occasionally clasping my hand in his. He followed my career right up until his death and wrote to me whenever a work of mine was published. To receive encouragement and perhaps even occasionally some circuitous and qualified praise from this critical man always meant a great deal to me.

Another outstanding figure among our teachers was the New Testament scholar Julius Schniewind. Due to his patrician background in Wuppertal, Schniewind had a rather aristocratic appearance. His cultured home was always open to us students. In evening conversations there, we would not only take up the themes of the previous lecture, but also discuss literature and music. (He was, by the way, a pianist of concert standard.) And what enchanting stories he could tell! How vividly a piece of theological and philosophical history would come alive for us in his portrayal of his teachers! He was, however, first and foremost the pastor of his students. He possessed an infallible instinct for discovering what was troubling a student and, without being obtrusive, would address the problem directly. This could also take the form of severe criticism if he sensed that a student was talking pious waffle that had no foundation in personal experience. When one of us once spoke of "our sinful flesh," he sharply told him to shut up and forbade such parrot-fashion repetitions of pseudopastoral clichés. Should he one day attend a service conducted by that student, he added, he very much hoped that he would not be showered with such hackneyed nonsense.

Schniewind knew how to interpret the Gospels and, in particular, to present the person and words of Jesus in a way that brought their truth alarmingly close to us—even when we were engaged in complex philological work. In our eyes he seemed like an "original Christian" in the literal sense

of the word. It was as if he had been present at the events described in the
New Testament and could speak as an eyewitness. In his lectures there were
sometimes moments of such prophetic power that they took our breath away.
Nevertheless, his lectures were always rational and factual, and never indulged in wild religious ecstasy. When his words flashed like lightning
through the fog of false piety, as was the case in the scene I described earlier,
it was not the attack of a mocker making fun of certain Christian clichés from
a position of indifference, but a reprimand from an eyewitness. His mere
presence was enough to convey to us how spurious much of our conventional
Christan vocabulary was and how much was simply the regurgitation of
secondhand platitudes. He trained us to distinguish the true from the false.
He was for me *the* great religious teacher. He also remained true to himself in
the Third Reich and was on several occasions transferred for disciplinary
reasons.

We held him in great affection, not least because we sensed his love for us
students. He even joined in with our pranks and follies. He had a particular
predeliction for my friend and fellow fraternity member Hans-Martin
Helbich, who was later to become Superintendent General of the Berlin
Diocese. Schniewind was partly shocked and partly amused by Helbich's
cheeky Bavarian wit. I would like to relate a typical example of this.

Even in the bitterly cold winter of 1928–29, Schniewind used to pause for
a few moments on his way to his lectures at a crossroads in the hope of
meeting one of his students and conversing with him for the rest of the way.
On one such occasion, he bumped into Helbich who, since he was only
wearing a thin loden coat, was completely frozen through. Schniewind tugged
at the student's sleeve and said sympathetically, "Your flimsy coat is not
keeping you very warm, is it?" To which Helbich replied, "Well, of course I
can't afford a fine fur coat like yours!" That was a bit too cheeky for
Schniewind. With a stern countenance, he reminded Helbich of the respect
that should be accorded to someone of his age and status. "Mr. Helbich," he
said, "Please remember that I am a man who fought in the war!" "Aha! So the
coat is stolen!" Helbich then blurted out. By taking the bull by the horns in
this way and being yet even more cheeky, Helbich managed to transform the
situation into one of general merriment. All Schniewind said was, "One of
these days I'll stop that insolent mouth of yours!"

Schniewind saw an opportunity to do just this in his oral examinations on
the Epistle to the Romans at the end of the semester. As a rule, these
examinations consisted of brief, individual conversations in which the candidate had to translate and interpret a passage from the relevant text. Helbich

was summoned to Schniewind's apartment to take this examination, where he was kept waiting for a long time.

He had done practically nothing for the examination and knew very little about the subject. He relied on talking his way out of the situation, especially since he knew that the examiner had a liking for him. Nevertheless, the long wait was beginning to make him nervous.

At long last, the double doors leading to the neighboring room were opened. Despite his strong nerves, the Bavarian's blood froze in his veins at the utterly unexpected sight that greeted him, for there in front of him sat the entire faculty dressed in their ceremonial gowns. He got to his feet, completely nonplussed. The Dean, Hermann Wolfgang Beyer, then informed him in a short speech that university regulations required that one examination a year had to be taken in the presence of the whole faculty. This year Helbich's examination had been chosen for this purpose. "Dr Greeven," the Dean continued, "would you please take the minutes of the proceedings. Please begin the examination, Professor Schniewind." The terrified Helbich then began to stutter out a dreadful translation. It was a dreadful fiasco that prompted constant expressions of disapproval from the professors. Suddenly he noticed, however, that some of them were winking at each other in amusement and that Schniewind had great difficulty keeping a straight face. Scarcely had he realized that they were playing a trick on him (recalling Schniewind's ambition to shut him up one of these days), when he jumped up and began to make a speech. "Dean! Professors!" he said, "I thank you for granting me the honor of assembling before me today and think that we may now let the curtain fall on these proceedings!" In the midst of the amusement which followed, Helbich could just hear the voice of Schniewind complaining, "So he's had the last laugh after all!"

So what was all this about? The answer was that Schniewind had been appointed to a chair in Königsberg. He had then invited his colleagues around for coffee to bid them farewell and had taken this opportunity to enlist their support for the masquerade he had planned. They had all agreed to take part with great enthusiasm.

With the cheeky Helbich in the middle, they now all made their way to the dining table to celebrate Schniewind's promotion with afternoon coffee. The following night we were rudely awoken by someone furiously ringing the doorbell of our fraternity house. A postman had brought a large envelope sent express delivery for Helbich. Inside were the minutes of his examination. Schniewind had made one last attempt to get his own back on him.

I do not wish to relate any further student pranks. I felt I had to extract

Helbich's little caper from the recesses of my memory because it shows the idyllic life of a small university town in the late twenties, that is, in the brief period between the overcoming of inflation and the disaster of Nazism. It was as if history had held its breath for a moment and for a few years allowed *homo ludens* to flourish.

During the Second World War, shortly before I was banned from travelling and speaking in public, I saw Schniewind again in Halle—it must have been 1941—and spent a day at his house. This meeting gave me great support in the difficult years that lay ahead.

Literally the whole day consisted of people arriving to report some terrible event to him. Former students brought news from the front of fellow students who had been killed in action. Clergy wives reported that their husbands had been arrested or that a pastor had been transferred to the "suicide squad" of a punishment batallion or had been given a particularly rough time by the Gestapo. And so it continued the whole day long. On hearing the report of a particularly brutal case, Schniewind uttered with great emphasis a sentence that reminded me of the New Testament concept of "Exousia" (power): "The Lord will scatter them in a *single* moment."

I have never forgotten this prophetic moment. In those days just about everything Hitler did seemed to meet with success. We felt that the noose around our neck was slowly being pulled tighter and tighter. There was no end in sight. And then in such circumstances to hear this statement on the fall of titans! From then on I was able to follow the story of Hitler's terror with the calm certainty that his tyranny would one day come to an end. A higher power was holding the reins and would continue to guide us. Only the secretly cirulated poetry of Reinhold Schneider was capable of speaking of this end with similar prophetic authority. And when I read of the end in the abyss described by Goethe in his "Epimenides Awakes," I received a comforting confirmation of this prophecy. Goethe too had known something of the swing of fate's pendulum.

> That which has boldly ascended from hell,
> at iron fate's behest
> Half the world or more may quell—
> but return to hell it must.

After the war, Schniewind was also appointed provost of Halle-Merseburg alongside his teaching post. He was by this time a broken man, for the war had exacted a heavy toll from his family. His son, an eminent concert pianist, had lost all his fingers to frostbite in Russia. During this period of famine, he made his official visits by bicycle, until one day he collapsed. I always think of him whenever I come across the passage in the Book of Daniel where it is written that "The teachers shall shine like the glory of heaven."

My portrayal of this much-loved teacher has caused me to get far ahead of myself. I return now to the beginning of my university career in Greifswald.

After doing well in my high school examination, I enrolled for the theology course at the University of Greifswald with a completely unjustified sense of self-esteem. The silly comments of one of my schoolteachers who had read my essay on Demetrius played a major role in leading me to hold this exalted opinion of myself. On reading my work, he told me that there was really no need for me to go to university. Even today I am still ashamed of the vanity this created in me. My inability to distinguish between school and university, and the naive illusion that I had indeed already written one "great work" may have been the reason why I was not content with the introductory exegetical tasks Martin Noth set us in his Old Testament seminar for first year students. I thus asked for a "weightier" topic. This great Old Testament scholar—later one of the world's leading authorities in his subject—showed no derision whatsoever at my audacious and ignorant request. Instead, he granted my wish and allowed me to write on a topic of my choice. In my indescribably amateurish artlessness, I conjured up the essay title, "The Development of Israelite Religion from Adam to Christ." I still keep this piece of work as an example of the follies of my youth. Despite this, Professor Noth took the work completely seriously and even gave me an embarrassingly good mark for it. In his discussion of the essay with me, he did not look down on me as a stupid boy, which was what I deserved, but treated me as a youthful partner. Nevertheless, he made it clear to me that my essay was pure nonsense and that without first acquiring the necessary skills it was inevitable that I would make such foolish errors.

In this wise and gentle way he brought my intellectual adolescence to an end and showed me what it means to stand before a completely new beginning. I fell into great despondency when I realized the true extent of my ignorance and felt myself to be a charlatan. From that time onwards I regarded fraternity life, despite the good friends I had acquired there, as a torment which hindered me from dealing with the real issues of life.

I now know that the illness that lay ahead was a disastrous attempt to escape from my problems. I had suffered for some years from a massive swelling of the thyroid gland (goiter), which impeded my breathing. This problem could have been treated medicinally with some chance of success.

Although I was warned by various doctors against having an operation—especially in Greifswald where goiter hardly ever occurred—I employed all my cunning and energy to force them to give me one. It was not only my delight in dramatic and quick solutions which drove me to this decision (and was later to drive me to many other acts of folly as well), but above all the desire through pain and the dulling of consciousness to distract me from the horrible emptiness and dreadful lack of direction I was feeling.

The Illness

The operation took place at the end of February 1929 and ended in disaster. Besides a suppurating pulmonary embolism (empyema), which made the removal of a rib necessary, I was also taken ill with a serious postoperative tetany which was to remain with me for the rest of my life. Through the various case studies made of my condition I acquired a sad fame. I would fall into terrible and painful tetanic paralysis, which spread to the respiratory center and each time brought me to the point of death. These attacks were preceded by a feeling of animal anxiety. When in later years I often had to speak and write on the phenomenon of anxiety, I always had these fits in my mind's eye. Calcium injections, which helped temporarily, were soon no longer possible because the veins in my arms had become inflamed.

Although I went from one university hospital to another—Marburg, Erlangen, and Bonn—in my four years as an undergraduate, none was able to help me. Numerous attempts were made to replace the epithelial cells. These cells control the level of acidity in the body and had been destroyed in the operation. The doctors tried implanting the glands of people killed in accidents, which had to be implanted as quickly as possible beneath the skin of my abdomen. Several attempts were also made to implant sheep glands. At such operations, I had to lay next to a sheep on another operating table. Because rumor of this got around Marburg Hospital—not least because there was always plenty of mutton afterwards—I became known there as "Mutton Thielicke." Finally, they attempted to replace the epithelial cells by using a human fetus. For six weeks I was the sole male patient in the Bonn gynecological clinic, waiting for the sad moment when a fetus could be obtained. When the waiting finally became too boring, I arranged to be taken secretly to a cinema in Bonn for two hours. To be on the safe side, however, I left my name at the box office. And, of course, exactly what I feared might happen actually happened. A torch beam suddenly fell upon me and the usherette told me to go quickly to the telephone. The doctor was furious and asked what had possessed me to leave the clinic without permission. Case X had just occurred and speed was of the essence. When I arrived, I could see the doctors at the entrance of the hospital. Scarcely was I in the building when they began to rip my clothes from my body, before rushing me to the operating theater. There I had to pay dearly for my misbehavior. The scolding I received was the least of my troubles. Far worse was that I had to suffer an implantation of the glands into the peritoneum without any anesthetic. I always got caught on the very few occasions that I did something wrong!

All these torments were of no avail. Ferdinand Hoff, who was at that time a lecturer in Erlangen, was at least able to provide me with temporary relief by treating me with high doses of ammonium chloride. This resulted however, in severe symptoms of paralysis, caused by crystals being deposited in the muscular system. This in turn inflicted considerable damage on the kidneys. I was neither able to walk nor to bend down. I eked out my existence in a wheelchair and, in despair, continued my work. My fellow students brought me their notes from lectures and seminars, which I was only rarely able to attend personally, and understanding hospital managers allowed me to transform my room into a small study.

I recall Ferdinand Hoff with particular gratitude. This was not only because he was at least occasionally able to help me. His humanity was also a great boost to me. In the evenings, we would often discuss philosophy, above all Plato, for hours on end. He was constantly asking me to tell him about the Ph.D. in philosophy I was writing under Eugen Herrigel on the relationship between the ethical and the esthetic. Despite the poor state I was in, I worked zealously on my research topic. It was an agreeable distraction from my agonizing condition to be able to concentrate on a piece of creative work.

It was only very rarely that I saw Eugen Herrigel himself, my supervisor in Erlangen during this period. When I did meet him, he exerted a strange fascination over me. He had been a professor in Japan for several years, and had immersed himself deeply in Zen Buddhism. He even looked almost Japanese! Whenever anyone spoke to him, he appeared to wake from a deep meditative trance. When I gave a series of lectures in Japan many years later and mentioned that Herrigel had supervised my doctoral dissertation, the eyes of the audience lit up. I was also informed that Herrigel had understood the mystery of Zen better than any other European.

I had concealed my intention to do a doctorate from my parents in order to spare them the disappointment should I be unable to carry it through. It thus came as a complete surprise to them when I sent them a telegram informing them that I had passed my doctoral examination with flying colors. It was one of the few happy moments in those dark years when, after my move from Erlangen to Bonn, a copy of the book, which had been beautifully printed by Felix Meiner Publishing House, was brought to me in hospital. To get the book published, my father had had to contribute what was in those days the enormous sum of 1900 marks towards the printing costs. He did this because he and my mother believed that, in view of the desperate state of my health, it would probably be the only thing I would leave behind.

When I sat for my first theology examination at Koblenz University, which I took in Bonn, I was in such a dire state that Werner Tzschachmann, a loyal friend from school and university, had to accompany me and look after me. I was not even capable of dressing myself and only my strength of will enabled me to sit through the examination. Meanwhile, the Americans had developed a hormone preparation produced from animal glands acquired from Chicago abbatoirs. This preparation, which was called "Collipian Para-T-Hormone," was supposed to work veritable miracles in cases like mine. Unfortunately, it cost 1200 marks per month. In the economic plight of the time, no health insurance company was able to provide such a sum, especially since the costs had to be paid in dollars. Paul Martini, the Bonn specialist for internal medicine who was treating me, fought doggedly for government money to pay for this medicine, which, by the way, I would have to use for the rest of my life. I thought very highly of him for never leaving me in the dark about the seriousness of my condition. We spoke quite openly about this being my very last chance. He even gave me a copy of the report he had sent to the Prussian Minister of Education and the Arts requesting the financing of the expensive preparation. It concluded with the words: "Your decision in this matter will determine whether this capable and courageous young man may continue to live or whether he faces severe agony and certain death in the near future. As far as his capacity for work and his zest for life are concerned, there is nothing to distinguish him from other healthy human beings." After despatching this request, Martini discharged me at the beginning of April 1933, for it was now only a case of waiting for the Ministry's acceptance of our request or for the end.

While I was waiting for this fateful decision at home with my parents in Barmen, a brief interlude took place that awoke false hopes in me. The well-known specialist for internal medicine, Hans Eppinger, who in those days was working in Cologne, had come to hear of my case. Because he was at that precise moment engaged in research relevant to my case, he invited me to his clinic for about a month. He lured me with the promise to use his budget to supply me with the expensive Para-T-Hormone preparation for the period I was there. Although there were, of course, some disadvantages in being their guinea pig, I was not able to resist the offer. After all, it meant a further month of life.

So, one Sunday afternoon my friends took me to Cologne hospital. I sought to get through the first rather miserable evening there by filling capsules with ammonium chloride. I did this by weighing the ammonium chloride with the precision scales I always had with me. This was the way I prepared my "daily bread" for the following day. I did not after all know whether they were going to give me the benefit of the American medicine on my first day. Then, suddenly and without knocking, a person I had never seen before in my life entered my room with a large, growling dog. Without introducing himself as the head of the hospital—for it was indeed Eppinger in person—and without even inquiring who I was and how I was feeling, he curtly asked me what I was up to. Even today I cannot forgive myself for letting my surprise get the better of me. Instead of requesting him to follow the usual formalities and introduce himself, I obediently answered his question. He then described all my pharmaceutical equipment as nonsense and took them away from me. At this I explained to him, "If I don't get my dose now and tomorrow morning, I'll suffer a very severe tetany attack by ten o'clock at the latest. I should know. I have after all had many years' experience." With a scornful glare he replied, "Kindly leave that to me!" And while I was reminding him of his promise to supply me with Para-T-Hormone, he left the room without a further word.

After a bad night, I could feel a terrible fit coming on the next morning. My thorax tensed up, as did the rest of my musculature. In great pain, I struggled for breath and had a cork thrust between my teeth to stop the convulsions of my jaw. The ward doctor called the boss. Eppinger watched me with complete indifference and, once again, without uttering a word. He then ordered all the doctors who were not busy and all the psychiatrists to be rounded up so that they could watch the spectacle of my writhing in agony. When the room was so full with doctors that they spilled out into the corridor, Eppinger explained that what they had before them was a classic case of psychogenic tetany. With a genuine tetany of this degree, he said, the patient would scarcely still be alive and would certainly not have completed a doctorate, sat for examinations, and so on. He seemed to assume that I was not present and was incapable of taking in his supposedly plausible explanations.

While he was speaking, everybody continued to gape at me. Then he suddenly turned towards me, bent over my bed, and, in an unexpectedly mellifluous voice, said, "But now we want to free you from your pain by administering the liberating calcium injection." He was passed an enormous hypodermic syringe, which he then inserted into the veins of my arm. During the slow infusion he kept assuring me in the false sympathetic human voice he had put on for the occasion, "Look, your fingers are already relaxing. . . . Your chest too is now expanding. . . ."

But nothing of the sort was happening. The convulsions had already agonizingly paralyzed all my muscles and I was gasping for breath in a struggle against asphyxia. They had deceived me with a placebo. Despite the gravity of my condition, they had deliberately caused me great pain by injecting me with a simple saline solution. After this failure, Eppinger turned again to his doctors and said, "We will now take a blood sample to ascertain the calcium level." It was several days before I learned from a doctor I was on good terms with and who had contacted the hospital, that the calcium level in my blood had been so dangerously low that no doubt remained as to the authenticity of my tetanic fit. At last I received the calcium injection, which, as it had done on many previous occasions, rapidly restored me to my normal condition.

However, I now gave vent to my rage at having been so mistreated and berated these "gentlemen" for behaving in a manner unworthy of their profession. It was incredible, I said, that they could immediately diagnose me as "psychogenic" without first determining the level of calcium in my blood. Furthermore, I had been deceived. I had been lured into the clinic with the promise of being supplied with the American preparation, a promise which on the basis of the diagnosis they had just made could not have been meant seriously.

Then came what was for me the most objectionable aspect of this affair. While I was voicing my feelings in this way, these "gentlemen" continued to observe me, some with indifference, others with light irony. They saw in me the psychopath who was not to be taken too seriously. No matter what I said, it was regarded as a symptom of a psychological disorder. In later years, I actually became quite grateful that I had had such an experience. Since then, I have controlled my facial expressions whenever I have met somebody who was suffering from a psychological illness. I did not want to be guilty of insulting their human dignity.

After I had returned home, a message arrived from Martini on the same day I received notification that the Prussian Ministry for Education and the Arts had turned down my application for assistance. He informed me that he had received a recently developed German medicine which, although it had not yet been tested, was at my disposal if I wanted to make one last attempt. That did not sound very encouraging, especially as I had already tried out a large number of such medicines without any success. I was also too weak to feel motivated to make another attempt. In the end, however, I gave in to my mother's despairing insistence and allowed myself be taken to Bonn.

When I arrived at the hospital, the ward doctor gave me a small bottle. It had only been supplied to a few large hospitals for testing purposes and was not yet available commercially. On it was written "AT 9" (antitetanicum) and below that "poison," which was probably intended as a warning in view of the fact that the medicine had not yet been tested. This warning was also the reason why the doctors dared only to administer the very smallest dose to me. When that did not help, I drank the whole bottle in despair. I wanted to force a decision: either this maximum dose of the medicine would help me or the "poison" would kill me. That evening I bid farewell to my life. I sat there gazing constantly at the crucifix opposite my bed. (After I was discharged from the hospital, I was allowed to keep it and it still hangs above my desk to this very day.) I was only vaguely aware of the tremendous alarm my action had caused in the hospital. When I awoke the next morning, I was at first astonished at the mere fact of being alive and felt happy in a way I cannot explain. I had the feeling that I had been saved and could feel a sense of euphoria running like an electric current through my limbs.

This resurrection took place on Good Friday, 1933. I have always regarded my recovery as a miracle. I do not mean that a hole had been torn in the causal nexus in some miraculous way. No, it was something quite different. Two chains of cause and effect had taken place independently of each other. The one consisted in the development of my illness, which was heading towards death. The other consisted in the progress of a research project in the Berlin Hospital Laboratory of Friedrich Holtz, the discoverer of the medicine that saved me. What I understood and still understand to be a miracle was solely the stroke of fate that caused both lines of causality to intersect at that decisive point in my life, at that point where it stood immediately before its end. A quantifiable sequence of events suddenly acquired a personal quality by saving a human life. To designate this intersection as a "miracle" is admittedly only evident to those who believe "that there is one who governs" (these were Karl Barth's last words when he telephoned his friend Eduard Thurneysen immediately before his death). Even the New Testament never understood miracles as objectively demonstrable proof of the existence of God.

My deliverance gave me the friendship of Ferdinand Hoff and Friedrich

Holtz, two great doctors who have my eternal gratitude. For doctors like them it was a fulfillment of their profession when they succeeded in saving a human life despite the apparent hopelessness of the case. They accepted such successes with humility.

Anyway, after waking up the next day, things improved dramatically. What did it matter that I would be dependent on this medicine for the rest of my life like a diabetic! I continued to take it for more than four decades until it was replaced a few years ago by another still more effective medicine. Less than a year after my recovery, I was awarded a certificate for sport. It is impossible to describe the joy I felt at being restored to life after years of dreadful and demoralizing loneliness. I now knew what faith meant and everything that had previously fascinated me about theology was swept away by completely new impulses.

Meetings with Karl Barth

The last phase of my illness and the beginning of my recovery occurred during my two semesters at Bonn. In 1932, whenever I was well enough to live in my student digs in Quantius Street, some good friend would help me to attend Karl Barth's classes every now and again. In this way, I was at least able to come into some degree of contact with the great master.

From the very beginning, I had an ambiguous relationship with Karl Barth. On the one hand, I was impressed by the tremendous force and one-sidedness with which he emphasized the infinite qualitative distance between eternity and time, God and humankind. I was also enthralled by his ironic polemics, which darted like tongues of fire from the precipitous towers of his theological system. And woe betide the person upon whom he hurled his firebrands! He combined profundity with cheekiness, a combination that is as a rule irresistible to the student temperament. Despite my admiration for him, however, I opposed his thought because I believed him to be living in a theological ivory tower.

Barth did not concern himself with the concrete—either inward or outward—situation of the human being, and yet it is precisely to such a situation that the Christian message is addressed. Any consideration by a preacher of what degree of receptivity he might presuppose on the part of his congregation, what questions, hopes and fears they bring into church with them, which of their feelings and thoughts he should "pick up on"—all reflections of this kind he regarded as highly suspect. He believed that it was the preacher's duty to refrain from all attempts at making the Christian message relevant to the modern age. This was because, in his opinion, it was *the Word* alone and nothing else that created an audience. There was thus no need for the preacher's (manipulative) assistance. From such a standpoint, the mere attempt to search for "common ground" with the audience could only mean that one no longer believes that the Word of God possesses a power *of its own*. If a person subscribes to such view, then he must indeed be keen to rush to the Word's assistance with all manner of tactical tomfoolery and to consider whether he should employ direct or indirect methods to force an entry into the human mind and soul for the Word of God.

In this way Barth—at any rate in his earlier period and during his time at Bonn—eliminated that discipline which could be described as "natural anthropology." When we asked him on the eve of the Third Reich to say something about Christianity and National Socialism just for once, he refused to do so with his usual argument that current political problems were "not a subject for theology." He did, of course, have a personal opinion on all of these matters and was, he said, very happy to disclose them to us privately in individual tutorials.

That was typical of him. He understood the *political* significance of the enormous number of unemployed during the last stages of the Weimar Republic, the catastrophic state of the economy, and the predicament the Treaty of Versailles had caused German foreign policy—but *theologically* all this was of no importance to him. His strict adherence to an "infinite qualitative distance" between time and eternity placed these themes firmly in the sphere of our temporality. For this reason, there was no theologically guided *ethics* in his thought, at least not at that stage of his development. Due to the tremendous influence Barth came to exert on Church policy during the Nazi dictatorship through the increasing importance of his school of thought, this deficit increased the vacuum that existed in respect of the question of Christianity's relation to the world. The demented philosophy of National Socialism was then able to fill this vacuum almost without resistance. Because Barth became the intellectual leader of the Church's resistance and *de facto* the chief theologian of the Confessing Church shortly after Hitler came to power, this anthropological deficit also had an influence upon its program. It was to become a severe handicap to the Confessing Church that in essence it spoke merely *pro domo*—that is, on behalf of the continued existence of the Church and its creed. Characteristic of this was its slogan

"The Church must remain the church." For the Confessing Church the issue was almost exclusively one of preserving church identity.

Thus in the early stages of the Third Reich they were content with repelling the penetration of Nazi supporters—that is, the "German Christians"—into the leadership of the Church. In adopting this course of action, it was all too easy to overlook the fact that Nazi strategy was aimed at seizing power precisely in those *anthropological* areas, in the Church's *worldly surroundings*, so to speak, that they regarded to be outside the Church's domain. The Nazis aimed at ousting the church from the schools and universities by means of ideological indoctrination, from the upbringing of children by giving a monopoly to the Hitler Youth and disbanding church associations, and from social and domestic policy by eliminating political parties and trade unions. But all this, essentially through Barth's influence, simply was not regarded as a theological issue and did not appear to touch the taboo of the church's creed.

As a result of this, attention was fixed on issues whose only relevance was to the inner life of the church. (Only on exceptional occasions—as was the case with Bonhoeffer, the Kreisauer group, and the Freiburg resistance movement—were voices raised which understood the church's duty to be to offer resistance in a much broader sense.) Now, if Hitler had impugned the Augsburg Confession or the Heidelberg Catechism or any other confessional documents, *then* they would have willingly allowed themselves to be burned at the stake! But anyone who waited for this moment of *status confessionis* waited in vain. The Nazi bosses, of course, did not have the slightest inkling that such venerable documents existed.

So, within the church they resisted the supporters of the Nazis with courage and self-sacrifice, while in the outside world Hitler was endeavoring to destroy both human and Christian values and was laying siege to the city of God with ever greater ferocity. It was only much later—and this was probably prompted primarily by the Nazi oppression of the Jews—that members of the Confessing Church began to look beyond their own borders and at last grasp the comprehensive strategy of the Antichrist. This also led Karl Barth, from about 1937 onwards, to make a theological *volte-face*.

Of course, these developments could not be even remotely foreseen when I was studying under Barth in 1932. The reservations I had towards the master at that time and which prevented me from becoming a "Barthian" were founded primarily on my instinctive feeling that his theology did not take the secular framework of human existence seriously and would therefore inevitably degenerate into dogmatic speculation. Even at this early period, I began to work on an alternative theological program. I was soon to hurl this rival theological position at the great man on what for me was to be an unforgettable evening.

Once a week, Barth used to hold open evenings at his home, where he would discuss the lectures of the previous week in cheerful dialogues with his students. On one such evening, I summoned up all my courage and launched a vigorous attack on the anthropological deficiency in his theology. I had just been awarded a Ph.D. in philosophy and sought to make clear to him by means of numerous quotes from Kant and with my own ideas that neither a theology nor a philosophy of education could legitimately ignore with such contempt as his did the structure of human consciousness and the existential position of the person to whom it was addressed. At the basis of his position lay something like a magical understanding of the Word which robbed the Gospel of its concreteness and brought back the old heresy of docetism in a new and extreme form. He thereby barred the way toward the development of a Christian ethics and left the human being with no theological guidance in life. Instead of providing such an ethics, he transferred his doctrinal endeavors to remote metaphysical spheres, expending his intellectual energy in speculation on the Holy Trinity and other "heavenly" themes.

It was certainly a rather youthful and overly tempestuous attack. The students present, most of whom were loyal disciples of Barth, listened with embarrassment, for in general these evenings consisted of faithful recapitulations of what the master had said in his lectures. But Barth appeared to enjoy somebody stepping out of line for a change and attacking the foundations of his thought. At any rate, a sharp battle of words took place between us, which, of course, was unable to end with the victory or defeat of either of the adversaries. Anyway, at the end of our debate, he thanked me and said that such penetrating philosophical discussions had not taken place for a long time at his evening meetings. He even asked me to keep coming to them and to play devil's advocate for him. This request annoyed me a little because his friendly praise could not hide the fact that my attack had not shaken him in the slightest. For him, I was merely the advocate of an opposing position he had ruled out long ago. However, he had admitted that he "could not refute me but at the moment could only address (!) me." By this he probably meant that a point had been reached in our dialogue where it was simply a matter of opposing convictions. My arguments, however, made absolutely no impression on him. He was far too certain of his position for that. He just needed someone to rub himself up against in order to produce lively conversations and avoid getting bored with the eternal agreement of his chorus of disciples.

At these open evenings, Barth would allow the whole spectrum of his copious mind, namely, his charm, wit, and above all his humor, to blaze forth. What was merely rude impudence on the part of the young hooligans and other obsequious characters among his followers—who acted according to the principle that the more impolite they were, the more clearly they indicated their discipleship—was sublime irony in the case of the master himself. He once said in a seminar on Paul Althaus' book "The Last Things" that one could still hear in Althaus' theology the sounds of the harmonium that had resounded through his parents' house. It was impossible for students not to be delighted by gibes of this sort!

At the last open evening of the semester, no serious discussion took place. Instead, the highlights of the semester were relived in songs, poems, and sketches. A short time after Barth's comment on Althaus' book, we were treated to a revue on Althaus' upbringing. The scene was a Christmas evening, complete with a Christmas tree adorned with candles. The first thing we heard was the rattling of a model railway set, followed by the solemn sounds of a harmonium. Suddenly, in the midst of all this, the boyish voice of little Paul called out, "Mommy, I can feel my religious consciousness awakening!"

This story, which was just one of a wealth of Barth anecdotes that I could serve up, had a sequel. When I had fully recovered from my illness, I left Bonn at the end of the semester and moved to Erlangen to study under Althaus for the doctorate in theology. I contemplated my first visit to his home with some trepidation. I was afraid that I would lose my composure if I saw his harmonium, and was all the more worried that this might happen when I was invited with a friend who had also been present that evening at Barth's house. Unfortunately, we both caught sight of the harmonium almost simultaneously. I caught my friend's eye, with the result that we both had to struggle to keep a straight face. Unfortunately, our outburst did not escape Paul Althaus' attention. "Are you laughing at my harmonium?" he asked with raised eyebrows. We went as red as a beetroot and, praying for the earth to open up and swallow us, denied it vigorously—in those days a great professor was still treated with respect! So, it came as a relief to us when Althaus, noticing our embarrassment, continued, "Do you know that this harmonium has a history?" We replied, of course, that we did not. As he spoke, we watched him with rather exaggerated curiosity, so relieved were we at this diversion. "My famous colleague may well be a great man," he said, "but he is also sometimes rather tactless. I have only just heard about the comments he made about my harmonium in his seminar." And then in indignant innocence he told us about Barth's gibe. At this we completely lost our composure and burst into gales of laughter. Althaus was clearly taken aback by this reaction. Fortunately, my friend saved the situation. Bravely taking the bull by the horns, he told Althaus the even worse sketch about the "awakening of Althaus' religious consciousness." For a moment, it seemed to hang in the balance whether Althaus would take offense and throw us out or whether he would manage to transform his indignation into laughter. Only when his wife Dorothea burst into laughter, did Althaus reluctantly join in. Humor was not one of his strongest points.

Barth's wit was sometimes so engaging that it even forced a smile from the victim of his mockery. This once happened to me shortly after the end of the war. An American press officer had tracked me down in Korntal, which was a little village near Stuttgart where I had fled to escape the bombing, and asked me to write an essay for some American newspapers on how it had come about that the land of Goethe and Beethoven should have sunk to the inhumanity of National Socialism. In view of the overweening arrogance of the Americans during the first days of the occupation, I did not intend to help them boost their egos by providing them with one-sided confessions of guilt. Instead, I portrayed National Socialism as model case of what can happen to a nation that has become insecure and disoriented for some reason. As a result of such insecurity and disorientation, the German people had not recognized in Hitler the "beast from the abyss" but had taken him to be an angel of light. Americans should take care that they do not find themselves in a similar position and should learn from Germany's dreadful experience, for—and I concluded with the rather dramatic words—"we had come face to face with the Devil." Soon afterwards I heard that Barth had seen the essay and had remarked in a lecture, "Down in Swabia lives Thielicke, the man who has come face to face with the Devil. I expect the Devil got a nasty fright!" This witty remark, which was made all the more amusing by being spoken with a Swiss slur, compelled even the butt of the joke to join in the general laughter it caused as it circulated rapidly from person to person.

In the first years after the war, Barth and I occasionally held discussions with each other, either in letters and in speeches, or sometimes face-to-face in Basel. The main issue was for the most part Barth's politicotheological statements, above all the way he interpreted the historical guilt of the German people and constructed a general line from Luther via Frederick the Great and Bismarck to Hitler. He once said to me after we had disputed for hours in his study at Basel, "The reason that you are often so aggressive towards your contemporaries (regardless of the consequences!) is probably because you are still young. But now you're a professor and really ought gradually to quieten down a little!" He then listed a few of the basic points that divided us, but concluded with the conciliatory remark, "There is at least one thing that unites us: We can both enjoy a good laugh with each other." That was indeed the case, not least because we both loved anecdotes.

In the last years of his life, Barth spoke of me in milder and occasionally even affectionate terms. That was probably because his friend Eduard Thurneysen had in the meantime also become my friend. Thurneysen was an enthusiastic admirer of my theology and often attended my sermons in Hamburg. I was extremely grateful for the good reception he gave to everything I did, especially since I had a much higher opinion of his rank in the history of theology than many people, who regarded him as a sort of lackey of Karl Barth. He must have put in a good word for me with the great man in Basel.

In Erlangen

To leave Barth for Althaus in Erlangen was not only a dramatic theological change, but also a dramatic change of personalities. It would be hard to imagine a greater contrast of teachers. I did not go to Althaus because I wanted to become his disciple—I had too many reservations for that—but because he would allow me completely free development of my own entelechy. There was no such thing as an "Althausian." I was even allowed to choose my own topic for my theological dissertation. And later it did not bother him very much that I adopted an extremely polemical attitude towards his theology in my dissertation.

In those days in 1934, Althaus was in his prime. He had a narrow head (praised as "nordic" in the Third Reich) and a fresh complexion. He was very kind in his dealings with his colleagues and students, but was also very anxious to cultivate a certain pontifical image. For example, he liked us to stand up when he entered the seminar room and not greet him with the usual tapping and stamping. Before the first seminar of the semester, he would ask me to remind the students of this. He was quite aware that he was the star of the university and that it was primarily because of him that students flocked to Erlangen. In a conversation he once let slip the sullen complaint that a colleague from another university had not stopped off to visit him, the "*genius loci*," on his way through Erlangen. At an open evening at his home shortly afterwards I succeeded in deflating his sense of self-importance a little. I noticed that a student was desperate to use the bathroom but, in the house of this great and rather solemn theologian, did not dare to ask where it was. I announced to him, "Mr. X, it's the second door on the left! If you're in the house of the *genius loci*, you must become acquainted with the *locus genii*!" Althaus certainly did not take offense at remarks like this, although he always had to overcome a brief moment of shock, which amused me greatly.

In general, I enjoyed listening to his sermons in the church at Neustadt. They came from a pious heart. When on a later occasion we both vented our anger at a pathetic sermon given by sloppy preacher, he said, "Do you know, I've long since given up expecting to hear a good sermon in church. I've also grown less demanding with regard to exegetical thoroughness or cultured language. There is just one thing, however, that I cannot give up, namely, the personal touch." I always sensed this personal touch in his sermons. There was nothing artificial about him. The truth he preached was part of his life.

There was good reason why so many people attended Paul Althaus' lectures and listened eagerly to him. His lectures were didactically skillful and were structured in a way that made them easy to remember. Subject matter and careful commentary were held together in equilibrium. The pleasure he took in linguistic and rhetorical formulation was unmistakable. When, at the climax of his exposition, the sentence "I formulate . . ." flowed (there is no other way of putting it!) from his lips, then every pen without exception burst into activity in order to capture the succinctness of the maxim that was now to follow. Mind you, precisely this great elegance of expression frequently led him to embellish a thought he had not fully thought through with a formulation that was so captivating that less-critical listeners would marvel at his supposed solution. In this elegant way, he occasionally obscured difficult and controversial questions. I recall his discussion and assessment of the argument between Luther and Zwingli on the real presence of Christ in the Eucharist. On such occasions, he liked to give the appearance of great resolution. At the same time, however, he loved to grind down all the edges of opposing positions and resolve their differences in mild agreement. That was the case here. With the cry of "I formulate" resounding through the lecture hall, he coined the unforgettable maxim, "The issue is not the real presence of Christ but of making the presence of Christ real." Spontaneous applause greeted this formulation. For centuries Lutherans and Zwinglians had struggled to establish a correct understanding of the

Eucharist, and now—at last!—a man had arrived who had found a formula which both solved the problem and made clear the Eucharist's redemptive significance. And all those present were witnesses of this great moment. When we came to discuss this maxim, however, it emerged that nobody could envisage what it meant. But when we first heard it, it enchanted us.

Walther von Loewenich once spoke of Althaus' ability "to see the 'for and against,' the 'on the one hand and on the other,' the 'both-and' and the 'yes, but.' " This could be extremely annoying in situations where a clear decision was called for. I can well understand Karl Barth when he once said, "I would like to shake him again and again until he at last expresses an unambiguous opinion." Perhaps it was his fate not to be born in the more peaceful climate of the nineteenth century. Instead he was condemned to live—of all times!— during the Third Reich, where what counted was not the synthesis of opposites but the making of strict distinctions.

When I came to study under him at Erlangen in 1934, he was struggling to come to terms with National Socialism. Like many other people, he was at first full of hope and trusted Hitler's assurances concerning "positive Christianity" with innocent naiveté. His nationalist background in conjunction with his development of a doctrine of "creational hierarchy" and his tendency to harmonize everything, induced him to integrate the Nazi doctrine of "blood and soil," nation and race, into his understanding of creation. The young up-and-coming members of the theology faculty, which included Wolfgang Trillhaas, Wilhelm Schwinn, my future brother-in-law Walther von Loewenich, and Kurt Frör, were in this respect much more skeptical. This led to my one and only clash with Althaus, a clash which even made me temporarily consider making a complete break with him.

The cause of this clash was a disgraceful and pitiful pseudo-Lutheran work intended to rival the now famous "Barmen Theological Declaration" of the Confessing Church. The work I am referring to is the so-called "Ansbach Recommendation of 1934." This had been inspired by the Erlangen arch-Lutheran Werner Elert, and had been given the blessing of "the Association of National Socialist Protestant Clergy"(!) in "deep brotherly respect for our fellow clergymen—Heil Hitler!" Althaus—*horribile dictu*—had also put his name to this document. It pretended to give "at long last the genuine Lutheran voice a hearing." In reality it was nothing other than an evil theological sanctioning of Nazi ideology. Among other things it contained the sentence: "As believing Christians we thank the Lord our God for giving our nation in its time of distress the Fuehrer to be our 'pious and loyal sovereign' and for wishing to establish good governance with discipline and honor through the National Socialist system of government."

All this was intolerable to us young men. We organized a protest meeting in Uttenreuther House (a few days before the Röhm rebellion on June 30, 1934), which even Lilje took part in, and attacked this opportunistic monstrosity in numerous speeches. Althaus sat, as I noted in my diary, "in the first row as if he were in the dock." He was certainly not motivated by opportunism, since this was alien to his nature, but had been taken in by Elert, the man behind this document and, despite his high academic position, the evil spirit (and dean!) of the theology faculty at Erlangen. In stating his approval of this document, Althaus had doubtless fallen victim to his naive doctrine of creation, which held that God's eternal order could be ascertained empirically through observation of the world. Were the Nazis not doing the same when they clothed nation and race with the dignity of an order established by Providence? My dissertation—which was an attempt to construct something like a reformed theology of history—stemmed to a large degree from my protest against this questionable form of natural theology. It sought to make clear the ambivalence of the creative order as something which lay between creation and fall. That Althaus accepted this work, which both criticized the regime and questioned his own position, at least proves that he was not guilty of opportunism. His character was beyond reproach, at least as far as his motives were concerned.

Werner Elert, on the other hand, never forgave me for rebelling against his concoction and denounced my adherence to the "Barmen Theological Declaration" as evidence of my hostility to the state and above all of an alienation from Lutheranism that could not be tolerated in Erlangen. He did everything in his power to thwart my *habilitation** for the University of Erlangen and in doing so often drove Althaus to despair. This review of my life is too important to me to demean it with a list of his various attempts to prevent my being awarded the degree. It was sometimes a test of faith for me to see a theologian—and one of high standing at that!—employ such methods.

It was a great comfort to me and many others at this difficult time to see a man so full of character and so resolute in his resistance to the Nazis as the Erlangen New Testament scholar Hermann Strathmann. He had been a member of the Reichstag for the Christian People's Party and as early as 1931 had, in his pamphlet "The National Socialist World View," published a clear

---

* A postdoctoral degree that qualifies the holder to teach at university level. *Translator's note.*

diagnosis and prognosis of what was happening around Hitler. Even *after* the advent of the Third Reich he continued to voice his opposition to the regime in his sermons at Neustadt Church. He did this with a resolution, courage, and openness that sometimes made his listeners catch their breath. When I was suffering at the hands of my great adversary in the faculty, I turned to him for refuge.

The Nazis attacked this steadfast and stubborn man as soon as they gained power. Nazi students organized disturbances in front of his house, demanded his dismissal, and demonstrated against him in the town. They even disrupted his lectures. However, his supporters also organized themselves into a group, of which I was, of course, also a member. The most important man in this operation was a young theology student by the name of Rupprecht von Gilardi, one of the leaders of the Nazi Youth Movement (if I remember rightly he was head of its cultural department). He was very fond of making grand appearances in an ostentatious brown uniform. Particularly impressive and commanding of respect were the colored cords that adorned his cap. Even in those days I suspected that they were his own private invention. Whenever he chose to play the mysterious and influential party member, he did so (with a twinkle in his eye!) primarily in order to intimidate the local branch of the party and help the Church and the faculty. On some occasions he took effective and courageous action against baying mobs. He also tried to find a professor willing to go with him to persuade Schlemm, the Nazi Minister for Education and the Arts and one of the few politicians who was regarded as a decent man by opponents of the regime, to support Strathmann and exercise his authority to secure Strathmann's protection. None of Strathmann's colleagues was prepared to take a prominent stance in such a precarious situation. Only the old, disabled, and frail privy councillor Procksch immediately declared himself willing to travel with Gilardi to see the Minister. This duo—the one young and tempestuous, the other noble and dignified—managed to obtain something like a letter of safe conduct for Strathmann, who continued to go his clear and consistent way.

Procksch, the privy councillor I mentioned above, loathed the Nazis for different reasons than those of us younger men. He was still living in the age of the Kaiser, which in his eyes had become transfigured into a golden age. Every January 27—that is, on the Kaiser's birthday—the lecture hall was full to bursting with people who wanted to hear him. This was because, well into the Third Reich, he would make a speech in honor of his imperial master in faraway Doorn Castle. His students would listen to these speeches with amusement but also with a hint of emotion, while the Nazis let the old gentleman, who was soon to be dismissed from his post, get away with it. His public explanation of why he could not make the Nazi salute also gave us great delight. "I would be risking my life," he would say. This was indeed the case. At each lecture, two students had to assist this seriously disabled man to the lectern, to which he then clung for support. How, then, could he have raised his hand to give the Nazi salute! But his long, white beard was unable to conceal completely his mischievous grin when he made such announcements. His audience proved that they had understood him by their thunderous applause.

My Doctorate in Theology and My Struggle to Gain the Habilitation

As soon as I arrived in Erlangen, I set to work on my dissertation with gusto. I was very troubled by the prospect of having to live my whole life—so it seemed to me at the time—under Hitler's thumb and to witness his destruction of church and culture. At first, however, this worry was simply outweighed by my personal happiness at still being alive after my illness. In addition to this, I had the joy of working on an important topic which I myself had been able to choose. I entitled my work: *Geschichte und Existenz: Grundlegung einer evangelischen Geschichtstheologie* (History and Existence: Outline of a Protestant Theology of History). This quite extensive opus (the 370 printed pages of the book published by Gerd Mohn Publishing House of Gütersloh constitute only an excerpt from a much more extensive manuscript) formed the intellectual basis for my later four volume work on ethics. It was reprinted thirty years later in 1964. Because it was diametrically opposed to the Nazi understanding of life and history, it was later one of the reasons for my dismissal in 1940.

I had the good fortune of being able to move back into my old student digs in Friedrich Street. My landlady was a maternal, plump, extremely witty, lower-middle-class widow by the name of Babette Gehret. She lived only for her "gentlemen" and did all she could for them. Every now and again she felt obliged to write to my mother and assure her that I was leading an extremely respectable life. She once wrote: "Doctor Thielicke must have been praised by his professor yesterday. I could hear him chuckling and giggling on the stairs, so I knew immediately."

When I was writing up a large section of my thesis in the summer semester of 1933, I used to get up at one o'clock each night and usually worked on the balcony. As morning approached, I would listen with a sense of moral satisfaction to the life that was awakening all around me, especially to the shrill ringing of alarm clocks and the groaning and yawning of those having difficulty getting up. When Mrs. Gehret brought me my breakfast, I would sometimes complain that I did not know how to proceed with my work or that I had deleted a whole page. On such occasions, she would always have a word of comfort. She would make some such comment as "I've also just gone and dropped a stitch again." I would work until midday and, if the weather was not too bad, would travel with friends to Dexendorf pond to go swimming. At seven o'clock in the evening, I would go to bed so as to be fit to resume my work shortly after midnight. This was a rather unusual and very intensive way of life. Above all, it enabled me to work without being disturbed. Such a life is only possible when one is young and has no job or social commitments. Anyway, I made enormous progress.

I would certainly not have been able to put up with this monastic isolation from the world if I had not been filled with enthusiasm for my subject. I was concerned with a problem that was to remain an essential theological issue for me from that time on. This was the question of how the vertical dimension of revelation is related to the horizontal areas of life in which our natural life takes place; that is, how is revelation related to the state, culture, and personal life. The question which has always interested me most of all is whether and to what extent the Christian faith brings about a new under-standing of our *life*. In my research into this issue, Luther's statement that *"persona facit opera,"* that is, "it is the person who does the works," became my leitmotif. In all that the human being thinks, plans, and achieves, regardless of the sphere of life in which he carries this out, he is engaged in a process of self-actualization. I was never interested in the first instance in political, economic, and cultural programs as such, but was deeply con-cerned with the question of the nature of the *human being* who expressed and actualized himself in such things. I cannot even watch a film or observe a circus artist performing his tricks without asking myself the question of how the human being expressing himself in this way understands himself and to what extent these self-portrayals are thus "fragments of a great creed." I was also interested in the corresponding theological question of the change that occurs in the human being and, following on from that, the forms in which he expresses himself when he finds God and thereby discovers himself and arrives at his true identity. For I was quite certain of one thing, namely, that the human being does not find himself when he searches for himself. He only gains and actualizes himself when he loses his life to God.

In this way my theological work acquired from the outset a motif which freed it from becoming esoteric and dogmatic, and gave it the character of a *dialogue*. When in some of my later works I conducted an impassioned conversation with the present age and wrote my book *Man in God's World*, I never thought of myself as an apologist defending the Christian faith from a secure position and anxious to prove to the secular human being his errors. Rather, I always regarded the lack of truth and the wretched ideological surrogates I observed in the "outside world" as something present in *me* from which I had been saved through no merit of my own. To me, the neopaganism of the Third Reich was merely a gigantic projection and objectification of what *my* "blood" and *my* "soul" were also continually bringing forth. For this reason, I was only able to overcome this by withstanding the temptation into which this neopaganism thrust me. It possessed a bridgehead in me. I was myself susceptible to it. I was not at all sure of myself and knew only too well that I could not regard myself as Christ's representative and the Antichrist as something outside of me. Rather, I myself was the "battleground," and I was well aware that wild wolves were howling in *my* subconscious too. I regarded it as a confirmation of this position when neopagans told me that I had understood them and sometimes asked me if I was one of them. Consequently, I conceived of theology not in apologetic terms, but as a conversation between the spiritual and natural sides of my personality. And only after I had thrashed out this dialogue in my own person, could what I had to say to the outside world gain credibility. This is more or less the process that led me to write the aforementioned *Man in God's World*.

The manuscript of this book was, by the way, smuggled in diplomatic baggage to Switzerland during the war. It was then published anonymously in Geneva, before being sent to the education courses in all enemy prisoner–of–war camps. After the war it was published in several editions by J. C. B. Mohr of Tübingen. It was again my Erlangen dissertation that provided the theoretical basis for these attempts to converse with the secular world as a Christian.

I was very pleased when Althaus expressed his satisfaction with this first theological venture by his twenty-five-year-old student. As a result of his approval, the *viva voce* ended with my being invited to submit myself for the habilitation. It was also agreed that the extensive dissertation I had written for the Ph.D. should be regarded as my habilitation thesis. In view of the systematic character of this work, however, the faculty felt that I ought to take an additional examination in historical theology. That was fine by me, especially as I was again allowed to choose my own topic. This time I chose to examine the theology of Gotthold Ephraim Lessing, primarily with reference to the relationship between reason and revelation in his thought. In this work, I came to some astonishing results that were not reconcilable with previous research on Lessing. I did not interpret Lessing as a simple rationalist, although this was the conclusion most scholars had drawn in light of his opposition to Goeze, the chief pastor of Hamburg. Instead, I tried to prove that Lessing's concept of reason itself contained the principle of transcendence and that the structure of his thought had a much greater affinity to Kierkegaard than it did to Reimarus, the archrationalist whom it was assumed Lessing resembled. This book on Lessing was later published in five editions by Gerd Mohn Publishing House and earned me more approval than disapproval from Lessing researchers and enthusiasts.

Of the many conversations I had with Karl Jaspers during my time at Heidelberg, there was one that made me especially happy. In this conversation, he confessed that my book had led him to revise his previous understanding of Lessing. I must admit, however, that this great man, whom I greatly admired and who, like me, suffered the fate of being dismissed from his post, did not always regard my work with such friendly approval. I will have more to say about this later.

It took me quite a while to gain the habilitation. It was Dean Elert who was chiefly responsible for this delay. He was constantly finding new objections to my poor person. His main objection was that I was not Lutheran enough. This was because I came from the Calvinist parish of Gemarke and, as a supporter of the Confessing Church, ardently supported the "Barmen Theological Declaration." It infuriated him when in February 1935 I gave (together with Karl Barth of all people) a militant lecture on Christ or Antichrist at a large Rhineland-Westphalian Parish Congress in Gemarke Church. He was particularly enraged by the fact that I emphasized in the preface of the published lecture that "we of the younger generation" had to conduct the argument quite differently and more radically than the older generation was for the most part doing. Elert was annoyed at this "incitement to war between the generations" and felt that it was a personal attack on him. His exaggerated attitude of "If you're not for us, you're against us" had led him with some justification to feel that I regarded his stubbornly Lutheran, polemical denominationalism as hackneyed, obsolete, and anachronistic and that I saw the real arguments as taking place on quite different levels.

He never one approached me *directly* with his feelings of resentment. I only ever heard of all his troublemaking through Althaus and Strathmann. When one day I asked him in writing if he would be prepared to engage in an open discussion with me and said that I did not mind if it took place as a private conversation or as a debate in the presence of those colleagues of his that he was constantly endeavoring to stir up against me, he curtly rejected this suggestion. No matter what I did, the powerful dean would never condescend to have anything to do with this insignificant novice.

Despite all his efforts, he did not succeed in preventing my being awarded the habilitation. The only thing his enervating delaying tactics accomplished was to drag out the years until the habilitation examination and ministerial confirmation of its award at last took place, in the summer of 1936. This was a strain on the nerves, not least because the regime's strategy of strangling Christianity turned a habilitation in theology into a race against *time*. Would a habilitation be at all possible a few months hence? It was also a constant test of my faith to see a theologian and a representative of an orthodox, chemically purified Lutheranism to boot, make use of such underhand tactics.

Finally, Elert attempted to put a last stumbling-block in my way in the habilitation itself, namely, by his choice of the topic of my test lecture. I only had three days to prepare for this lecture. Everyone who knows anything about theology will be able to appreciate the cunning trap he set by giving me the topic: "Is its Aristotelian foundation constitutive of or only of marginal significance for Thomistic metaphysics?" It was my good fortune that the problems relevant to this topic had occupied me for some time. Elert certainly had no inkling of this, with the result that I did not fall into the trap he had laid for me. This highly abstract topic certainly demanded some intellectual effort on the part of the listening faculty members. I remember Hans Preuss, the church historian, remarking in the colloquium that followed, "I would certainly have come to grief in the icy regions of this abstract subject if I had not held firmly onto the rope of my personal interest in our candidate for the habilitation." But he had to ask himself in all seriousness, he added, whether I would ever be able to make myself intelligible to the average student—and this factor should at least be taken into consideration. This was all grist to Elert's mill. But then Althaus roused himself and overcame that gentle nature of his that was so averse to any form of aggression. Shaking with anger, he replied that it was without doubt solely the fault of the *topic* that the candidate had been forced to climb into the icy zone of metaphysics with its glaciers and thin air. He also found a word of approval for the didactic successes of my first year seminars. So in the end, I was able to leave the battlefield victorious.

An Inner Conflict

My dissertation had one other consequence which was to be important both for my theological development and also for my maturity as a person.

Althaus staunchly supported my intention to embark on a career as a university teacher. One of the most important preconditions of such a career was obtaining a post as a professor's assistant. Such a post not only secured one's livelihood but also guaranteed the freedom to pursue one's own research. Furthermore, the possibility also arose of running first-year seminars and of gaining teaching experience. The only such post at Althaus' disposal, however, was occupied by my friend Wilhelm Schwinn.

Schwinn was not only a highly gifted theologian but also possessed a considerable general knowledge, especially in literature and the history of art. Furthermore, he was also a very humane and friendly person. It was his misfortune to suffer from inhibitions in writing, a sort of paper phobia. At any rate, after five years he had still not handed in his doctoral thesis. When, with much moaning and groaning and under constant pressure from his friends, he finally managed to write something, it was in both quantity and quality only a remote indication of what he was really capable of. This was the reason why Althaus gradually lost patience and wanted to appoint me as his assistant in Schwinn's place. Schwinn, however, was such a strong and self-confident personality that his mild-mannered boss did not dare to announce this to him openly and put off the decision for several months. I myself, of course, neither wanted nor was able to exert pressure on Althaus, firstly, because Schwinn was my friend, and secondly, because I knew how much he loved his academic job and had hopes of an academic career. So I took no action whatsoever, but secretly waited for Althaus eventually to stir himself into making a decision one way or the other. After all, both my fate and Schwinn's depended on it.

Then at last the day arrived. Althaus sent my friend a letter of dismissal and appointed me in his place. Then something happened that I would never forget. I was on my way to the university restaurant for lunch, when I ran into Wilhelm Schwinn. With unaccustomed coldness and having great difficulty in controlling himself, he said to me, "You know that Althaus has kicked me out and appointed you to take my place. I know that you have not done anything to cause this. You've got a clean slate. I can't reproach you with anything. But just the mere fact of your existence has ousted me. If you didn't exist everything would have been different. So my academic career is in ruins and I don't know what will become of me. Please understand that for the time being I can no longer see you. I simply can't bear it. Goodbye!" With that he turned on his heel and entered the restaurant, while I quickly retraced my steps.

Whenever we ran across each other in the following weeks, he greeted me formally from the other side of the road and avoided meeting me directly. I certainly suffered from this estrangement as much as he himself did, and perhaps even more. One day, however, he suddenly came over to me, smiled and said, "I can now see you again. I've got over it. Let's be friends again like we were before!"

Schwinn later took holy orders. I was a little worried by this decision because, in view of his rather elitist education, he hardly seemed capable of dealing with ordinary people. But in this I was very much mistaken. His lovable and warm-hearted nature very soon won everybody's heart. A previously unknown side of his sense of humor also developed, enabling him to enjoy dealing with and painting delightful portraits of unusual human beings. Later, when he was Dean, he had a decisive influence not only on the church life but also the cultural life of Würzburg. He was also a worthy partner for Bishop (later Cardinal) Döpfner. After the war, he achieved great things in the reconstruction of Würzburg and was given the honorary title of "Wilhelm the Builder" by its citizens.

But at the time of our parting, this future fulfillment was still shrouded in darkness. It was this very darkness that acquired a far-reaching and even creative significance for my life and thought. Although I had not consciously pushed my friend out, let alone intrigued against him, I had nevertheless become his rival and had—"through my mere existence," as he put it—shattered him. That did not leave me without some feelings of guilt. "Who am I really?" I asked myself. Am I merely an individual, endowed with will and consciousness, and responsible only for how I employ them? If that is so, then I bear no guilt for what happened to Schwinn, for I was very fond of him. I had a high regard for him, and certainly did not want to do him any harm. But was I not also at the same time the exponent of historical structures determined by the principles of achievement and competition, and consequently by the law of the survival of the fittest? How, then, could I have denied or circumvented the law that determines history? Perhaps by pretending to be more stupid than I was in order to give Schwinn a chance? But that would have been absurd! Obviously, the conflict between us had been produced by the autonomous laws of historical structures, and nobody can simply withdraw himself from these. This was a theme of oppressive—and theological!—relevance.

Virtually all my theological problems have emerged not as the result of purely intellectual processes, but have grown from situations in my life—mainly from conflicts. That was also the case here. The basic concept that gave rise to my later works on ethics received decisive impulses from this conflict with my friend. This basic concept at the same time brought me into theological opposition to my boss. You see, a neo-Lutheran like Althaus regarded historical structures as something like a "creative order." For him the fall consisted primarily in the human being's rebellion against and misappropriation of the fundamental laws ordained for this world. In light of my conflict with Schwinn, however, I could no longer regard the world in this way. That I had had to oust my friend and appeared to have ruined his life was *not* the result of my having violated the laws ordained for this world. No, this conflict was already *laid down* in the very structure of the world. And did this not apply to history *in general*? For instance, was not politics dominated by the *sacro egoismo* of nations? Did not politics also confront me on all sides with the laws of self-assertion and survival of the fittest?

But if this were the case, then I could not possibly continue to regard the historical world as neutral. And if this conclusion were correct, it would mean that the fall was not only present in the corruption of the individual's will but also had an institutional dimension; that is, that it had also come to acquire an objective existence in historical structures. Moreover, because I myself was a historical being, I could not distance myself from this transsubjective sphere. On the contrary, I had to identify myself with it. After all, I myself was and am this history! This was the reason for my feelings of guilt towards Wilhelm Schwinn. I could not say, "Here I am, the innocent Helmut Thielicke, who only wishes for the best, and over there is the 'evil world' that has carried me off to where I do not want to go. I myself certainly wish for the best, but 'the circumstances won't allow it' (Bertolt Brecht)." No, I myself *am* these circumstances by virtue of my "mere existence."

All this resulted in my developing a quite new conception of good and evil, creation and fall, self and history. Virtually everything I have produced in the way of theological theory is based on this conception. The more I pursued these thoughts, the more numerous became the analogies I found in literature. I found references to this problem, for instance, in Bergengruen's *Der Großtyrann und das Gericht* (The Tyrant and the Court), in Jochen Klepper's statement that "kings have to commit more sins than other people" (because entanglement in historical necessities increases in proportion to one's public activity), and above all in the suffering caused to Frederick the Great by the conflict between personal and political morality. Even Bismarck's statement to his pious friends in Lower Pomerania could be cited as evidence of this. When they reproached him for adhering to the *sacro egoismo* of the statesman, he shouted at them, "Just *you* try doing this job!"

I had now been granted the same experience in my little corner of the world and henceforth sought to make it the subject of my theological reflections. The main aim of these reflections was to interpret the totality of human historical existence (politics, economics, culture, technology, and so on) in light of its ambivalent position between creation and fall.

I have dwelled on this conflict with my friend Wilhelm Schwinn at some length because I felt constrained to make clear at some point the existential drive at work in my thought. My theological work was always only a superstructure placed upon the experiences and sufferings of my life, and *one* of its nodal points was my conflict with Schwinn.

This relation between life and thought was later to reveal itself more immediately and openly in my sermons than it did in my systematic thought. It may be that the congregation sensed this and as a result listened more intensely and were more affected by my sermons. I was often asked to explain the effect of a sermon, but as a rule, I avoided giving an answer. There is no "human" interpretation of the "effect" of a sermon. However, in my description of my conflict with Schwinn, I may at least have given a hint here of the direction in which I was seeking one of the possible (but usually impossible!) answers.

My First Experiences with the Nazi Regime

I gained my first significant experiences of National Socialism while I was still in Erlangen. Erlangen was in the area where Julius Streicher, a primitive brute of a man, circulated his newspaper *Der Stürmer*.* You could not help but notice the innumerable posters for this pornographic and sadistic publication. It was not actually due to any merit of my own that I pursued a fairly clear line (I will explain what I mean by "fairly" in due course) regarding Hitler right from the very outset. It was due, on the one hand, to the fact that I found the "fuss" surrounding Nazism and the type of people it attracted

* An anti-Semitic weekly periodical edited by Julius Streicher from 1923–45. *Translator's note.*

physically repugnant. Having said this, I did also meet a few idealists I respected and who later even tried to help me when I was dismissed from my post at Heidelberg. On the other hand, it was due to the fact that I was one of the few people who had actually read Hitler's *Mein Kampf.* The style and content of this book had to a certain extent immunized me against Nazism. A further reason for my antipathy was that, in the very first days of the Third Reich, I had to attend an "ideology course" for budding lecturers, lasting several weeks. This gave me the opportunity of staring into the bottomless pit of Nazism, an experience which exorcized any susceptibility to this political gospel that was left in me. First of all, I found myself as the result of a general collective decree suddenly put forward (if I remember rightly, on the grounds of my fraternity membership) for "candidacy" of the SA.* By means of a few tricks, however, I managed to leave this bunch soon afterwards and was able to devote myself to my doctoral studies without interruption. At all events, I resolved—and remained true to this resolve—that I would under no circumstances swear an oath to the Fuehrer.

Then, one after the other, we budding university lecturers were ordered to report to a military camp for lecturers. This camp was situated in Dambritsch, a village between Liegnitz and Breslau, and held 150 young academics of all faculties. During our time there, we once again had to put up temporarily with being addressed as "SA men." At the morning roll call the leader of the course would greet us with a shout of "Heil, SA!" to which we had to reply in unison, "Heil, Sergeant-Major!" Our boss was a former grocer, a very simple and decent man who had never seen a university from the inside and had great difficulty understanding the profession of the men under him. Incoming mail was only delivered to us when it replaced our academic titles with the insignia of the SA. We were ordered to inform our family and friends of this procedure. Only when our "superiors," who were very obsequious and primitive characters, wrote postcards to their numerous sweethearts, did we, as "their subordinates," have to sign with our titles.

I was the only one of us who kept the hated SA uniform on for the whole of the course, even when we were off duty. I was like a man who had got sore feet from walking and preferred to keep his boots on because he could not bear the thought of forcing his feet back into them after a brief rest.

What I described earlier as my "immunization" against Nazism was at first based not so much on the fact that I had fully understood the depravity of

* SA is an abbreviation of *Sturmabteilung*, i.e. "Storm Troopers," a division within the Nazi Party led by Ernst Röhm until his execution in 1934. *Translator's note.*

Nazi doctrine as on the sum total of many individual experiences that had disgusted me. I saw—apart from a few positive exceptions—how the petty-minded characters at the camp enjoyed bullying the academics and giving free rein to their lust for power. How often we would hear constantly new modifications of the statement, "If you carry on like that, I'll ruin your career!" It was unbearably humiliating to know that our future depended on a good or bad report from these homunculi.

Our day-to-day work consisted of a kind of elementary military training. It was certainly very much harder for the older ones amongst us to tolerate our treatment there than it was for a young pup like me, the baby of the course. Some of them were highly decorated front-line officers from the First World War and found it hard to endure being ordered about by these dubious characters.

After the future lecturers had "passed" basic training, the regime subjected them to a sort of advanced examination. This was concerned with their basic "ideological" position, their didactic ability, and their personal qualities (!). This second course took place in the so-called Academy for Lecturers, which was situated in the pleasant setting of a villa in Kiel-Kitzeberg. Despite its dubious goals, this academy was a pleasant experience and was sometimes even quite impressive. The reason for this was probably that in 1935 the reign of terror had not yet reached its peak. As a result, it was still possible in some places—such as this academy for example—for astonishingly open discussions to take place. The attitude of the head of the academy, the Königsberg philosopher Hans Heyse, also contributed to the freedom we enjoyed there. He would sometimes read from his book *Idee und Existenz* (Idea and Existence), which was published shortly afterwards. The tenor of this book was that Christianity had shattered the unity of *bios* and *logos* represented by ancient Greece and that, as a result, the history of Europe constituted one long mistake. However, through the racial ideology of Nazism, he argued, Europe was now experiencing a revolutionary *volte-face*. In appearance Heyse was a rather leptosome and anemic man of study. He was certainly anything but the nordic hero figure he introduced to us as his model. I always had the feeling that his adherence to Nazi ideology, which he appeared to have adopted for reasons of expediency, gave him a bad conscience.

In the academy, we had to give lectures from memory (!), without the aid of notes. We were obviously supposed to show what our inner thoughts were and to reveal our true selves through our spontaneity. This at first seemed pretty grotesque to us, but in fact turned out to be a very productive exercise and led to a symposium of great intellectual profundity and energetic dialogue lasting several weeks.

Heyse planned to form study groups on an interfaculty basis. There were to be groups on the natural sciences, history, and law. The leader of each group was to hold a series of lectures on his subject, which were then to be thrown open for discussion. The intention of distributing the faculties among the various study groups was to force each lecturer to make his subject intelligible to those not specialized in his field. Each person was free to join the group of his choice.

When Heyse announced this plan, I asked whether there was anybody who might be interested in forming a *theological* study group. I will never forget Heyse's dismissive shrug of the shoulders and the ironical tone in which he asked if there was anybody who wished to participate in such a group. And look what happened! Hands shot into the air and we were all of a sudden the largest group.

But even better was to come. There were four theologians on the course. Apart from me, there was the young New Testament scholar Heinrich Greeven, who later made a name for himself primarily (but not exclusively!) through his philologically exemplary synopsis of the gospels. Then there was the Catholic New Testament scholar Donatus Haug, an earthy Bavarian held in great affection by us all, who was killed in action at Stalingrad. Finally, there was a German Christian church historian who, precisely because of his conformism, was not usually taken seriously. I can still see the joy with which Donatus shaved every Sunday morning after breakfast. Then, between finger and thumb and with as little contact as possible, he would take off the obligatory brown shirt and put on his cassock to celebrate mass.

The other members of the academy spoke of us as "our three theologians." We also formed a front against the position of the head of the academy. In addition, we not only had to deal with our theological study group and its tremendously lively debates, but were also constantly being summoned to take part in the other groups. I am not exaggerating when I say that the whole academy almost "degenerated" into one long discussion on religion. I myself dealt with the theme of "the unity of life and Christianity." This was chosen in deliberate opposition to Heyse. When we presented the summary of our work at the plenum at the end of the course, the audience pointedly received us with seemingly neverending applause. We had the feeling that the others—regardless of different or even opposing positions—wanted to re-ward our efforts to achieve clarity and our willingness to stand up for what we believed in. A considerable number of our colleagues even asked us to start the day with an act of worship before work began. We would have loved to have done this but our request was flatly rejected by the course leadership. It would really have been far too massive a provocation for an academy under the patronage of Alfred Rosenberg and which regarded his *Mythos des 20. Jahrhunderts* (Myth of the Twentieth Century) as the Magna Carta! However, we found a way around this. In place of an act of worship, Heinrich Greeven, who was a gifted musician, played a hymn on the piano each morning, the sounds of which streamed through the open doors of the building. An ever greater number of our colleagues assembled to listen in silence. In this building, this meant more to us than a conventional church service. I do not believe that anything like this was still possible in the years of Nazi rule that followed. We had made use, as it were, of the last remaining freedom.

When the time came to leave Kitzeberg, we were especially moved by the way in which our secular non-church going and even "German Christian" colleagues bid farewell to "their" theologians and expressed their gratitude. The mask of joviality was unable to conceal their emotion. Thus a member of the SS, whose confrontation with the Christian faith had visibly shaken him, said to me, "My dear Thielicke, when you next meet the good Lord, give him my kindest regards and ask him not to leave me in the lurch." We shook hands for a long time. I had understood him. For me, the people I met, the intellectual discussions and not least my work of proclaiming the Gospel in the Kiel Academy were the strongest inner experiences that were granted to me in the first years of the Third Reich.

Growing Conflicts

The camp and academy for university teachers had provided me with a profound knowledge of Nazi ideology and had increasingly opened my eyes to the apocalyptic terrors it held. This in turn led to an increased determination on my part to dissociate myself from it. I thus found myself in the dilemma of being a young man pursuing a much desired career while living under a dictatorship. This continually confronted me with the problem of either being consistent and refusing to compromise, which would mean giving up the goal I had set my heart on; or of pursuing my chosen profession and seeing to it that, without selling out, I maneuvered myself past the obstacles in my way. Today, many years later, it seems obvious which was the right course. Although I have undeservedly come to acquire the reputation of advocating the policy of no compromise towards the Nazis, I was not at all absolutely certain that I had adopted the right course. For this reason, I feel it is important to show clearly the difficulty of my decision and to solicit some understanding for a mode of behavior that is scarcely comprehensible to anyone who has not lived under ideological tyranny. My purpose here is not to solicit understanding for *my* position but to make clear the problems confronting the *whole* of German youth in my generation.

I wanted to become a university lecturer and longed fervently to devote all my energies to the truth and to pass this truth onto young, alert, intellectually active and inquisitive people. I had a great passion for teaching, and the hour I spent at the lectern was the high point of the day for me. Should all of this come to nothing? And if it did come to nothing, what was then to become of the deserted lecterns?

I also noticed how fond the young students were of their lecturers. It plucked at my heartstrings to see their despair when one of us was dismissed and left them on their own, that is, *abandoned* them to some dubious characters. They were a flock that had to be led. Should not the shepherds do something to avoid being picked off too easily by the marksmen waiting to discover a chink in our armor? In the following years we wore ourselves out with such thoughts.

On the other hand, the truth we proclaimed would lose its authority and credibility if we employed dubious methods to propagate it. When one has a "vocation," any concessions one makes in order to further the cause one believes in tend to compromise and rob it of its power. Was not a great silence better than a shady, amputated truth? But what if the Third Reich were to last for many decades, as it sometimes seemed it would? Should one remain silent for the whole of one's life, should one extinguish the flame that burned within one's heart? I often envied the old men who had done their work and could now retire with a "clean conscience." But I despised them all the more when they were not even capable of ending their careers with decency.

I opted for the following solution. I decided that there were certain things that I would not do under any circumstances. I would never join the party, regardless of the pressure the Nazis might exert upon me and any promises they might make. And I would never—either orally, in writing, or in print— express any support for the regime or even make a positive remark about it. For I felt that to betray one's *principles* and to do so by means of *words* was much worse than affiliation to or formal participation in an organization. Statements of principle ought to be the means by which the representative of a vocation, a "professor" (in the true sense of the word) proves his credibility. Concessions were not possible *here*. I could forgive a friend his membership of the Nazi party as long as his principles remained inviolable. Conversely, I despised those who, though they avoided giving public support to the Nazis, were unscrupulous opportunists as far as their principles were concerned. A professor must be judged by his principles. They are his deeds.

This was the reason I was often annoyed at how foolish the criteria were for establishing the guilt of individuals after the war. It was a source of constant irritation to me that membership of the Hitler Youth was deemed defamatory, while political "virginity" was considered to possess heroic status. The question that should have been asked, indeed the only legitimate question, was "What did you say and what did you publish?"

Although I remained "chaste" in my principles and thus had no revelations to fear later on, I did not go around telling every Nazi about my political convictions. Mind you, I also never lied to them, not even in critical situations. Despite this, I sometimes felt I was guilty of hypocrisy—or "camouflage," as it was rather euphemistically called—and was occasionally quite disgusted with myself. Indeed, I sometimes felt a need to wash my hands. I was also conscious of the fact that small, harmless concessions can lead to a gradual retreat from one's convictions. To avoid this, I decided to give constant signs by which I and others like me could be identified, and to say, "Do what you want with me. I'll go so far and no further!" To help me achieve this, I studied the temptations of Jesus. My work on this book (*Between God and Satan*) helped me and some other people to strike the right balance in the confusion of the times.

Head of the Student Hostel at Erlangen—New Obstacles

At the end of 1935, a student hostel was established for theologians. When the Nazis dissolved the fraternities, "Uttenruthia," an ancient fraternity with a rich tradition, was also closed down. The Church then acquired the beautiful, spacious building that had belonged to this Christian fraternity and, in accordance with its new theological purpose, filled it with life. As *"Abbas illustrissimus,"* as the students liked to call me, I resolved to organize in these rooms a kind of monastic life that had both spiritual content and a festive human atmosphere. The first intake of students, which I chose very carefully, offered the best chance of achieving this. As far as I know, only one of them is still alive. The others were either killed in the war or died later. Time and again my letters came back from the front with the comment stamped or handwritten on it "He gave his life for Fuehrer and Reich." But in those days, when we first met, we were a happy bunch. We engaged in long discussions, cracked problems together, and held glittering parties. At the ceremonial inauguration, my passion for planning perhaps got rather the better of me. It must have seemed to the people assembled there as if I regarded our monastic circle as ushering in a new life for Erlangen theology.

It was thus all the more sobering to be brought down to earth with a bump by the dean of the faculty. He stood up and—looking me up and down inquisitorially—said that his only wish for the new hostel was that we should not let anybody outdo us in loyalty to the Fuehrer. But that sort of comment made no impression on us. We knew that we were an island in the sea of Nazism, and enjoyed our sense of community.

The final part of the examination for the habilitation consisted in an obligatory public lecture. To fulfill this stipulation the Berlin Minister of Education and the Arts referred me to the German Christian–dominated faculty in Breslau of all places. I could only suspect at whose suggestion this new stumbling block had been placed before me. That certain people were hoping that I would suffer a disaster there was only too obvious. This was also the unanimous conclusion of my friends and supporters at Erlangen.

When I arrived in Breslau, I was received with great coolness. My "bad" reputation had somehow preceded me. The only comfort was that I was able to live in the vicarage of my friend Heinrich Benckert, later to become Bishop of Rostock, and enjoy the hospitality and friendship of people who stood close to me both in human affection and in their convictions.

The Breslauers had gone to great lengths to ensure that my "public" lectures were not publicized. Consequently, I spent the first lecture staring into the inscrutable faces of my "examiners." Oddly enough, however, news of the lectures had circulated, with the result that an increasing number of students came to the next two lectures. They obviously disapproved of their teachers' subservience to the regime, for they received me with thunderous applause and were clearly inspired and delighted by my protest. For some incomprehensible reason the intended stumbling block failed to work. The examiners were at any rate decent enough not to veto my being awarded the habilitation.

When I returned to Erlangen, I discovered that a new and last hurdle had been placed in my way. Elert informed the faculty and the ministry that in his opinion Erlangen had enough lecturers in my subject and that they therefore could not offer me a position. The regime's strategy of starving the church and theology did not prevent him from preferring to ruin a young academic rather than—as Althaus interpreted it—tolerating an up-and-coming rival.

When my boss failed in his attempts to thwart Elert's machinations, he asked his friend Emanuel Hirsch to arrange for me to be transferred to Göttingen. This was, of course, touchingly naive, for the great scholar Emanuel Hirsch (he was without doubt the most important church historian of his age) was regarded as one of the chief ideologists of the German Christians and was a notoriously fanatical National Socialist. We used to translate his first name "Emanuel" as "May God be with us." When Hirsch then asked Paul Althaus to send me to him, I made my way—albeit with no great hope—to Göttingen.

Of all days to be invited to Hirsch's home for dinner, it had to be on a Sunday prescribed as a day of economy by the NSDAP.* On such days, stew was the only permitted meal. As his guest I was treated in a friendly way. Even back in those days he was a sickly, bent man with very poor eyesight. The SS emblem he wore in the lapel of his jacket made a macabre impression on somebody of his phenotype. We had scarcely finished our meal when he engaged me in a conversation aimed at both extracting information from me and examining me. It took such an absurd course that I fear my readers will shake their heads in disbelief when I relate what happened. Nevertheless, I can vouch for the veracity of what occurred.

The only question he asked me was, "What do you feel when you press your ear against the stomach of a pregnant cow?" As grotesque as this "examination" question may sound, I caught on immediately and knew what he was driving at. He was aware from my publications that I took an extremely critical view of so-called "natural theology" and knew that "blood and soil" theology with its Lutheran variant in the "Ansbacher Recommendation of 1934" had sharpened my criticism still further. So what Hirsch wanted was the reply that, as a Christian theologian, I would hear the creator's voice in the calf embryo's heartbeat. Had I conceded this, his next move would have been to employ his famous diabolical dialectic to push me into the fold of Nazi biological doctrines. The rather insolent reply I gave him was that I had come to him on the assumption that he would examine me with regard to becoming a university lecturer in theology and not a veterinary surgeon. After that I quickly set off for home.

Emanuel Hirsch was always both a fascinating and frightening figure for me. What was fascinating was his enormous learning, especially his knowledge of German Idealism. I am also thinking of the colossal edition of Kierkegaard's works that he undertook later, and above all of his multi-

* Nationalsozialistische Deutsche Arbeiterpartei (National Socialist German Workers' Party). The official title of the Nazi Party. *Translator's note.*

volumed history of theology, which he wrote from memory after losing his sight. At the same time, however, he was and remained (right up until his death) unwaveringly loyal to the Fuehrer. Even when the Allies had entered Göttingen, and the professional Nazis had long since beaten a hasty retreat, he called his family and the refugees he was housing to sing the Horst Wessel* song with him. In a conversation with me, Georg Merz, the former editor of the Barth journal *Zwischen den Zeiten*, formulated the ambivalence of this strange man in the following way: "Hirsch does not believe in the Gospel accounts of Christ's resurrection but he believes every word that Goebbels has uttered and every line of the *Völkischer Beobachter*."* Hirsch never forgot the rather cynical snub with which I had taken leave of him in Göttingen. In August 1943, he came close to putting my life in danger with a letter that almost amounted to a denunciation. (Mind you, he was no ordinary denunciator, his behavior had more to do with his subjectively honest conviction that it was his duty to expose me as an enemy of the Third Reich). The problem was as follows. When I was banned during the war from speaking in public and publishing my work, a number of church organizations, including a rather weak German Christian bishop who was trying to cultivate goodwill on both sides, sold my duplicated speeches and essays. They reached all fronts in large numbers. One of these works dealt with the theme "The limits of intercession." In this essay, I criticized the all-embracing prayer made in church for the blessing of the Fuehrer as our divinely ordained leader. This political and liturgical criticism of mine aroused Hirsch's intense anger. In his letter of protest to the German Christian bishops, he wrote the following sentences: "As a German and a Christian I reject such an insane formulation of this question. For me the Fuehrer and his state are the most precious, beloved, dear, and holy possessions we have. . . . And if somebody asks me whether I ought to pray for these things, I turn my back on that person as a sick, poor, but also repulsive fellow who lacks all natural human instincts. I am also disgusted by any German who can question whether we ought to pray for such 'antichristian people' [he is referring to the Nazi comrades of his son, who was killed in action—the author], and who qualifies this prayer with a prayer for the downfall of these

---

* Horst Wessel was the composer of a Nazi hymn sung in the Third Reich after the German national anthem. Wessel was killed in a brawl with the Communists in 1930 at the age of 23, thereby becoming a Nazi "martyr." *Translator's note.*

* A newspaper. It began life in 1887 as the *Münchner Beobachter*, before being acquired by the Nazis in 1920 as their party organ. *Translator's note.*

antichristian powers." In spite of everything, I always pitied rather than hated this eminent man, who had been led by his fanaticism onto what turned out to be a hopelessly false path. In view of the cowardly opportunism of former Nazis who denied their Nazi past after the war, Hirsch's consistency even gained my respect, even if it did stem from his blindness. He was determined to remain true to himself, even when this caused him extreme loneliness after the war.

After my fruitless journey to Göttingen, all roads to achieving my hoped-for career seemed to be blocked. Then, at the end of October 1936, I received a letter from the Minister of Education and the Arts of the German Reich, completely unexpectedly appointing me to a chair in Heidelberg as the replacement of someone who had been suspended from his post (because disciplinary proceedings were being taken against him for a nonpolitical matter). Unprepared as I was, I had to take up the post in Heidelberg within eight days and assume all the teaching duties of a full professorship. I thought of the proverb, "An unexpected end puts your sorrow to shame," as I happily mounted my motorcycle and set off for an unknown but certainly challenging future in Heidelberg.

Professorial Beginning in Heidelberg

1936–1940

MY HEIDELBERG YEARS constituted my first test in my actual profession. I now had to fulfill the duties of a full professorship and hold four lectures and one seminar each week. That alone was a watershed in my life. In addition to this, Heidelberg was the place where I fell in love and in 1937 got married. During my first years of married life, I came into serious conflict with the Nazi Party, eventually leading to my enforced dismissal from the university in 1940. Karl Jaspers shared the same fate and had to give up his post on the same day as I did.

Without yet knowing what subject I would have to lecture on—which was a very delicate position for a beginner to be in!—I arrived in Heidelberg with a few manuscripts in my saddlebag and with my motorcycle laden with books and the usual necessities. For want of another address, I stopped off at the Theology Student Hostel to ask for advice. This proved to be the right place for me to begin. The hostel was run by Dr. Ernst Köhnlein, a scientist who later became a theologian. He and his wife very kindly took me in and, in the form of a brief survey, gave me my first report on the situation in Heidelberg.

There were, he informed me, some world famous authorities in the theology faculty, such as the New Testament scholar Martin Dibelius, the church historian Walther Köhler, and the Old Testament scholar Gustav Hölscher. The Dean, he said, was absolutely loyal to the regime. I would certainly run into problems with him and should not allow myself to be deceived by his affable bonhomie. In the church at Heidelberg, as everywhere else in Germany, fierce clashes were taking place between the Confessing Church and the German Christians. Although the "famous old gentlemen" of the faculty were inwardly on the side of the Confessing Church, they refrained from getting directly involved in the dispute. Only the brave old pastoral theologian, Renatus Hupfeld, was prepared to put up a fight. As a result, Köhnlein continued, Hupfeld was something like a father figure to the students, the vast majority of whom supported the Confessing Church. Hupfeld's extreme hospitality played an important role in keeping the Confessing Church together.

Of the younger members of staff, Köhnlein continued, the Patristic scholar Baron Hans von Campenhausen was the star of the faculty. He not only fascinated his audience with his immensely lively and original lectures, but also impressed them by adopting an open and unequivocal stance in the conflicts of the day. The students were delighted that this stance was now to be reinforced by two young scholars, namely, Günter Bornkamm who was soon to arrive from Bethel to take up a lectureship in New Testament, and myself. The air, Köhnlein added, was full of rumors that the theology faculties were soon to be closed and transformed into theological colleges.

My first solemn inaugural visits to the "big names" of the faculty were enough to allow me to gain an impression of these dignified gentlemen. In the period that followed, they became fatherly friends to me. Later they and their wives also took my young wife under their wing and touchingly took care of her. In order to increase the solemnity of the occasion, it was customary to wear top hats to such introductory visits. Because this type of headgear could not exactly be said to have an aerodynamic form, I could scarcely wear it on my motorcycle. Furthermore, I also had considerable difficulty finding another place on my vehicle to store it. To solve this problem, I bought myself a so-called opera hat, a collapsible construction that fitted snugly into my saddle bag and only needed to be popped open in front of the relevant house. This hat was to cause Walther Köhler considerable astonishment. Köhler was a dignified man who looked very much like an English Lord and whom one could easily imagine arriving at such occasions in a horse-drawn carriage. As a gentleman of the old school, he accompanied me, the humble novice, to where I had parked my motorcycle. By continuing our conversation for a while longer I put off the dreaded moment when I would have to confess that I had come to such an official event on this sporty and casual vehicle. This was made all the worse by my being in the presence of a man who, by virtue of his age and fame, was entitled to expect the proprieties to be observed.

The dreaded moment arrived and he gazed at me and my motorcycle in disbelief. "And what are you going to do with your top hat?" he asked, visibly confused. Seizing the bull by the horns, I replied, "No problem, my motorcycle's got a cylinder-head." With this I folded my hat together, bowed one last time, and put my foot down. In my rear mirror I could see him gazing after me in bemusement.

Gustav Hölscher was a dainty old gentleman of noble intellect. He had a magnificent scholarly profile that was reminiscent of Erasmus of Rotterdam. The evening gatherings at his home were characterized by a formal, indeed, almost ritual character, but despite this, they were never stuffy. The hosts' friendly attention and playful command of etiquette simply did not allow any awkwardness to develop. Only once, when my attire did not quite correspond to the norms appropriate to his home, did he look me up and down with a hint of lofty disapproval.

People of Hölscher's intellectual sensitivity, of course, suffered especially under the Nazi barbarism. It worried me when I saw that his house too hoisted the swastika flag on important days in the Nazi calendar. At the same time, however, I was amused by how tiny the flag was. It was about as big as a handkerchief, and compared with the size of the neighbors' flags was in itself a statement of opposition.

The real star of the faculty was Martin Dibelius. Together with Bultmann, his form historical research enjoyed international reputation. From the very beginning, I was constantly being invited to his home. Later, whenever one of us was ill, we could rely on his radiant wife with her infectious vitality and positive attitude to life to give us motherly assistance. Even the gloomy days in which we were living were unable to darken her constant cheerfulness.

Among the many things that united Dibelius and me was our love of anecdotes and memoirs. At first, my respect for this famous man made it difficult for me to grasp the strength of his predilection for gossip and the delight he took in relating countless pieces of scandal about the members of large and small royal courts or other important people. He was especially fond of telling stories about the wives and widows of famous men. Such women were particularly numerous in Heidelberg, and Dibelius was marvelous at portraying their vanity and hostility towards their rivals. He even went so far as to say that some widows, whose defense and propagation of their husbands' legacy was so overpowering that it got on everyone's nerves, gave one a certain sympathy for the Indian practice of *suttee*. I often attended his lectures, which delighted me not only because of the splendid way he gave them, but also because of the jokes he made during them. When his lectures were over, Dibelius loved to travel home on the back of my motorcycle and revel in the astonishment of the students when they caught sight of him. When I stopped in front of his house, he would occasionally ask me to sound my horn so that his wife and children would see him on the imposing machine.

Günter Bornkamm and Hans von Campenhausen became two of my closest friends in Heidelberg. Today I marvel at how much time we had for each other, especially since all three of us had to slave away at preparing the huge amount of material necessary for our classes on time. We often used to drive out of town in Bornkamm's tiny Opel P-4 and go rambling. Sometimes, we laughed so much that the little car swerved all over the road and we had to stop until we had regained our composure. We would make fun of the odd characters among our enemies and took pleasure in relating the quick-wittedness with which many people reacted to their evil attacks. No period is capable of creating such a cascade of jokes as a tyrannical regime. Even the cabarets, which in our day are so colorless, were bursting with high spirits and often crossed the boundary of what was acceptable. Thus, for example, the Munich comedian White Ferdl once began his act by breaking off at the word *Heil* in the obligatory greeting *Heil Hitler*. Then, holding his head with embarrassment, he stuttered out, "I've gone and forgotten the name!"

My friend Campenhausen made me realize what aristocracy can really mean. He lived with his enchanting wife and four flaxen-haired children in a large but rather shabby apartment in busy Rohrbacher Street. They had no money to reupholster the once noble chairs, and their financial situation was generally difficult. Despite this, a festive splendor lay over each frugal meal. The ceremonial of the Baltic lord of the manor had become second nature to my friend (which was why it seemed natural and was more likely to inspire than to inhibit) and even the children behaved like well-bred princes. They were, thank heavens, not *always* well behaved. When their father had to spend long periods away from home because he had to stand in for someone at another university, his high-spirited sons would sometimes get so out of hand that their mother was forced to call for my assistance.

When, quite in accordance with proper procedure, Campenhausen was called to a chair, he discovered on making his inaugural visit to the Rector that the Party had vetoed his appointment. Although his life underwent a radical change as a result of this, he never uttered a word of complaint. He was then shamelessly sent as visiting professor to theology faculties at other universities. On one occasion he was even sent to be fifth (!) church historian at the little university of Greifswald, where he was completely superfluous. But this too he endured without complaint and with much self-irony.

Indeed, self-irony had become second nature to him. Because of a foot complaint, he had difficulty in standing for long periods. For this reason, he asked his students not to bring their questions to him in the corridors of the university, but to visit him in his office, where he would be able to sit down.

When despite this request a student spoke to him in the corridor shortly afterwards, he simply asked him to take a seat. He himself then sat down on the floor, compelling the embarrassed student to do the same. This then forced the passing crowds of students either to climb over them or to go to the trouble of finding another route. That was typical of him and his superior nature. He always did what he believed to be right and always had the last laugh.

Because we held our lectures at the same time, I always used to meet Karl Jaspers in the lecturers' common room. We had many lively discussions there and often arranged to continue them at his house. Because he was married to a Jewess, he lived in constant fear and hid her as much as possible from strangers. He had an enormously profound intellect and was constantly surrounded by an aura of thought. He avoided even the slightest allusion to the menacing political situation even though it was of particular relevance to him. He knew that it was only his fame that protected him and his wife, and that this protection was hanging by a thread. The order that had obviously been made to spare him would be immediately revoked if he dropped his guard in the slightest.

With a regularity that bordered on monotony, Jaspers was constantly bringing up theological problems at our meetings. For him such problems were of almost absolute and vital importance. He could not cope with the fact that Christianity claimed to be absolute (at least in the sense in which *he* understood it). His arguments were always variations on the same theme: Faith, he argued, was an existential act and in this respect was absolute for our subjectivity. Consequently, a religious truth—such as, for instance, the belief that Christ is our Savior—stands or falls according to the faith of the person who witnesses to this truth. If this person fails and denies his faith, this truth perishes with his denial. That is why Giordano Bruno had to suffer being imprisoned and burned at the stake in order to ensure the continued existence of the truth (belief that this and other worlds possess a soul) in which he believed. Galileo, on the other hand, was calmly able to renounce the astronomical truth that the earth revolves around the sun and then secretly append the ironical comment, "But the earth really *does* move!" Galileo could do this because he was not advocating an *existential* (and *ipso facto* a vulnerable) truth but an *objective* truth that did not require a witness to die for it. With regard to objective truths, it is the evidence that determines their validity. Jaspers then went on to argue that if the Christian faith claims to be something like an unconditional absolute that is valid for everyone, then it ceases to be solely an existential, unconditional truth that exists "for me" alone. While laying claim to being an existential truth, it is at the same time claiming an objective universality for itself. In other words, it wishes to unite in itself the types of truth espoused by Giordano Bruno *and* Galileo. In doing so, however, it ceases to be a thoroughbred religious truth, as it were. It was this and this alone that had always prevented him from becoming a Christian, despite his wish to do so. More than once during such discussions he would with great emotion take up Lessing's statement that this alone was the "infinitely wide chasm which he was unable to cross. Whoever helps me to cross it will earn my undying gratitude." In these dialogues I for my part pursued the goal of making clear to him the fundamental difference between Bruno's panentheistic belief and Christian testimony. I cannot pursue this debate with Jaspers any further here but have devoted a chapter to it in my work on dogmatics, *The Evangelical Faith*.

Our dialogue on existential truth intensified in Jaspers' seminar on Kierkegaard. One day he invited me to dispute with him in the presence of the other participants in his seminar. He regarded Kierkegaard as the pure existentialist philosopher whose commitment to a historical (and in this respect objective) figure like Christ was absolutely incomprehensible in view of the nature of his thought. For this reason, Jaspers rejected Kierkegaard's Christian commitment and regarded everything that nevertheless pointed towards it as mere ciphers, and as the mythological coding and circumscription of purely existential pronouncements. Because I held this to be an almost grotesque misunderstanding, a fierce battle of words resulted, which culminated in fundamentally different analyses of the text. The undergraduates and Ph.D. students present listened keenly to this debate, which, however, was unable to reach agreement.

This all had an extremely odd epilogue. Jaspers, who by his standards had got very heated during our debate, said at the end of the meeting that, if I would allow him to speak frankly, he would like to confess that he was not too keen on conducting this form of dialogue with a theologian. In his opinion, I had argued like one of his colleagues in the philosophy faculty. I had impressed him not so much as a theologian, but as an advocate of hermeneutical questions, in other words, as someone who reflected on the premises involved in comprehending Kierkegaard, but who went no further. Precisely *that* which he, Jaspers, valued most highly in a theologian had been absent, namely, the voice of the witness. I replied that, because he had addressed subtle questions of interpretation in his Kierkegaard seminar, it was my task to meet him on the same level. I did not consider it to be an adequate method of dealing with such issues simply to content myself with

stating my adherence to an opposing conviction, as he obviously expected
from a theologian. On the following evening, I continued, I would be dealing
with the text on the temptations of Jesus (Matthew, chapter 4) in the Students'
Christian Union. There he would be able to hear me in another role, namely,
precisely that of the witness.

When I casually made this rather brusque remark, I never expected
Jaspers to understand it as an invitation and even go so far as to accept it. But
lo and behold, the next evening he sat among the audience together with the
members of his seminar and even followed the text of the hymns in his hymn
book. I was very moved when he said to me afterwards, "This evening I have
indeed heard the voice of a witness."

I have got ahead of myself again. In my first days at Heidelberg I was
concerned only with my lectures and my student audience. According to the
faculty's teaching program the next subject on my agenda was ethics. To
lecture on this subject, I first had to work out a basic framework. There was
no way of getting out of my lectures—and I really was a greenhorn! I had to
give them on time immediately after my arrival. I made things easier for
myself by first fishing out all my old manuscripts that were of any relevance
and then sought to get myself and my students to believe that these were
precisely the right themes with which to begin. I had a wonderful response
from my audience, which in turn gave me the momentum to work on the
further systematic construction of this large lecture course. Altogether it was
to last two semesters.

We had splendid students. They were a small group who, in defiance of all
the obstacles, came together to do theology. They were an élite (I use this
word with pleasure, despite the abhorrence with which it is regarded today!).
When August Winnig one day made the strange but sensible attempt to
obtain the advice of young students on a matter of church policy, he was very
much impressed by the passionate and decisive statements of these young
men, saying afterwards that he "felt like a naked little child surrounded by
knights in armor." These young men saw to it that one did not wilt under the
strain and the energy one gained from them was then reflected back onto
them. Most of them were later killed in action.

I would like to describe a few characters from my first generation of
students. However, I am afraid that if I began with one student, I would soon
not be able to stop. One of them (despite what I have just said, it now looks as
if I am after all about to begin telling stories about my former students, but I
promise to bite my tongue as soon as this story is finished!) was an energetic
child of nature from Munich by the name of Gerhard Scholler. His satirical

folk songs and Bavarian folk dancing were the highpoint of every party. When he returned from the war after a long period in captivity, however, he was in such a desperate state that he was hardly recognizable. Soon afterwards he was struck down by the dreadful disease of multiple sclerosis. This meant that he was very soon only able to perform his duties as army chaplain from a wheelchair. He loved his work dearly and persevered with it as long as was humanly possible, which greatly moved his soldiers. But the day came when his ill-health forced him to give up his work. He spent the last years of his life in a nursing home together (!) with his elderly mother. When I visited him in his tiny room there, I was confronted by a completely paralyzed and bowed white-haired old man. Despite this, he still beamed at me with the last sparks of his old cheerfulness, a cheerfulness that was due to his faith. I used to call him every Sunday from Hamburg. His voice, which had by this time become cracked, was full of goodness and wisdom until the longed-for silence arrived at last and he was able to begin singing God's praises in another world. What an eventful life! What it is to be a human being!

Each semester I would take my students for a weekend in Spöck. This little village in Baden was truly one of Germany's most special spots. It was still under the lively influence of a revivalist movement founded in the previous century by Pastor Aloysius Henhöfer (1789–1862). As soon as the church bells rang out on Sunday, something like a Pavlovian conditioned reflex took place in people's legs and propelled them towards the church.

The magnet that attracted us to Spöck was Urban, the village priest. He was a very unusual character, a marvellous combination of primitive Christian and comedian. In his deep bass voice we believed we could hear the voice of the ancient prophets and the first witnesses to the faith. It was an elemental cry that was not to be heard either in a theology lecture or in an academic church service. That such elemental naturalness still existed in the lousy twentieth century was for us a comforting counterbalance to the barbarism of the Nazis. We always returned to Heidelberg uplifted, even when we did not always agree theologically with everything Urban said. Thus he once set aside two evenings to speak on "Law and Gospel" (which in this divisive form was a rather dubious undertaking). The first evening consisted of a judgmental sermon of such ferocity that many of the intimidated audience did not turn up for the second evening, when he spoke in much softer and milder terms on the Gospel. I can still hear the constantly repeated refrain of the evening when he spoke on judgment, "Even the savior first has to bash your heads in!"

There was considerable turmoil in this quiet village when a high-ranking leader of the Hitler Youth dared to attack the clergy. Of all places, he chose a milieu saturated with Christian tradition. He accused the clergy of seeking to make the people submissive by propagating the imaginary fears of death and hell that had been invented by the Jews. As an alternative to this vale of tears mentality, he offered the Nazi slogan, "Die standing, die laughing!" We had the good fortune of being present when Urban replied to this Nazi attack. His deep voice shook with rage and scorn as he repeated the Nazi slogan. He then went on to relate how Clemençeau had similarly wanted to die standing and to this purpose had arranged for his coffin to be lowered into the ground vertically. "My dear congregation," he roared at the top of his voice, causing the congregation to cower in their seats, "I would not like to have heard the din he made when his kneecaps popped out." That was what he was like in full flight. And with this comment, the Nazi attack was crushed. It is only with considerable difficulty that I resist the temptation to continue with a series of similar anecdotes.

The earthy quick-wittedness we encountered in Urban was the antithesis of the somewhat overdeveloped intellectuality of the academic tradition at Heidelberg, at least in the form it took in the old days when the university's magnificent traditions were still observed. It is hard to believe in these more sober days the extent to which the academic moguls of those days held themselves to be the center of the universe. Even today, Heidelberg is still full of all sorts of anecdotes about them, although the distinction between historical reality and legend has naturally become increasingly blurred over the years. A good example is Kuno Fischer, the famous historian of philosophy, who is perhaps the most popular object of posthumous stories. Fischer attached great importance to being addressed by his title "Excellency" and not simply as "privy councillor." Moreover, he insisted on this title being used in the third person, which resulted in such sentences as, "Would his Excellency be so kind as to. . . ." This affected behavior is indicative of the cult hero status he and his star colleagues attributed to themselves.

Now one day, Kuno Fischer suffered a slight stroke. This prompted his servant to fetch a doctor who lived nearby and, with blue light flashing, as it were, drag the elderly physician up the stairs. Gasping for breath, the doctor asked him, "What have you done with his Excellency in the meantime?" Whereupon the butler replied, "Yes, what should I have done with him, doctor? I just kept calling to him, 'Won't his Excellency return to his former excellence?!' "

A somewhat macabre relict of this need to behave like a public monument occurred in the drawing room of Mrs. Marianne Weber, Max Weber's widow, while I was still at Heidelberg. Marianne Weber belonged to a circle of rather stuck-up women—Mrs. Weber preferred the term "high-natured"—who liked to believe that they formed a distinguished "intellectual" élite. I was constantly evading invitations from this circle because from what I had heard it seemed likely that these old ladies, irrespective of whether they belonged to the aristocracy or to the bourgeoisie, would send a shiver down my spine. In her biography of her husband, Mrs. Weber also devoted some space to her mother-in-law, Helene Weber, and described how the latter nursed her daughters during childbirth. But this priestess of the intellect spiritualized everything and could not bring herself to say a word like "childbirth." Instead, she wrote that Mother Helene played a very active role in the "wifely duties" of her two daughters.

My First Years of Marriage

I had already experienced how easy it was to fall in love in Heidelberg. At first, this happened in quick succession, and since I had decided to enter into holy matrimony sooner or later, I was torn this way and that by the torment of having to choose. Then I met Marie-Luise Hermann from Karlsruhe, and something clicked between us immediately. This caused the conflict raging within me to intensify. I myself am not sure whether it indicates particular responsibility or whether it is rather evidence of questionable bourgeois behavior on my part that I then attempted to weigh up systematically the merits of the three "candidates" in the hope of coming to a decision. Although Marie-Luise, whom I later came to know as Liesel, immediately went to the top of my list, I had to take as my criterion an as yet unknown factor of considerable importance. Both my profession and my political convictions were possibly leading me towards a serious conflict with the authorities. Up until now, I had only been responsible for myself. A wife would not only have to be on the same wavelength as me but would also have to be brave. The thought that she could perhaps be inhibited in her actions and anxious to appease, perhaps giving her husband's career priority over his convictions instead of encouraging him in moments of despondency, was too dreadful to contemplate. A "scaredy-cat" would certainly be of no use to me. But how could I find this out?

This train of thought was what led me to the rather adventurous idea of setting each of the three women a sort of test of courage. (Fortunately, none of them knew either of the existence of the other two women or of my plan). I decided to take each of them for a ride on my motorcycle and race around a sharp bend I knew well at top speed. Whoever then uttered a squeal of fright when our angle with the road was at its sharpest had failed the test. Only one of them—and it was precisely the lady I hoped it would be—did not utter a sound. Although this was certainly a dubious, perhaps adolescent way to behave, the result of this experiment has proved its validity throughout the whole of our life together, which now amounts to almost half a century. My wife valiantly endured all the crises of our more-than-eventful life. She never opposed those convictions of mine that threatened to endanger our position. On the contrary, her calm, quite unfanatical, but resolute manner ensured a straight course on her part. I do not know how I could have faced her if I had resorted to opportunism for the sake of my career or through sheer cowardice. I also had my moments of weakness. After I was dismissed from my position at Heidelberg, I wrote to various churches in the hope that they would offer me a post. When it emerged that nobody wanted a person who had compromised himself politically (and could in turn compromise them!) I temporarily considered changing faculties and toyed with the idea of studying medicine. Again, it was my wife who enabled me to regain my feet and who remained undaunted. Also as the mother of our children she found, in contrast to me, the correct combination of love and strictness. It may well be that my odd idea of a motorized test of courage was nothing more than a chance decision akin to casting lots. Nevertheless, a higher and gracious hand saw to it that this lot fell "on that which was most delightful," as it says in the Psalms.

Before our wedding in October 1937, I went on a tour to visit all my old friends. When I returned home two or three days earlier than I had intended, I discovered several subpoenas from the Gestapo waiting for me, the last of which sounded urgent and threatening. I simply sent them a copy of the announcement of my forthcoming marriage in the expectation that this would provide them with a sufficient explanation. Among the wealth of wedding congratulations we received, we then actually found a card with a picture of two cooing doves and the printed words, "God's blessing on your Wedding," signed "The Gestapo."

We had scarcely started out on our honeymoon—on my motorcycle, of course—when the Gestapo called on my mother-in-law and asked after me. When she replied that we had not informed her where we were going, they pushed off back to where they had come from. When we had returned home to our new apartment, our first guest was the Gestapo, who surprised us with a house search. Sometime earlier I had quoted in a lecture a few spine-chilling sentences from Julius Streicher, the "Leader of the Franks," which a friend had noted down for me. The Gestapo now wanted me to divulge the name of my source. When the official finally discovered a few lists of names such as, for example, the names of the students taking part in my seminar, he ran his finger down the list, constantly asking, "Is it him? Is it him?" My reply was just as mindless. I simply repeated the sentence, "No comment, no comment." Once during this the good man groaned loudly and said, "Oh, if only I could catch you out!" He was really a good man, an honest and normal policeman who, without himself having had a say in the matter, found himself transferred to the mob that made up the Gestapo. He found having to discriminate against "respectable gentlemen" extremely embarrassing, as he openly confessed to me. "If only I was back with my villains," he said wistfully at the end, before taking his leave of us with a simple "goodbye" instead of the usual "Heil Hitler." After the collapse of the Third Reich, I met him again in an American concentration camp for Nazis. Even poor wretches like him were locked up there.

Our landlady was an old Nazi and a dragon in every respect. I was a thorn in her flesh and she felt permitted to harrass such a politically notorious character as myself in every conceivable way. If anything in the building got damaged, she always regarded my students, who were constantly our guests in our little attic apartment, as the culprits. This was what prompted her to go so far as to take legal action against me over a burst toilet drainage pipe. All she received at court, however, was a severe rebuff. That this damage, along with broken door handles and upturned trash cans, could be put down to an attack by my students was not at all obvious to the judge. I do not know where she picked the expression up, but in the abusive and accusatory notes she kept putting in our letter box she was fond of speaking of the "*ecclesia militans*"(!), which was allegedly responsible for this or that act of destruction. We kept our spirits up through laughter and by adopting an ironical and exaggerated politeness towards her. We were even prepared to give a particularly energetic Hitler salute when we met her. Sometimes, however, it did become a little too much for us. I mention our experience with our landlady to show how even the trivial side of everyday life could provide opponents of the regime with some small but special pleasures.

Much more humiliating than these petty gibes was the totalitarian state's interference in certain aspects of one's private life. After we had been married a good two years and still had not yet produced any offspring—we had suffered the tragedy of several miscarriages—we received a letter marked "confidential" from the Ministry of Education and the Arts. In this letter we were informed that the Fuehrer expected young married couples to produce many healthy children to ensure the continued existence of the Nordic race. In the enclosed envelope, which only the Minister himself was permitted to open, I sent an explanation by return of post as to why our marriage had not yet been blessed with children. An irresponsible action of this kind could not remain without consequences for the career of the guilty party.

This letter reached us just after my wife had arrived home from hospital after yet another disappointment. In my reply I made clear in the strongest possible terms that I was not prepared to tolerate questions and unreasonable demands of this kind. I do not know of any reaction on the part of the authorities to this.

The first days of our life together were overshadowed by an event that distressed us greatly. A friend of my youth, Horst Erbslöh, had accepted our invitation to spend Easter (1939) with us. He had been a few classes below me at school. Because his parents' villa was on my way to school, we often met each other and went part of the way together. It was his athletic figure, the grace of his movements, and his beaming smile that first drew my attention to him. He liked being led and advised a little by an older boy like me and also enjoyed being occasionally licked into shape when he complained about his poor marks at school. I would tell him that he had brought it upon himself through his charming tendency to be lazy.

It later became clear to me that this friendship was colored by a tender eroticism, although this was never openly expressed, not even in words. This restraint had less to do with our natural chastity than it did with the limits imposed upon our behavior by the collective taboo with which that age protected the erotic sphere. For this reason, our friendship did not proceed beyond an enthusiastic affection for each other. This affection still gives me great joy, even when I look back on it half a century later.

Once, not long before his expected visit to Heidelberg, I dreamed of him. I saw myself standing suntanned before his coffin holding a funeral oration in his honor. This dream came true. He did not arrive as expected on that Easter morning but sent instead a long letter in which he informed me that he had embarked on a journey from which he would never return. I was the only person to be informed of this, he said, and asked me not to search for him. He thanked me for what I had told him about faith and for all the friendship I had shown him. He said this would be of comfort to him when he went to his death at the most beautiful place on earth. As a young businessman, he continued, he had suffered several disappointments for which he held himself responsible. He did not feel at all capable of coping with life. Even his girlfriend, he complained, recoiled from entering into a life-long relationship with him and was constantly coming up with new excuses. (He did not know that another man had entered her life and that *this* was the reason for her reluctance). He specified the person to whom I was to bequeath on his behalf the most beautiful pieces in his collections. He closed with the words that he hoped that God would forgive him for fleeing from a life that had become unbearable to him and asked me "to pray that God might forgive him." The last sentences were smudged. I believe his tears had fallen upon them.

After I had recovered from the paralyzing shock that this news caused me, I concentrated all my energy on whether I could still save him and, if so, how I was to go about it. I then remembered that he had the previous year sent me a postcard from Berchtesgaden, where he had been a mountain soldier. On it he had marked with a cross a spot in the Watzmann massif and had commented, "This is in my opinion the most beautiful place on earth. This is where I would like to die." At the time I had thought nothing of it, but now this statement suddenly acquired a new significance. I picked the card out from my archives, reached for my train schedule, bundled together the most necessary utensils, and took the next train to Berchtesgaden. There I intended to persuade the mountain troops to place a search party at my disposal to help me look for Horst.

It was already late evening when I arrived in Berchtesgaden. I went straight to the barracks. I do not know what obscure entrance I had arrived at, but at any rate I did not meet a single living soul. It was Easter after all and most of the soldiers were on holiday. Eventually I came across a sentry, who nearly arrested me as an intruder. At any rate he listened to my explanations of the whys and wherefores of my visit with great suspicion. After a lot of to-ings and fro-ings, I was at last taken to an officer. He at least believed me when I introduced myself and explained my profession, and was prepared to listen to me with an open mind. After I had completed my story, he asked me with some resignation how I envisaged my plan being carried out. He could hardly scour the whole of the Alps just because my friend had been a mountain soldier. After all, I did not even know that he had not chosen another place to die! I then showed him the mark on the postcard and asserted with great resolution that we would find him at Hocheck and nowhere else. The captain knew this spot and promised to send out a search party at first light. Unfortunately, his orders prevented him from accompanying me.

On the following day, the search party found Horst at the exact spot I had predicted. He could not have been dead long. A shatteringly serious expression was etched into his features. I had to identify him. My friend's body was then transported to his home town of Barmen. There I conducted his funeral service and for one last time conjured up the radiant picture of earlier days and the hazy picture of his last days for those who had loved him. I did not conceal the fact that he had deliberately sought death, but I also quoted his last statement, in which he had said that he was certain he was not going into hopeless darkness but was convinced that a compassionate figure would receive him on the other side.

During the days we had spent looking for Horst, the mountain sun had given me a suntan, exactly as it had appeared to me earlier in my dream.

Under the Threat of Ideological Dictatorship

The two Nazis at the university with whom I had the most extensive dealings were the temporary rector, Ernst Krieck, and the dean of the theology faculty, Theodor Odenwald.

Ernst Krieck had worked his way up from the position of elementary school teacher. He had made a name for himself with sound educational books—and this was before the advent of the Third Reich—before becoming the chief ideologist, so to speak, of National Socialist educational theory. In comparison with similar publications of that period, his multivolumed *Völkisch-politische Anthropologie* ('National-Political Anthropology') was at least notable for its independent style and Krieck's aversion to swimming with the tide. He was at any rate no streamlined career man but a sullen character who could not easily be pigeonholed in any single group. He was thus at least respected for being genuine in his beliefs, even if one did have to fight against feelings of revulsion when he appeared at academic ceremonies in his SS uniform and kept clinking the golden rector's chain against the belt buckle of his uniform. He made it quite clear to me that he regarded me as a dissident, which must certainly have played an important role when I was later thrown out of the university. For this reason I was very moved when, after the collapse of the Third Reich and not long before his death, he wrote to me from the internment camp at Moosburg begging my forgiveness and hinting that he had found his way back to what had earlier once given his life meaning.

Theodor Odenwald, the dean of the theology faculty, was a plump man of medium height who radiated good naturedness and bonhomie. He used to behave in a somewhat forced comradely way towards his students, but was also capable of giving them an extremely severe ticking-off if he was displeased with something. Because he was a good-natured and helpful man, he was generally well liked among the students, even if they did take a largely critical view of his theological and political pronouncements. He seemed to me to be living proof of the fact that a certain subjective decency is simply not enough when difficult decisions are called for. If one bases the norms of one's behavior on a dubious system of values or is prepared to come to an arrangement with the *zeitgeist,* such decency is not sufficient to prevent one from leaving the straight and narrow. As a result of this, Odenwald eventually lost any fixed standpoint he might have had and it became impossible to ascertain his position on anything. This instability could be clearly seen in his literary productions. He had never written an original and independent theological work but had merely published occasional essays on the contemporary situation such as, for instance, his essay on *The Current Crisis of Christianity,* or an essay imitating Nietzsche's polemical style on "emasculated Christians." He wrote nothing but publications in support of the system, in which he endeavored to create an aura of modernity, progressiveness, and of being up-to-date with all modern developments.

At first, Odenwald was always extremely friendly towards me. But then, during my last semesters at Heidelberg, an event occurred that triggered off in him something similar to Saul's resentment of the younger man, David. Because we both taught the same subject, it was a source of some embarrassment that virtually every student preferred my lectures to his. Eventually, the number of students fell so drastically that his lectures had to be canceled. After what I later suffered at his hands, I sometimes wondered how I would have behaved in a similar position. This thought was enough to dampen the self-righteousness that was threatening to overtake me.

The beginning of the end of my teaching career in Heidelberg began with a great scandal. In the summer of 1939, all the students in Germany were called upon to take part in the harvest. The approaching war was beginning to cast its shadow. To this purpose, a propaganda event took place in the hall of the university, which was given a big spread in the press. At this event, a representative of the German student leadership gave a speech containing the words (I paraphrase): "The only people who will be excluded from this operation are the theologians. They have dissociated themselves from our nation and its renewal. We shall therefore also dissociate them from the service of this nation." At this, our students, who were scattered through the hall, left their seats as one man, pushed their way through the packed aisles, and left the hall *en masse*. In those days, this was an unheard-of, virtually unique demonstration and was the talk of the town for days. The speaker was so disconcerted that he stopped speaking and for a long time stood helplessly watching the events taking place around him. As a result, the walkout took place in complete silence. Not a single cry of protest was heard.

This incident was extremely depressing for our students. What actually was their country and their nation? Defamations of the Christian faith had been occurring with ever greater frequency. And now this public expulsion! In an age where people are free to demonstrate and oppose the government, as is the case today with our mild-mannered democracy, it is difficult to comprehend what this angry exodus meant back then and what a provocation it must have been in the climate of terror of that time.

After that evening, we sent two student representatives to Gustav-Adolf Scheel, who at that time was the German student leader in Stuttgart. Scheel was one of the few pleasant and decent characters in the higher echelons of the Nazi hierarchy. Our people made such an energetic, spirited, and drastic protest to him that he actually enjoyed it. Indeed, he made what almost amounted to a declaration of love to them before ordering the edict against the theologians to be revoked. This order was unique in the Third Reich, which usually never revoked anything and whose customary reaction to protest was to harden its position still further. When three special trains were subsequently laid on to take the students to the harvest, the theologians were on each occasion given a special welcome over the platform loudspeaker.

On the morning after the scandal in the hall, I gave a special lecture in which I fiercely attacked the student leader's speech and also sought to help my audience in their distress. I wanted to make clear to them (and to myself) how a Christian copes with such disparagements. I conjured up the "other Germany," whose place had been usurped by the contorted countenance of our present fatherland. Nazi Germany, I declared, was a mere caricature, cruelly concealing the *Germania invisibilis*. This speech, too, was to play an important role in my dismissal. It was later published as a contemporary document.

The Enforced End: The Events Leading to My Dismissal

My dismissal took place in two stages. The first stage was the sudden and to my eyes mysterious reappearance of the professor (Jelke) against whom disciplinary proceedings had been taken and whose chair I had been representing all those years. As a result, I was now in danger of becoming superfluous unless another teaching post was found for me. The dean of the faculty at Erlangen, of which I was still officially a member, got wind of the new situation almost before I did and hastened to inform me that Erlangen had absolutely no use for me. I found it scandalous that in an age in which a noose had been placed around theology's neck that was constantly being pulled tighter, a young theologian who had not yet had the time to prove himself should be pushed out in such a callous way.

In this respect, the faculty at Heidelberg behaved quite differently. It decided unanimously to find a nontenure lectureship for me. Dean Odenwald revealed this decision to me with a broad smile and offered me his congratulations. He then went on to assure me that he would push this measure through and that he already saw a promising opportunity to do just this.

Despite being a member of the Nazi Party, the integrity of the oral surgeon K.F. Schmidhuber, who was the local Head of Lecturers, gained him everybody's trust. He was constantly trying to assist us young theologians. When I visited him in his clinic and told him that the fate that had been menacing me had fortunately been averted, he gave me a nonplussed and rather sad look. "I've just been reading your file," he said. "Unfortunately, it contains exactly the opposite. Your dean writes that it is now no longer possible to keep you on here. In his opinion, the unpleasant stir some of your recent lectures have caused makes your continued presence at this university undesirable. In addition to this, he felt that it was important to reduce the burden on the faculty caused by reactionary elements." "But Mr. Odenwald has only just promised his support!" I replied. "Then he's been playing a double game," Schmidhuber responded, "Please go to him and demand an explanation. You're quite welcome to tell him what I have disclosed to you. I always thought that clergymen didn't lie, but, as we now see, that's not the case. Oh well!"

I do not want to give a detailed account of the report I wrote on the pretty stormy argument with the dean that then followed. With a scarlet face and close to collapse, he accepted the reproach Schmidhuber and I made that he had been playing a double game with me. After a few excuses, which I swept aside, he was forced to admit his intrigue and then said in the embarrassing silence that followed, "What stress the likes of us live under! Please take into consideration that a theology dean cannot have any principles nowadays."

I will never be able to forget the moment Odenwald made this remark. He had completely disarmed me. The burning rage with which I had approached him was extinguished at a stroke. The tragedy of his good-natured but unsteady character and finally the candor of his capitulation overpowered me. The conflicts of the day were simply too much for him. I felt sorry for him and the triumphant feeling of moral superiority that had previously inspired me evaporated. I saw that the integrity of the theologian—and especially that of such a feeble one as Odenwald—was under much greater threat than that of the indifferent contemporary into whose inner vacuum Nazi ideology could flow unhindered. The dean's Christian faith caused him to suffer from powerful inhibitions and he was plunged by his pact with the Nazi system into a gruelling conflict. Because he recoiled from making clear-cut but painful decisions, the only way he could escape from his dilemma was by suppression and denial. This reluctance to take a decisive stand was founded on his inadequate theology, which did not provide any real counterbalance to the rival ideologies of the day. I also suddenly understood something I had previously thoughtlessly disregarded, namely, why his last lectures had been canceled owing to lack of students. I was overcome with pity for a failed human being.

The second stage of the end of my career followed soon afterwards. Even before the decision on the agreed nontenure lectureship had been made, I received notification that "the Fuehrer's deputy" had exercised his veto on behalf of the party against my being allowed to continue to work as a lecturer in any form. This letter also contained the demand to pay back the income I had already received for that current month. I do not believe that even a maid would have been dismissed in this manner. Up until then, we had had to manage on my monthly salary of 350 marks, which was not enough to have made any savings possible. Consequently, we now found ourselves in serious financial difficulties.

No sooner had Schmidhuber heard of all this than he came to my assistance in a way that touched me greatly. He was in charge of a clinic and was snowed under with work. To alleviate some of his workload, he had just been assigned a new chief assistant. For my sake, he did without this urgently needed assistant for three months and gave me the latter's salary. He could not bear to see me treated unfairly, although our ideological views were anything but close. Yes, there were even Nazis of this kind! During the later denazification process they were lumped together with their evil comrades. When this happened to Schmidhuber, I fought for his rehabilitation with all my might. I have always remembered him with gratitude and respect. My treatment by the Nazi Party went too far even for the university, as I can report to its credit. The then rector, who was also a medic, registered his protest and succeeded in obtaining an interim payment for me.

News of my dismissal spread very quickly, and all of a sudden I felt like an outcast. Some of my acquaintances no longer dared to greet me on the street or crossed the road to avoid meeting me. This was not the case with my faculty colleagues, however, who remained loyal to me. Also, a few professors from other faculties made no secret of their solidarity and even demonstrated it publicly. Thus the neurologist Viktor von Weizsäcker and the jurist Karl Engisch were constantly inviting me to take walks with them. There were also other ways in which I received some agreeable signals that heaven had not forgotten me and that my wife and I were being looked after. One of my students had heard of my dismissal and sent me his complete savings of several hundred marks. Only with great difficulty was I able to persuade him to take the money back again. The great Old Testament scholar Gerhard von Rad, who at that time was teaching in Jena and whom I did not know personally, wrote me an extremely sympathetic letter and invited us both to live for an unlimited period at his family's estate on the Chiemsee. We would, he said, be provided of in every respect and could live there free of worry and with no need for an income. I would have to compile a very long list if I wanted to enumerate all the signs of friendship and helpfulness that were shown us in addition to those I have cited.

I used the free time I suddenly had on my hands to write my fingers to the bone—I still have a whole file from this period in my archives—and to protest against my dismissal to every conceivably relevant authority. I was above all concerned to find somebody who could gain me access to the Brown House* in Munich. I was determined to speak to the Fuehrer's deputy or one of his advisers. Access to this house, however, was protected by a wall of iron. Old Pastor Scheel, the father of the German student leader, was also extremely concerned for my welfare. But despite his son's influence even he was not able to gain admittance for me, although he made a genuine effort.

Then, one day, Hans Heyse, the boss of the Academy for Lecturers I had attended and with whom, as I mentioned earlier, I had had many heated debates, paid a completely unexpected visit on me. Now an officer in the army, he was in Heidelberg on official business and just wanted to look in on me. He had not yet heard of my fate. Despite our opposing roles in the Academy, I had always the feeling that he liked me. On this occasion, too, he

* Nazi central office in Munich. *Translator's note.*

reminisced on our days at the Academy with great affection and spoke warmly of our "productive opposition." When I told him about my vain attempts to storm the Brown House, he encouraged me simply to go there and not allow myself to be turned away. This seemed a good idea and I resolved to attempt it.

My Visit to the Brown House in Munich

This was no sooner said than done. I travelled to Munich and entered the Brown House's threatening and cold walls. I had only got as far as the porter when I experienced my first "halt" because I was unable to show him either a summons or an invitation. And when I said in all naiveté—it was really very naive!—that I had to speak to the Fuehrer's deputy, his only reaction was a quizzical smile as if I had said that I had come in the name of the Emperor of China. Anyway, he then ignored me completely and proceeded to leaf through some papers. However, I refused to budge an inch and stood watching the uniformed big shots that were going in and out. A young civil servant, one of the few civilians in the building, stopped for a moment and fixed me with his gaze. I do not know why. Perhaps I looked rather helpless and lost. At any rate, he suddenly approached me and asked whether he could be of any assistance, informing me that he knew his way around the Brown House. "I don't believe you can help me," I replied, "It seems that nobody here can help me." "Well!" he said with a smile, "That remains to be seen. Who is it you want to see, then?" "The Fuehrer's deputy," I replied. "Good heavens," he exclaimed, laughing out loud, "That's aiming a bit high. It's very difficult to get hold of Mr. Hess. But if you tell me what the problem is, perhaps I can advise you on somebody else who might be able to help you!"

The man was so kind and helpful that I quickly spluttered out my story to him. While I was doing this, I immediately gained the impression that our basic views were perhaps not at all so far apart. At any rate, he took up my cause with astonishing commitment. "I have an idea," he said and pulled me into a corner. "I can gain you access to the adviser for the arts. I know her well. We'll see how far that brings us. The real key figure for your case is the National Head of Lecturers. He's pretty inaccessible. But who knows? If the girl manages the situation skilfully, perhaps she can get you an audience with him."

He telephoned briefly from the porter's telephone and then lead me to the aforementioned lady who, in view of the responsibility of her position, struck me as very young and inexperienced. To my surprise, she was informed about my case and began immediately to find fault with my concept of history. I ought to understand, she said, that an understanding of history in which the fall played such a dominant role and which refused to predicate a "hierarchy of creation" for nation and race is unacceptable to National Socialism. As a pupil of Hans Heyse, if I had ever heard of him, she went on, she certainly had no sympathy for such a theology.

When I heard Heyse mentioned I intervened immediately, deliberately dropping the casual remark that I knew him very well and that Mr. Heyse had had tea with me a few days previously. Her reserved physiognomy lit up as if an electric impulse had passed through it. If her revered master had dignified me with a visit—she immediately asked about the whys and wherefores— then there must be more to me than this rather obsequious creature had suspected. This fan of Heyse's had scarcely thrown me an almost reverential glance when I exploited the favorable impression I had created by saying, "Well then, if Hans Heyse respects me despite my theology of the fall, then I really ought also to be worthy of an appointment with the National Head of Lecturers, don't you think? Of course, I don't know if your influence reaches far enough to gain me an audience with him." She was immediately prepared to dispel my doubts about her influence and asked me to take a seat for a moment in the waiting room. A few minutes later she appeared again, saying, "The National Head of Lecturers will see you now," and informed me of the corridor and room number of his office.

Still slightly stunned by the suddenness of my success, I made my way to the stronghold of this Mr. Big and after marching past a few receptionists suddenly found myself standing before him. To the outside world he was know as "Laddie Schulze." I had already been told that he was a typical apparatchik and had himself never been a lecturer. He wore a glittering (diplomat's?) uniform covered with innumerable medals that were unknown to me. (It crossed my mind that they might have originally belonged to foreign potentates.)

I wrote up my notes on the pretty dramatic and occasionally loud conversation that followed in a café immediately afterwards. I can only give an account of a few moments of this model case of contemporary history here. (Despite immediately making a record of this meeting and despite the quotation marks, the following is, of course, not an absolutely literal account, but is an attempt to give the most accurate report possible.)

"So you made it!" he said in greeting, before immediately showering me with a wild torrent of words. "I was expecting a fat, little priest, but instead I find a nordic youth before me! You should be ashamed of yourself for being a Christian. It shows that you're still wet behind the ears! It is outrageous that someone like you can still talk about sin and such pathological nonsense and make the whole of world history dependent upon Adam's having eaten an apple!" All this and more was hurled at me in an extremely loud and wildly staccato voice.

It suddenly became clear to me that any discussion with this man would be utterly pointless. He would just throw me out. This being the case, I wanted at least to try to make a dignified exit. It was thus not a courageous act on my part when I snapped back at him in the same high volume, "That's just typical of National Socialists like you. You present us with some nonsense your advisers have talked you into believing and fling a caricature of Christianity at us. It's enough to make us blow our tops. This discussion is really quite pointless. I think I might as well leave right now." I was so angry that I had completely forgotten where I was.

But then a strange thing happened. These people were so used to (and disgusted by) fawning subservience that they often reacted affectionately to violent opposition conducted in their own style. This was also how I fared. After my outburst, the official beamed at me and said almost sentimentally and thoughtfully, "Oh, when I look into your blue eyes, it's clear that you belong to us! I did of course express myself somewhat drastically. I'm a blunt sort of person and like to speak frankly."

He was at any rate suddenly very much more friendly and listened quietly to me. However, because he was only superficially informed of my case from hearsay, he was not able to make much of a response. Finally, I even sensed a certain barbaric goodwill on his part—I do not know how else to describe this crude character's good mood—and, in simple terms and taking his primitive nature into account, was able to tell him something about my Christian faith. "At the beginning of our conversation, you said that my Christian faith was proof that I was still wet behind the ears. But I have not always been a Christian. I only acquired my faith later. I have then, as it were, deliberately chosen to be wet behind the ears. This choice alone and not the relicts of pious traditions is my faith!"

The atmosphere had meanwhile eased to such an extent that I could say to him, "After all that we have discussed and after correcting a few things your advisers have told you, I find it very odd that I was thrown out of the university and see no reason why this decision should remain in force. I would be grateful if you would inform me of your precise reasons for this decision."

"I'm sorry, old man, but the decision stays and, what's more, I'll tell you why," he said. "Strictly speaking, it has nothing to do with you personally." And then came the decisive sentence, which I can repeat almost word for word. "As long as theology faculties still exist—and that won't be for much longer, I can tell you!—I will make sure that only sucking pigs and no wild boars are appointed to professorships. You belong to the younger generation of lecturers who have most influence with the students. We don't want lecturers like that. We'll deal with the older lecturers later." "I have understood you very precisely, Sir!" I said and got up to leave. He accompanied me to the door and took his leave of me with the words, "We'll talk again in ten years. By then you'll be one of us." To this I replied slowly, thoughtfully, and with very clear enunciation, "Yes, in . . . ten . . . years, Sir." Long before the ten years were up, no one could tell me where he was and what had become of him. "His own home knew him not."

A few months later, he inquired whether I would be prepared to accept a professorship in philosophy, should one arise. He obviously wanted to help me. But because this was unmistakably part of the strategic goal of closing theology down, I rejected his offer. Althaus described this offer as a "diabolical temptation."

Unemployed

So now I stood in a professional void and considered what move I should make next. For a brief moment, a chance appeared that caused me great excitement. I received an inquiry from Hamburg whether I would be willing to accept a candidacy for the post of main pastor at the Church of St. Nicolai. You bet I was willing! This was a special post that had a long tradition lying behind it. Its duties consisted exclusively in preaching, teaching, and running the church. Above all, the teaching aspect of the post (the preparation of candidates for confirmation and the holding of public lectures) bore at least some resemblance to my previous work. This offer seemed like a sign from providence to me. Such assumptions, however, often prove to be human, all too human speculations. This was also to be my experience.

As soon as the church authorities at Hamburg found out that I had been dismissed, they retracted their offer, saying that they could not afford to burden themselves with someone like me. The former German Christian but now long since "converted" Bishop of Hamburg, Franz Tügel, a keen and sympathetic reader of my works, tried to intervene and reinstated me on his list of candidates. This caused us yet more days of nerve-racking tension. But then everything was suddenly brought to an end in one fell swoop. A letter signed "Heil Hitler" arrived from the parish council containing the curt message that the selection committee had rejected my candidacy. I was in great despair and suffered a crisis of faith when I saw this last chance destroyed. Later, when I was summoned in a quite different way to a wonderfully fulfilling job in Hamburg, I thought back not unashamedly on how easily we insignificant human beings identify our wishes with the will of God and are then vexed when "higher thoughts" deal with us according to quite different and much wiser principles.

I now sought a church that would be willing to entrust me with a clerical position. I possessed the necessary educational background and had taken the necessary examinations for such a post. But my application met with no success and I received rejections from every quarter. I was *persona non grata* and was regarded as a liability. The State Church of Baden, with which I had had very close relations from my Heidelberg days, sent me a very warm invitation. However, the Church had had a governmental and therefore Nazi "financial department" forced upon it. It was this department's duty to approve every church living, every church event, and even every transfer. It simply used its veto to prevent my being awarded a post, describing me as "politically suspect." From Bishop Meiser, the head of the Bavarian State Church, I received a letter that contained neither a salutation nor a polite closing sentence, informing me that I could find "temporary" employment in his State Church. How welcome I was to him was made crystal clear by the following statement: "This does not entail acceptance into the list of candidates for a church position or inclusion in our health insurance scheme." For somebody who, after all, had been a professor for three years, the style and manner of this brotherly helpfulness appeared so "untempting" to me that I did not bother to respond to the letter. From other quarters, too, there only came rejections, or I was put off, which again was of no help.

But I had to do something and do it fast. Not only was our money on the point of running out, but the Gestapo was also beginning to make threatening noises. Nowhere did there appear to be a light at the end of the tunnel. During these weeks I wrote, primarily for my own consolation, a little book entitled *Wo ist Gott* (Where Is God?) This little book was later printed in several editions. It was concerned with the problem of Job and dealt with my own religious doubts in the form of letters addressed to an imaginary "Sergeant K." I always found working through my personal problems in literary form very therapeutic. By imposing intellectual order upon my chaotic worries in this way, I sought to bring them under control. I received many letters in response to this book, especially from the front. Some of these letters occasionally caused me a little embarrassment. The imaginary Sergeant K had become so real to quite a significant number of people that they requested his army postal number so as to get in contact with him.

Emergency Accommodation in the Army

In the midst of this awkward situation, God's gracious hand once again reached into my life and sent Major Klein to my home. Klein's reason for visiting me was that he had read some of my books and wanted to discuss a few issues with me. When I told him of my apparently hopeless situation, he advised me to enlist in the armed forces. "Your wife will then receive enough financial support to live on. And in the army you'll also be safe from the Gestapo." I had to explain to him that I had unfortunately been declared unfit for military service on the grounds of my illness and, furthermore, was permanently dependent on medicine. "That doesn't matter," he said, completely unimpressed. Because he occupied an influential position at the records and recruiting office of the regional headquarters at Heidelberg, he saw a few (rather crooked!) possibilities of making the relevant alterations to my military records and getting me into the army. I very soon received my call-up papers and was drafted into a special division of the aircraft recognition corps at Wiesbaden. After the customary basic training, which I had no trouble in passing, we learned how to identify and report invading enemy aircraft. To apply what I had learned, I was later transferred to Evreux, a town between Paris and Le Havre that had been almost completely destroyed by German aircraft.

I will spare the reader my military experiences. They were nothing out of the ordinary and did not involve me in any military engagements. Until my enlistment, I had spent my whole life in an academic ivory tower. It was a very enjoyable change to be able to associate with ordinary people. The camaraderie often made me forget the desolateness of my life as a civilian. For some of my fellow soldiers, I was a welcome assistant in the writing of letters, primarily to girlfriends, fiancées, and wives, but also to mothers-in-law. Before putting pen to paper, I would first ask exactly how large a dose of emotion—from a soft purring to fiery passion—the individual wished to have in his letter. I was always proud when I was told that the letter had had the desired effect. I also enjoyed thinking up all sorts of unusual answers and modes of behavior for my often rebellious dealings with my superiors. Unable to fit these into their routine, they were reduced to helplessness. Such embarrassing situations also gave my comrades a lot of pleasure. I can remember that a particularly fierce and much feared sergeant, an individual who truly loathed Christianity, once interrupted his lesson to tell a joke that was not only dirty but also blasphemous. Now you really cannot and should not be prudish when you are in the army. But this combination of two obscenities was going too far. I put up my hand and said with the routine curtness, "Sir, I would ask you to refrain from such inappropriate jokes while on duty!" This was one of those cases for which there was no provision in his rules of behavior towards subordinates, and consequently caused him a verbal block. In addition to this, the added threat that he had also done something impertinent "on duty" may have thrown him off balance. At any rate, he gaped at me dumbfounded and, grinding his teeth and thinking frantically, paced up and down in the deathly silence that filled the room. What would happen now? Then abruptly and without making a single remark, he continued with the lesson. Afterwards, I received a small ovation from my comrades, who hated the sergeant because of the sadistic pleasure he took in tormenting the less skillful among us.

After about nine months, life in the army became deadly boring. I also knew from Liesel that the Gestapo had in the meantime fallen silent. I longed for meaningful work. So I decided to bring about my discharge from the army. A simple trick was all that was needed to achieve this. All I had to do was to reveal my illness to the army doctor. After I had done that, I would be immediately included in the discharge proceedings. The first stage in achieving this consisted in getting myself transferred to barracks in Frankfurt where hundreds of candidates for discharge were assembled. There, however, the process then ground to a halt. Horror stories were told about how many weeks one could be detained there. And that was indeed what happened to me.

Every morning at the barracks there was a roll call. At these, fatigue-parties were detailed to clean the latrines in other barracks and attend to other extremely unpleasant duties. So I concentrated the whole of my acumen on how I could escape as quickly as possible from performing this inspiring service for my country. Then I had an idea. At each morning roll call, anyone with venereal disease had to fall out to the left. I made a mental note of a few faces and discovered that they no longer turned up the next day. So one morning I also joined those suffering from venereal disease. The sergeant on duty had meanwhile got to know me reasonably well during my stay there. At any rate, when I fell out to the left with those suffering from venereal disease, he bawled at me, "What are *you* doing here?" adding ironically, "Alright, which venereal disease have you got?"

That by-now-familiar moment when an unexpected answer paralyzes the military mind arrived once again, for when I told him about my "chronic postoperative tetany," instead of giving him the usual familiar information, his inventory of routine jokes for such cases failed completely. Furthermore, he probably did not want to reveal that his knowledge of venereal diseases was incomplete and that he found himself confronted with a new and unknown disease. After giving me that rather helpless look that I love so much in military men, he let me remain with the V.D. crowd and gave me my identity papers shortly afterwards. I was now a civilian again and was very pleased to be able to return to my young wife.

Maturation in Parish Ministry

1940–1942

J UST AS I RESOLVED to redouble my efforts to find work and earn my keep, a letter arrived from Bishop Wurm, the Swabian Primate. In a cheeringly fraternal tone, he invited me to Stuttgart to discuss how the Swabian State Church might aid me. Yet we had never met, and knew of each other only from hearsay. I knew of his resistance to the Nazi regime, of course, and had also heard the amusing quip with which the Swabians made fun of the bishop's permanent quarrel with Murr, the Governor of Württemburg: "Murr groans when Wurm moans." He had also read some of my publications, but this can hardly have been what prompted his letter. The fact that a fellow Christian had got into serious difficulties was sufficient reason for him to offer his help. As a result of this attitude, a whole army of people who had been dismissed or driven from their posts congregated in his church, and it was a matter of complete indifference to him if this incriminated him with the authorities.

Full of hope, I made my way to the "Bishop's Palace." This was a set of rooms in a block of rented apartments high up in Silberburg Street in Stuttgart. If I remember rightly, one had to climb more than ninety steps to reach it. When I arrived, I was received by a sweet old couple, who reminded me of Philemon and Baucis, with a table set for teatime. Their warm-heartedness made it impossible for any feeling of awkwardness to arise.

During the lively conversation that immediately developed, I gained my first impressions of this truly remarkable man. In the years that followed, these acquired increasingly clearer contours. I came to know his unwavering courage in defying the Nazis, after having been taken in by them for a brief moment; his warm sense of humor, which enabled him to make fun of the pettiness of the local bigwigs and also to smile, full of self-irony, at Swabian idiosyncrasies; his ability to bear the burden of having to make each decision not only with an eye on his own personal position, but also with view to the fate of the great State Church of which he was the leader; finally, his wide education, above all in history, which enabled him to find historical parallels for almost every current issue. When we discussed the tribal characteristics of the German people and I voiced the opinion that the Saxons suffered from feelings of inferiority whereas the Prussians were convinced of their own superiority, he reacted promptly by saying, "We Swabians suffer from both. It is important that you know that, if you join us." This adage was indeed sometimes of assistance to me!

So we got on well with each other from the very beginning, and this great bishop's care for me, a young nobody, was a source of immeasurable joy and strength to me.

"When the war is over and the Nazis have gone, we will need to have you back as a professor," he said in his homely Swabian accent. "That's why I'm thinking of giving you a minor position in the Swabian mountains. There you would have time to study and keep yourself in the picture." That was typical of him. He was always thinking far ahead while at the same time concentrating on the insignificant personal fate of the person who at *that* moment was his neighbor.

After we had talked about other things for a while, he returned to his plan to give me a post in the Swabian mountains, and said that his idea would probably not work. "With your High German you wouldn't understand a word of the dreadful Swabian dialect the farmers speak up there, and they wouldn't understand you either. But I'll think of something." I did not mind where he sent me. I felt I was in good, caring hands, and was prepared to do anything to avoid disappointing this generous man. When he then soon afterwards found a position for me in the Swabian uplands where the Swabian dialect was not so bad—at least not in his opinion!—he had without doubt made the right choice.

Before we took our leave of each other, we both went onto the balcony. Stuttgart lay below us in the evening twilight. Soon the blackout regulations would spread a lightless night over the city. We were quietly absorbed in this sight when Wurm suddenly stretched out his arm and, with a broad wave over the panorama before us, said, "All this will go up in flames and perish in rubble and ash. Let's enjoy once again what it was like and still is today!" When I later lived through the inferno of Stuttgart's destruction, I looked back on this statement as a prophecy of doom.

Settling Down in Ravensburg and Langenargen-by-Constance

The Neckar sparkled enchantingly in the moonlight as I bid farewell to Heidelberg. After a last melancholy evening in the snow-covered city, I set off in mid-January for my new post at Ravensburg, not far from Lake Constance.

The old town, which was notable for its many towers, had something homely about it. When I left the station and made my way to where I would be staying, my apprehensiveness abated. The path I was taking led me past the old town hall, with its magnificent Renaissance oriel, and across the broad market place, with its venerable patrician houses. From high above the town, ancient Veitsburg Castle called down its greeting.

I was given a room in the apartment of the Sterkels, an elderly married couple. Until my arrival, young curates had used to live there. This elderly couple, who were always very touchingly concerned for my welfare, could not quite understand how they had come to have a "Parish Locum Tenens" (to use my official title) of my rather advanced age staying with them. They lived through the war almost in the spirit of August 1914 and were politically unutterably naive. Nearly every month, old Mr. Sterkel would gleefully tell me in his cracked old voice how many tons of British registered shipping had been sent to the bottom of the sea. I thus spared him and his wife a more precise account of my past so as to avoid confusing them. I was later very moved when their small, innocent, and harmless world was destroyed by the most terrible catastrophes. Both their sons were killed in the war and their daughter, a young doctor, fell to her death in a mountain accident.

My room reminded me of my student days. It was where I slept, studied, and received my visitors. At first, Liesel stayed in Heidelberg to break up the household. When I sat alone in the clean but very simple room, which was furnished with pictures that did not appeal to me, I felt terribly lonely and was seized by fear of the future. I could not conceive that I would never again have any students. In my inexperience, the clerical post I was about to assume, with its sermons, house visits (how would the people receive me?), and teaching duties, lay before me like a frightening *terra incognita*. How would I cope with it all?

When Liesel joined me after a few weeks, we were given an additional room in the vicarage opposite. But then the child we had been yearning for so fervently, Wolfram, was born, and my little family moved into the vicarage at Langenargen-by-Constance. Because I retained my job at Ravensburg, this meant that we often had to live apart. Only once a week after the Sunday service was I able to travel to Langenargen to discuss all my joys and troubles with my wife and to have the pleasure of seeing our little boy.

As far as outward appearance was concerned, our residence at Lake Constance nestled in an area of considerable beauty. From my study, where I was surrounded by my beloved books and familiar furniture, one could gaze across the lake into Switzerland, a happy illuminated land of peace where blackout regulations did not apply, as far as the majestically towering Mount Säntis. Behind the house there was a veritable Garden of Eden. When spring arrived in all its glory, the effusive southern light caused the flowers positively to explode into bloom. "The magnificence of exile!" I sometimes thought. The people in the village also proved to be friendly and helpful neighbors to my family.

Despite this, however, we had never felt so lonely in our lives. Not a single person knew why we had come. Nor could we tell them, because in their innocence they would not have understood. As a result, there was nobody, apart from my old headmaster, Paeckelmann, who had retired to Wasserburg, with whom it was possible to have a serious conversation. We often said to ourselves that it would have been better to have lived in the concrete jungle of some big city and to have had good friends that were on our level.

I was welcomed with open arms in Ravensburg vicarage on the other side of See Street, and also in the house of the dean, the Reverend Kommerell. The occupants of these houses were sensitive enough to put themselves in my shoes and did their utmost to make my transition to my new career easier for me. The Reverend Gestrich, whose replacement I was, was a soldier at the front. Every now and then he would come home on leave. Shortly before his arrival the old flower woman, Mrs. Meyer, who was well known in town and quite a character, used to turn up at the vicarage and announce, "The Savior has telephoned me to say that the reverend is coming home on leave!" When Gestrich one day unexpectedly turned up *without* this advance notice, she was visibly indignant and said with a threatening look towards the heavens, "Our dear Savior could've telephoned me this time, too!" Wolfgang Gestrich was a thoughtful man who was well versed in the fine arts. His wife was a practising doctor. She and her mother, the *belle mère* loved by all, were wonderful conversationalists. I was impressed by the discipline with which these women coped with their terrible anxiety for their menfolk and their refusal to let this anxiety get them down.

I was also often the guest of the Daurs, the other clergy family living in the house. Reverend Daur was my closest colleague and, in my inexperience, I could always go to him with all my questions and troubles. I often felt ashamed at the humility and, indeed, fraternal joy he showed at the ever-increasing church attendance that occurred during my ministry. I often wondered whether I would have remained so pure in heart and free of resentment towards a rival as this selfless man did towards me.

The place where I felt most at home in Ravensburg, however, was first and foremost the home of the churchwarden, Kromer, who was a sort of manager and accountant to the parish. I sensed immediately that both Mr. and Mrs. Kromer were very fond of me. They uncritically approved of everything I did, an otherwise not exactly laudable but rather dubious mode of behavior. In my uncertain and often despondent moods, however, it was just the right medicine. Under their touching care, I would bloom again after some disappointment or another had laid me low. Even today I get a warm feeling in my heart when I think of these friends.

The Greenhorn Vicar

I will never forget my first task in my new job. It was the weekly Bible evening in the parish hall. My landlady had already assured me how much she was looking forward to me holding "bedtime." Her lady friends, she informed me, would also be there, so we would be completely by ourselves which would be very cosy. But why, I asked myself, did she describe the Bible evening as "bedtime?" Was I expected to sing the old ladies to sleep? Going by my landlady's remarks this almost seemed to be the case. The cause of this confusion was the dialect my landlady spoke. In the local parlance the word for "Bible evening" (*Bet-Stunde*) was pronounced exactly the same as the standard German term for "bedtime" (*Bett-Stunde*). This only dawned on me afterwards, however.

About twenty old ladies were waiting for me in the small hall. The baby of the group had, if my memory serves me right, just celebrated her seventy-second birthday. The organist was an old man of eighty-two whose harmonium playing suffered considerably from his gouty fingers. He was scarcely capable of striking a single key without making a mistake. The singing of the old ladies, however, seemed to me to be very lively, at least in comparison with the harmonium accompaniment that tried in vain to catch up with them. I was reminded of the singing of my students and was overcome by a feeling of melancholy. But then I plucked up courage and decided to see the funny side of the matter. So I spoke to the old ladies as if they were a group of eighteen-year-olds, used a few ribald and highly worldly expressions, and also worked in one or two anecdotes. One of the old ladies, all of whom were soon crowing with delight, said at the end, "But you weren't at all like a vicar, Vicar!" Now I did not know what the old ladies said about this evening at home or in the shops, but at any rate, the number of ladies gradually increased and, lo and behold, the average age dropped considerably. Furthermore, after a few rather shy members of the male sex had made a first appearance, more and more men began to attend my prayer evenings. Finally, a large number of adolescents even turned up and we had to use the neighboring hall as well. I was very happy at this because it made me feel that I was probably on the right track. Later on, I sometimes revealed my method to younger theologians. This was as follows: "You must speak to the type of audience you would *like* to have, even if there is not a single such person there. Many people make the mistake of bowing to the dictate of the people present."

It is also the *first* impressions I had that stick most firmly in my memory with my other official duties. This is the case, for instance, with my shy attempts at making house calls. I was very nervous about these. The thought of ringing somebody's doorbell and having to reckon with the possibility of being unwelcome filled me with horror. And even if people were friendly and let me in, what was I supposed to talk to them about? Merely to indulge in small talk about the weather, headaches, or the latest reports from the front, seemed to me to be a betrayal of my profession. But how should I best go about steering the conversation onto more important things? Would it not be an all too abrupt transition if I read them something from the Bible or hymn book?

I considered various ways of conducting a conversation and naively decided to begin my housecalls simply by visiting every house in the whole of a single street. The parish had a large, multicolored index card system for housecalls. I attributed this colorfulness to my predecessor's esthetic sensibilities, not suspecting that the white cards indicated Protestant parishioners while the other colors referred to mixed marriages of various kinds. This misinterpretation of the index system was the first mistake I made. More were to follow.

The first two visits, which were recorded on white cards, went well, even if it did depress me that I did not get much further than introducing myself. But then I rang at the next glass door, this time with a red card in my hand. When I introduced myself as the new vicar, an elderly dragon of a woman, probably the domestic help, snapped back at me, "Master's in the cellar," and slammed the door in my face. I now made my second mistake by going down into the cellar, which was something a man in my position should never do. I carefully groped my way forwards in the half-darkness and listened for any sound that would indicate the presence of a human being. Eventually I thought I could hear the humming of an electric machine and knocked on the door, without, however, getting any reaction. When despite this I cautiously entered the room, my glasses immediately misted over. I just had enough time to notice that a stream of blood was flowing beneath my feet. During the moment of shock that resulted from this sight, I heard a male voice rant, "How the hell did you get in here? Can't you see I'm working?" I was in a butcher's workshop. Instead of beating a hasty retreat, I made my third mistake and introduced myself. At this, the voice bellowed, "You can see that you're of no use to me. And what's more I'm a Catholic!" I removed my glasses, immediately regained my composure and almost began to enjoy the grotesqueness of my situation. I wanted at any rate to make an appropriate exit. "You're right, please forgive me," I called out to him, "it's just not on for a Protestant clergyman to set foot in the workshop of a Catholic butcher, which, as even the neopagans know, stands under the seal of the confessional. Goodbye!"

Even my first christening was not without its problems. I was particularly afraid of such venerable official duties because they consist of many different kinds of liturgical formulae which, if one muddles them up, make it very easy to cross the boundary between solemnity and ridiculousness. The child to be christened belonged to a large family, each member of which had gathered in front of the house to receive me. When I arrived, they greeted me respectfully in an obviously well-rehearsed chorus of "Good day, Reverend!" I was encouraged by the fact that they appeared to regard me as an experienced professional, and I immediately became more self-confident. But then the problems began. First of all, I inadvertently omitted the main part of the service, the creed. Then to my horror I forgot the name of the child, as a result of which I began to stammer. The family, which was well acquainted with the baptismal service, naturally noticed my amateurishness and let me know it, for when I took my leave of them, it was no longer "Good day, Reverend" but "Heil Hitler, Vicar!"

So my curacy brought me many memorable and amusing encounters that I would hardly have had in the homogeneous and comparatively rather colorless social stratum in which I had lived until then. After my first fright at the hitches that befell me, I began increasingly to enjoy the robust and unique characters among the common people.

The task that caused me the most problems was the propagation of the gospel from the pulpit, that is, the *sermon*. Because preaching was to play a very important role for me in the later decades of my life, and because many of my homiletical and meditative works have appeared all over the world in various languages, I feel compelled to devote a little space to describing the difficulty in which I found myself in those early days.

Up until that time, I had lived under the foolish illusion that I could only set foot in the pulpit when I had got the theological theory completely clear in my mind. It was for this reason that I had always avoided preaching whenever possible. It was only after I *had* to preach because of my job that I gradually realized how false my previous conception had been. In other words, I learned to understand that faith comes from preaching and that theology is merely the result of later reflection on this faith. Thus theology does not, as I had previously imagined, *precede* preaching but *follows* it. In retrospect, I now know that I could not have written the eight volumes of my systematic theology—ethics, dogmatics, and the history of theology—if I had not had the spiritual experiences I owe to my preaching duties.

There was also another reason for the fear I felt when I made my first visit of inspection to the Ravensburg pulpit from which I would soon have to preach. I have already mentioned in the account of my habilitation that I gave earlier that I tended to express myself rather abstractly in my early period. I would descend into the depths of profundity and move simultaneously in the rarified air of pure intellectuality. I still have in my archives a letter from Emil Brunner, who kindly drew my attention to these dangers in a helpful and paternal way. He has played an important role in my career as a red warning light. After a few sentences declaring his support for my work and speaking of the hope he placed in me, he wrote the following words: "There is one thing I as the elder man and as a genuine admirer of your work might perhaps say to you: I am a little afraid of your virtuosity and, if I may say so, of your intellectual cleverness. You dissect everything that falls into your hands. I feel quite uncouth and clumsy in comparison, but I cannot really believe that my inability to dissect and analyze is really a deficit. . . . That is why a quite immense responsibility rests upon your shoulders. You have to step into the breach that Barth has torn open and which I cannot fill. You are still full of youthful energy whereas I am almost sixty. You are clever enough to talk to the German people, whereas I cannot. For this reason, you must at all costs beware of your ability, your insatiable analytical intellect. May God grant you the necessary simplicity."

It did not escape me that Emil Brunner had overestimated me in many respects. But precisely because it was his *goodwill* that had driven him to this exaggerated appraisal of my talent, I was also prepared to accept his criticism. Thus his letter is one of the documents that have had a decisive influence on my life.

His critique of my esoteric and academic style caused me to worry whether I would be able to preach in a way that would be intelligible to ordinary people. I resolved to concentrate all my intellectual energies on this task. Because I had to look after the outlying districts of Ravensburg and the surrounding villages (Weissenau and Mochenwangen) and consequently had to travel long distances by foot, I used to think on the way about what images and stories I could use to illustrate my sermons. I attempted to use all the various experiences I had had in my preaching—from a sunset to conversations at the sick-beds of my parishioners. I also decided to begin by preaching not on texts from Paul's letters but on the stories in the Gospels in order to remain close to the narrative form. In doing this, I strove to find the point where the members of the congregation could identify themselves with the figures surrounding Jesus.

Even as early as my first attempts at preaching, I had a good feeling, and my enjoyment increased each time I mounted the pulpit. Gradually I also acquired a certain rhetorical élan, which I let myself be carried away by, especially since I noticed that the congregation responded in a favorable and lively way and that attendance increased. The thing I enjoyed most was gazing into thoughtful young faces. While I spoke, I always fixed my attention on a select group of people. It was mainly to these that I addressed my sermon. I even learned that a good method of public speaking is to concentrate on a *single* member of the congregation and to enter into an intellectual dialogue with him. All the other people in the congregation would then listen of their own accord. If, on the other hand, one wants to include everyone and to give something to all of them, one's sentences dissolve into generalities, and one produces the most dangerous reaction possible in preaching, namely, the feeling on the part of the listener that the sermon is not addressed to him.

The thing I found most difficult was having to preach when I was undergoing a *spiritual crisis*. If on the previous day I had been walking along See Street, and had again bumped into the Nazi schoolteacher, I had difficulty in coping with my anger at the contemptuous way he had treated me. How could I then preach a sermon on the text: "Love your enemies"? One Saturday I received news that *four* of my former students, to whom I was particularly close, had been killed in action, and on the next day I had to preach on "Joy in the Lord." How could I do that without hypocrisy? I was afraid I would lose my credibility. Simply to call the whole thing off—"Sermon cancelled due to spiritual crisis!"—was, however, not a viable alternative. I would cope with a distressing situation of this kind by openly confessing my spiritual crisis from the pulpit: "If I have to preach on joy today, then you should not think that my heart is so overflowing with joy that it is merely a case of opening my mouth and allowing it to flow out. I cannot speak 'lyrically' of joy because I am dejected and depressed. . . . The text on joy stands like an alpine peak high *above* me while I flounder about in the depths below. So I will try to make clear what message is being sent down from this peak to us in our grief. . . ." I thus always attempted to be completely honest and not to say anything to the congregation that I was not at the same time prepared to say to myself. I was consequently *also* prepared to admit to them that I did not feel equal to a certain Biblical passage. I was always strangely moved by the fact that it was precisely this honesty that made the congregation listen attentively to the sermon! Stranger still was the fact that I myself left the pulpit comforted and with a renewed capacity for joy.

Once, after a sermon in which I had made some aggressive remarks about the contemporary political situation, a sixteen-year-old member of the Hitler Youth stormed into the sacristy and was so enraged that he was almost prepared to tear the bands from my cassock. After this incident, I repeatedly invited him to come for long walks with me so that I could talk to him at length. This sixteen-year-old Wolfgang was a really special boy. He was something like the Hitler Youth's leading pianist, a true child prodigy. For the journeys to his concerts, Goebbels placed a special railway compartment at his disposal, and he appeared at each concert in a smart soloist's uniform.

Never again was anyone's piano playing to thrill me in the way his did. A few weeks later, he was playing the organ in a church service at A, the town where he lived (he only came to Ravensburg on visits). He then decided to study theology and later came to me in Tübingen.

He soon got so excited by theology that I feared for his psychological equilibrium and suggested to him that he ought rather to study a completely down-to-earth and secular subject such as, for example, economics. I put him in touch with my colleague Carl Brinkmann. Brinkmann took a liking to Wolfgang, gave him special support, and soon made him his assistant. He later became a well-known, indeed famous, professor of his subject. Our friendship has continued to the present day.

I once shocked the Ravensburgers from my pulpit. On the Sunday before

Reformation Day, the choir had to drop out of the service, and many other places also remained empty. There was a pathetic reason for this. The Nazi Party liked to arrange its meetings to take place at the same time as the Sunday church service. When it did this, it also exerted considerable pressure—and on Reformation Day this was particularly strong—on people to attend. Consequently, many gaps appeared on the church pews. I was incensed at the compliance of the congregation. I found it intolerable to allow them a week later to sing Luther's hymn with the bombastic accompaniment of trombones and trumpets. I had always found the final lines of the hymn rather frightening: "If they take your life,/wealth, honor, child and wife,/ Stand not in their way,/Their actions will not pay,/For from us God's kingdom will ne'er go away." But now these words had become a grotesque lie! I could not tolerate such insincerity and made a confidential arrangement with the organist so that I could make clear my protest. At the final hymn, "A stronghold is our God," I made the congregation stand up and announced that I would say something after the third verse. When we had finished the third verse, and everybody was putting away their glasses and closing their hymn books, the organ suddenly stopped playing, and I said, "A large part of the last church service had to be canceled. Many people were too afraid to come to church and went instead to a political meeting. That was nothing less than a denial of our faith. As long as this shame hangs over us, it is forbidden for us to sing the last verse, 'If they take your life, wealth, honor, child and wife. . . .' It would now be a lie to sing it. Therefore, the organ will now play the verse on its own while we remain standing and consider our failure. Woe betide anyone who sings along!" Then the organ played the last verse in a very muted way. The congregation was profoundly shaken by this and a sob went up through the church. When exactly forty years later, my former confirmation candidates, who were now respectable citizens and parish councillors, invited me back to Ravensburg, they had still not forgotten this "punishment."

A good deal of my time was taken up with *teaching*. Because religion was no longer taught in the schools, this task was undertaken by the parishes, as a result of which I had to teach hordes of small children. How was I to go about this? I had, after all, never been trained in this area. For my second theological examination, which the governing body of the Bavarian Church had kindly permitted me to take despite the fact that I had had no practical training, I had to leave Erlangen and give a test lesson to a class of little girls. They cheerfully went along with the lesson, and I convinced myself that my pedagogical talents must have greatly impressed the examiners. At the postmortem, however, the leader of the church assembly told me that I had done just about everything wrong. When I shyly made the objection that a forest of hands had shot into the air every time I had asked a question, he said, "That was only because of your exotic accent. That was something interesting and new for the children." So I must have made quite a fool of myself. And with this experience behind me I was now supposed to teach a horde of little children. I was in a difficult position.

I decided to tell as many colorful stories as possible and to do my best to portray the biblical characters as modern figures. But then I remembered a cautionary tale the Freiburg economist Constantin von Dietze, a colleague and old friend of mine, had related to me on the way to Ravensburg. His children's religious studies teacher had also striven to portray the stories of the Bible as vividly as possible and had even gone so far as to set them wherever possible in Freiburg. An example of this was the teacher's lively account of the resurrection of the widow's son at Nain. When the young man died, the teacher said, his brokenhearted mother ordered a coffin for him from Mr. Einhenkel the master carpenter. (The name has stuck in my memory, there must really have been a person of that name in Freiburg at that time.) When the funeral procession was crossing Dreisam Bridge, the teacher continued, Jesus met them, raised the young man from the dead, and returned him to his mother. The children were impressed. When the teacher asked them if they had any questions, a little boy put up his hand, wanting to know just one thing, namely, "Did Mr. Einhenkel then take his coffin back?"

So I remembered this story and it served as a warning to me. It illustrated that too much fantasy and imagination could unintentionally fix the children's attention on a triviality. I tried to steer a middle course, but this too was not always successful. I remember my attempt to acquaint the children with the story of Zacchaeus in the mulberry tree (Luke, chapter 19).

Zacchaeus, the chief tax collector, very much wanted to see Jesus. However, he was of such diminutive stature that he had to climb a tree to do this. Jesus then called him down and even called in at his home (which in view of Zacchaeus' contemptible profession caused an unpleasant sensation). The gospel describes the conversation that Zacchaeus had with Our Lord and closes with Jesus' wonderful love for this man, who had previously tried in vain to appease his bad conscience.

I now wanted to present the scene to the children as vividly as possible and played the mulberry tree myself. I placed a little boy, who had volunteered to play the role of Zacchaeus, at the top of the tree, in other words on my shoulders. Another boy, playing Christ, then had to pass by the foot of the tree and wave to Zacchaeus to come down. At this point, however, my Zacchaeus lost his balance and I was only just able to catch him. Since he did not have any branches to hold onto, he grabbed hold of my glasses when he began to fall, sending them tumbling to the floor, where they were dashed to pieces. I was very unhappy about this because the glasses were expensive and I was on quite a poor salary. I then had the bright idea of lodging an application for their replacement with the church warden, who was a friend of mine, on the grounds that I had had an "accident at the workplace." He, however, said that this rule was intended for physical education and not for religious studies teachers. However, I did not give in, but told him of a clergyman I knew whose dentures had once flown from the pulpit during his rather overenthusiastic sermon. They landed on the chancel and were smashed to pieces, forcing him to finish his sermon by "speaking in tongues." Could that not perhaps be regarded as a workplace accident? And if so, was it not in principle related to my case? I was actually reimbursed for the expense of new glasses.

The problems I had with the Ravensburg dialect caused me much embarrassment, especially with the smaller children. At the beginning of each lesson I had the tiresome duty of taking the register. When, in a class of little girls, I discovered that someone was absent, the children would keep calling out, "Must be a nanny!" Because I did not understand what this was supposed to mean, I made the mistake of asking for an explanation of the expression "nanny." The answer I received was as follows: A nanny was a child who had to take care of its smaller brothers and sisters because their father was at the front and their mother was frequently at work. I rejected this as an excuse for nonattendance and told the girls to bring their little siblings along in such cases. Furthermore, I continued, they should in future bring a *Heftle* (exercise book) to school—I did my best to speak Swabian—because I wanted to dictate some exercises to them.

When Liesel, who was going to play—or rather, maltreat—the harmonium in class, and I neared the parish hall for the next lesson, we were met by an indescribable sight. The children were lifting heaven knows how many baby carriages up the steps and every one of them—including those without brothers and sisters—was carrying a chamber pot. This was something I did not understand at all. In the classroom some girls were holding babies in their arms, others were pushing baby carriages to and fro, little children were running around, and the floor was covered with chamber pots. The first thing I did before we began singing was to ask them why they had brought these objects along. "You yourself told us that we should all bring a *Häfele* (chamber pot) with us," they cried in chaotic unison. They had misunderstood my pseudo-Swabian *Heftle* (exercise book) as *Häfele*, which in these blessed pastures meant a chamber pot. "My mother was very surprised," said one of them. "Mine too," added others. It was dreadful. When on top of everything they produced very poor work in class—perhaps the confusion and din was also to blame for their useless performance—I am ashamed to say that I lost my self-control and bellowed at them in a stentorian voice. The children of Ravensburg were not used to this sort of thing, certainly not in religious studies lessons, and were struck dumb with fright. The babies, however, woken up by my bellowing, now began to cry with all their might.

At this I was overcome by such an elemental sense of my professional failure that for the first time in my career—and I believe also for the last time—I panicked and fled the classroom. I grabbed my wife by the arm and ran with her to my room. There overcome by the misery of the new situation, we bewailed our misfortunes and did not leave the house for several hours. Meanwhile, news of the events in the classroom must have spread like wildfire, for wherever we went, whether it was to the vicarage, to the deanery, or to the Kromers, everywhere people had difficulty controlling their laughter. The public was unanimous in its opinion that nothing as funny as this had taken place at Ravensburg in living memory. This helped us to see the funny side of this event.

Although I generally had good relations with my candidates for confirmation and was often able to have a good laugh with them, I occasionally also had difficulties. Some Nazi teachers appeared to loathe the fact that the children liked coming to my lessons and made clear their ideological opposition. Three boys in particular were considerable troublemakers. One of them, a *Jungvolk** leader of enormous stature, once put his hand up during class and said, "Yesterday at school Mr. X said that everything we learned here made the nation stupid and that Christianity was a Jewish religion which would merely make people weak." I then decided to confront this head-on by ridiculing this teacher, ending with a request to the boy to convey my answer to him with my regards. Even back in those days I was well aware, of course, of what dubious educational procedure it was for so-called figures of authority to conflict openly with each other in the presence of young people. In more

---

* A subsidiary organization of the Hitler Youth for boys aged between ten and fourteen. *Translator's note.*

peaceful times it would have been appropriate to have had a word with such a teacher in private and not in front of the children. In the ideological struggle of the day, however, that was quite hopeless. For this reason I preferred to make sure that I had the last laugh.

Sometime after the aforementioned incident, I took a chest-expander into my class. I then got the *Jungvolk* leader to come to the front of the class and reminded him of what he had said about Christian weakness. I then asked this boy, who was a really strong young man (otherwise it would have been rather unfair), to pull the chest-expander apart. But he was unable to move it a single centimeter. "Now I'll show you just how weak Christianity makes people," I continued and stretched the expander to its full length. From then on there were no more objections of that kind. This all took place, of course, on a level which was far below that of sensible discussion and could hardly be said to be an ideal example of Christian witness. All the same, it left a lasting impression. Even at a cheerful reunion decades later, my old confirmation candidates would still replay this scene.

One of the three "Nazi" boys annoyed me in a particularly cunning way. He learned all his exercises very well and reeled them off with deliberate indifference. If I met him on the street he would greet me with an intentionally rigorous but also clearly ironical "Heil Hitler!" Although I took a great deal of trouble over him, he remained inapproachable, indeed frosty. Some years later, when I was a professor in Tübingen, he was the last of a particularly large number of students to come to see me in my weekly consultation session. I recognized him immediately. (I cannot remember what he was studying.) He wanted to apologize to me for having been so unpleasant towards me and, looking back on those days, he made them much worse than they had really been. This moved me beyond measure, especially since I had in those days implored God to help me think well of him and pray for him, and to preserve me from falling into the trap of answering hate with hate.

After the collapse of the Third Reich in 1945, I could not get my three "Nazi" confirmation candidates out of my mind. I wondered how they coped now that the ground had been cut from under their feet and they had been plunged into the void. So I wrote a long letter to all three. Avoiding any gloating at having been proved right, I assured them that I was always there for them and that I was upset by the inner distress they must now certainly be feeling. At that time there was no postal service or rail connection, and my letters only reached them after many detours and by means of couriers. The three boys sent detailed and moving replies to my letters.

When describing my *official duties*, such as funerals, I will have to be careful not to allow the narrative to expand excessively. One event carved itself particularly deeply into my memory. One day, a mother whose twenty-year-old son, a member of the SS, was dying, came and asked me to pay a visit to the military hospital. She told me straightaway that she and her whole family followed the Fuehrer with all their heart and soul, and had left the church. For this reason, she continued, she was sure that I would not want to listen to her. But, she said, she was in great distress. She knew no one in this strange town and needed someone to whom she could pour her heart out. I was, of course, always there for her during the next few days. What she was utterly unable to understand and what tortured her most of all was that this radiant and combative son of hers was not giving his life for the Fuehrer on the battlefield but was dying wretchedly of leukemia. This did not fit into her understanding of life. From this point, our conversations ventured into areas of unforgettable profundity. Before I went to the hospital with her, she confessed to me still with some apprehensiveness that her son had thrown a hot water bottle at the crucifix in his room a few days earlier. That had unsettled her, but I comforted her by telling her that the Crucified One Himself always embraced with love those who were against Him and who perhaps "know not what they do." When I approached the young man's bed, he was already in his death throes and was no longer able to respond. I read a few verses from the hymns of Paul Gerhardt for him and his mother. These verses meant a lot to me, and the mother, hearing them for the first time, listened with astonishment and great emotion. Afterwards, as I was leaving, I told her how profoundly moved I was by her courageous attitude in the midst of such pain. She then replied, "Yes, perhaps I do have a courageous attitude. But please don't probe any deeper; it has no substance behind it what-soever." I was thunderstruck by these words. It was as if the foundations of the "heroic worldview" had suddenly been revealed to me. When after the war I spoke in many American concentration camps on behalf of captured SS men and former Nazi activists, I kept taking up this distinction between attitude and substance and sensed that this struck a chord with the men. I continued to correspond with the mother of the SS man for many years, and had the feeling that she slowly regained the substance she had lost.

Soon afterwards, a judge, who was still quite young and whom I did not know, died in Ravensburg. His profoundly unhappy widow, who asked me to conduct the funeral, told me that she had not been living in Ravensburg long and that her husband had been mostly in military service. It was for this reason that I had not met him, although he came to listen to my sermons from time to time. He had always remained true to his faith, she said, even if he had for idealistic reasons joined the Nazi Party and the SA very early. When she announced that the aforementioned organizations would be present at the funeral, I insisted that the ceremony at the graveside should be a self-contained religious service at which no commemorative speeches by the Party would be tolerated. What happened afterwards was none of my concern.

I prepared myself to address the Nazi hordes, who were indeed present in large numbers at the grave. In my address, I took up some set phrases I had read in an SS pamphlet on the conduct of Nazi funerals. I can still remember what I said quite well: "We constantly hear in our country that the life of the individual is of no significance when compared with the life of the nation. And when it comes to dying, we are told, then it's only as if a leaf had fallen from the tree of the nation. The living trunk, however, constantly brings forth new leaves in a process of creative renewal. I have a question with regard to this. Does anyone of you gathered here today *dare* in front of this grave and in the presence of the widow, parents, and three children of the deceased to repeat this and to maintain *here* (not in the pub or at the safe distance of one's desk) that this man, loved as a husband and father by his family, is merely an interchangeable and replaceable leaf on the tree of our nation?" I had said all this with considerable vehemence and then used what I had said as the peg on which to hang a brief meditation on the infinite worth of the individual in the eyes of God. Before the commemorative speeches began, I left the cemetery. As I left, I thought I saw them gazing after me not so much with anger as with embarrassment.

Towards the end of my time at Ravensburg there occurred more serious clashes with the Nazi Party, which culminated in my being repeatedly interrogated by the Gestapo at Friedrichshafen. This also began in quite an amusing way at first. One day I received an inquiry from the coal mining district of the Ruhr Valley asking whether it would be possible for a number of sixth-formers wanting to study theology to come and spend between eight and fourteen days of their holidays with me at Ravensburg. In this way they would receive something like a first introduction to their subject from me. Would it not be possible, I was asked, to arrange this in such a way that it appeared to be a period of recuperation for the students in an area not subject to bombing-raids?

I was filled with enthusiasm at being able to work to some extent in my old profession again and sought to find a way of avoiding the allergic reactions of the Gestapo to such courses. Without disclosing the background to my plan, I asked the people attending my evening Bible classes to try to find accommodation for "young refugees from the bombing-raids" in the Rhineland. I wanted to avoid any fuss, I said; everything should be done discreetly.

While everybody was nodding their heads at this, I noticed an almost deaf old lady who was constantly attempting to pick up my words with an enormous ear trumpet. (In those days we did not have the chic hearing aids common today.) She even put her ear trumpet down for a moment so as to be able to nod particularly vigorously. However, as was soon to become clear, her intense agreement was based on a horrendous misunderstanding, for a few days afterwards I was visited by a prosecuting attorney with whom I had become very good friends. We had similar literary interests and agreed in our political opinions. He was quite agitated and revealed to me that the prosecuting attorney's office was about to initiate legal proceedings against me, and that he regarded the matter as pretty serious.

What had happened? It was precisely that deaf old lady who was the cause of this commotion. In earlier days, she had held an honorary office and had collected money for good causes. Since the advent of the Third Reich, however, this had been strictly forbidden and reserved exclusively for the Nazi national welfare organization. The old lady, however, had understood nothing of what I had said about "refugees from the bombing" but thought that I was at long last once again asking for a street collection to be made. So she set off posthaste, was received like an angel on all sides with cries of "at last someone is collecting for a decent cause again," and had soon filled her old collecting box. Unfortunately, Nazi collectors were to scour the same street a few hours later and were confronted by nothing but grumpy faces. Eventually they found out who had been there before them and the trouble began. I was accused of violating the collection law. When I at first burst into laughter at these errors and confusion my friend severely rebuked me and listed the possible legal and penal consequences. In addition to this, he said that I had caused considerable embarrassment to the whole of the Ravensburg judiciary. At my astonished "How's that then?" he told me that his department was responsible for my case. He had, however, withdrawn from my case because he was befriended with me and therefore prejudiced. The district attorney had then said that he was in the same position because his son was one of my confirmation candidates and that I had from time to time visited his home, including for private conversations. Eventually, my friend continued, my case was passed on to an articled clerk with a few comments on my behalf. Fortunately, the case then petered out.

In my later Ravensburg days, it was a source of constant annoyance to me that even letters from my wife in neighboring Langenargen took eight days or longer to arrive. This was because, together with my other mail, they were obviously opened and checked. My anger at this prompted me to write an extremely ironical letter to the post office with the request that they forward my few lines to the department responsible for checking mail. I also sent a copy of the letter to the church assembly in order to provide it, as I wrongly imagined, with some amusement. In contrast to the simple letter of denial I received from the post office, however, the assembly's reaction was one of annoyance. In its opinion, I wilfully put myself in danger by such escapades and should therefore kindly desist from making them. Even Daniel in the lion's den, the letter continued, had only been given the task by God of remaining steadfast in the presence of the lion. He had not been given the added task of going and pinching the lion's tail. Would the leadership of the church react in a similar way in the humorless age in which we live today?

During my ministry at Ravensburg I received invitations to speak in many different parts of Germany. The church leadership was constantly giving me time off work for the most important of these. So I spoke, sometimes on several occasions, in Marburg, Heidelberg, Tübingen and Berlin. I am forced to pass over all the anecdotes I could tell of these sometimes adventurous journeys, which were made under war conditions, and will only describe the decisive journey I was to make in September 1941 to the cities of East Prussia, concluding with a series of lectures in Danzig.

When I arrived overtired in Königsberg after the long journey (and worried that I would not be fresh enough for the service in the cathedral that was to take place that evening), I had hardly set foot on the station platform when I was snatched away from the reception committee by the Gestapo, who then subjected me to a three-hour interrogation in their office. The first sentence with which they greeted me there was: "Your propaganda and rabble-rousing journey through East Prussia is canceled." They had my itinerary in front of them right down to the smallest detail, but despite this they went through the agenda with me. They then reproached me for all my political "sins" since my Heidelberg days. They were astonishingly well-informed. Their peremptoriness and hatred made clear to me that any discussion of detail would be pointless. I just said a few sentences to them about the Confessing Church and its mission. But even then their distorted picture remained unshaken. As a summary they formulated the following (as usual only verbally, of course, they never put anything in writing): "*First*, you will leave East Prussia this evening with the 21.40 train to Berlin. If you ever return to East Prussia you will be sent to a concentration camp. *Second*, you are forbidden to speak in the cathedral this evening." They most graciously permitted me to attend the service as a member of the congregation until the departure of my train.

The reader will be able to imagine how dismayed and sad my hosts were on hearing the result of my interrogation. They were battle-tried men who had manned their barricades with courage in the fierce polarization that had taken place in the church in East Prussia.

The memory of that evening in the cathedral, which the authorities were not able to cancel, still moves me today. After the opening hymn, a fellow clergyman mounted the pulpit of the overcrowded house of God and announced the Gestapo's decision. A profound wave of emotion passed through the crowd like when the wind wafts across a field of corn. "He's sitting over there," the speaker said, "but he is not allowed to speak to us. He has to leave East Prussia forever with the 21.40 train. For this reason we will finish earlier than originally intended and accompany Helmut Thielicke to the railway station." The Gestapo had certainly not expected such a demonstration. There then took place an enormous pilgrimage to the station, where the people stood shoulder to shoulder on the platform and began loudly to sing hymns. We waved goodbye to each other for a long time.

In an overexcited and alert state of mind, such as easily sets in when a state of exhaustion is violently interrupted, I decided not to follow the Gestapo's orders never to return but merely to leave their immediate sphere of influence and bring forward the visit to Danzig with which I had originally intended to conclude my lecturing tour. I thus alighted from the train in Dirschau, spent the night writing and dozing in the waiting room with numerous other travelers, and traveled with the first early morning train, between four and five o'clock, to Danzig. Although daybreak was not an appropriate visiting time, I made my way to the vicarage where I was to be put up. It was only my exhaustion that gave me the courage to seek admission at such an unsuitable hour. The Polish maid who after a while opened the door and who hardly understood any German, was very frightened by the strange and unknown person who stood before her and tried to slam the door in my face. Not without the use of some force, however, I forced my way in, expressed my need of sleep to her by means of a gesture and simply lay down on a couch that I had spotted through the open living room door. I then lost consciousness. When one or two hours later I gradually began to wake up after a period of confused dozing, I suddenly felt like a dead man in a coffin. For when I awoke, I found the whole family standing around my couch looking at the intruder, who because he had not introduced himself was still very much of a mystery. After I myself had regained an awareness of my identity and had introduced myself, there was great joy at my appearance, despite the regrettable cause of my early arrival. The agenda that had been planned for the visit I had intended to make the following week was quickly rearranged. I was now able to enjoy some wonderful days of intensive intellectual exchange and magnificent, merry celebrations at the homes of hospitable people in the evenings afterwards. Nevertheless, in the conversations I had with various people, a fearful anticipation of approaching doom would every now and again suddenly break through. These visions of expulsion, flight, diaspora, and the end of the old world were all fulfilled.

One morning, Mr. Edel the organist took me to the belfry of St. Catherine's. There I sat next to him in the chamber while he rang the bells. I was allowed to choose the hymns. I was moved by the devotion with which this man let the gospel ring out high above the city into the world beyond. Every now and again I walked up to the parapet of the tower and looked down into the depths. The bells resounded in my ears and heart and the powerful sound filled me to such an extent that no other tone could disturb me, including the noises from the depths below me where an air-raid shelter was being built. I could only see, but not hear, the rattling of the excavator, the droning of the pneumatic drills, and the rush of the traffic. I did not catch sight of anyone who might have looked up and heard something of the richness of tone that was carrying me along like a powerful wave. I saw how the people were completely absorbed by the noises of the world, how they were wrapped up in their daily tasks, and the question leaped up at me as to why what moved me as an expression of the Gospel did not also ring in *their* ears.

Soon after returning from my trip to East Prussia, I was again summoned by the Gestapo in Friedrichshafen. I must confess that it was always worrying to be summoned by the Gestapo, because one never knew beforehand what they were going to interrogate you about and because one was dealing with an organization where the rule of law did not apply. In a state where the rule of law is observed, even somebody who has once had to go through something like this cannot appreciate the butterflies in the stomach one suffered in those days. On this occasion, the Gestapo imposed a strict and indefinite ban on my traveling, speaking in public, and writing for the whole of the German Reich. The only exceptions to this ban were my local work in Ravensburg and the train journey to my family in Langenargen. When changing trains in Friedrichshafen, however, I was forbidden to leave the railway station. But all this was not enough for them. Soon afterwards I was supposed to give up my job as vicar and be sent to work in a munitions factory. Intervention on the part of the church authorities was able to prevent this. The parish, incidentally learned nothing of all this. They had no idea that I was, so to speak, "interned" in Ravensburg.

Offer of the Schleiermacher Pulpit at Berlin

During these weeks a new event took place which seemed to push my life in a quite new direction. I received the offer of succeeding Bronisch-Holtze as occupant of the Schleiermacher Pulpit in the Church of the Trinity at Berlin. This was the church of the government quarter. The only active parish member among the great men, however, had been President Hindenburg, who used to follow the church service from a seat specially reserved for him.

Because this church, which was steeped in tradition, was surrounded by government buildings, administrative buildings, and office blocks, the local congregation consisted for the most part only of janitors and their families. This rather dismal prospect was, however, brightened up by the fact that there was a sizable body of people present in the German capital whom it might be possible to win for the Gospel by "preaching them into a community" (as it was explained to me). The situation may have been similar in Schleiermacher's day, whom, despite all our theological differences, I have always held in high regard. This job did have its attractions, of course, especially as the student community and work at the Friedrich Wilhelm University in general was still assigned to it. The spokesman of the parish council, who was very fond of me and with whom I had to negotiate, was, by the way, the famous builder of the Olympic stadium, the architect Werner March.

I do not need to explain why I was attracted by the prospect of this job in Berlin. However, the difficulties began with my ban from traveling. It required a great deal of laborious paperwork to obtain a one-off special permit from the "central office of the Reich's internal security service." This finally met with success and I was allowed to travel to Berlin for the negotiations and for a church service, which I then held with great joy in front of a large and receptive congregation. Very soon, however, the other vicar, who was responsible for looking after the local community and whose loyalty to the regime I had been warned about, initiated an unbelievable intrigue of denunciations against me. He had made thorough investigations into my political past, which he then passed on to the appropriate authorities. While everyone who belonged to the Church of the Trinity loyally supported me, his intrigue met with success with the Prussian church assembly, which had been infiltrated by German Christians. Very soon the moment arrived when I felt it would be undignified for me to continue to be, on the one hand, an object of attack and, on the other hand, an object of delaying tactics. I cut through the Gordian knot and refused the post on my own initiative.

Dramatic Times in Stuttgart

1942–1944

W HEN I RECEIVED THE OFFER FROM BERLIN, Bishop Wurm had already promised me a new field of activity in Stuttgart geared to my special situation, if I decided to remain in Württemberg. Yet he was so high-minded as to leave the decision completely up to me. He never even hinted at the fact that it was he who had saved me from my catastrophic job situation and that I was thus under a moral obligation to him. I myself, however, was well aware of my indebtedness and had thus not traveled to Berlin unaccompanied by pangs of conscience.

As soon as these plans had fallen through, Wurm came out with what he and his colleagues had had in mind for me. He wanted to establish *ad personam*—that is, tailor-made just for me—a "Theological Department of the Württemberg State Church," which I was to head. Above all, he wanted me to act as his theological adviser. In addition to this, he thought I ought to preach a sermon once a month in Stuttgart and, over and above that, found it desirable if I would visit the individual deaneries every second Monday and stimulate the clergy with some theological lectures (the topics of which I could freely choose). When I voiced my surprise at the modest scope of my duties, he repeated what he had already said at our first meeting, namely that he wanted me to continue to devote myself to my academic work so that I would remain fit for a chair in theology "after Germany has lost the war" and Nazi rule was over. "So do whatever you want," he continued, "I am confident that you will not disappoint us."

I was impressed by the generosity of this offer and his confidence in me. At the same time I felt it to be absolutely binding on me and resolved to give it my best. Wurm was also able to arrange permission for me to move freely in Württemberg to carry out my duties. Mind you, when a few months later my weekly lectures in the cathedral began to draw large crowds, the Gestapo seemed yet again to regret its "liberal" attitude. During one of the many subpoenas they served on me, they threatened to expel me from Württemberg if I persisted with my "malicious agitation." They also informed the church assembly of their intention and requested it to urge me to show restraint. But then the old bishop once again showed his mettle, declaring to these gentlemen, "If you do anything to Thielicke, I will take his place in the pulpit myself and in case you then also force me to silence, I have another ten replacement preachers in reserve." Wurm's loyal resolution was a wonderful source of strength to me. When I thanked him for it, he just laughed and said, "The crowds you've been drawing have now reached such a size that they have become your protection. People like the Gestapo are afraid of that form of mass emotion. And it would definitely come to some sort of mass emotion if these meetings were to be banned. Rest assured. Compliance is much more dangerous."

Liesel and I were allocated an apartment on the ground floor of a large vicarage (Kanzlei Street) immediately next to Schloss Square in Stuttgart. Altogether, three families lived in the vicarage. Above us lived Prelate Hartenstein—after Wurm, the most important figure in the religious life of Württemberg and heavily involved above all with the state's pietistic circles. Although we were very different in mentality, he helped me with my work wherever he could.

On the top floor lived the cathedral's parish priest (and later Prelate of Reutlingen) Pfeifle and his family. Whenever there was an air-raid warning, he would run to a shelter high up in the cathedral tower and keep watch. After every raid he had to crawl through the huge and confusingly labyrinthine roof beams of the church and search for incendiary bombs or extinguish smoldering fires wherever possible. That was a task which required enormous courage, for the flames could, of course, flare up and encircle him at any moment. When the church finally met its end and the tower was burning like a torch, Pfeifle only escaped the blazing funeral pyre by the skin of his teeth. He had held out in his dungeon up in the tower until the venerable cathedral finally collapsed, from where he also witnessed the destruction of our house, powerless to salvage any of his possessions. Later, after the destruction of the church, Pfeifle, with no thought for himself, held out in a burning house until he had managed with enormous effort to rescue a mentally retarded and completely helpless boy. Only then did he think of his own safety.

To enter our house in Kanzlei Street, one had to cross a large paved courtyard which was adjoined on the other side by the propaganda office of the Nazi Party. There the "golden pheasants" (as we called the important party bosses with their insignia) strolled about at lunchtime without either side taking any notice of the other. Mind you, that did not apply to our children. Little Wolfram was pampered by them. Berthold, who was born during our time at Stuttgart (actually at Urach, where his mother had sought a shelter from the bombing to give birth), later lay in his cradle surrounded by mountains of rubble. This contrast between destruction and new life exerted such a strange fascination that people who had otherwise had nothing to do with each other gathered around his little bed to watch him smile. Not only the Nazis left what was later their half-ruined office to visit him, but also conscripted Russian women came at every free moment to play with him and to cuddle him. We were shaken by these scenes. What longings this cheerful child could awaken in these exiles!

Although the real bombing had not yet begun, our apartment was in a dreadful state when we moved in. Our predecessor had taken with him everything that was at that time in short supply and which would either itself be necessary in his new accommodation or might be a useful bartering counter for other necessities. That included not only the stoves, which it was extremely arduous for newcomers in a strange town like us to replace, but above all the faucets, which had all been unscrewed. During our first days in the apartment we had to fetch water for drinking, cooking, washing, and bathing from our neighbors.

The Planning and Realization of a Public Dogmatics

As early as my time in Ravensburg it had become apparent to me what disastrous results the Nazis' ban on religious education in the schools had effected. The makeshift institutions with which the church sought to compensate for this deficit could not fail but to be inadequate. Very soon the up-and-coming generation was ignorant of the most simple knowledge of the Bible and of the tenets of the Christian faith in general. I thus became increasingly convinced that there was a need for the development of a sort of *dogmatics for adults*, lessons aimed at combining information and interpretation. Above all, however, these lessons had to bring faith into relation with people's experience of life and to the problems life poses. In brief, they were faced with the task of making the relevance of Christianity as clear as possible. The person taking part should learn that he himself belonged in the

world of faith. He should discover his position in this world and that it was
here that an answer to his questions was to be found. If this could be
achieved, then secularized and aloof people would probably also sit up and
take notice.

To the distress of many of my pietistic friends in Swabia, I did *not* think
much of the normal type of mission to the people, the effect of which was
supposed to spread from the circle of conventional churchgoers to the
secularized public. As a rule, it was only the familiar "little crowd"—I mean
no disrespect by this!—that felt addressed by such missions. This faithful
minority flocked together from many surrounding parishes and through this
accumulation gave rise to the deceptive impression that a real "expansion"
had taken place.

I also became increasingly aware of the deeper reason for this failure. The
mission to the people was very subjective and appealed to sentiment and a
willingness to make a decision for Christianity. It presupposed that its
audience already had various biblical associations at its disposal, that it was
acquainted with the creation and fall narratives, and that biblical characters
such as Moses and Jeremiah, Peter and the Ethiopian chamberlain were
familiar figures. This biblical scenario, however, was a *terra incognita* for
aloof and secular people, even for people with a tenuous relationship with the
parish! They were thus bound to remain just as unmoved by this sort of
gushing evangelical testimony as someone who has never been to an opera
and has an opera lover describe the stage and sing him snatches of melodies.

What mattered to me was to impart to the people of our age first of all the
basic *material* of which they had been deprived. I thus wanted to give them
instruction in the facts and thereby provide them with the foundations—that
is, the *premises*—for a possible decision. I did not, of course, intend to do
this indifferently and objectively. I wanted rather—in a clearly recognizable
manner!—to speak as a *witness* and not to conceal my commitment. Only
commitment—this was how I saw it in those days and still see it today—
ought not to be a thematic end in itself but a constant undertone restricted to
the background of my factual instruction.

I knew all kinds of didactic theories on teaching the catechism to adults,
but could not see any evidence that this theoretical waffle had had any
practical effect. In those days I was guided by the instinct—an instinct
which has now been confirmed by my experience of life—that only concrete
and practicable *models* give out effective signals and achieve anything. So I
arrived at the plan of employing this method in the attempt to teach the

catechism to adults. Should my plan succeed, it might perhaps also stimulate others to devote more attention to a new kind of "didactic sermon."

There was one other thing that motivated me, namely the fact that people in those days were completely consumed by worries about the war—nearly everybody, after all, had relatives at the front—and fear of the future. I suspected that the thought-provoking experience of concentrating on factual questions of faith would help them—especially when these questions did not simply distract them from their everyday troubles or even serve to suppress them, but when the medium of faith helped them to confront their problems from *another* perspective. I had been mulling over all this for quite some time and had given it thorough consideration.

When I shared my ideas with Bishop Wurm and eventually came out with a concrete plan, he was immediately as keen as mustard and promised to do everything he could to help me. He also immediately suggested a suitable venue for my undertaking, namely the Church of St. Mark, a favorably situated and very spacious building, the vicar of which, Rudi Daur, was a highly respected man who was favorably disposed towards such things. Wurm had in any case had this church in mind—together with the hospital church—as the place where I should give my sermons.

After I had drawn up a complete plan for this Christian dogmatics of mine, the first meeting was announced in the press (which at that time was still possible) for Thursday evening. Wurm had engaged state parliament stenographers for this and all following evenings, so that the collected lectures could be published verbatim in book form after the war—indeed, over the years several new editions appeared. In that age light was shed on many questions of faith, human nature, history, and life in general with a profundity that is scarcely possible in peacetime. I wanted to be certain that such a moment so productive of knowledge was preserved.

I awaited the first evening of my experiment with understandable stage fright. I was thus all the more grateful when I looked down from the pulpit and saw a seething mass of people, including many soldiers in uniform. As early as after the first evening there was no longer even any standing room, forcing us to change the venue to the enormous cathedral. Theodor Bäuerle, who in those days was cultural consultant to Bosch and was one of my most faithful friends, thought that the move was a mistake and warned me, "An overcrowded Church of St. Mark is better than a three-quarters full cathedral."

But this fear, too, was unfounded. With approximately three thousand people in the audience, the cathedral was soon just as overcrowded as the Church of St. Mark had been. I often had to push my way laboriously to the pulpit. To the annoyance of the organist, some people even sat down on his bench beside him. Once, when the audience arose, someone even accidentally trod on the pedals, causing a horrible discord to roar through the church. I can still hear in my mind the powerful singing that surged in on the pulpit from all sides.

I kept the devotional setting brief, for I wished to keep the inhibitions of people unfamiliar with the church as low as possible and to give them the more comfortable feeling of attending a "lecture." However, I also did not wish to dispense altogether with the character of a church service. People should be clearly aware of the context in which what I sought to offer them belonged, even if this often included reflections they were not used to hearing from a pulpit. For this reason, a hymn was sung at the beginning and at the end of the lecture. I concluded the evenings with Luther's evening blessing, from which—particularly during the time of the air raids—there proceeded an inexhaustible power. Thus I remember an evening when the air raid sirens began to wail in the middle of the lecture. When I said the Peace, it had a calming effect, enabling the church to be cleared quietly and calmly. During this I remained standing in the pulpit. The organist also remained at his post and played a hymn taken from the evening service.

What a special group of people it was that gathered there on those Thursday evenings! The audience included virtually every class of society: from generals to privates, from big businessmen to workers, from university professors to school children. Large numbers of people from the Hitler Youth and other Nazi groups were also present in civilian dress. Although it made me happy to be able to tell all these people about what was for me the most important thing in life, I was weighed down by the burden of responsibility. From my large mailbag and from my many visitors I learned of the problems of my audience. I became aware of their great longing for security and how much this encounter with the Gospel, which for many was their first, meant to them.

While the lectures were still being held in the Church of St. Mark, many members of the audience had expressed the wish to have an abridged version of the lectures to help them remember what they had heard. In my mail, which increased dramatically, I received many letters from people who wished to send such an abridged version to their husbands, sons, and fathers in the field. These requests were expressed in such an urgent and touching manner that I passed them on to the audience and announced that I would dictate such an abridged version from the gallery each Thursday after the lecture. I urged in particular people who knew shorthand and who were able to duplicate the lectures—secretaries, for instance—to assemble there and asked businessmen to supply paper, which was a scarce commodity at that time.

The effect of this appeal was enormous. Each week I dictated the abridged version of the respective lecture to approximately two hundred secretaries and other people. Whole mountains of paper were donated to me by the relevant businesses and carried into my home. The dictations were duplicated, passed on to other people, who then duplicated them yet again. I never discovered how many copies were published, of course, but I believe the number exceeded that of many publications printed in peacetime. I noticed this from the large number of letters I received, which soon reached me from all fronts and from the whole of the German-speaking world. All this happened at a time when it was extremely difficult to get anything else published—especially for somebody like me, who was excluded from every normal avenue of publication. To me it was like a miracle of God, similar to the miracle of the loaves and fishes. Many people bound the lectures into simple booklets. These still have a place of honor in my library today.

In retrospect I can hardly believe the excessive amount of work I had to cope with in those days. I always put the greatest effort into preparing my speeches and sermons. In addition to this, I also had to read the ever-increasing flood of mail, which took a long time on my own. I felt the trust of the people, not least that of the soldiers at the front, to be so binding that I could not leave their letters unanswered. Although the church authorities had placed a secretary at my disposal, I never felt able to dictate a letter that had anything to do with spiritual welfare—and that was mostly the case— but always wrote a reply myself. I did not want other people, even the most trustworthy, to see these replies.

On top of that, I also had many other duties. I had to make a lot of journeys to the various deaneries. The higher forms of a grammar school requested religious studies lessons of their own accord, and I could not and did not want to refuse them this request. I was also soon monopolized by the Christian students at the technological university, eventually becoming their vicar. In addition, the church assembly in Stuttgart organized clergy meetings all over the state at which I had to speak. The theology faculty at Tübingen was constantly requesting me to give lectures, which, despite being pressed for time, I always accepted with particular joy. Sometimes I had to speak three times in a single day. Many days the workload, as I noted in my diary, often

wore me out, sometimes leading to a full-blown collapse, which understandably caused my family to share in my suffering. And yet time and again I was
carried away by the greatness of the task and the yearning of the people. How
a moment of tiredness could suddenly burst into new life when a letter
revealed that my work had helped someone to find faith, or make his peace
with God, or come near to Christ (whichever way one wishes to express it).

The movement that developed out of the evenings in the cathedral naturally also brought our enemies into the arena. Reverend Pressel, a member of
the church assembly and a man who was particularly supportive of my work,
warned me one day about a spy who every evening took notes of the lectures
for the Gestapo. The church authorities knew exactly who he was, Pressel
continued, and previous experience indicated that he would also turn up at
my home one day in order to sound me out even more thoroughly. What made
him particularly dangerous was the fact that he was Jewish and everyone
therefore assumed that they could be unreservedly open with him because he
was by birth an enemy of the regime! He had already informed on several
people. Pressel told me that he himself and some of his people always sat
near him in order to follow exactly which passages he wrote down.

This Jewish spy then did indeed come to see me, not just once but several
times. Although I was on my guard against him and was, so to speak, larded
with prejudices, his autobiographical stories nevertheless got under my skin.
In him I was confronted by a special case of the Jewish fate. He told me that,
despite being a Jew, he had had a picture of the Fuehrer hanging in his room
for years. He came from one of those conservative and upper-class families
which felt themselves to belong to the German nation. Although he himself
made no reference to it, I grasped the conflicts into which he had been
plunged by a regime that wished to represent this nationalism but excluded
its Jewish supporters *cum infamia*—indeed went very much further than
mere exclusion. In now placing himself at the Gestapo's disposal—which
was, of course, something he did not disclose to me—Dr. G may have been
prompted by the almost masochistically perverse motive of gaining access to
the "National Movement," at least by means of this back door, despite his
Jewishness. At the same time, however, he was also seeking to save himself
in this dubious manner. But in doing so, he had entered into a Mephis-
tophelian pact that could not but corrupt him to the core. One event shows
this particularly clearly. After his house had been destroyed by bombs, a
neighbor I knew well, Mr. N, took Dr. G in, although, as he knew very well,
this act of kindness towards a Jew would certainly incriminate him with the
Nazis. In his innocence, he made no secret of his anti-Nazi convictions,

especially as he regarded it as self-evident that his Jewish guest was of the same mind. Because these conversations were handicapped by his hardness of hearing, Dr. G asked Mr. N to put their discussion in writing. Mr. N agreed to this, especially since he was fond of developing his thoughts in written form. When Dr. G had got together a bundle of these essays, he handed them over to the Gestapo, who immediately arrested Mr. N. A few days later, I too was taken away for interrogation. Dr. G had passed the whole of my correspondence with Mr. N, which he had been permitted to examine under the pretext of his interest in theology, on to the Gestapo.

All of us who knew and thought highly of Mr. N racked our brains as to how we could free him from the clutches of the Gestapo. Wurm eventually achieved this with the aid of some doctored reports a psychiatrist friend of his had written. These saved Mr. N's life.

After the collapse of the regime, I was tortured for a long time by the question of whether I ought to inform the authorities of what I knew at that time of the atrocities this man had committed. I could not bring myself to do it, however, although it was hard to bear the thought of seeing him continue with his medical career as if it were the most natural thing in the world. But I was so shaken by the beginning and end of the fall that he had undergone that I felt too inhibited to throw the first stone.

Teaching in Swabia

At the beginning of my time in Stuttgart, I had imagined that my fortnightly journeys around the state to the various deaneries would be a minimal burden, almost a leisurely enterprise. But after all the tasks I had been given in the meantime, or rather after all the tasks I had imposed upon myself, this theological work caused me a certain breathlessness. Nevertheless, my encounter with the Swabian clergy, above all with the many unusual characters among them, had something refreshing about it. I also believe that they welcomed and were stimulated by my work. At any rate, I felt myself to be openly and trustingly accepted wherever I went.

At the evening celebrations afterwards, I enjoyed the Swabian sense of humor, which even the seriousness of the age was not able to stifle. At first I expressed the wish that a native clergyman should hold the spiritual meditation which was supposed to take place at the beginning of each of my conferences. I was not very keen on acting as a spiritual "one man band" and thus pressed for a collaborative effort. For a reason that I was not at first able to grasp, this suggestion met with resistance. I kept on being asked to lead this meditation as well and was thus forced into the unfortunate position of having to conduct a continuous monologue. When one day I revealed my misgivings to an old dean, he disclosed what lay behind the reserve of my fellow clergymen. In broad Swabian he explained, "You know, these men have been together ever since they started secondary school here (Urach, Maulbronn) at the age of ten, and since that time they know everything there is to know about each other. Now that they're fully-grown men, they feel embarrassed if they have to talk piously in front of each other. You can understand that! So please, could you hold the meditation? As an outsider you're not affected by all this!" I was so touched by this that from then on I gladly complied with his request.

If I wanted to relate all the typically Swabian experiences I had, I would have to devote a special chapter to them. There is only one that I cannot easily pass over, an experience that at the same time brings to the fore a characteristic feature of the age. If I remember rightly, it took place when I was visiting Gaildorf Deanery and was invited by Count Pückler, the former ruler, to dinner at his castle. In my room at the village inn I was instructed that I had to address the Count as "Your Lordship" and his wife, who was a princess by birth, as "Your Highness." In the honest intention of behaving in a refined manner, I rang the bell at the gate and was admitted by a young liveried servant who was so cross-eyed that this must certainly have been the reason that he had been preserved from military service. I was warmly received by this patrician couple and was introduced to a few elderly lady aristocrats. After a little small talk, the cross-eyed butler flung open the double doors, revealing a glittering table covered with a bright white table cloth from which crystal glasses and silver cutlery sparkled back at us. As was to be expected in war time, the meal that was served on the beautiful china was meager. The little slices of meat were so thin that one could almost have read a newspaper through them. I was nevertheless impressed by the fact that, far from relying on their contacts with the top people, the lord and lady of the castle paid for their comestibles with food ration-cards like everybody else. The old ladies showed their breeding by pretending to be overwhelmed by the opulent meal and kept uttering such pointed cries of delight as, for instance, "Exquisite, my dear!"

Still under the impression of the splendor I had witnessed, but also suffering from unappeased hunger, I found it difficult to get to sleep in my room at the village inn. While I was forcing down my war breakfast of coffee substitute and a stale black bread roll the following morning, the landlady announced to me that his lordship's servant wished to speak to me. And, sure enough, there he was approaching the table, dressed again in livery but this time carrying a silver tray which he held out horizontally to me. "His Lordship respectfully requests Dr. Thielicke to provide a 50g meat token for yesterday's dinner," he said. Thinking rather than whispering the words "There's nothing like bowing out in style," I cut out the token, which was about half the size of a postage stamp, and with a genuine effort at making an elegant gesture laid it on his tray, where it then lay in complete isolation. For the reason I mentioned earlier, I was not sure whether the butler was looking at me or the meat token when he departed. At any rate, he carried the token away on its bed of precious metal with a stiff and upright posture as if he were carrying a monstrance. After the war, Her Highness told me sadly but calmly that His Lordship and she had buried the Count's silver in the grounds of the castle before the Americans arrived. The soldiers had discovered it with radar devices, however, and had taken it with them.

Of the theological activities that came particularly close to my earlier profession, there are two events in particular that I have never forgotten. On the one hand, there were the lectures in Tübingen, which I was only able to give in churches and halls. I especially remember the debate I had in the hall of Schlatter House before an audience of professors and students with J.W. Hauer, the leader of the German Religious Movement. This was, of course, a small sensation in those days and attracted so many students that many had to stand outside in front of the windows, confronting us with the problem of making ourselves as intelligible as possible to them. In the first years of the Third Reich, Hauer had created the German Religious Movement as a large umbrella organization for a number of neopagan groups. It merged in about three hundred local branches the motley variety of German religious life, from Odin worshipers and followers of the grand prophetess Mathilde Ludendorff and her dark thunderings to the race mystics of widely differing provenance. What had at first begun with mass rallies and a flood of propaganda, however, very quickly disintegrated back into mutually hostile sectarian groups.

Disappointed by the absence of any long-term success, the NSDAP eventually dropped this ideological and religious auxiliary army of theirs. When I spoke to Hauer, he was already a disappointed, rather lonely and bitter man, but was still a personality in Tübingen. Only a little of the former demagogic zest that had inspired him in the Berlin Sportpalast stadium as the harbinger of a new religion could still be detected. But precisely this may have furthered our discussion, a discussion which although passionate was nevertheless factual and sometimes even touched the depths of profoundity. When we shook hands after the debate, I thought I could detect something like sorrow, or at any rate a somber earnestness in his eyes.

My Encounter with Bultmann

Another great event for my theological work occurred with the publication of Bultmann's essay on the demythologization of the New Testament in 1941. This essay caused a sensation and was to dominate discussion for many decades. In February 1943, Bishop Wurm convened a symposium in Stuttgart on this topic, which people attended from far beyond the borders of Württemberg. Sometime prior to this he had already requested me to write a lengthy theological report on this subject, which he then had duplicated and sent to a large number of church leaders and theologians. I was to give a shortened form of this report at the symposium. This was how one of the first commentaries on this exciting subject came about. Bultmann himself commented on my report in the *Deutsches Pfarrerblatt* (German Clergy News) and wrote me several friendly and appreciative letters. At the same time, however, he employed the same old argument in these letters that he had used for decades, namely, that he had been "misunderstood." It was not by chance that Barth gave his later polemic against Bultmann the sublimely ironical subtitle of "An Attempt to Understand Him." As a martyr to permanent misunderstanding, however, Bultmann will certainly have again shaken his head at this too.

Formulated in a shortened and consequently somewhat misleading way, this debate was concerned with a fundamental problem, namely—and this was Bultmann's starting-point—that the form of the statements in the New Testament was tied to ideas and concepts that were conditioned by the age in which they were written. This form was dependent above all on late Jewish apocalyptic ideas and the gnostic myth of redemption. The object of our faith, however, can only be the "message" itself that is enclosed in these structures, not the external appearance conditioned by the age in which it was formulated. With this he had indeed formulated a fundamental question, one which in differing forms has occupied theology ever since the Enlightenment.

The considerable theological flurry Bultmann caused with his pithy and emotive term "demythologization" resulted from the question of where the boundary ran between the core message and its external appearance. Might not the Incarnation, for instance—the "Word made flesh"—and consequently the figure of Christ himself, perhaps fall under the verdict of being merely a mythical linguistic form conditioned by contemporary history and no longer belonging to the core of salvation history? There can be no doubt that the problem Bultmann has thrown on the table will outlive his theology, for the problems that great theologians and philosophers have formulated have a much greater longevity than their answers, which are more likely to be closely bound to the time in which they were written.

The controversy surrounding Bultmann interested and fascinated me first of all, but not exclusively, for practical reasons. I had studied under him at Marburg and experienced his powerful personality as a teacher. In his seminars, we were all afraid of him, at least when we had not done our preparation properly. He was one of the great intellectual leaders of our age, and served as an example of how a scholarly or ideological school originates, irrespective of the faculty or political and ideological sympathies involved. Such a school originates along the following lines.

The master must above all construct an original conceptual apparatus which exudes the intimacy of his group and is easy to use. The cogs and hinges of this apparatus must do duty for only a very few basic axioms of his doctrine so that more-modest and less-eloquent minds can also set it in motion and keep it going. Thus, for example, Bultmann did not like it at all when a member of the seminar spurned the master's original conceptual apparatus and answered the question "in his own words." I can still hear his indignant reaction on such occasions, "That is not quite wrong, it is true, but please use my terminology—not because it originated with me (which it for the most part did not, but was rather borrowed from his philosophical colleague Martin Heidegger), but because it is appropriate to the subject." Thus it came about that empathetic and adoring female students sitting in the first row were constantly asking permission to speak. These young ladies then deliberately served the master with the jargon he desired (*existentiell* and *existential*, *coming-across-ness*, *thrownness*, and many others), although their intelligence quotients struck me as being in no way outstanding.

During my Heidelberg period, I once accompanied Jaspers to one of Bultmann's lectures. Jaspers was strangely excited. Bultmann had been a few classes below him at school, and Jaspers described to me his boyish charm, especially his sparkling eyes, with great enthusiasm. Later he read

Bultmann's publications with considerable reserve and contemplated his reunion with Bultmann after so many decades with a certain degree of anxiety. After the lecture, he expressed his great disappointment. "He's still doing the same old thing," he said. "There are no surprises and no developments with him. He has learned nothing new. No criticism has ever caused him to revise his position in any way. He sits securely like a windowless monad in the shell of his terminology." This was certainly a correct observation, and later on I sometimes recalled this statement on occasions when Bultmann was indeed apparently extremely "accommodating" in discussions with his colleagues but did not deviate one iota from his course. Despite all his stupendous learning and his intellectual acumen, I was repelled by the cast-iron, inflexible material from which his system seemed to be constructed.

To both my astonishment and joy, I heard a few years ago that he had had the first volume of my dogmatics read aloud to him during the last years of his life. Perhaps this too did not take place without him shaking his head—I would expect that anyway—but I was honored that this great man deemed my efforts to be worthy of his attention.

Literary Output

During my time at Stuttgart I attempted to develop a long-term plan for my work so as to protect it from the danger of being determined by chance causes. For the same reason I also wanted to avoid the many lectures I had to give in Stuttgart and the State of Württemberg becoming thematically independent of the various wishes that were brought to me. I resolved to continue the work I had begun on two books, which were completed while the war was still on, and largely organized my lectures around their subject matter. By this means I was able to work within a comprehensive and ordered framework and simultaneously kill two birds with one stone.

The first book was a general diagnosis of the intellectual situation, a sort of "critique of contemporary culture," which was published after the war under the title of *Man in God's World*. The other book, which was written under the influence of the war, was about death.

Both books had an adventurous beginning. One day, a representative of the World Council of Churches in Geneva, a man of exceptional experience, appeared at my home. He had heard of the books I had been working on and had come to ask for the manuscripts of both volumes. By means of his personal connections, he said, he would have them smuggled across the border in diplomatic baggage and—anonymously, of course!—get them published by Oekumene Publishing House in Geneva. From there they would be sent to the Allied prisoner-of-war camps all over the world. So-called prison universities had been organized in these camps and my books, the representative said, could be extremely useful to them. And this is indeed what happened.

When my identity was divulged after the war and letters concerning the books were able to reach me, I learned of the enormous response these two books had received in the prisoner-of-war camps. When I am lecturing somewhere or other—sometimes even on other continents!—I am still approached even today by people for whom these books meant a great deal during the intellectual famine they suffered in prison. While I was writing these books, of course, I still had no inkling of all this. For me this desk work, for which I had to find time alongside my many other duties, was above all a source of strength and joy. While working on these books I also came to know myself better. I was after all working without any concrete hope that it would ever be possible to publish the manuscripts. I was writing for my desk drawer, so to speak. In the process, however, I became aware that writing was something like a natural process for me. I discovered that I *had* to write and that not to express my life in this way would be like floating in unreality. Following Descartes, I said to myself: *scribo ergo sum* (I write, therefore I am).

The Burden of the Air Raids and the Threat from the Regime

Before the bombing war struck our city with all its might, I received a telegram from my parents in Barmen informing me that they had lost everything in a large-scale attack on my home town, and were now homeless. After wandering about helplessly at first, they came to us in Stuttgart, carrying only a small suitcase and still visibly shocked by their experience. The only comment my mother made was, "I didn't even have a handkerchief to dry my tears." Their happiness began to return again when I took them with me to my evening lectures in the cathedral. Above all, the powerful singing there moved and comforted them. They later went to live with members of the Loewenich community at Erlangen. In our imagination the parental home forms, of course, something like a secure anchorage in our lives. It took a long time to come to terms with the knowledge that this—father's large library, the clock on the mantlepiece, mother's china, the familiar beds—had all been destroyed.

The more frequent the attacks upon us became, the more we trained ourselves in the art of "letting go." In the process I made a strange discovery that forced me to revise many of my previous opinions. I had always thought that the early Christian expectation of the impending end of the world necessarily engendered something like a scarcely comprehensible escapism, an indifference to everything that was of this world. I myself now stood before the impending destruction of my and our world—and now observed that my emotions took a completely different course than I had expected. Sometimes I gazed lovingly at the rows of books in my study and thought to myself, "I still have you. Perhaps you'll go up in flames tomorrow, but today is today." While I was striving to detach myself emotionally from my books in an attempt to fulfill the Pauline demand "to have as if one did not have," I experienced not the eschatological dissipation of the moment I had expected but an enormous increase in intensity of life. The "beautiful moment" acquired a heightened luminosity. The early Christians who were convinced of the imminent end of the world perhaps did not despise the world at all as much as I had previously thought.

After I had taken a great deal of trouble to evacuate large sections of my library to hiding-places in the country—including to a mortuary in Korntal cemetery!—I was visited by a colleague who was a well-known author. He was surprised at my relatively small reservoir of books and obviously assumed that I wrote my own productions off the top of my head. As his eyes scanned the pitiful remnants of my library, I explained to him that I had stored all my vital literature in a safe place. "Well, well," he said, visibly indignant, "So you want to let my stuff burn, then!" With that well-known expert eye that authors have he had to my horror caught sight of his own works on my bookshelves. "Whatever I need for my immediate work has, of course, remained here," I said, seeking to take cover from the vanity to which he and all authors, including myself, are prone. Even against such a somber eschatological backdrop, there was almost always some cause for amusement.

Apart from the menace of the air raids, which escalated both in frequency and in severity, the political hindrances also increased, although I do not wish to go into all the Gestapo interrogations here. It was also no longer permitted to advertise my cathedral lectures in the newspaper. At first the Gestapo forbad *every* mention of the lectures, even in church notices. Later the church assembly was at least able to gain the concession of being allowed to hint at the lectures. The permitted notice, which was printed in very small letters, ran as follows: "T. 8 P.M.," and as the air raids increased, "5 or 6 P.M." Despite the inadequate advertising, people continued to come in the thousands, a sign of the highly sensitive response of readers in those days. This was another expression of the same phenomenon that had already become noticeable in the acute sense of hearing people had developed. The smallest hint was sufficient to trigger off immediate associations with the present in the mind of the hearer. When today one reads some of the articles in the old Frankfurter Zeitung criticizing the regime and commenting on contemporary issues, one might think one was confronted by a somewhat embarrassing conformism. In those days, however, these articles could make one's blood run cold, because we understood what was clearly being said *between* the lines.

We had another experience of how restrictive press censorship was when I wanted to place an announcement of the birth of our second boy, Berthold, in the newspaper. The text I submitted was "God's goodness has blessed us with our second child. . . ." The man behind the counter in the editorial office was so taken aback by this that he disappeared to consult his boss. The boss himself then rushed straight in and made clear his refusal with some animation. They could not publish such an overtly Christian announcement, he said; because of my influence it would be copied by every road sweeper. "Please write just a factual piece of information on the birth!" he cried on his way out and disappeared. I sought to wrest at least the wording "With grateful joy . . ." from the servile person with whom I then continued my negotiations. The adjective *grateful*, however, again made him so uncertain that he once more disappeared to see his boss. After lengthy consultation, I was granted this profession of our gratitude "as a special exception."

Deep below our old house we had an air-raid shelter. Its thick walls gave us some protection during the bombing, although in the end it too was reduced to rubble. The detonation of high explosive bombs caused it to sway like a ship. What was uncanny was that we noticed nothing of the incendiary bombs when we were down there. As soon as the worst was over, the prelate and I would hurry to the surface. Time and again we had to climb through broken glass and the remains of doors and window frames that had been ripped out and torn to pieces. We were often able to extinguish the smaller fires—at least in the early days.

It was awful having to wake the children and to lug them into our cold vault when the alarm sounded. Berthold was still too small to be afraid. All that happened when the shelter shook particularly violently was that his little arms would shoot up into the air. Pfeifle's smallest child, not yet three years old, was more aware of what was going on. Despite this, he did not really understand what was happening and seemed more to enjoy our night adventures than to be afraid of them. During the bombing he would smile at all of us and want to play—a reminiscence of how God had actually intended his creation to be. Wolfram, however, was old enough to understand the danger. He sat on my lap and cuddled up close to me. I did my best to tell him a story and tried to keep my voice as calm as possible. I was nevertheless afraid that my pulse, which had of course quickened, might unsettle him. It was above all our concern for the children that caused us parents the most anxiety. In this respect some things were even harder for us than for the soldiers at the front. Because the light went out every now and then, I always held a lighted candle in my hand and watched closely to see if it trembled. That was like a sort of training for me.

Of course we prayed quietly. This experience too provided me with some new insights. To pray against every bomb and to be constantly thinking of one's own safety only led to a sterile and panic-stricken prayer which could not possibly reach our Heavenly Lord. Such prayer remained fixed on the object of fear, on the bombs. I increasingly stopped thinking of my own life and prayed for the children and the people around me whose last hour had now come. I regarded this as a priestly action, which helped me to achieve a greater calmness.

Once, before the sounding of the all-clear, the police shouted down into the cellar and ordered us to come out immediately. A huge fire was raging all around us and there was only *one* escape route left. These sorts of fire were especially dangerous because they were accompanied by a hurricane-like storm and often led to a fatal lack of oxygen. We seized our children and tore to the escape route we had been shown through the sea of flames. I can no longer remember where we spent that night.

Gradually our house—badly damaged, it is true, but still inhabitable— was just about the only house in the neighborhood still standing. After all the surrounding buildings had been reduced to rubble in a single night, and we could see the ruins of the cathedral through the smoke on the following morning, I took Wolfram by the arm and showed him the scene of devastation that lay all about us. "All broken," he said offhandly before turning again to his toys. It seemed to mean no more to him than when his little hands knocked over a tower he had constructed with his building blocks. He would build a new one. This analogy had something immensely comforting about it. The children helped the grownups to see the superior power confronting them in perspective. That too may be part of the praise that God receives out of the mouths of babes (Matthew 21:16).

No matter how much I mobilize my imagination, my memory of those terrifying air raids remains fragmentary, and I ask myself how these unfillable gaps have come about. I can still see everything before me exactly as it was: the streets strewn with rubble, the scorched ruins, bizarre fragments of what used to be bathrooms. I can also still hear the bang of the bombs' impact and the crackling of the huge blazing fires, the earthquake-like tremors of collapsing buildings, and above all the wailing of the sirens. But today it is only my reason and not my memory that is able to reconstruct what none of these optical and acoustic memories is any longer able to reproduce, namely the smells of fire, burnt wood, and water that filled our nostrils and pursued us wherever we went. These smells of burning, cold sweat, and decay from mass burials heightened our horror at what had just passed over us and simultaneously increased our fear of what would lay hands upon us again in the coming night. The nose is the organ for the irrationality of terror, for everything that cannot leave its mark on our needle-sharp *visual* memories. What a miserable skeleton so-called historical facts are! The enormous range of what one has experienced makes it impossible to bring the past into the present. If this is the case with one's own memories, how much more serious its effect must be when looking back on the history of the human race! What do we really know of the Egyptian plagues or the Platonic Idea, what do we know of just a single day when "all was quiet on the Western front"?

The wild drama of these nights and days, during which we also had to do our daily work, was interrupted once a week by a small oasis of relaxation. This took place when we visited our friends Mr. and Mrs. Knoll in their cultured house high above Stuttgart on the Feuerbacher Heath for a few hours. It is difficult to express in words the debt we owe to the loyalty and hospitality of these two people and the joyful breathing-space they gave us in that breathless age. As an industrialist, our friend Mr. Knoll had all sorts of resources at his disposal that were not available to normal mortals. Thus we were able to enjoy ground coffee and black tea with a group of friends there and pass the time talking about the pressing questions of the age or discussing my lectures. Because we were unaccustomed to these pleasant stimulants, they used to induce a state of euphoric zest in our minds and kindle scintillating battles of words. When one terrifying night a number of houses on this hill were also hit, Martha Knoll filled her large house with her homeless neighbors, improvising by hanging curtains throughout the rooms so as to provide the families with a provisional and modest remnant of their own living space. Then one day all that remained of this magnificent house was the ground floor, and that was full of rubble, ashes, and water used for extinguishing the flames. Just as I was rolling up my shirtsleeves, I was greeted by the master of the house, impeccably dressed and with a flower in his buttonhole. With a gesture of invitation and with complete composure he led me to a poky little corner near the kitchen. In this single undestroyed room stood a tiny coffee table laid with a dazzling white table cloth and fine china. From a narrow vase a rose greeted us as a sign of life. To see such a sight in the midst of the chaos of destruction filled me with a greater happiness than any other meal I have ever enjoyed, no matter how magnificent. It was culture's protest against the negative powers surrounding us; it was the self-assertion of a humanity that kept itself in form when all around it was coming apart at the seams and sinking into a frightening formlessness. I realized, perhaps for the first time, what a "gentleman" is: not just someone who knows how to handle lobster, oysters, and caviar in a refined manner, but someone who also upholds the insignia of his dignity externally; a person who still remains himself when the standards and rules surrounding him break down and are distorted in alienation.

We also had a few other places of refuge with other loyal friends. Later, they even took us in when our house had been destroyed.

What one could call "the general mood" of those years was extremely complex and certainly could not be reduced to a common denominator. Apart from the fear of the night to come, everyone was troubled by the apprehensive foreboding that a great catastrophe would accompany the downfall of Nazi rule. But what would come *afterwards*, the future's future, so to speak, was absolutely inconceivable. The vengeance which would descend upon us from the nations we had tortured exceeded our powers of imagination. Consequently, the impending end of Nazi rule aroused not so much the hope that freedom was drawing near as the horror of the unknown. At the same time, reassuring delusions were constantly being cultivated. Rumors that the Fuehrer still had fantastic wonder weapons at his disposal were whispered from ear to ear and vouched for by many people. These weapons, it was believed, would crush all our enemies in one fell swoop and make them beg for mercy. The most extravagant rumor of this kind I can remember assured us that the Fuehrer possessed a device capable of freezing the whole of England into a single block of ice. "We're gonna freeze'em," was on everybody's lips, this pregnant statement being accompanied by an expression to show that the speaker was indeed in possession of such esoteric and secret lore.

Religious people, too, gave themselves over to apocalyptic ideas of the most fantastic kind, particularly the Swabians, who have a predilection for the cryptic. They firmly believed that true believers would be miraculously translated from the worst distresses of the Last Days—for this, it was believed, was indeed the age in which we found ourselves. Everybody was talking about the "translation." It was held, for instance, that we would one day be traveling in a streetcar and discover that the pious driver had suddenly vanished, or we would be sitting in church when the vicar would all of a sudden disappear in the middle of a sermon. Is it still possible to comprehend these apocalyptic hopes and fears today? They are just as unrecoverable as the smells of that age.

On the other hand, these wild eschatological expectations had to go hand in hand with the very down-to-earth process of making provision for the coming night and providing food and drink on the following day. This not infrequently led to a grotesque schizophrenia. Thus I recall a vicar's wife who sought to impress on everyone she met her conviction that we would witness the Second Coming of the Lord *before* the end of the war. Despite all her fanaticism, however, I knew that she was at the same time a down-to-earth housewife and mother concerned with the daily provision of her family. Now, when the general demand was issued before the Wehrmacht's first winter in Russia that all available skis should be placed at the disposal of the armed forces, I could not resist asking her the somewhat smug question, "Have you done your duty and donated your skis to the Fuehrer?" (She and her family were keen skiers.) "No, I haven't," she promptly replied, "Who knows if we'll ever get any again after the war!"

Reinhold Schneider's sonnets were very popular among thoughtful people in those days. Leaflets of his poetry were constantly being copied out and circulated, above all those with the following magnificent verses:

Only those who pray can succeed
In preserving us from the sword
And wrest this world from the powers of judgment
Through lives that are sanctified.

For wrongdoers shall ne'er force heaven's gate:
What they unite shall again be rent,

What they renew shall be swiftly spent,
And all they do brings disaster in its wake.

Goethe's poem "Epimenides," originally aimed at Napoleon, was also passed from hand to hand and had a comforting effect that is difficult to imagine today:

That which boldly ascends from hell,
At iron fate's behest
Half the world or more may quell,
But return to hell it must.

I gained my most profound comfort from the spiritual core of my job. In my memory there are a few fixed points—scenes of symbolic constancy, so to speak—in which the good and evil of those days are concentrated to a heightened degree. I shall now describe some of these.

Not far from us there was an underground antiaircraft battery manned by an officer and forty-seven female auxiliaries. During the bombing it suffered a direct hit. Not a single corpse could be found in the huge crater, just scattered pieces of human limbs. Severely shaken, I stood before this enormous hole of total annihilation. A woman with a string bag then approached me and asked whether I was such and such a person. Because of my scruffy old clothes and blackened face she was not quite sure. When I answered her question in the affirmative, she said, struggling to maintain her composure, "My husband was the officer in charge of this antiaircraft battery. They couldn't find a single trace of him, nor could they find anything left of the girls. All they gave me was this cap of his [she pointed to her bag]. While he was still alive, we both attended your lecture last Thursday. I would now like to thank you before this hole for preparing him for his death." It was now my turn to struggle to maintain my composure. One could be granted such moments of consolation in the midst of the most severe of tests, in the midst of being overcome by a paralyzing sense of futility. Such consolations were not the result of frantically striving to think up theories that would bring about an artificial harmony. They were unexpected gifts. Nevertheless, some time was required to open these gifts and to appreciate the treasures they contained.

A young student who had once been a member of my university congregation had some time earlier been drafted into the armed forces. He had now been granted a brief home leave because his parents had been bombed out of their homes. During his visit, however, he had himself been killed in a bombing raid. This upset me greatly, for he had been a cheerful boy whose infectious laughter I believe I can still hear today. When his father asked me to give him the last rites and to hold a funeral address for him, I immediately accepted. I then traveled with the father to the cemetery in a van that usually had the sad task of removing the bodies of those killed in the bombing. It was an adventurous journey. Time and again we had to drive over mountains of boulders and make detours around larger obstacles. At the cemetery, mass burials had already been going on for hours. Everywhere there were coffins, certainly several hundred of them. These used to be retrieved after the funeral because when "business was booming" it was totally impossible to give all the dead a coffin of their own. This was not the only respect in which the large number of victims made a macabre "rationalization" necessary. When there were a large number of dead to be buried, a common ceremony was held at several mass graves by clergymen of various denominations. Strangely enough, a catholic priest and I were allocated two individual graves, one for my student and one for a member of the Catholic community, whose relatives had gathered for the walk to the grave. An extremely awkward situation then arose. There was considerable confusion in the cemetery because fresh air raids had to be reckoned with at any moment. This created the problem of what to do with all the people—that is, with the people who were still *alive*—in the event of such an attack. Due to this confusion and the huge number of coffins, the second dead man could not be found quickly enough. Eventually, we were requested in no uncertain terms "not to hold up the work" and to make our way to the grave, which was quite some distance away. The coffin, we were told, would be brought along afterwards in time for the ceremony. So off we all went, my Catholic colleague and I, the two families of the dead men, and a small military deputation behind the coffin of my student. Eventually, we all stood before the two open graves. My colleague asked me to take my funeral service first, certain that the coffin would come before it was his turn. So I began the service. While I was still speaking, I noticed that there was some agitation among the members of this sorely afflicted Catholic family. After my last amen, a messenger from the cemetery authorities hurried over and disclosed to us that there was in fact no second coffin. It had just that moment been ascertained, we were told, that the body of the other dead man had been completely blown to pieces and that a burial was therefore out of the question. I felt bitterly sorry for my colleague, who now had to tell this to the dead man's wife, parents, and children. Profoundly shaken himself, he then broke the news to the family in kind and comforting words. He blessed the earth that should have covered the dead man's body and which would now serve as a little burial chamber for someone else, saying, "Even if we are unable to find our dead, there is Someone who knows about them all and who never loses them. The dead will recognize him by his voice, the voice of the Good Shepherd."

Much of what we experienced was too immense for us to cope with in one go. Shock and consolation continued to whirl about within me for a long time after that day in the cemetery, until that comforting saying about the One who knows his dead despite the atomization of their bodies gained the upper hand. Nothing was a routine Christian statement or cliché any more. Everything gained in specific weight, in substance. The events we experienced were, so to speak, tailored for long-term effect and only bore fruit after a long process of maturation. But whatever grew in such a way was never forgotten, not even in a long life.

One Sunday morning I had to hold a church service in Plochingen. After the introductory words "In the name of the Father, the Son, and the Holy Spirit," the sirens began to wail, forcing me to dismiss the congregation immediately with the concluding blessing. A medical officer then approached me, introduced himself as the head of an SS military hospital, and asked me to hold the canceled sermon in front of his patients. When the air raid alarm was sounded, he said, the men had been taken to a large cellar, which was where I would now be able to talk to them. I was astonished and asked him whether he could afford to allow such a "clerical invasion" of an SS hospital of all places, and whether he would not get into serious trouble. He responded by saying curtly, "That's my problem!" and invited me to get into his car. During the short journey I quickly worked out a sermon for this special situation.

The cellar we then entered was laid out in the form of a cross, and the head doctor asked me to speak from the point where the corridors crossed since this was strategically the best place. All around me there were camp beds built on top of each other in sets of three. After a brief announcement of my visit had been made, many inquisitive eyes peered down at me from these beds, intrigued by the unusualness of the situation. On the top bunk above me on my left, an SS man was sitting and eating cherries, spitting the stones into a large tin can with a loud plunk. He continued to do this with pointed nonchalance, probably wishing to make clear his indifference to such religious waffle. In a moment of inspiration, I now concentrated all my attention on him, telling an anecdote I thought might interest him, and speaking animatedly to him as if he were my only listener. The plunk of cherry stones into his can grew slower, and every now and again he looked expectantly at me for a few moments. He then put the can completely to one side, rested his head in his hands, and gave me his full attention. That was a wonderful moment in my career as a preacher.

In a conversation with the head doctor afterwards, who I had sensed thought very much as I did, I told him of a dangerous situation I had got into after the attempt to assassinate Hitler on July 20, 1944. He invited me to come to his hospital if the danger became acute. There he would put me completely in plaster and make me unfit to be arrested. This thought was a source of strength to me in the following months.

At the end of a season of lectures in the cathedral, in early December 1943, I organized a large communion service for my audience. I felt that after all the talking, this large audience should for once have the experience of being a *congregation* and celebrate a real church service together. Altars were set up at various places in the church, where the sacrament was administered by eight priests. This time I was able to speak quite directly from the pulpit and address the distraught flock as a pastor. In the sacristy we then donned the majestic albs over our black cassocks and went solemnly to the altars to administer the sacrament. At this unconventional communion service, the members of congregation were called away from their pain and sorrow by the wonderful sense of community. It was as if a radiant joy had spread over them, as if the transient world around them had sunk into oblivion and the foundation of all things had led them into certitude and trust. When we then got together with many of our friends in our apartment after the service, all this continued to linger on in us for a long time afterwards. Spiritual joy—what else can I call it?—and human cheerfulness overflowed in a small oasis in time.

My lectures in the cathedral and the conversations afterwards also allowed me to discover that a good many supporters of the Nazis, above all the younger ones, had some quite different personality traits from those one would expect. A few journal entries written immediately after the events they describe and taken arbitrarily from my diary bear witness to this.

A few weeks ago Bäuerle (head of cultural affairs at Bosch and later minister of education and the arts) read me the letter of a member of the *Leibstandarte*,* which described the appalling mass shootings. In his letter this man spoke of his approval of these murders in the hope that everything would be different after the war. He was now in a military hospital here, had attended the lectures

---

* Originally Hitler's bodyguards before becoming a division within the SS. *Translator's note.*

in the cathedral, and now sends all his guys from the Hitler Youth (he was a Hitler Youth leader) en masse to my evening meetings. He went up to Bäuerle and told him that the scales had fallen from his eyes and that he had seen the light.

A young engineer from Daimler, a former Catholic who had left the church, visited me this morning. He says he now realizes that there is "something in" Christianity after all and would like to return to the church again. But which one? He also wants to have his children—five and two-and-a-half years old— christened, but when, how, and where? Long conversation. Happy to experience this homecoming.

SS captain Lothar F and his friend SS man Roland Ö—both formerly well-known top class sportsmen—visited me. They have been charged before a Nazi Party court with 'infecting Nazi Party youth with Christianity' because they sent a number of their young people to the evenings at the cathedral. They await their trial with composure and regret nothing; on the contrary, they have the feeling that a gate has been opened and that they have now found the right path. They were now also determined to be true to their principles and draw the attention of the people who had been entrusted to them to this path. They felt they were under an obligation to their comrades.

Pressel, the head of the church council, told me that a young Hitler Youth leader had been stopped by the police after last Thursday evening's lecture and asked where he had been. After he had answered "At the cathedral," the police took down his particulars. On the following morning he was informed "It is unworthy of a leader of the Hitler Youth to go to see Thielicke. You are herewith forbidden to attend any further lectures." Thereupon the boy tore off his epaulettes and cords and left the room with the words, "I can live without being a leader of the Hitler Youth and I'm still going to go to Thielicke's lectures." I would like to make this boy's acquaintance.

Yesterday evening I had a conversation in my study with a party member who insisted on remaining "loyal to the Fuehrer" but who had come to have doubts. He had been moved by Christianity and did not know how he could reconcile this with his National-Socialist convictions. I reacted cautiously because precisely this kind of question was also typical of an agent provocateur. Eventually I gained the impression that he was genuinely troubled. Sometimes I sat like a cat on hot bricks because five of my "most vulnerable listeners" were secretly present in the next room but one. These were Dutch forced laborers who had introduced themselves to me after one of the last lectures and whom I allow to meet in my rooms once a week.

Happily, I was also constantly finding other ways of gaining access to young people. I have already mentioned that I used to teach religious studies in a grammar school. One day, however, this came to an end because the boys were called up to be antiaircraft auxiliaries and had to man some cannons in the Zuffenhausen hills. Despite this they were determined to continue with the lessons and asked me to visit them once a week. This, however, was most strictly forbidden by their superiors. The Luftwaffe, under whose jurisdiction they now came, did not recognize any need for the pastoral care of the armed forces and consequently any need for lessons in religion. The boys did not give in, however, and lobbied—always in vain—one authority after the other, gradually working their way up the hierarchy. Eventually they managed to get an audience with a real live general, who took pleasure in their energy and honesty. "It's true that it's forbidden, lads," he said, "but if you really want it, I'll take responsibility for it." They sent a messenger to me with the good tidings, and from then on I cycled one afternoon a week to see them. Because they had to be constantly on stand-by near their cannons, I was never able to see them as a single group, but had to go at alternate hours to each unit in turn and talk to them while they were sitting down on the fortified rampart surrounding their cannon. In all my work with young people I have hardly ever encountered such attentiveness and participation as I experienced then. A corporal, who obviously imagined religious studies to be a very depressing subject, once asked me in some astonishment what there was in religion to cause our constant laughter.

One day, one of the boys telephoned me in great agitation. Would I come straightaway, he asked, something terrible had happened. He then immediately replaced the receiver. Full of dark forebodings I set off and found my young men utterly distraught. During the visit of one of the boys' fathers, a low-flying American aircraft had strafed their antiaircraft position, hitting and killing the father. The boy had to take his father's body to the cemetery himself in a handcart. The boys were, after all, only about sixteen years old and still half children. They crowded around me, some crying, others stunned. I put my arms around those who stood closest to me. A long time passed before I could bring myself to say a word.

A good twenty years later I gave a lecture in California—I can no longer remember in which town—and afterwards the host professor invited me to a bar to relax. When I asked him where he had learned such good German, he told me that he had spent a long time at Stuttgart with the occupying army. I found that very interesting, I interjected; I had also spent a few years there during the bombing war.

"I deliberately volunteered to go there," he said, continuing his story, "I was a member of a low-altitude fighter squadron for the last two years of the war, you see." Among the targets he had been assigned to attack he also mentioned the antiaircraft battery at Zuffenhausen. "Do you know it?" he asked. "You bet!" I replied and told him what his work had looked like down on the ground. . . . He looked at me with horror. "Perhaps that was my bomb. . . ." I did not contradict him. And this was a man who radiated goodness and who had told me previously how devotedly he looked after the young people in his congregation. During this conversation I became painfully aware of the wickedness of long-range weapons, which Konrad Lorenz describes in his book *On Aggression*: because we cannot see the victims of our aggression, our natural inhibitions against committing violence are not mobilized. In this way, a man who would otherwise devote himself to serving human life with all the fibers of his heart, can commit cold-blooded murder.

Relaxation was no longer possible that evening. He paid the bill and we went silently to my hotel.

Resistance Groups

Through Bishop Wurm I was kept informed of the military and civilian resistance groups working for Hitler's forced removal. The church in Freiburg had set up a sort of parallel organization for this purpose. A circle of well-known Freiburg professors of various faculties were to work out within the framework of Christian ethics a draft document on the comprehensive reorganization of political, economic, and cultural life after the war. Wurm was now approached with the request to send me as his delegate to this circle. The reason for this request may not only have been my subject area but also the fact that I had known some of the leading figures of this circle for quite some time, such as the economists Constantin von Dietze, Walter Eucken, Adolf Lampe, as well as the historian Gerhard Ritter and the jurist Erik Wolf. Other members of this circle were the well-known industrialist Walter Bauer and the theologian and later Bishop of Berlin Otto Dibelius. Carl Goerdeler, who it was intended should become the first German Chancellor of a post-Hitler government, regularly took part in the meetings of the Freiburg group. He was executed after the attempt on Hitler's life on July 20,

1944. Dietrich Bonhoeffer was the circle's intermediary to the church committees and to friends abroad, especially to the Bishop of Chichester. Theophil Wurm had certain misgivings about entrusting me with this task because I was still strictly forbidden by the Gestapo from traveling outside Württemberg. Despite this, however, I was able to persuade him to send me to Freiburg.

For me the most important meeting of the Freiburg circle was the gathering that took place at von Dietze's house on November 17, 1942, lasting several days. It was an intensive interfaculty discussion on the preparation of our document and was, above all, a theological controversy. I, for my part, found Ritter's draft all too idealist (in the philosophical sense of the word) and attempted to push through another theological approach that was at least in parts closer to Reformation thought. In an otherwise frantic age it was a pleasure to experience how everybody present listened to each other and took criticism seriously. I later published the document that materialized from these meetings under the title of *In der Stunde Null* (The Zero Hour) (J.C.B. Mohr Publishers, Tübingen 1979).

Of all the people present, Carl Goerdeler made the strongest impression on me. He enjoyed an unofficial authority in our circle as a matter of course. Not only did he possess remarkable skills of expression, which often enabled him to find a formulation that solved many of the tangles we got ourselves into, but he had above all a clear understanding of the facts and immensely more information at his fingertips than we did. At that time he was formally employed by the firm Bosch in Stuttgart. This gave him the necessary pretext for making countless journeys around the country and abroad—despite the war!—and during these to call on important personalities in the military and civilian spheres. He made these journeys with astonishing uninhibitedness, scorning the suggestion that he should adopt a disguise. When we urged him to be more careful, he refused with a smile, saying that it was precisely this free and easy openness that was his protection. He avoided everything that the Gestapo associated with the lifestyle of the conspirator.

Goerdeler had an infectious personality. If one overlooks the banal overtone that usually accompanies the term, one could describe him as an optimist. Even in the darkest analyses of the situation, he never got bogged down in diagnosis but always kept the future in mind and the necessity of molding and protecting it from the worst. He was a person who was constantly making plans, engaging in dialogue and seeking and finding contacts of the most varied kind. The thought that he was to become German Chancellor after that unknown time in the future when the war was over was a source of strength to us. Surrounded by nothing but academics who had been forced to venture into politics but who—as is always the case—discovered their limitations there, he had an invigorating, truly political mind that did not get bogged down in theoretical concepts as we were in constant danger of doing. He was an expert in the art of the possible and for all his receptiveness to abstract principles nevertheless possessed the necessary quantum of pragmatism.

That he may have been overly conservative or even reactionary was not something I ever noticed. In an age that was usually very sensitive to such things I doubt very much that this would have escaped my notice if it had indeed been the case. Perhaps he was "conservative" in the good sense, if we avoid understanding this term in the trivialized sense in which many people use it today. For many of our contemporaries it merely seems to evoke the image of a can full of stale, vitamin-deficient vegetables. He was conservative in the sense that he was scornful of that naiveté, or rather infantilism, that believed it was possible to begin without presuppositions *ab ovo* or which made change a goal in itself. Goerdeler's historical and cultural sophistication was far too profound to allow him to overlook the value of tradition and of what our forefathers had created and inherited. At the same time he was far from having an uncritical attitude to the past. The suggestion that he had had the reactionary intention of merely allowing the past to continue to roll mechanically into the future on the conveyor-belt of tradition is nothing short of grotesque. On the other hand, however, whatever had come through the fire of criticism and self-criticism was for him the basis upon which his vision of a different future for foreign policy, social policy, and cultural affairs was founded.

How critical he could be of some traditions became clear when he came to speak of some of the generals he had sought in vain to win over to his plans. His comments made me realize for the first time the conflicts and almost insoluble entanglements the military must inevitably get caught up in when they are trained to be unpolitical and then have the only ground upon which this unpoliticalness was meaningful cut away from under them. This ground, of course, was an authority figure to whose moral status one could reassuringly (at least fairly reassuringly) delegate one's personal responsibility. There was no provision in the military's mode of thought for the possibility of criminals being at the head of the state.

As a result of this, there had also been little or no reflection on the problem of the *oath of allegiance*. Previously, the oath had, of course, been unproblematic because it had not been sworn—as was now the case—on a person but on a symbolic figure such as the king or the constitution. That the oath of allegiance always involves a reciprocal bond between both the recipient and the giver of the oath and that the oath lapses when, for instance, the recipient of the oath breaks out of this bond was, of course, one of the reasons for the plan to kill Hitler, since only in this way could the bond imposed by the oath be canceled (at least in the contemporary understanding of this bond). But these considerations also failed to impress the generals, for traditional officer training certainly did not countenance the idea of rebelling against the commander-in-chief with the intention of committing "tyrannicide."

Goerdeler was confronted with this time and again when he spoke to high-ranking officers about their responsibility and tried to prick their consciences. His desperate and futile endeavors could cause him to lose his temper and led him to the conviction that the appeal to one's unthinking duty to obey was an escape into mere formalism, indeed was cowardice. Goerdeler knew that it would not be possible to overthrow Hitler without the assistance of the military. Consequently, his failure to persuade the generals was the point at which he was momentarily overcome by feelings of hopelessness. Our circle seemed to do him good. Here at least he did not have to struggle with such problems. It was only much later and after more mature reflection that I came to see that the generals' conflict in fact went very much deeper than I was able to understand at the time, so that I had to be on my guard against self-righteousness.

My last encounter with Goerdeler took place a few weeks before July 20, 1944, when he visited me in my apartment in Stuttgart. He hinted that an important decision was shortly to be made and asked me to write a passage on the state's attitude towards Christianity and the churches for the inaugural speech he intended to make on forming a new government. I sent him my rather turgid text through the post and he dropped me a few lines expressing his gratitude. That was the last I heard of him. Gerhard Ritter later told me that he had met Goerdeler after both of them had been taken into custody by the Gestapo. Goerdeler seemed, he said, to have lost his identity. Ritter then told me some details of the meeting, which moved me greatly. What tortures and terrors must this strong and cheerful man have undergone to have been reduced to such a shadow of his former self?

As the youngest (and sole surviving) member of our circle, it depressed me—clearly very much more than the older gentlemen—that our policy outlines were mere empty fantasies. We had, after all, no idea what the end of the Hitler era would look like. I could not get the uncomfortable thought out of my mind that the great authorities sitting around our conference table were reproducing the past they had lived through in a purified form, merely adding to it the nuance that it formed an antithesis to the Third Reich. Thus it is only with mixed feelings that one can read the document today. Its inviolable dignity, however, consists in the fact that it was an intellectual testimony to the "other Germany."

We knew what would happen if the Gestapo ever got wind of our conferences. Part of the document actually fell into the Gestapo's hands after the assassination attempt on July 20, 1944, without us ever finding out how. As a result of this, most of us were arrested. Because they were involved in other aspects of the conspiracy, Bonhoeffer, Goerdeler, and Perels were executed, after having spent several months in a concentration camp and having sometimes suffered cruel maltreatment. Walter Bauer, von Dietze, Lampe, and Ritter were later saved from certain death by the Allied entry into Berlin.

Gerhard Ritter described it as puzzling why the remaining collaborators and conference members had not been arrested. Walter Bauer later told me the solution to this puzzle as far as my own person is concerned. In a Berlin prison at the beginning of 1945, the Gestapo had confronted him with a list of the people present at the main meeting of November 17, 1942, one name of which was illegible. It was mine. Walter Bauer pretended not to know who it was. The Gestapo reacted by whipping his naked body, while secretaries stood around watching the scene drinking coffee and smoking cigarettes. But he remained steadfast and spent a night in dreadful pain. When the procedure was repeated the following day and he was beaten on the wounds that had opened up in his skin, the pain became so unbearable that he was forced to divulge my name. He was quite appalled at his weakness and was happy that I understood and approved of what he felt he had to confess to me. That the Gestapo took no action against me was probably due to the fact that I had moved to the rather remote village of Korntal after our home in Stuttgart had been destroyed and, moreover, that the communications network was already very badly damaged. I was often interrogated by the Gestapo, but the Freiburg document was never mentioned.

It was always a nerve-racking experience whenever I took the train to or from Freiburg, because I had to avoid having my papers checked. Once, when I was travelling back from a meeting, I sat down in a compartment occupied by three SS officers, because I assumed that their papers would only be cursorily examined, if at all. I kept a firm grip on a small briefcase containing my Freiburg notes as well as my identity papers and ration cards.

Unfortunately, shortly before we arrived in Stuttgart, I fell fast asleep and only awoke when the train was about the leave the station again. Startled, I managed to leap out at the last moment, forgetting to take my little briefcase with me. I do not wish to describe the frustration and trouble it took to get replacements for the lost papers from the authorities. Very much worse was the fear of my illegal journey being discovered and, even more tormenting, the question of what would happen if my notes were found. The following weeks were darkened by a debilitating fear. It was after all not just only my own fate that was at stake but also that of my Freiburg companions. Whenever a car stopped anywhere near our house, Liesel and I were almost paralyzed with fear. Were they coming to get us now? But nothing happened. The briefcase had obviously fallen into the hands of a common thief who had only been interested in the ration cards. It took a long time for the fear gradually to abate and for us to be able to think of the putative thief with hearts full of gratitude.

Stuttgart's End

The day on which the severely wounded city of Stuttgart was completely destroyed was July 26, 1944. We heard about it on the radio on the last day of our holiday at Lake Constance. We had stopped off at the Kroners in Ravensburg before setting off for home and now had to reckon with our house and all our remaining possessions having been destroyed. We had left the children in a reliable home at Ravensburg we knew well, so that we could get some peace for once. What was going to happen to them now? We were paralyzed by a deep depression. For the moment we had to promise not to go and see them so as not to cause them any homesickness. We could not bring ourselves, however, to forgo one last look at the catastrophe that was Stuttgart, where, of course, we could not take the children. So we crept into the garden of the children's home and, standing behind a tree, watched little Wolfram playing with the other children, on one occasion seeing him cry when someone tried to take away his little horse. We also saw Berthold thrashing about in his cot. With an inexpressible sorrow, we slipped away and set off for Stuttgart.

Our train journey to Stuttgart was interrupted time and again because of damage to the track. We then had to change over to omnibuses and—again, after long delays—back to the train. Eventually we arrived at Cannstatt.

There the journey came to an absolute end because the rest of the track was completely destroyed. I asked the stationmaster if it might still perhaps be possible to reach the center by foot. The man merely raised his hand slightly and said, "Hardly—that is Stuttgart!" All we could see were gigantic clouds of smoke darkening the sun and making it appear like a reddish ball. Stuttgart was still burning.

We set out towards this inferno. The further we advanced, the more the smoke brought tears to our eyes. We pressed handkerchiefs to our mouths in order to breathe. Hardly a single person was going in our direction and we had to fight our way arduously through swarms of desperate refugees streaming towards us. I can still see an elderly couple leaning against a wall in exhaustion, their daughter desperately clasping her hands towards heaven in a gesture of prayer. We ought to have stopped and made some comforting remark to them, but we just did not know what to say. The dreadful suspense drove us forwards.

At last we came to the final corner—or rather, its last remnants! Behind it we ought to have been able to see our house. All that was left was a few fragments of wall. Smoke billowed from fires amongst the ruins. Part of the furniture that had been saved was standing in the street. We were moved by the fact that the other occupants of the house had taken care of our possessions as well and that some of my students had also come to help. They described to us the drama of Stuttgart's final hours. What a comfort it was that we still had each other! Princess Urach, whose house on the hill had not been destroyed, took my family in, making it possible for us soon to fetch our children and take them there. During the day we worked in the ruins, above all in the cellar, looking for anything that could be salvaged. Most things, however, had been looted. Even my cassock was nowhere to be found. In the evenings, Liesel was often so exhausted that I had to pull her up the hill to the princess's house in a little handcart.

One of the following days was a Sunday. There were no longer any bells which could ring out and no church in which a congregation could gather. Only the little church on Doggenburg hill was, despite letting the wind in, still usable to some extent. There a frightened congregation still numbering some thirty people met. On that Sunday I heard the most powerful sermon I have ever experienced. It was given by Prelate Issler, a prince among Christian preachers. Some of the sentences still resound in my ears as if I had only just heard them: "When did we suffer more? Now, when we look at our burned city through the empty windows of this church and think of the terrors from which we have just escaped and which have robbed most of us of all our possessions? Or did we not suffer still more in past years when we rushed with instinctive assurance from victory to victory; when there was no God to command our arrogance and our sinful torture of our fellow men to stop; and when we dared with impunity to refer to the so-called 'blessing of providence' which permitted everything, but everything, to succeed? Were we not in danger of losing our belief that God rules over the world if he had allowed this *via triumphalis* to continue unchecked? But now the Lord has spoken in the storm, he has spoken through fire and blood. And terrible though our city's catastrophe is, God has at least broken his terrible silence, he has spoken in thunder and lightning. Although this lightning may also have struck much of what we hold dear, he has at least made himself known, he has spoken in storms."

This cut us to the quick. Nobody had ever spoken of us or to us in this way before. It was a speech of the final hour, the hour when the infernal beast was about to return to its abyss after its flight to the upper world.

Our Time in Korntal as Refugees from the Bombing

1944–1945

WE HAD NOW LOST OUR HOME in Stuttgart and I had to search for a new place for my family to live. It was, of course, impossible to find anything in the devastation that was Stuttgart. My work, however, required me to remain near the town. But where? The huge number of refugees fleeing the bombing had long since flooded all available accommodation. When I was just about to give up all hope, one of the leading figures in the Korntal Brethren, Wilhelm Simpfendörfer, who at that time was a teacher but was later to become Stuttgart's minister for education and the arts, told me that he would do everything in his power to find us somewhere to stay in Korntal. I had come into contact with him through his sons, whom I knew well from my work with young people and students and with whom I even had a close relationship. When I then visited the Simpfendörfer family, we became friends at first sight, a friendship which deepened in the period following. This friend's house was like a place of refuge and a new home for me and my family.

Admittedly, Simpfendörfer's first attempt at finding us accommodation ended in bitter disappointment. All his efforts were in danger of foundering on the resistance of Korntal's Nazi mayor. The mayor did not want to get himself into hot water by taking in an "enemy of the state," and thus refused me permission to settle in Korntal. Simpfendörfer was furious at this refusal and took it very seriously. Nevertheless, he refused to give up the struggle and endeavored to find new allies to help him break the mayor's stubbornness. Before I began my cycle ride back to Stuttgart, I went for a last stroll through the village, which was now blacked out for the evening. My anger at the rebuff I had received culminated in an extremely unfair collective condemnation of all members of the establishment and was directed against the whole village. Narrow streaks of light filtered through the edges of the blackout blinds in the quiet, peaceful houses. Behind the blinds families would be sitting and enjoying their evening meal. But this did not arouse any idyllic feelings on my part. No, as a refugee I envied them their possessions and their contentment. Although there were many things much worse than this temporary vagabond existence, I still experienced an element of sympathy for the proletariat's resentment of the propertied classes. When shortly afterwards my friends in Korntal did indeed manage to wrest a reluctant approval from the mayor, I felt ashamed of myself for having had these feelings. I would not, however, have liked to have forgone this experience.

Aided by Russian prisoners-of-war, we loaded the remainder of our possessions onto a van. When we were near the main railway station, the drawer containing our china, of all things, toppled from the van. I leaped down and began to brush the pieces to the side of the road with my feet so as to avoid damaging the tires of other vehicles. At that moment, a bomb exploded a few hundred meters further up the road we were traveling, leaving a large crater. If it had not been for our mishap with the china, we would probably have been at exactly that spot when the bomb exploded.

Until we found permanent accommodation in Korntal, we had to live at the home of a teacher's wife. Apart from pious thoughts, this woman's heart was full of an extreme pride in owning her own house. She and her husband had made many sacrifices to save enough money from his modest wage to buy this house. When we moved in with our two boys, who were ill with a feverish influenza and severe earache, she showered us with religious quotations. All that now mattered, she said, was "to clothe the naked and to give shelter to the homeless."

But it quickly emerged that all we were hearing were pious noises and we were very soon to get to know this lady from another perspective. She demanded board that came to more than my monthly wage, and moaned loudly when our sick children once wet the bed because her precious sheets would inevitably suffer even in the most careful wash (my proletarian instincts rebelled again: after all, we no longer had any bed linen whatsoever!). This pious woman made clear to us how dependent we were on her by harassing us in many other ways. When we later heard that during the occupation Moroccan soldiers had lolled about with their muddy boots on in the beds our former "hostess" had been so anxious to protect, we were unable to resist briefly enjoying a truly unchristian gloat at her expense.

A *providentia specialissima*, for which we were profoundly grateful, then led to our being taken in by Mrs. Cläre Scheytt. In this energetic and charming woman we met with the true piety of the Brethren, a piety that was averse to all sham religiousness. We became good friends and together endured the difficult final stages of the war and the new terrors of the first period of occupation.

Our New Life in "Exile"

We gained many friends through church services with the Brethren, where I was constantly being invited to preach, and soon came to feel at home and safe in our place of "exile." During this period, we developed a particularly close relationship with the Simpfendörfers and a few other intellectually and spiritually open-minded families. Because I was not allowed to publish anything, a number of manuscripts had accumulated in my desk drawers, which on many evenings I read aloud to a circle of friends. Conversations on vital topics that went beyond the depressing events of the day helped us to avoid becoming absorbed in brooding about the present and the ominous future. When we were later all able to work in freedom again, we sometimes looked back nostalgically to these hours, in which we grew into a close community and in which eternity and time fulfilled our life together.

This circle was enlarged still further by my calling together at regular intervals a group of "frustrated authors" who were in a similar position to me. Bishop Wurm, the historian Gerhard Ritter from Freiburg, the India expert and publicist Friso Melzer, Friedrich Delekat, the biographer of Pestalozzi, my theological colleague and friend Edmund Schlink all gathered there, as did other theological exiles who had been taken in by the Church of Württemberg, namely Hans Asmussen and Günter Dehn. Strange as it may sound, it was the free time forced upon us by the trials and tribulations of the war that made these meetings possible. In all the later years of my life, when we were again completely engrossed in our professions, I never again had such a happy experience of this form of community.

Despite everything, my most loyal assistant was my Dutch secretary Diny Lipp. To reach me in Korntal she had to cover distances by train and foot that are truly inconceivable today. She always remained cheerful and never let any of the strain show—including the fears she had to endure.

The people of Korntal were very fond of us and were constantly slipping us food for the children. Time and again we discovered that even the worst times have a good side to them. Such times of crisis are accompanied by joys and experiences that are unknown in normal life. A good example of this is the lady who owned a small private swimming bath and to whom we were indebted for the enormous enjoyment of hot baths. One day, she called out of the window to me, "The Savior told me in a dream last night that each week I have to give you three fresh eggs from what my hens produce." I was unprincipled enough not to go into any theological explanations of the validity of such dreams, preferring just to shake my head thoughtfully and gladly take delivery of the eggs. Similarly, when approximately two months later she assured me from the same window that the Savior had now told her that she had given me enough eggs, I at least showed enough character to accept the dream's command without protest.

Working from Korntal I now attempted to resume my duties in Württemberg. Because of constant interruptions in the rail link and the threat of air raids during the journey, this was becoming more and more arduous. Often the train had to stop because of attacks by "low-level fighter aircraft." People were particularly afraid of these, and during such attacks we passengers had to seek cover on the railway embankment to escape the bursts of machine gun fire. But the warm welcome I received everywhere, the joy of a sense of community, and the support and strength I gained from concentrating on factual matters compensated for many troubles and dangers.

Lecture Tours Under the Burden of Air Raids

People were constantly asking me about my lectures in the cathedral and I was determined to continue with them. Because Stuttgart Cathedral had been totally destroyed, I had to be on the lookout for an alternative and (so far, at least!) undamaged venue. In Stuttgart, only the hall of the Southern German Fellowship and in neighboring Bad Cannstatt the town church still came into consideration. The Church Council circulated a small leaflet inviting people to the lectures, news of which was then passed on by word of mouth, a form of communication that was highly developed in those days. The invitation ran as follows:

DR. HELMUT THIELICKE
is continuing the lectures previously held in the Cathedral. For the time being they will be held in pairs at the following venues:

Stuttgart   Every Wednesday at 7.30 in the main hall of the Southern German Fellowship, 4 Eugen Street. Lectures begin on September 13th.

Bad Cannstatt   Every Thursday at 8.30 in the town church. Lectures begin on
                 September 14th.

Subjects include: the puzzle of God's government of the world; on the meaning
of history; freedom of will or predestination; the meaning of suffering.

After a strenuous bicycle ride through the devastated landscape—time
and again I had to dismount and climb over mountains of rubble—I arrived
at the Southern German Fellowship on the Wednesday as advertized. There I
discovered that the hall had been completely destroyed. A few members of
the audience who had arrived early looked over this awful place with me.
After an emotional farewell, we sadly made our way home again. A few weeks
later, our venue in the church at Bad Cannstatt was also completely destroyed. This time, however, provision had been made for such an eventuality. The hordes of listeners were directed to Luther Hall, a large and still
undamaged hall where the people sat and stood packed unimaginably
closely together. I was clearly aware of the great sacrifices all these people
had made to get to the lectures. Most were without any means of transport and
had often had to walk for hours through the dust of devastated landscapes to
get to the hall. It is very difficult to grasp this intellectual hunger in our
comfortable and overfed age.

A short while later, the lectures in Cannstatt came to an abrupt and
terrible end. One evening we were taken unawares by a sudden, full-scale
alarm. I concluded the evening with a blessing and asked the audience to
make their way quietly to the air raid shelters. I had arranged with the
organist that he should play a few quiet evening chorals during such an
evacuation. Despite the narrow exits and the slowness of the exodus, this all
took place without any panic. Meanwhile, I stood at the lectern constantly
waving to members of the audience. Next to me stood the student Gerhard
Simpfendörfer, or "Truxa," as I called him, who never left my side. Truxa and
I only left the hall after the last person had departed. Scarcely were we
outside when we saw the flares that bombers discharged over an area they
intended to attack, burst over the city and illuminate everything as bright as
day. We both raced to a nearby concrete bunker, nicknamed the "sugarloaf,"
and, with the first bombs exploding around us, hammered with all our might
on the bolted gate. For a long time nobody seemed to hear us or perhaps no
longer dared to open the gate, until at last two men quickly pulled us inside.

A fairly large section of the audience had gathered there. The terrified
silence in our bunker was in stark contrast to the noise of the bombs

exploding all around us and causing our concrete castle to sway like a ship on a choppy sea. It was only after the attack that I learned that two of the people who had attended the lectures had been killed. One of them was the organist, who had continued to play right up to the last moment.

When the attack was over and we had left the bunker, the town was ablaze. I immediately set off on the long journey by foot to Korntal. On the way, I passed a piece of ground on which there stood a number of small temples created from side and roof ashlars. Was it not the Wilhelmina* with its Moorish arcades? I am no longer able to reconstruct the way I took home. A young girl was squatting in front of one of these little temples, which had collapsed into a pile of stones. Beckoning to me, she said, "A mother and her four children are buried beneath this rubble. The children are already dead. The mother is still alive but is trapped and suffering dreadful pain." I could hear her whimpering and screaming, and I doubted that she would last much longer. The girl shouted touching and comforting words to her while I tried in vain to lift the heavy ashlars away. I cried for help at the top of my voice but there was no other human being for miles around. While we squatted despairingly and helplessly on the stones, the dreadful moaning grew quieter and quieter and eventually ceased altogether. There was nothing more for us to do.

So I continued to wander through the night, which was eerily illuminated by the flames of the city. I crossed a meadow strewn with a herd of dead and dismembered cows, and passed by some huts for foreign forced laborers, who were trying hard to save their burning lodgings. Nobody laid a finger on me. In that night there existed a sort of a brotherhood of the terrified. Towards morning, I arrived home utterly exhausted. My arrival ended hours of worry for Liesel. She had seen the sky over Cannstatt ablaze with light, and had even been able to pick out the columns of smoke rising from the city. She knew that I was in the middle of it. Scarcely had we gone to bed when the sirens began to wail in Korntal and we had to take the children down into the cellar. Feeling very cold from exhaustion, it was then that I noticed that I was almost on the edge of a nervous breakdown. For the first and probably only time in my life, my teeth began to chatter.

From then on it was only possible to hold the remaining lectures in Ludwigshafen. My loyal audience even made their way there.

Despite the difficulties of the journey, we were constantly being visited by

---

* The Wilhelmina (now known as the "Wilhelma") was a zoological and botanical garden founded by Wilhelm I and adorned with miniature temples. *Translator's note*.

our friends and above all by former students of mine who were on holiday and
wished to have a heart to heart talk with me. These conversations were both
comforting and disturbing at the same time. They were dominated by the
monotonous and tortured question that had held us in its clutches for years,
namely, how were we to cope with having to wish a terrible end upon our
fatherland rather than see it suffer neverending terror? What was the point of
military service under the command of this despicable system? We were
fighting for a criminal who was destroying all that we held dear. Why should
we continue to go along with this? But what was the alternative? To abandon
the comrades one loved and who had in many cases lost their home towns,
houses, and even families? And *where* should one then escape to? It was part
of the demonic nature of this system that it had not even left any deserts
where one could have found refuge. Wherever we looked and whatever
questions we asked, the result was the same—we were surrounded by
precipices and a future so dark that no eye could pierce it. When they took
their leave of me, it was a last farewell, a departure to a fate which nobody
knew whether we would survive. There the blessing I gave them for their
journey into the unknown outgrew all the harmless formalities of friendship
and found its way back to its origin. It became an effectual word that
accompanied and supported them. I do not wish to say any more about these
farewells.

The End of the War

At last the war came to an end. Preceded by reports of their atrocities, the
Moroccans flooded into our villages. The screams of women being raped
could be heard. Two heavily armed guys even pushed their way into our
house and, gesticulating wildly, demanded that I hand over my wristwatch
and pocket watch. I had prepared a reaction to such an eventuality and had
learned an appropriate French sentence I shouted at them in a very sharp
tone, "Does Allah permit marauding? *Allez-hopp!*" and pointed to the door.
And they actually left quickly and with some embarrassment. One of our
neighbors, who had hidden her daughter from the Moroccans, also succeeded in driving them away, but in a much nobler way. When the guys
arrived, she played "Take then my hands . . ." on her harmonium. At this, the
dreaded warrior said with tears in his eyes, "Mama godly," took a few
nourishing things from a haversack and sat down to eat with her. So many

moving scenes of human kindness took place alongside all the cruelties and prevented one from making an adverse judgment of the Moroccans as a whole.

The worst reports came from the neighboring village of Ditzingen, so that I felt duty-bound to help if possible, especially since the parish had no vicar. By making use of my own official stamp and any other stamps I was able to get my hands on, I issued myself with an impressive permit. We were, after all, not allowed to leave the village! The permit's ultraofficial appearance certainly made the desired impression on the guards who inspected it, even if they did hold it upside down and were unable to understand a single word.

So I fought my way through to Ditzingen and found the worst confirmed. Many girls and young women had been raped in the presence of their parents and children. I visited the families that had been particularly badly affected and found them distraught, sometimes in a state of shock. They were terrified of the next night. I discussed with some of the leading figures in the village how we could protect the women and we decided that they should spend the next few nights in the church. The children were to remain with their mothers. A number of men were prepared to keep guard in front of the church portals. We could calculate on the Moroccans respecting the holy place, a calculation that was then indeed confirmed. So for the next few hours beds made from blankets and straw mattresses were shipped into the church. When I then held evening prayers from the pulpit in this strange enclosure, the women had already plucked up courage and for the next few hours felt secure and were even quite cheerful. The many children present also certainly contributed to the women's sigh of relief. Children, of course, always enjoy exceptional situations and it is extremely difficult to get them to quieten down on such occasions. I reminded my listeners of the stable at Bethlehem where there had also been a bed of "hay and straw." I was pleased to notice that a few faces had begun to smile again, and I sought to adopt a cheerful rather than a melancholy tone. When we then went on to sing together the evening hymn of the *Wandsbeker Bote**, "The moon has risen," everybody in that quiet chamber knew that they were protected, and that "you should sleep and forget the misery of the day."

---

* Newspaper published by Matthias Claudius from 1771 to 1775. Here Claudius published his hymn "The moon has risen." *Translator's note.*

An Adventurous Journey to Eisenhower's Headquarters

Only a few weeks after the capitulation, the church leadership together with the mayor of Stuttgart began to consider what could be done to establish contact with leading representatives of the military government—above all with the Americans—and to make suggestions for the reconstruction of the devastated cities, the reflation of economic life, the removal of the worst and often absurd severities of the denazification process, as well as the reopening of schools and universities.

Because the Nazi regime had left behind a total vacuum, and no political representatives whatsoever were available on the German side, the church, as the only surviving "authority" and as one held in respect by the occupying power, felt obliged to become a sort of stopgap representative. Because of his courageous resistance to the Nazis, we thought that Bishop Wurm was probably regarded as the most respected German. So the decision was made to establish relations through him and with his assistance with Commander-in-Chief Eisenhower at his headquarters in Frankfurt.

We zealously went to work on putting this plan into action and persevered even when we were confronted by one difficulty after another. These difficulties consisted above all in technical problems with the communications system. Mayor Klett, who supported us resolutely, was able to pull a few of the meager strings he had at his disposal and believed that he had detected indirectly via a few intermediaries a rough, pretty vague consent on Eisenhower's part to receive the bishop. It was not possible to determine much more than that. That was sufficient, however, for us to begin making preparations for an adventurous journey with Wurm to Stuttgart. I myself was only a little cog in this affair. Apart from Pressel, who was Wurm's personal consultant, the main players were three brothers from the Müller family from Stuttgart, namely Manfred Müller, diocesan youth officer and later head of the Church Council; Bernhard Müller, a well-known and successful industrialist who had spent a few years in the United States and had a magnificent command of American slang (we called him our "American"); and Eberhard Müller, who was later to become the first director of the first Protestant Academy in Bad Boll and to spread with unparalleled vigor the academy idea all over the world, including as far as Africa, the United States, and Japan, founding branches everywhere.

The Müller brothers had managed to persuade the military commander in Württemberg to place two luxurious black Mercedes limousines from confiscated stock at our disposal, complete with full gasoline tanks. In addition, I succeeded in getting hold of a student together with motorcycle. He was supposed to drive in front of us with the church flag when we arrived at Eisenhower's headquarters. We did this because in order to have an effective meeting with the Americans, who at that time were rather snooty, we had, of course, to make as prestigious an impression as possible, despite all our wretchedness. To this end we promoted Wurm, who was after all also the chairman of the Council of the Protestant Church, to archbishop, which he tolerated with a smile. Privately, of course, we were not permitted to address him as archbishop.

Because the church leadership had, since the destruction of Stuttgart, been resident at emergency quarters in the countryside, news of the bishop's planned journey quickly got about amongst the farmers. And when he merely hinted in a sermon that our main problem was the food question (although it was possible to find a place to sleep in Frankfurt, there were no hotels where Germans could eat) these devoted people placed such an impressive mountain of the most magnificent victuals at his feet that the trunks of both of our limousines were filled right up to the last cubic centimeter with food. We were given loaves of bread, ham, drippings, sausages, jam, and other magnificent things we had not been accustomed to seeing in this quantity for a long time. There was even a healthy quantity of invigorating cider. In those days, it took two days to travel from Stuttgart to Frankfurt. Time and again the expressways and roads we wished to travel had been destroyed, forcing us to make time-consuming detours. As a result, we only got as far as Heidelberg on the first day. There we distributed ourselves amongst the families of our colleagues from the theological faculty to spend the night. In those days, every reunion of people who had survived the war was a celebration. And when we then unpacked our grub and each took a generous portion to where he was staying, our hosts' eyes nearly popped out of their heads. In our Frankfurt hotel, which only had emergency accommodation at its disposal, the grotesque situation arose that it was not the waiters who asked us but *we* who asked the waiters to take their places for dinner. Glittering symposiums ensued, especially since our Frankfurt friends soon joined us as well. The old bishop was so carried away by all these reunions and all the fuss and bother that he insisted on travelling through the city in the sidecar of our motorcycle. During his trip he wore a light, rather worn, woolen jacket, which was the cause of a little argument we had with Mrs. Wurm. To make a good impression on Eisenhower, we wanted to see our archbishop dressed up as solemnly as possible in his best frock coat and wearing his golden cross of office. Marie

Wurm, however, had little appreciation for matters of prestige and sent us packing. She thought Theophil would suffer a stroke if he wore his heavy clerical gear in such hot weather. Furthermore, the snooty Yanks did not deserve his getting dressed up just for them. When we visited Eisenhower's headquarters, the bishop did indeed keep his jacket on. Marie had got her way and trusted in the power of his personality.

Although we supposedly had an appointment for an audience with Eisenhower on the following morning, all sorts of problems now arose, which was only to be expected for Germans in those days. The first thing we discovered was that Eisenhower was at that moment not even in the country but was in Washington, and that at best a deputy would be able to receive us. That was naturally disappointing. On top of everything, it was uncertain whether the deputy would at all be prepared to see to us. Our "American" was at any rate suspicious and decided to do some reconnoitering. When he returned, he told us a truly bizarre story.

Eisenhower's headquarters, which were situated on the grounds of the firm IG, were protected by numerous roadblocks, checkpoints, and barbed wire fences. Despite his energetic actions and his impressive American slang, our man only got as far as the outermost perimeter. He nevertheless succeeded in getting the guard to telephone other sections. After endless to-ings and fro-ings, he was eventually informed that Lieutenant H had been instructed to receive the Archbishop and deal with his requests. At this our friend Müller nearly burst a blood vessel with rage. In a spontaneous reaction, he exceeded his authority and replied, "His Grace the Archbishop regrets that he cannot permit himself to be received by a lieutenant. He must decline this invitation."

That was, of course, very daring and could have gone badly wrong. But because in the situation at that time the victors were used to Germans behaving for the most part in a pretty sycophantic and servile manner, this haughty and superior answer obviously made an impression on the Americans, who called Müller back after he had already begun to take his leave. After renewed telephone calls, we were informed that Eisenhower's political advisor, the distinguished and later very well-known diplomat Robert D. Murphy, would receive the Archbishop and his "entourage" on the following day. What a triumph! Now our friend really got going and took his demands even further. It was not in keeping with the dignity of the Archbishop to be stopped at every checkpoint, he said. The Archbishop must be given free passage. After yet more telephoning the Americans even agreed to this. Old Wurm enjoyed all this immensely.

The good bishop's complete inexperience in dealing with foreigners, let alone with Americans, now caused us some anxiety. To avoid any blunders or embarrassing situations arising, we had worked out precise tactics for the conversation and strove to rehearse the bishop for his part in it. After the greeting, Wurm was supposed to say a few weighty sentences on the state of our country and the duties of the victors towards the conquered nation. He was then to conclude this brief speech with the sentence, "My advisers will discuss the remaining issues with you." Each of us was then to speak to the General about his special subject. It was intended that my contribution should be on the theme of "the reopening of the schools and universities."

The next day, it was clear that Müller's energy had borne fruit. Our motorcyclist traveled ahead of our limousines with the church flag. The bishop sat alone in the first, while the rest of us followed in the second. At the first checkpoint, we were received by an officer, who politely saluted us and stepped onto the running board of the bishop's car. He then took us past all the intermediate checkpoints without stopping, where the sentries even saluted the bishop's car. Old Wurm waved at them, smiling sweetly. Murphy was waiting for him on the steps of the headquarters dressed in a sort of diplomatic gala uniform (that, at least, is what it looked like to me), and we grinned appreciatively at our "American."

However, there now began a series of blunders due to our good leader having forgotten everything we had taught him. It was probably only his personal dignity that prevented the absolute worst from happening.

Scarcely had Murphy invited us to sit down (during the period of "no fraternization" Germans usually had to remain standing throughout!) when, beginning with a little polite small-talk, he asked how the bishop and Mrs Wurm were. Not realizing that this was merely a routine set phrase, the bishop now indulged in a detailed description of his wife's illnesses, telling Murphy that while she was still suffering from leg pains the catarrh that had been troubling her recently had fortunately cleared up. I will never forget either the American's perplexed expression at this unexpected catalog of illnesses or the horrified look of my companions. Wurm had still not mentioned the sentences we had rehearsed with him and with which he was supposed to take his leave. There was even a brief and embarrassed pause, during which the diplomat recovered to some degree from his shock. He then got straight to the point and inquired as to the wishes of His Grace the Archbishop. The bishop's answer prompted us to seek cover in the depths of our seats, for as the first point on his list of requests he announced that we did not have enough gasoline to continue our journey. Could Murphy, he asked, perhaps help us with this problem? (We had unfortunately told him about this problem shortly before the meeting. It was afterwards neatly solved by our "American" craftily stealing the gasoline we required from a military filling station.) Murphy now seemed to be struggling hard to maintain his composure.

I can no longer remember which of us it was that saved the situation by calling out a few key words to our bishop on the subjects we wished to discuss. At all events there could no longer be any question of a dignified exit. He stayed until the end and the rest of us said our little pieces as best as we could. We never learned whether they bore fruit and hurried things along a little. In spite of everything, Murphy was obviously impressed by Wurm's personality. He at any rate accompanied him to the entrance of the house and respectfully bid him farewell.

Because news of Wurm's presence in Frankfurt had circulated quickly, the day still came to a conciliatory and moving conclusion. People both known and unknown to us, people who had been listed as missing or even thought dead, streamed into our hotel. There were unforgettable scenes when we were reunited with Martin Niemöller, who had just been released from temporary American custody after spending many years in a concentration camp; with Hans Asmussen, who at that time was still friends with Niemöller; and with Eugen Gerstenmaier, who had been saved from the death sentence passed by the People's Court and freed from prison by the Americans. Among all those delighting in our richly laid table were also a few representatives of the World Council of Churches, who happened to be in Frankfurt. They had a special surprise for me. They enabled me to see for the first time those books of mine that had been published anonymously in Switzerland after the manuscripts had been smuggled out of the country in diplomatic baggage, namely *Man in God's World*, *Tod und Leben* ("Death and Life"), as well as a collection of sermons.

Less happy than this conference in Frankfurt was the first conference of church leaders after the war, which had been arranged for the end of August 1945 in Treysa and in which I was supposed to take part. Bishop Wurm, who was leading the conference, had entrusted me with a major paper on the role the church had played between the ghetto and the public, and in particular on the disastrous role a misunderstood two kingdoms doctrine had played in the Lutheranism of the Third Reich. When I then appeared with my extensive manuscript for the car journey to Treysa with my colleagues, I discovered that the car had already left due to a stupid misunderstanding. In those days, the trains were still not yet running. Even if it is true that my paper would not have marked a watershed in the history of the church (although it might perhaps have been quite useful as a corrective to a certain tendency to return to a denominational way of thinking), I still found it extremely painful to have to relinquish my role in a decision-making process of such importance.

First Signs of Interest from Tübingen and Other Tempting Offers

My last months in Korntal were accompanied by preliminary discussions on my appointment to a chair in Tübingen and thus my return to my actual profession. Time and again in the coming decades I had the opportunity of embarking on other careers in the church or in politics. But offers and appointments of this kind were never able to make me seriously doubt my feeling that I was meant for the profession of university lecturer. I was fond of my students and the hours I spent lecturing and running seminars were a joy to me. I derived great pleasure in exchanging ideas with colleagues from other faculties and in having the freedom to write books. I also enjoyed the dignity of the alma mater—at least until its frightening decline from the late sixties onwards. Almost every day I have thought gratefully of that *providentia specialissima* that granted me a career in which duty and inclination came into almost complete congruence. I endeavored never to forget that for countless people—and not only for production-line workers—their way of earning a living was a bitter and meaningless drudgery, whereas my work was not only my "hobby" but was something I even got paid for.

So I did not find it difficult to resist calls to other areas of life and work. There was only *one* aspect of such offers that sometimes tempted me. You see, I often felt the urge to act, whereas in my profession I only had the *word* at my disposal. Mind you, in the following decades I made ample use of it in many public statements; not always successfully, by the way, and in the early years often all too vociferously, polemically, and also probably too frequently. Every time I said or wrote anything, I received clothes baskets full of letters for and against, indeed I twice received almost one thousand letters. This, as well as the discussions I caused in the press, led to a lot of trouble in the family. Sometimes my wife would return from her shopping expedition carrying a newspaper, which she would then thrust threateningly under my nose and say, "What have you gone and written now!" Indeed, I wrote some things in secret, under the table, so to speak, because I knew that I intended to turn a deaf ear to her well-meaning admonitions to exercise restraint. Especially in the first post-war years I found it very difficult after so many years of silence to refuse the press and radio when they kept on interviewing me on the often delicate issues of the day or asking me for my comments. The subjects concerned were, after all, connected with my profession. During this period the desire sometimes came over me to go beyond making speeches and writing books and articles and to acquire the capacity of direct action. This quickly wore off again, however, as soon as I stepped up to the lectern. The temptations of St. Anthony were certainly more severe. So as not to interrupt the flow of the narrative later and having now reached the point in my story where I was expecting to return to my beloved job, I will take this opportunity to name in advance some of the offers I received to leave the career for which I had so happily been predestined.

I was asked a few times whether I would be prepared to accept a bishopric. In my very first months in Tübingen, a delegation from the appointments committee consisting of Dürr, head of the Church Council; Professor Gerhard Ritter, who had fortunately escaped from Nazi imprisonment; and Erik Wolf, arrived from Freiburg with the aim of persuading me to become head of the State Church of Baden. Similar approaches were later made on the part of other state churches. In my first few years at Tübingen, I was offered outright the post of minister of education and the arts for North Baden-Württemberg, but turned it down after a brief period of consideration.

Finally there came yet another offer which, however, did not become public knowledge, and which I myself also treated with discretion. At Whitsun 1965 the then foreign minister Gerhard Schröder telephoned me from his house "Atterdag" on the island of Sylt. As I knew, he said, Bonn was about to establish diplomatic relations with the state of Israel. Because this was a particularly delicate task after the fate of the Jews in the Third Reich, the government was contemplating offering the post to a man from the academic world who, moreover, was not incriminated by anything from the Nazi period. He had now been instructed by the Cabinet to ask me, he continued, if I would be prepared to accept the post of first ambassador in Tel Aviv. Gerhard Schröder was of the opinion that I ought not to decide immediately but to think the matter over. He would, he said, telephone again the following day. Nevertheless, I asked him if he would inform me of his personal opinion of the matter. Quite frankly, he replied, his opinion differed somewhat from that of the Cabinet, although he respected its motives. The German representative in Tel Aviv would above all have to deal with economic problems, and these, he said, were, after all, not my department. He was thus afraid that this post could wear me out. He himself, he informed me, had for that reason pleaded for a professional diplomat but had not been able to get this through Cabinet. They simply absolutely wanted a professor.

The opinion of such a competent and well-meaning man was very important to me. When he telephoned again the following day, I declined the offer, which he seemed to greet with some relief. Nobody was in any doubt that the appointment which then followed of the experienced diplomat Rolf Paul was certainly the best possible choice. His services in Tel Aviv, above all his stamina in the first difficult period and his diplomatic tact, won high recognition. Golda Meir found words of grateful appreciation for him in her memoirs.

I have got ahead of myself with this last paragraph. At first I waited to see whether the vague rumors that had been floating about for weeks that the French had the ambition to reopen the first German university in Tübingen and that the faculty wished to appoint me to a professorship were indeed true.

Then the time came at last. Adolf Köberle, the dean of the faculty and a special colleague with whom I was later to become good friends, cycled from Tübingen equipped with an authorized armband and important permits to convey officially the faculty's intention to appoint me to a professorship. Then, towards the end of July, an official from the ministry of education and the arts brought news of my provisional appointment for August 1st—exactly a year after the destruction of our house. When the occupying power likewise gave its blessing to this sometime afterwards, I was finally a member of the academic staff of Tübingen University. The sentence "I appoint you as full professor with life tenure" in the certificate of appointment signed by Carlo Schmid, the president of the provisional government of South Württemberg-Hohenzollern, seemed like a fairy tale after all the years I had spent doing temporary jobs.

It was old Wurm who provided the most beautiful finale to my period of exile when he wrote the following letter to me sometime later.

I am proud that I was able to give you refuge [i.e. in our Swabian State Church]. None of the others to whom we also extended our hospitality has shown his gratitude through such devoted work in both the academic sphere and in the preaching of the Gospel as you have done. Above all, I will never forget your evening lectures in the Cathedral. There in Stuttgart's darkest hour you stood both as a herald of the truth and an intrepid witness to the Gospel in

the chaos of battle and were simultaneously a bringer of peace to a frightened
people. May the Lord bless all your future work for his glory and for the good of
our church and nation.

These words of this revered old man meant more to me than being awarded
a medal. They also caused me some embarrassment, for I knew better than
anyone how earthen and fragile the vessel was in which I had to keep safe
and to manage the treasure.

The Tübingen Years

1945–1954

AFTER AN ADVENTUROUS JOURNEY, I arrived at Schlatter House on Örsterberg Hill, equipped only with the most necessary clothes and an iron ration of books. Schlatter House was a hostel for Christian students, and it was here that I was to stay in a student room that had been placed at my disposal. Because no trains were running, my Korntal friends had ordered a taxi for me, which I now loaded right up to the roof. During the journey, the driver disclosed to me that he did not dare enter the French zone. He told some horror stories about how some of his colleagues had had their irreplaceable taxis confiscated. What a prospect!

And look what happened! When the zonal border, which lay a short distance before the Tübingen suburb of Lustnau and was guarded by Moroccans, came into view, my taxi driver pulled up about one hundred meters in front of it and said cordially, "I'm afraid I have to throw you out now!" He then put my belongings on the side of the road and, as if that were not bad enough, I had to help him. "You'll get to your destination somehow," he assured me before beating a hasty retreat.

I sat there at the roadside looking a picture of misery and with no idea of how I was to get myself and all my things to the place where I had such ambitious plans for my life. Nearby there was a solitary farmhouse. For want of a better idea, I wended my way towards it and sang the ballad of my helplessness to the plump and, judging by her appearance, good-natured farmer's wife who lived there. While I was speaking, I noticed what a magic word the title "professor" is for the Tübingen disposition. That a person with such a title should have been left by the wayside like a gypsy who had been robbed of his wagon, shook her deeply. After she had recovered from her initial shock, however, her face lit up with an idea of how we could save the situation. "I know what we'll do," she said in her charming Swabian accent. Her female cunning produced a fantastic plan straight away. She called her daughter, a sweet little thing called Annele, who was about six years old, and ordered her, "You take the professor across!" As she explained to me, the Moroccans were very fond of children, and the guards knew her Annele. We would now load all my things on to a little handcart, she said, and Annele would then pull it past the sentries. After a hundred meters, I could then take over the cart myself and pull it to Österberg Hill. She was, she said, quite happy to lend it to me for a day.

Everything went smoothly! The Moroccans even tenderly stroked the little girl's head and pushed the cart a little way themselves. I took over after the next corner and pulled the cart as far as Schlatter House, where the house-keeper, Miss Reich, received me with some amusement and with a shake of her head. The thing that annoyed me most was that when Annele left, I did not have anything to give her as a sign of my gratitude.

Lunch was ready when I arrived at Schlatter House. In keeping with the times, it was a very frugal meal. Dr. Ewald Katzmann and his family were also still residing at the house. Like myself, Katzmann also came from Barmen, and we enjoyed the intimacy of conversing in our common idiom. As a newly fledged publisher, he wanted to publish Ernst Jünger's first postwar publications (the Paris diaries, *Strahlungen* ("Radiations"), *Heliopolis*, and others). When he told me about this, I regarded his plan as somewhat fantastic. When he then one day returned triumphantly with the manuscripts from Kirchhorst, which was where Jünger was living at that time, I was pretty flabbergasted. But there was a simple solution to the puzzle. After the long period of shortages, Ernst Jünger and his wife, Perpetua, whom I also greatly admired, had a lot to catch up on in the way of everyday items. Katzmann, however, had been a tax and business consultant to Swabian industry before he had begun to scale the loftier heights of intellectual creation. He thus had a tremendous number of contacts and sources of supply at his disposal, which he was crafty enough to mention when attempting to persuade Jünger to part with his manuscripts. A publisher, who simultaneously had night-dresses, knickers, and underpants at hand, was irresistible in those days, even for someone like Ernst Jünger.

In the following years, it was remarkable the people he was able to lure into his house and bring together in festive evenings with his blue-eyed charm and large, cheerful, and musical family. On one occasion, almost the whole of the Parisian Company of St. George, which had gathered around General Hans Speidel, met at his house, including Ernst Jünger, Carlo Schmid, and the fascinating Armenian authoress, Banine. In his fantasies on the piano, Katzmann could pass from "Wait, my soul" to "Little Ann from

Tharau," to "Hail to you in victor's laurels," causing a stringently mathematically minded colleague from the music faculty who was present to turn away in agony. I, on the other hand, felt great pleasure on being reminded of the sentimental pietism of our home town of Barmen.

The Tübinger Theology Faculty

I was given an extremely friendly reception by my faculty colleagues. Even Karl Fezer, who had been quite heavily involved in National Socialism and who had initially been a zealous accomplice of the German Christian "Reich's Bishop" Ludwig Müller, gave me an almost emphatic welcome and expressed either directly or in a roundabout way his expectation that I would act as a sort of patron saint during the process of denazification that was threatening him. Prior to 1933, he had been an important teacher of homiletics. The aura of his then obviously powerful personality and above all his profound, spiritual nature had for many years attracted large crowds of students to Tübingen, who learned a form of preaching from him that was both saturated in the Bible and open to the present. There was now no longer any sign of all this. He made a boring impression in the pulpit and seemed like an extinct volcano to me. I believed I had discovered the reason for this decline, namely the fact that he never recanted or expressed any remorse for the false path he had taken and down which he had carried many of those who had trusted him. As a result, there seemed to be a sort of spell hanging over him. As the much younger man, I was unfortunately unable to find the words that I certainly ought to have said to him; time and again I bounced off the wall he had erected around himself. It shook me that a Christian—for he was indeed a Christian and also wished to remain such—refused to claim forgiveness for himself and so break through the spell of the past; and when I was sometimes angry at this hardness of heart, I sought to combat my anger with compassion.

Above all, the church historian Hanns Rückert, without doubt the central figure in our faculty, became an elder friend to me. He was a great teacher. His lectures were worked out in what was often a tortured quest for the truth and he would not rest until he had found a suitable linguistic form for the subject under discussion. I was fascinated by the succinctness of his prose and his style, which he was constantly refining. At the same time, he suffered from a certain "papyrophobia," which had resulted in his having only published a little, and even the little that he did publish only came out, apart from a few exceptions, through the efforts of his students. During our friendship I was sometimes disturbed by the fact that our theological interchange did not quite match the intensity of our friendship. Our intellectual constitutions were probably too different. All the same, his rather caustic sense of humor enabled us to have a good laugh together—and that is by no means the worst form of friendship.

We were later joined by the New Testament scholar Ernst Fuchs. Because of his provocative questions and aggressive intelligence, which caused many frightening legends to grow up around him, Fuchs was something of an *enfant terrible*. The students, too, immediately divided themselves into friends and foes and were almost rabid in their arguments for and against him. In complete contrast to his teacher Bultmann, whole sections of Fuchs' speeches would be given over to sibylline cascades of words that nobody understood. That did not make his followers lose faith in him, however, because the prophetic fervor of his lecture led them to assume that they were being given insights of cryptic profundity which until then had merely been a mystery to them. The rest of us also realized that some meaning did indeed lie hidden behind these esoteric and dark sayings, for a pearl of thought could suddenly light up in the midst of the amorphous flow of words. Fuch's formulation of this thought also often compensated for much of what would have otherwise rushed emptily past the listener. I was one of Fuchs' few colleagues who liked him despite or, perhaps, because of his strangeness. For me he was a typical example of Swabian eccentricity. The good Lord had simply made him that way and if one wished to find a key to his volcanic nature, one had to look to the chthonian-tellurian elements of the Alb hills.

At Tübingen I met friends from earlier days with whom I shared many common memories. Among these were the New Testament scholar Otto Bauernfeind, whose introductory seminar in Greifswald I had attended and who had for months visited me with touching loyalty during my serious illness, as well as the lecturer in mission studies, Gerhard Rosenkranz, with whom I had been close friends since my old Heidelberg days. The broad horizons of the much traveled man surrounded him, and his gifts as a storyteller succeeded in taking his listeners with him, as it were, and turning them into witnesses of the ethnology and religious practices he had experienced.

To give an adequate sketch of the New Testament and Judaism scholar Otto Michel would require Thomas Mann's sublime descriptive skills. He attached no importance to being "dressed up to the nines." His loyal followers said that he gave the money he saved in clothes to the poor.

Michel was a respected authority in his subject and was later the author of some important commentaries. It was not unusual for his spiritual temperament to get a little out of control. He sometimes, for instance, had visions during his lectures and fell into an ecstatic silence. Shocked or enraptured by this, depending upon their point of view, his listeners also fell silent and waited with great suspense for the outcome of Michel's inspiration. Elemental cries then gushed forth from his tightly pressed lips, eventually venting themselves in a sirenlike wailing. Many people regarded him as a charismatic; others, who found his manner rather outlandish, preferred to explain his ecstasies as due to the restlessness of his soul. He liked to address his students as "my boy" and use the familiar form of address with them; occasionally he was also capable of conducting elegant discussions. At all events, he had many strings to his bow. Thus he was not only a prophet, but also a foil-fencer. I myself loved his unusual and eccentric nature.

The revered senior figure of the faculty, who, despite having been an emeritus professor for many years, still occasionally preached in the cathedral and gave lectures, was the systematic theologian Karl Heim. He was world famous and for many years was the magnet not only of the faculty but of the whole university. The hordes of students who crowded into his lectures were seeking not only the great teacher who knew how to present even the most difficult material with almost journalistic lightness, but also the pastor who was able to get to the heart of all those problems that were troubling his contemporaries. In the first decades of our century, but above all after the First World War, this meant dealing with the relativism that questioned every absolute on both a scientific and historical level, and most especially every claim that the Christian truth was absolute. It was precisely this controversy to which Karl Heim had devoted his life, and he never departed from this theme from his first youthful work right up to his last works.

Up until that time, Heim was the only theologian of rank who was carrying on a debate with the natural sciences. He sought to force them to lift their gaze to the transcendence that lay beyond the closed equilibrium of forces and self-contained finite system that formed their working hypothesis. The outcome of this debate was several important works, which physicists and biologists also took note of and which still have not been forgotten even today. The other front on which he did battle was against historicism as a worldview. Historicism demythologized, as it were, every truth believed to be absolute and attempted to show its functional

dependence upon constellations of historical events. Ever since Oswald
Spengler's sensational work, *The Decline of the West*, intellectuals in partic-
ular had been enchanted by this view of things. All this was taken up by
Karl Heim.

Consequently, in his heyday, Heim's classes were attended by students
and colleagues of virtually every faculty. That he conducted his debates with
the *zeitgeist* not merely as an exercise in clear thinking, but allowed his
background in Swabian pietism to show through on all sides, that he spoke
pointedly—though by no means importunately—as a witness of Jesus
Christ, imbued his lectures with an existential claim that was unparalleled in
its combination of intellectualism and spirituality and which captivated the
audience. It meant a great deal to me that this quiet old gentleman was
constantly turning up at my lectures and giving me kind words of encouragement.

Mind you, precisely at those moments when I admired and liked him most,
I always harbored a secret reservation about him. It was this that had
prevented me from going to study under him at Tübingen when I was still a
student. Only in the course of many years did I realize why I instinctively felt
a sort of barrier towards him. I had gained the impression that Karl Heim
himself was scarcely troubled by relativism. It seemed to me that he rested in
the peace of a certain and unshakable faith. He was, if I may express it in this
way, more of a "diaconal thinker" who took other people's troubles upon
himself and made them his own in order, as it were, to seek vicariously (since
he had been given the requisite genius for this) a way out of their intellectual
encirclement.

That Karl Heim was a diaconal, a vicarious thinker, became clear to me
when I observed him as a very old man. Everything that had filled his
intellectual life and had made him famous throughout the world now seemed
to have fallen away from him like a rotten garment. He was now only—the
word *only* is certainly not meant disparagingly!—a Swabian pietist assuming
responsibility for his fellow men in priestly intercession. He had overcome
the world and for him his dialogues with God had ousted all other conversations for him. I only mention these reflections because my relationship with
Karl Heim has occupied my mind so greatly, although I know full well that
what I have said is only a feeble attempt at penetrating the secret of this great
figure in the Kingdom of God.

Adolf Köberle, who was probably the most prominent of Heim's pupils and
a special colleague of mine, was the good spirit of the faculty and selflessly
and untiringly stood by me at the beginning of my time in Tübingen. The

students trusted his pastoral devotion, and his colleagues were always certain that there was no guile in him. Despite differing in certain respects, we felt ourselves to have much in common in the objectives of our work and our educational interests. Only with regard to his musicality—he was an accomplished violinist and his children had very successful artistic careers—did I feel terribly incompetent, despite my gratitude to him for all the enrichment he gave us with his music and his assistance in interpreting it.

Last but not least, I must mention Gerhard Ebeling. He was the youngest of us all and at first had to grow into the faculty. During my last days in Korntal, he turned up at my home one day. He said that he had heard of my appointment to a chair in Tübingen and wished to inquire whether there might be a position for him as an assistant there, since he wanted to embark on an academic career. Although he had published a significant work as early as 1942, I knew nothing of it because almost the whole of the edition had been burned in the air raids. I soon realized, however, that I was dealing with an extraordinary man, even if nobody could have at that time suspected the enormous importance he would later acquire as a church historian, Luther researcher, and systematic theologian in Tübingen and Zürich. In comparison with his immense learning and his extensive study of the sources, I myself felt like an amateur.

To me he seemed like someone sitting at an enormous microscope, constantly turning the micrometer screw and producing fine cuts. He was not very interested in conjuring up graphic portraits of emperors and popes, or giving dramatic descriptions of the rebellious masses, or describing everyday life—including the smells!—in a medieval monastery. The rarified air of rapt abstraction frequently spread across his later systematic works, but it was precisely this that enabled the themes he was treating to appear in their fine, immaterial structure. I always read his prose with great intellectual enjoyment.

I have never since met a person who worked as intensely as he did. This was probably due, above all, to his having an enormous amount to catch up on after all the interruption he had suffered as a result of the war. In his poky little assistant's room, the books were piled so high around him that one could not see him when one entered. Despite the hunger and cold, he got up at five o'clock each morning and only left the battlefield of his work late in the evening. "Each morning I look forward to the alarm going off," he assured me. He played the piano like a virtuoso, especially Bach. His wife, Cometa, was a concert violinist and greatly enlivened the musical life of Tübingen. We all felt it was a dreadful tragedy when she later went deaf and was banished to a world of silence.

On the weekends in those days, I often used to go for walks with Ebeling. During our walks we would each confess to the other our joy at having returned to our chosen profession. And yet there was sometimes also a quiet note of sadness in our voices at having become "soloists." We missed living as parish priests and being supported by a sense of community with ordinary people.

Despite the bonds of friendship that united some colleagues in this way, the faculty as a whole was strangely lifeless. There was no mutual theological exchange of ideas, and we did not get together in our free time. We only had meetings on the usual monotonous routine issues: problems with the reconstruction program, discussions about examinations and, above all, the tiresome subject of denazification. One moment this person, the next that person, would be suspended or sacked for good by the occupying power, which then demanded that a new professor be found. In the process, serious and foolish reasons were often jumbled together, causing our sense of justice to rebel and tormenting us with conflicts of conscience. Our communication with each other exhausted itself in these meetings around the faculty's green table; we were surrounded by an atmosphere of impersonality. This seemed to be connected with the *genius loci*, for Goethe had noticed many years earlier that Tübingen lacked what he called "academic circulation."

Friedrich Sieburg, Romano Guardini, Carlo Schmid

Fruitful contacts developed with colleagues from other faculties and with people outside the university. In those days, the enchanting scenery and undamaged city attracted above all many of the leading lights of the theater world. Paul and Traute Rose had transferred their Berlin theater to the Neckar. We used to be on friendly terms with both of them. Erika von Tellmann, Elisabeth Flickenschildt, and Theodor Loos lent big-city standards to the Tübingen performances. Apart from money, theatergoers also had to pay with a briquette* at the box office.

---

* Immediately after the war there was a severe shortage of heating fuel. For this reason people were often requested to bring a briquette to public events in order to heat the building in which the event was taking place. Indeed, a briquette was often a condition of entry. *Translator's note.*

Friedrich Sieburg, who also belonged to the new "immigrants," was splendid company, if one was content with the modest role of being a mere listener during his narrative monologues. As soon as another person opened his mouth, Sieburg had to fight against fits of yawning. One could then positively see him preparing his next attack to win back his role as star conversationalist. I discovered this very quickly and restricted myself merely to asking him questions about himself, to which he immediately responded. When he took his leave of us, he used to thank us in emphatic terms for an evening that had given him such a great deal and had stimulated him so much. And yet he was the one who had been doing all the talking and telling one story after another. He told stories about the Stefan George Circle and his tragic friend in Japan, the spy Richard Sorge, about the old Queen of Württemberg, whose chamberlain he had been and whom he had had to protect when the French invaded Bebenhausen because they believed her to be Hitler in disguise. He told us about Marshall Pétain's tragic loneliness—but also about the wives of Tübingen professors who hid behind their curtains waiting for the horses of the neighboring farm to defecate and then began a race to be the first to collect the dung for their little potato fields. Because he was a lover of the finer pleasures of life, a real gourmet and epicurean, Liesel was always seized by housewifely stage fright whenever we had him to dinner and, in keeping with the times, were only able to set an ascetic meal before him (at least until the currency reform).

Sieburg's entelechy at any rate brought to our gray republic of learning a glittering kaleidoscope of color from other cultural dimensions. Probably nobody has summed up this culture more trenchantly than Gottfried Benn, when he compared Sieburg's style with a *Baumkuchen*,* the "most noble and expensive cake there is. Not macaroons, not marzipan, but this soft, delicate texture in which one tastes so many concealed and hidden things." Benn alone succeeded in succinctly capturing Sieburg's nature with four adjectives, "sublime and epicurean, civilized and opulent."

Besides the learned, benevolent, and kindly Theodor Steinbüchl, my Catholic opposite number was above all Romano Guardini, who had accepted a chair in the European history of ideas at approximately the same time as I had. This was a chair representing the Catholic view of the world, so to speak, but was intended for listeners of all faculties. This new subject, which had not been previously represented at the university, was

---

* Literally "tree cake." This is a cake that when cut resembles a tree's annual growth rings. *Translator's note.*

deliberately established as a counterpart to my own chair. In the following years, Romano Guardini and I enjoyed many friendly conversations. From time to time he dined at our home. After dinner, this dignified man would often have to rush home at double-quick pace because Germans were not allowed to be on the streets after the ten o'clock curfew.

The first time we met was a chance meeting in the rector's anteroom. When we introduced ourselves, Guardini said, "This is a symbolic act!" At this I let slip the remark, "You mean that we meet in a 'waiting room?' " We laughed and expressed the hope that we would also meet in the "main" room. Because I began my lectures sometime before him, and he was still able to move about with a certain degree of anonymity, he came to listen to them. His sensitive observations concerning my style of speaking and also the reactions of the audience were very instructive to me.

Neither in his lectures nor in his sermons did Guardini leave anything to chance. Every gesture, every intonation, and every pause were calculated with the utmost precision. This became clear to me above all in his meditation evenings in the Catholic church, which were very well attended.

On entering the church, one was greeted by some deliberately simple organ music. There was no virtuoso church "concert." This music was intended to help the listener compose himself. In the meantime, Guardini sat self-absorbed in the chancel in full view of everyone, resting his leonine head in his hands. After at last mounting the pulpit, he behaved for a brief moment like a nervous manager, rummaging through his papers in an obviously futile search for something. Then, all of a sudden, he turned to face the altar and remained before it in peaceful composure for a while. As soon as the organ stopped playing he began his address in a meditative style. When he came to our house shortly afterwards and we had drunk a bottle of wine, he was obviously waiting in a relaxed mood to learn something about my impressions of that evening. Feeling my oats, I said to him, "I saw through you this evening." He gazed at me in astonishment, "What do you mean, you saw through me?" he asked. "You not only wanted to get your message across by what you said," I replied, "but were also intent on achieving certain results by performing various other demonstrations. I certainly do not mean this negatively."

Guardini now wanted to know exactly what I meant. "It was certainly intentional," I replied, "that the organist did not show off but just laid out a few structural lines in space and time. In the meantime, you were demonstrating through your statuesque peace in the chancel how one prepares oneself for meditation. When you were in the pulpit you then wished to make clear in allegorical form the transition from stress and agitation to composure. After rummaging through your papers, you suddenly turned to face the altar in silent concentration in order to illustrate the other dimension towards which you wished to lead us."

Guardini smiled and said, "You may be right." His enormous aura certainly stemmed not least from the opposites which his nature concealed. How spiritual and sublime Guardini could be when he was interpreting Hölderlin's hymns or speaking about the angel in Rilke's *Duino Elegies*, and how tactical and cunning when he wished to get something done! In the exuberance of a witty banquet I once blurted out, "You're not only a *homo spiritualis*, you're also a crafty devil!" Judging by his rather gratified smile, I thought I could detect that he did not at all mind hearing this. This crafty side of his nature can be seen very clearly in some of the photographs of him.

Another of the leading figures in Tübingen in those days was, of course, Carlo Schmid, who was soon to become chief minister of the provisional government of Württemberg-Hohenzollern. Before he reached this first peak in his career as a statesman, we made each other's acquaintance in a pretty grotesque way. This occurred some time before the reopening of the university and shortly after the first deliberations had begun on appointing me to a chair. I was still living in Korntal and had yet again undertaken to give another lecture in Tübingen. Shortly after my arrival, Köberle asked me if I would that afternoon receive a certain jurist by the name of Schmid, who wished to make my acquaintance. Schmid, Köberle said, was certain to play an important role in Tübingen in the future and was, incidentally, also a highly stimulating man. I really did not feel like seeing a new face that afternoon, for I was pondering over my lecture and was, on top of that, feeling hungry and tired. Because it was so important to Köberle, however, I rather sullenly gave my consent—completely unaware of whom I would have before me in the person of Mr. Schmid.

Schmid then duly appeared at the appointed hour. He was a very corpulent man—which was something that immediately stood out in those days!—and was wearing a rather crumpled suit, which did not make me think very highly of him. I told him straightaway that I had little time, whereupon he assured me, "You only need to tip me the wink and I'll disappear again." (I had never heard the figure of speech "to tip somebody the wink" before, which is why I can remember his words exactly.) "How can I be of assistance to you," I asked, in order to get straight to the point. "How's the formation of the government coming along in Stuttgart?" he asked in reply. I had assumed that he wanted to speak about personal matters and found his question rather farfetched. All the same, I knew a little about the plans for forming a government, for I had just returned from visiting Theodor Bäuerle in Stuttgart. From him I had learned that it was highly likely that he would on the following day be appointed the first minister of education and the arts, who in those days was still known as "state director," for the North Württemberg-Baden Zone. (Instead, however, Bäuerle only became head of a government department and was only later appointed minister, which was something I could not have foreseen.) When I then mentioned Bäuerle as the candidate for the post of minister to Carlo Schmid, he said, "You're wrong there, he won't get the job." How could this provincial from Tübingen, I arrogantly thought, make such a firm assertion, when I, after all, had just arrived back from the scene of the action! Consequently, I asked him rather indignantly and not without irony, "Who will get it then?" Schmid's answer was simple and brief. "I will," he said. I made clear my displeasure at this by falling silent and frowning sceptically.

He noticed this immediately and began to defend himself. In lengthy monologues, which I passively let wash over me, he steered the conversation onto various educational topics, quoting verses from Homer's *Odyssey* in Greek, from Baudelaire's *Les fleurs du mal* (he was at that time working on the German edition of this work) in French, and not least from Dante's *Divine Comedy*—in Italian, "of course." In the process, he made his points by means of nimble transitions and associations with all the skill of a *compère*. The more he sensed that I was switching off, the more quotations he pulled out from his educational baggage. When finally the name "Ernst Jünger" was mentioned and I—almost reluctantly—said that I had just had a look through the manuscript of "Radiations," he immediately claimed that, "Much of the book goes back to suggestions of mine." That was really going too far for me. I held him to be a charlatan and a boaster. So I "tipped him the wink," and he got up to go. Our parting was cool.

On the following morning, I immediately made my way to Hölderlin Street in Stuttgart to tell Bäuerle about the strange man who had introduced himself as the minister designate of education and the arts instead of him. In the hall Carlo Schmid came towards me and greeted me with a triumphant gesture, "I noticed that you weren't really prepared to believe me yesterday. But, as you can see, I did get the job after all. If you ever have a request that is in my department, let my secretary know and she will pass the message on. I will drop everything and place myself at your disposal." This time my mouth stayed open.

I later got to know him better and came to think increasingly highly of him.

In his period of office at Tübingen he showed much character in the way he defended German interests against the French. Here his perfect French, which had once been his mother tongue, came in very useful. I admired the universality of his education, which I had so thoroughly misunderstood in our first conversation, as well as his ideas for reforming the politicocultural sphere, and not least his ability to inspire his colleagues. Even today his memoirs reveal to the reader what a man of stature he was.

Whenever we met in the following decades, however, there remained a residue of awkwardness on both sides. Our first conversation was certainly one of the few in which he felt he was not being taken seriously—even if it was only for a short time. And I was embarrassed that my instinct for people had failed so utterly. When, about thirty years later, he received the Hanseatic Goethe Prize, I was sitting in front of him during the bus journey from the town hall to the Hotel Atlantic. He then tapped me on the shoulder and said, "Do you remember when I visited you in Tübingen . . . ?" He then smiled and I thought I could detect a hint of embarrassment.

Eduard Spranger

One of the truly great figures I have met in my life was Eduard Spranger, the famous philosopher of culture at Humboldt University in Berlin. In those days, Tübingen was so attractive that personalities of Spranger's standing followed its call, especially since the old gentleman had suffered greatly, both before and after the end of the war, and yearned for the relative peace of our republic of learning. He had played a considerable role in my development from youth onwards, and in his Tübingen years now deemed me worthy of his paternal friendship. I had read his *Psychologie des Jugendalters* (Psychology of Adolescence) as a young student—that is, as a youth who was not sure who he was and who was seeking a collective portrait in which he could recognize himself and thereby come to acquire a little knowledge of himself. I can still remember what a fascinatingly ambivalent impression this book made on me. On the one hand, I felt that I had been even better understood than I understood myself; on the other hand, I felt that Spranger had at the same time relativized me. All the oppressive uncertainties, all these ecstatic flights of fancy and puzzling feelings of sadness that I was prone to as a nineteen-year-old, were not an original and lonely fate after all but merely the expression of the laws of growth in which we all shared.

So Spranger was now coming to Tübingen, and I looked forward to his arrival with curiosity and trepidation. The joy of now being about to meet in person a myth from my youth was so great, however, that I wrote him a few lines of greeting. After his arrival in Tübingen, he paid a visit to the much younger man, thanking him with avuncular grandeur for the few lines of greeting and making no attempt to hide that words intended for the heart had indeed been received as such.

How often he sought in his modesty to overcome the distance that surrounds the superior man, and how strange it seemed—especially in his case!—that this very modesty now became the mark of his superiority and only served to increase his distance from other people. I remember how we once went for a walk on a rainy day together and talked about Luther. It was only later that this conversation acquired intellectual significance for me. He allowed the younger man to advocate theses which were obviously alien to him, and yet he raised his companion above himself by the way in which he listened, by means of a contrapuntal openness, as it were. I had no time to make such assessments during the walk itself because we were constantly having to jump over puddles, and I had a great deal of trouble fending off his attempts to push me onto the clean parts of the path while he himself took charge of the slippery loam. This little mud ballet of politeness has always remained for me a charming analogy of my personal dealings with Spranger.

The distance that this man created and which he was so touchingly at pains to overcome was based not on an "authority's" desire for prestige, but was his way of protecting himself from the vulnerability of his feelings. He felt that such self-protection was necessary in his constant dealings with young people and the ups and downs of their development. And because this imposing distance was not his real nature, he was able to get on well with simple people (a fact of which all those who only knew him through his lectures were unaware). One only once had to have seen how he treated the personnel at Tübingen University, or to have read the stiff and awkward poem he dedicated to "Emilie," the students' ersatz mother, and which, despite being the only poem this master of academic prose had ever written, was the sensation of a commemorative book. And with what warmth could he describe the prison officers and boilermen who took care of him while he was in prison in Berlin and for whom he felt such great affection!

During my later presidency of the West German Rectors Conference, I had to deal with a great many questions concerning university reform, and naturally I sought to harness to my wagon as strong and knowledgeable a draft horse as Spranger. Seldom have I been so sharply brought down to earth than when I made my proposal to him. With a look that can only be described as one of melancholy amusement, he said (I paraphrase): Nice how you young people can still get enthusiastic about something I went through decades ago. And then he gave me to understand that all this reforming business was only a sort of "eternal recurrence" in accelerated form. His words were touched by a tinge of sadness at the fact that a certain tendency to relativism and skepticism on his part, which is something that no knowledgeable person can escape, had robbed him here of the naive impulse to act. But he did not want to infect the naive exuberance of youth prematurely with the cancerous wisdom of old age, preferring to express in his book *Lebenserfahrung* (Experience of Life) what Luther says in his own way in the preface to his commentary on the *Römerbrief* (Epistle to the Romans), namely that every truth and all knowledge of the truth has "its time, its age, and its hour." That is, the wisdom of old age is legitimate for elderly people, but could become a paralyzing cancer for young people.

Yes, the wisdom of Eduard Spranger! He could employ the words of Jacob Burckhardt to describe wisdom as the *goal* of all experience. For "through experience we do not wish so much to become clever (for some future occasion) as wise (forever)." This wisdom enables one to see the transience of life relatively and yet does not lead to relativism, since it possesses a fixed point. Eduard Spranger only ever hinted, both verbally and in writing, at what this fixed point was in his case. It would be inappropriate to get analytical here. He was content with making visible by means of ciphers, as it were, the direction in which the core of his existence was to be sought. The Socratic aspect of his nature only permitted him to reveal hints because it is not good to bombard another person with objectives and to rob him of his own pursuit of these objectives.

Young people have an alert instinct for detecting whether an existence exhausts itself in the superficial or whether it possesses deeper dimensions, whether an author is expended in his work or whether he is more than this work. This is the only possible explanation for the fact that this man, whose thought originated in the idealist tradition, was able to thrill a younger generation that was developing along different lines well into a ripe old age, and why it was that students flocked to his lectures. When he occasionally acted with a directness that is only becoming for a great old man, they expressed their gratitude, their intellectual response with resounding ovations. Then his face, which normally showed no emotion, would be transfigured, and his audience was able to gain an impression of what he had looked like as a young man. Despite his distance, this reflective man was adept at liberating the youthful spontaneity of the reserved children of the postwar years, before going on to introduce them to the severity of his thinking and concepts. I keep his letters as a priceless legacy.

Back in the Lecture Hall

At first, only the two theology faculties were opened, because their academic staff had been less decimated by denazification than the other faculties. We began with a short semester from early September 1945 to the first half of December. If my memory serves me rightly, we had about three hundred and fifty theologians who had happily survived the selection procedure that had been imposed upon them. In obedience to the occupying power's orders, all theology candidates, and later candidates for other faculties as well, were filtered through various hard-working admission committees. Officers, especially high-ranking and general staff officers, had the greatest difficulties in getting accepted.

Before the lectures began, a strange feeling of loneliness came over me. Tübingen seemed to me like an occupied hinterland that had escaped the air raids. Despite being only a few kilometers from Stuttgart, I felt painfully cut off from the former companions with whom I had gone through so much. I prepared my lectures in my secluded room; but, of course, I did not yet know the people to whom I would be giving them. Because audience contact was an essential element of public speaking for me, I felt that I had been hurled into an unfamiliar vacuum. When I spoke to my loyal Stuttgart parishioners in the Church of St. Mark, which I continued to do even after I had moved to Tübingen, it seemed to me as if I had plunged into an other, familiar world. Was *this* world, was this homiletic dimension that had shaped my life during the past years, perhaps not to be my intended destiny after all? This was what I was asking myself. Furthermore, the large number of people attending these church services increased to such an extent in the following period that loudspeakers had to be installed in order to transmit the service from the church into the open air. The general depression that spread through the university as a result of denazification also certainly contributed to dampening my spirits. Every day the air was filled with new rumors about who had now been dismissed.

In early November we were able to move into a lovely apartment by the Neckar, in Garten Street, and were together as a family again. We glued together the remnants of our shattered furniture and were soon able to welcome students and colleagues to our home. Not long afterwards, a large headquarters for the provisional government's ministry of the interior was erected on the land opposite us by the Neckar. The government of the area, which the occupying power had marked out as South Württemberg-Hohenzollern, remained for the most part a foreign body in the consciousness of the population. Thus it sometimes came about that someone asking for the ministry of the interior could receive the information, "It's opposite the Thielickes, number 79!"

On September 4, 1945, the start of the new semester arrived at last. I held my first theological lecture in the smallest lecture hall. As a rule, my subject, systematic theology, is only attended by advanced students who have already completed the biblical and historical courses, quite apart from their linguistic studies. That there were initially hardly any such advanced students did not damage my enthusiasm at being back in my old job, especially since the crowds of students increased in number from semester to semester.

My most important teaching duty lay elsewhere, however. Among the ideas for reforming the university that were occupying us was the setting-up of a *dies academicus*, a sort of humanistic introduction to Western thought and culture. This was intended above all for the young people who were now returning from the war and captivity to the vacuum that the collapse of Nazi ideology had left behind. There thus arose an institution that seems almost like a fairy tale from the viewpoint of today's mad chase after qualifications and the idiotic overspecialization that accompanies it. Every Thursday was set aside exclusively for these general studies; no specialist lectures were held. From eight o'clock in the morning to eight o'clock at night, interdisciplinary lectures were held for listeners of every faculty dealing with the nature and purpose of human existence on the basis of each respective discipline. This Thursday *dies* was surprisingly well received by the homecoming generation, which was searching for new ways of living their lives. I myself held a lecture entitled "The intellectual and spiritual crisis of the West," a title which seems pretty pompous to me today! This basically dealt with the subject matter of my book *Man in God's World*, which at that time was still unknown in Germany.

I soon had to move to the main lecture hall. Then the lecture was broadcast additionally to two other lecture halls. When that also turned out to be insufficient, the ceremonial hall, which—in those days at least—was anxiously guarded, was opened for me. That too became overcrowded very quickly. Things remained very much like this for my remaining years at Tübingen. The much more indifferent students of today—there have in any case been hardly any general lectures since the sixties—will find it difficult to imagine how passionately interested the first generations of students after the war were in questions concerning the philosophy of life.

That is not to say that everyone was in agreement with me! There was also fierce criticism and a whole host of controversies. A colleague from the philosophy faculty, who for reasons unknown to me was my deadly enemy, got so worked up by the throng of students that he circulated the slander everywhere that I was holding demagogic, provocative speeches and was whipping up nationalist (!) sentiments among the students. After I had made a petition to the authorities with the support of the faculty, this even went to proceedings before a sort of academic tribunal, from which I emerged vindicated and without so much as a blemish on my character. My colleague was forced to apologize to me. Sometimes I also became aware of jealousy and various other inferior motives on the part of other people. With his purity of character, Adolf Köberle stood out all the more clearly from such people and was free of any resentment toward me. For him the most important thing was the success of the common cause. Cheval, the French university officer, also felt uneasy about this "parade" of young people. He was so agitated by the students' custom of stamping their feet in greeting when I made my way to and from the lectern in the ceremonial hall (and many of them were, of course, still wearing their heavy army boots), that he summoned me to him and spoke both anxiously and coldly of my putting the students into a "mood charged with magical and Dionysian elements" (!). This was displeasing to the occupying power, he said, and it was uncertain what consequences this might have.

Cheval was basically well-disposed towards me, and during our discussions was also occasionally capable of responding quite positively. He was constantly musing about the "structure of my personality," which remained something of a puzzle to him. He was, incidentally, a highly educated, sensitive specialist on German affairs, although he gave me the impression of being a rather nervous man. As a Frenchman, he was still struggling against certain feelings of inferiority arising from the French defeat in the Second World War, which he strove to compensate for by passionately emphasizing French cultural superiority. In general he cultivated polite manners, was honest, and was not without ambition for the advancement of "his" university. The only occasions on which he could become unpleasantly arrogant were when he felt that French prestige was being questioned. I still had to fight some battles with him, but in the intervening periods I also often enjoyed his intellectual conversation. Occasionally, at times of near intimacy, he even made some observations about me which both astonished and greatly assisted me. Thus I have in my diary the transcript of a conversation in which he had analyzed my effect in the lecture hall:

> He himself regards my basic intention as correct, and for the most part approves of what I am doing. The effect I have, however, although certainly unintentional, is often dangerous. Even my greatest gift has a bad effect on some people. (He said all this, incidentally, in a very friendly way and asked my permission to talk frankly about this matter on a personal level and as a colleague). In his opinion, I have the tendency to refine my "deductions" right down to the last detail and to give them a logically transparent structure in the form of large-scale reflections. But precisely by doing this I am preventing the students from thinking for themselves. On top of that, there is my love of pithy formulations that, together with the fact that I am a "strong-willed personality," has an extremely suggestive effect, causing the students to be satisfied with passively consuming what I set before them. He would like to see my lectures contain a stronger "maieutic element." I would do better, he thought, to throw something half-finished and fragmentary to the people for once. Then the "Dionysian mist" that surrounded me and disturbed him so much would rapidly disperse.

I still believe today, almost four decades later, that Cheval had recognized an important deficit in my work as a lecturer and had given me a piece of advice which I unfortunately did not heed sufficiently (and perhaps was unable to heed). None of my colleagues has ever spoken to me so openly and insistently. This Frenchman did, however, and yet he was the occupying power's university officer.

The critical reception of my *dies* lecture on the part of the French authorities intensified still further when Karl Barth gave a sensational lecture in Tübingen on recent German history and in particular on the question of collective guilt. I was on a lecture tour at the time and unfortunately missed Barth's lecture, but I studied very carefully several reliable transcripts that members of the audience had made and gave a detailed reply to his position in my next *dies* lecture. Although I tried hard to curb my temperament and deliberately spoke as calmly as possible, the general agitation caused by Barth's lecture was so great that every polemical point I made during my lecture was greeted with applause, which was something I did not at all welcome. The audience's response caused extreme annoyance to the representatives of the occupying power who were present and even

filled them with a sort of panic. Citing as their reason the agitation amongst
the audience, they were soon afterwards to take action against me, which I
will describe later.

First, however, I have to say something about the contentious subject of
guilt, which was causing feelings to run high at that time. The so-called
Stuttgart Confession of Guilt of the German Protestant Church, a thoroughly
moderate and level-headed document, was unable to prevent the Allies from
constantly expecting the admission of a wholesale and highly indiscriminate
collective guilt from the Germans. Many people fell in with this, often for
reasons of unconscious or even calculated opportunism, for whoever
ruthlessly condemned himself and pulled the German people to pieces was
well-liked by the occupying powers. When I was in Switzerland in 1947, I
noticed how congenial even the Swiss found this masochistic self-accusation
on the part of the Germans, and how greatly it reinforced a pleasant sense of
moral superiority on their part (and edited away, as it were, their own failure
to help the persecuted Jews). I had some alarming experiences of the
advantages to be gained through admissions of guilt and did not shy away
from speaking cynically of the "trick of admitting one's guilt."

There was something, however, that was much worse than this temptation
on the part of non-Germans to indulge in self-righteousness, namely, the
Allies' tendency to one-sided and wholesale condemnations, which caused
them to overlook the beam in their own eyes. This often provoked a furious
defensive reaction from the accused, which then prevented them from seeing
the guilt that *really was present*. Often these reactions merely led to the sins
of the Allies being offset against Nazi atrocities, such as, for instance, the
fact that they had not stopped Hitler, had flattered him at the 1936 Olympic
Games, or had committed mass murder by blanket bombing Hamburg and
Dresden, and that those held in Allied prisoner-of-war and punishment
camps had been maltreated. So both sides swung back and forth, each
ascribing guilt to the other, and seemed to have relieved themselves of their
own need for penitence.

Although Barth's lecture was incomparably milder than, for instance,
Niemöller's grossly indiscriminate self-accusations, his statements also
seemed to contain the irritating undertones of an accuser who had not
himself had to live under ideological tyranny, but had merely shouted his
critical remarks to the protagonists on stage from the sidelines, from the
auditorium of Switzerland.

It depressed me greatly that people's willingness to listen was blocked by
such outbursts. The Church and its message were even suspected of joining

forces with the Allies and as a result met with closed ears and hearts. To fight against this and to pursue a *discriminating* diagnosis of German guilt (which, of course, certainly existed!), and furthermore also to castigate the self-righteousness of the accusers and to expose their skeletons in the cupboard, was perhaps the weightiest task I took upon myself in the following years. This was all the more so after I had visited the Allied prisoner-of-war camps and heard with my own ears and seen with my own eyes the misery of the people incarcerated there. I experienced a profound spiritual happiness in learning from countless conversations and letters that *this method of discrimination* made possible not only insight into one's guilt and the readiness to repent, but also acceptance of forgiveness. At the same time, however, I exposed myself to an almost unimaginable onslaught of hatred. That these reactions could occasionally also take on curious forms was only a slight comfort. Thus I remember a postcard from Switzerland (where all sorts of transcripts of my comments had arrived and been published in the press) containing the words "I spit on your Barth lecture. Yours contemptuously, Pastor X."

For the French, this lecture was now the last straw, so to speak. Because I "stood up" for the Germans and instead of supporting the Allies was constantly finding fault with them, they believed—although nothing was further from my mind!—that I was whipping up nationalist sentiments among the masses. Obviously there were and are misunderstandings against which one cannot protect oneself no matter how hard one tries to strike a balance. I had just announced that I would consent to the many requests I had received to continue the *dies* lecture *after* the end of the theological semester, when the French banned my lectures because of the unrest in the town. I confess that I did not greet this news with a sense of inner superiority. Scarcely freed from Nazi oppression, I had again been served with a ban, this time straightaway in the first semester. I thus found myself sitting around in my study, "unemployed" again, as it were, with no inclination to do any serious work. I wondered what would now happen. My friends also shared my worries about whether the French would be content with just banning me or whether I would suffer a second dismissal, albeit this time under different circumstances.

News that my *dies* lectures had been banned spread through the town like wildfire. Meanwhile, Carlo Schmid and the Rector Hermann Schneider struggled with Cheval and Widmer, the governor responsible for Tübingen, in an attempt to clear up this misunderstanding and to persuade them to allow the lectures to restart. In doing so, they made very clear how great the unrest was, how quickly news of the events in Tübingen would circulate in the other zones and possibly compromise the French reputation for tolerance.

In January, the ban was surprisingly lifted again and the lectures were allowed to continue, albeit on new conditions. First, I was banned from the ceremonial hall on the grounds that this spacious theatrical forum did not exactly help prevent the build-up of emotions (so the French believed). Second, the lecture was to be moved back to the main lecture hall and broadcast to two other lecture halls at the most. Third, student cards had to be inspected at the hall entrances in order to exclude "nonuniversity elements".

I had a horrible feeling that there were going to be serious problems. While I was in the lecturers' common room, the rector requested me to step quickly up to the podium and begin talking immediately in order to forestall any demonstrative greeting on the part of the audience. You know, he said to me, how sensitive the French are. A few of them had announced that they would be coming to today's lecture, he continued, including a few gentlemen from the state government. In addition to this, some reporters from *Figaro* and *Corriere della Serra* would also be present.

The rector had scarcely departed when some students asked me to come immediately to the corridor in front of the main lecture hall, where there was a great deal of commotion and argument because of the refusal of the porters to let any more people into the overcrowded hall. I would have to go and calm the people down, they told me. My pulse beat faster as I made my way downstairs and pleaded with the people in the corridor to be quiet and show some understanding; otherwise, I pointed out, there would be serious consequences for the reopening of the university.

The tumultuous unrest did indeed subside to some degree, and I pushed my way, unnoticed at first, through the cluster of people to the lectern and immediately began my lecture, saying, "In the last lecture before Christmas I spoke about. . . ." Fortunately, there was no unwelcome applause this time. When I opened my manuscript after freely and briefly recapitulating the previous lecture, I saw to my horror that in the confusion I had brought my notes for the last lecture and had left the right manuscript in the lecturers' common room. For a few shocked moments I circled in nervous oratorical loops above the airfield and considered frantically whether I should admit my mistake and quickly fetch the correct manuscript. But then I thought of the restless crowd outside. An interruption could lead to renewed complications. That something like this had had to happen to me of all people at a time when so much was at stake and so many people were watching me sharply to see if I would make a wrong move! Then I pulled myself together and called out to my frightened soul, "With God's help, fly blind!" I put the wrong manuscript away and started to speak without the aid of notes. In doing so, I experienced the truth of what Christian Morgenstern wrote in his gallows song about "greaseproof paper," namely that fear can increase the mind's agility. The necessity of speaking without notes spurred me on to exceptionally clear formulations and arguments. Nevertheless, I continued to tremble at the shock and intense concentration for several hours afterwards.

Students and Other Good Souls

I have already mentioned that the response to my *dies* lecture led to a very large number of individual conversations, although these were less discursive than pastoral in nature. The personal problems, the earnestness of this sorely afflicted postwar generation, and the immense responsibility I carried enabled me time and again to overcome my exhaustion, an exhaustion which was increased still further by hunger.

There was a high level of attendance at the times set aside for students to come and see me. Schlatter House's kindly housekeeper always gave me a number of extra sandwiches, for in those days institutions catering for large numbers of people were provided with a more generous allocation of food than was the norm. I would have felt like a big shot, however, if I had eaten them myself; for this reason I slipped a sandwich to each of the students who visited me, as long as the supply lasted. It was only long after the famine was over that one of them divulged the secret behind these flourishing students visits. They were actually only interested, he said, in the sandwiches. Before they came to see me, they always thought up all the possible problems they could bring up with me in order to conceal the *true* reason for their visit!

Besides the many conversations I had, I also had to cope with an enormous amount of correspondence, with which my secretary was only able to help me to a limited degree. In particular, the circulation of copies of my reply to Karl Barth resulted in my receiving a large number of letters, many of which were concerned with the guilt question, often from a very personal aspect. Many people, including high-ranking officers, indicated that this discriminating way of tackling the guilt problem had brought them to admit what had been weighing upon their consciences. And they wrote to me about this almost in the tone of a confession.

When I think back to my Tübingen students, two faces still appear before me today. I first noticed them sitting next to each other at the church service commemorating the beginning of the new semester. The first was the theology student (and former lieutenant colonel and front-line officer) Konrat Weymann, his countenance deeply furrowed by the suffering he had experienced. Next to him sat a very young, little lad, "still wet behind the ears." Both were typical representatives of the first wave of students after the war.

A few students became close friends of mine in the following period, especially since we always let two of them live as guests in our home during the period when there was still a severe lack of housing and material shortages. I would very much like to present them all to the reader, but space will not permit it. Nevertheless, there are a few I feel I have to mention.

Firstly, there was Hans Schmidt from Esslingen, who had turned up at my home after one of the cathedral lectures at the age of sixteen. I immediately developed a close friendship with him, despite our difference in age, which lasted until his fatal traffic accident in 1981. From the very first moment I met him, I did my best to support and guide him. He later gained his doctorate and *habilitation* under me, went on to become my assistant, and was later a professor in Frankfurt. His great talent meant a lot to me because it both stimulated me and enabled him to make helpful criticisms of my work; his loyalty made my life easier.

I enjoyed a similar lifelong friendship with Heiner Paret, who brightened my Tübingen years with his charm and musicality. We are still in contact with each other even today; he is a pastor in Kusterdingen near Tübingen.

The third member of the group was Heinz Schladebach, whom we named "our boy Mozart" because of his ephebic delicacy and the way he played the violin. In the winter he used to go to bed in our unheated garret and read musical scores with the utmost enjoyment, despite the fact that he could hardly hold them in his numb fingers. During the student riots of the sixties, he was in charge of a rebellious seminary in Berlin and showed a staying power that we had hardly thought possible from somebody of his artistic and sensitive temperament. Even today he still displays fire and determination in intellectual conflict.

These difficult times were accompanied by much that united professors and students, even outside the university environment. Because there was still no coal, each of us was allocated a few trees that had been felled in the forests around Tübingen, which we were then permitted to make into firewood ourselves. Our students helped us unworldly academics with this; indeed they assisted us with great enthusiasm and cheerfulness, singing songs while they worked. The sawing and chopping, and finally the transportation of the wood home, was like a little carnival procession. I only regretted that we were completely unable to give these hungry and thirsty men the meal we owed them.

The everyday burdens of those first postwar years did not prevent us from holding parties of a splendor that seems almost unbelievable when compared with the modern preoccupation with recorded music, shallow discos, and the routine cheerfulness of professional entertainers. In those days, people's imaginativeness still expressed itself in poetry, plays, and songs composed by the students themselves. When the present priest-in-charge of the Church of St. Michael at Hamburg, Hans-Jürgen Quest, was a student, he was a virtuoso tap dancer and imaginative songwriter whose performances always formed an obligatory part of the program. Any professor who had not yet recognized his own failings had them drastically presented to him in the mirror of student cabaret. At these parties, all we had to eat and drink were brown rye rolls and an obscure tea. The mind did not yet seem to need any alcoholic stimulants; it simply lived from its own creativity.

The high point of the week, as least from my perspective, were our *Open Evenings*. Every Sunday during term, Liesel and I invited the students to our apartment. As far as external appearances go, these evenings too were rather primitive. We gathered our guests together in the largest room, which was also where the children slept. They were not disturbed by our singing. At various intervals they were placed on their chamberpots by expert student hands, and one student kept our little stove supplied with wood. The number of participants fluctuated between forty and eighty, which forced many people to sit on the floor, the table piano, and the rocking horse. At each open evening, I would propose a subject for discussion that was as far removed from theology as possible but always guided the conversation in such a way that it allowed us to keep coming back to theology. My ulterior motive here was to show the students that theology was not pursued in secluded ivory towers and that there was hardly a single aspect of life which did not fall within its boundaries.

I remember one evening in particular when we had to crowd together even more closely than usual. The subject I had announced for discussion was "Zarah Leander's concept of miracle." I was alluding here to this popular film actress and singer's hit "I know a miracle will happen one day," a song that everyone was singing, especially in the final phase of the war, and which had not yet lost any of its popularity. In those days it was regarded as the "wonder weapon song:" the situation was utterly desperate, our only escape was hope, only a miracle could save us. This song triggered off associations with the

wonder weapon that Hitler had announced would burst the chain of catastrophic defeats and turn the fate of the war around by one hundred and
eighty degrees. I had appointed two speakers to interpret this song, one for
the melody and one for the text. The person responsible for the text was
incidentally Jörg Zink, who was later to become a well-known author.

Everyone was expecting to have a whale of a time. This was probably the
reason why so many people turned up. Although there was indeed a lot to
laugh about, the basic tone of the evening was very serious. We encountered
a nihilism that regarded miracles merely as a desperate emergency outlet
and lulled itself into optimistic dreams with the aid of musical kitsch. So on
this occasion too we arrived back at our theological landing ground.

That particular open evening was accompanied by another amusing incident. As I was going to my seminar on the following morning, I saw on the
other side of the road a colleague who had always taken an interest in my
work and who from time to time asked me questions about it. This time I
rather shied away from this possibility. He was a typical Tübingen man,
molded by Swabian pietism and, despite all his understanding, would certainly have had little sympathy for *such* a bizarre "theological" topic. So I
hoped that he would pass by and not ask me about the previous evening.

But look what happened! He straightaway made a beeline toward me. We
chatted briefly until, to my horror, he asked me what we had discussed at my
latest open evening. What is a theologian, who alone on account of his
profession is not permitted to lie, to do when he at the same time believes that
the other person is not up to hearing the truth? I then had an idea of how I
could get out of this scrape. "Yesterday evening," I replied, "we discussed
the theology of Leander." (One would have to search for a long time until one
found mention of a Leander in a footnote of a work on the history of theology;
there are in fact no relevant theologians of this name whatsoever). My partner
in this conversation was visibly perplexed at this statement but did not want
to reveal a gap in his knowledge in the presence of a colleague. So he reacted
with a pensive and knowledgeable expression and acted as if he had the
whole of Leander's system before his eyes. "Very interesting, very interesting
indeed!" he said. He's fallen for it, I thought, and gloated a little that it was he
and not I that had had to lie (although I too would not have liked to have
embarrassed myself by revealing my ignorance in front of a colleague and
would thus have probably feigned knowledge in a similar way). A few steps
later he asked again, " 'Leander,' you say?" "Of course—Leander!" I replied. He then struck himself on the forehead as if he were embarrassed at
not having immediately recognized this well-known name. "Yes, of course!"

he added. I quickly changed the subject. I was nevertheless rather embarrassed at playing this despicable game with a professor's vanity. Suddenly, however, he once again returned to the dubious name. "Forgive me," he said, "but your open evening was concerned with 'Neander,' wasn't it?" (There actually is a Neander). "No, Leander!" I replied emphatically. "That's what I thought!" he said, concluding our brief dispute and shaking his head a little as if he were reproaching himself for having done the great Leander an injustice.

It was only when I left Tübingen almost nine years later and the faculty was holding a farewell party in my honor, that this colleague admitted to this embarrassing little episode. He described the occasion in a delightful poem before going on to describe with magnificent self-irony what had happened afterwards. As soon as he had arrived home, he had pored in vain over various encyclopedias in the hope of learning further details about the great, unknown thinker Leander. After these fruitless efforts, he steered his conversations with students onto the subject of my open evenings until he eventually discovered the truth. He certainly did not take too seriously the fact that I had misled him and that he had fallen for my trick, however. His sense of humor will have helped him to realize that he had fallen victim to a failing common to all of us professors.

A productive dialogue with colleagues from other faculties and with circles outside the university ensued when Theodor Eschenburg and I founded our Wednesday club. This was a carefully chosen company which met to eat together—at first meagerly, later more sumptuously—at Kaiser Restaurant and to discuss papers which we took it in turn to give. Besides various representatives from the business world, these evenings were attended by the head of Wunderlich Publishers, Hermann Leins, Mayor Mühlberger, General Hans Speidel, and my colleagues Gallas, Stadelmann, Spranger, Wenke, and Butenandt. These conversations were tremendously invigorating and extremely instructive. Butenandt above all made me realize how a great researcher is often able to describe the mysteries of his subject more simply and with greater transparency than a teacher working from second hand knowledge, no matter how well the latter has been trained to teach. If I have ever trembled in awe at the wonders of life it was when *he* spoke about them. At the same time he awoke in us a first inkling of what we today comprehend far more clearly as the dangers of gene manipulation and what we are now beginning to understand as *homo faber*'s debate on the nature of our creative purpose. Over and above that I was impressed by his modesty.

Hans Speidel, the future commander-in-chief of NATO land forces for

Central Europe, was also an outstanding figure in our circle. This was not only because he had been Rommel's chief of staff and had played a part in the officers' resistance to Hitler, but also because he possessed through his connections with American military staff information that was usually inaccessible to the likes of us. For all that, he had one endearing failing, namely his tendency to shroud his statements in an atmosphere of great mystery and to give his listeners the illusion that he was allowing them a look at the cards of the world spirit. When he once gave us a review of troops and weapons numbers in East and West, he had all the doors locked and ordered the landlord to keep all eavesdroppers away. We were also forbidden to take notes on his top secret communications. Despite this order, however, Eduard Spranger scribbled a few notes down under the table. Hardly had Speidel caught sight of this when he shouted at him in a sharp voice and ordered him to stop. I can still see Spranger dropping his piece of paper like lightning, obediently putting his hands on the table and blushing like a schoolboy caught red-handed. My friendly association with Speidel also continued in later years and was constantly finding expression in our correspondence with each other.

My Tübingen period was also marked by periods of severe depression, however. I do not wish to say any more about these and can only hint at the reason behind them. In the agitation and uncertainty of those first postwar years, all sorts of rumors flourished that often culminated in my being slandered, indeed denounced, to the occupying power. It is hardly credible what I was supposed to have said in my lectures and how damaging my influence on the students was supposed to be! Other people, however, praised me to the heavens and applauded me for having found the right words for the age and for helping that profoundly disturbed generation. These conflicting opinions, these reactions for and against me that reached me daily, resulted in a range of sharply differing moods with which I had great difficulty in coping. I was not, after all, a serene sage who was able to rise supremely above all this. Precisely because I was young and highly committed I saw myself dragged into the whirlpool of what I myself had partly stirred up. As a result I often suffered periods of extreme despair, with which I sought to come to terms by keeping a diary. How well I later understood Gerhard Nebel when he described the diary as "the literary form of the prison" and as an instrument of self-liberation. In addition to these personal troubles, there was the delicate situation in world politics, which constantly petrified us with the possibility that tomorrow or the day after tomorrow everything could come to an end. Would the tension between East and West not one day explode in a new world catastrophe? In the face of this apocalyptic perspective, Tübingen's petty local worries, which puffed themselves up with an importance utterly disproportionate to their true significance, simply did not matter. The communist takeover in Prague, the Berlin blockade of 1948, and the Korean War which began in 1950 were signals which prompted us to think about possible catastrophes. These fears were constantly at the back of our minds and sometimes completely drowned out our petty everyday worries.

Family Life

A ray of hope and a calming influence in my oscillation between euphoria and sadness were the children. Liesel was a mother who, unlike me, had the ability to strike a good balance between kindness and strictness. Wolfram and Berthold had already been born, of course, when we moved to Tübingen. Elisabeth, who to the jubilation of her little brothers came into the world in 1947, always retained some of the sunny May day on which she was given to us. Our family was finally complete when Rainer, who was quite a character even as a child, was born in 1949. I will have more to say about this later.

We sometimes wondered whether our two eldest children had retained some of the fear they had experienced during the air raids. Wolfram at least had had a conscious experience of the bombing, after all. When a violent storm broke over Tübingen one day and frightened the children, I took them in my arms and sought to calm them. Despite this, Berthold asked anxiously whether the thunderclaps were exploding bombs and whether everything was about to be destroyed. It was not I but Wolfram who found words of comfort. "These are *nice* planes, they won't hurt us," he said, "our dear Lord has sent them." He was generally a sensitive soul and had a tender, affectionate disposition. We sometimes worried, especially during the Nazi era, how he would survive in our egoistic world where everybody looked only to their own advantage, not suspecting what a fine figure of a man he would later become. I will never forget how I once took him into my confidence when I was feeling absolutely exhausted. I said to the little chap, who was fond of being with me in my study, "Father is *sooo* shattered, but has to work." He then pointed his little arm at Dürer's portrait of Christ's countenance, which hung above my desk, and simply said, "Savior!" We were upset when on one occasion during the famine the two boys found their mother's cookbook and proceeded to lick the colorful pictures of cakes and roast meat.

St. Nicholas' Day* was, of course, always a special occasion for the children. There were also always some students who took part in order to make it an enjoyable event for the children. One of them, Rainer Röhricht, who was later to become my assistant and was almost six feet six inches tall, was positively predestined to play Santa Claus. Beforehand, we had a detailed discussion about the various misdemeanors the children had committed, so that he could ask the children about them and get them to promise to behave better in the future. This worked as a rule and had a positive effect—at least temporarily. Berthold, however, once sought to forestall being confronted with his embarrassing list of sins by asking Röhricht, "You come from heaven, don't you, Santa? Can you then tell me who actually made God?" (He must have picked up something from conversations on "aseity.") I saw Röhricht, who was usually so quickwitted and endowed with native Berlin wit, momentarily struggle to maintain his composure before answering, "That is a question for earthly theologians, my boy. You'll have to ask your father. We in heaven have other things to worry about!"

Visits to the Internment Camps

As well as my work in Tübingen, I often had to go on lengthy lecture tours, especially when the semester was over. Occasionally I had to speak in ten different towns consecutively—both in the West and in the "Eastern Zone"—and be available for discussions and numerous personal conversations. Apart from the books I had recently published, the reason I was so often invited to speak, although I was by no means able to accept every invitation, was above all my statements concerning the contemporary situation.

Visits to the internment camps, where several thousand both genuine and merely putative Nazis were imprisoned, often in horrific circumstances, filled me with consternation. Because of my difficulties with the Third Reich, I was one of the few people who were allowed to enter the camps, if the prisoners called for us, which they could do either directly or via the camp vicar. In this way I came to visit the camp for captured generals in Ludendorff Barracks at Neu Ulm, the camp at Darmstadt known as the "extermina-

---

* Celebrated on December 6, when St. Nicholas places sweets in the shoes of good children and a cane in those of naughty children. *Translator's note.*

tion camp," and the "Kornwestheim VIP camp," where I had high-ranking SS leaders, generals, and other figures high up in the state and party hierarchy, including Prince August Wilhelm (nicknamed Auwi) of Prussia and the Reich's labor bosses Hierl and Hjalmar Schacht, sitting before me. Finally, I visited Ludwigsburg internment camp, where I encountered some old acquaintances again. There I met the former Reich student leader and later Gauleiter* Gustav Adolf Scheel, who at the request of his father had sought in vain to help me after my dismissal; I also met Seiler, the head of the Heidelberg district, who had likewise behaved decently towards me; and I also came across the Gestapo man who had been awfully embarrassed at having to carry out a house search after my wedding and who now touchingly and pitifully came up to me and said, "Do you no longer recognize me?" I was impressed by the way Scheel preserved his dignity. After I had given my talk, he described the background to his career in a long conversation.

Prior to 1933, he had played a leading role in the student campaigns against Gumbel, the Jewish pacifist and lecturer, and had got so involved in Nazi agitation that he had completely neglected his medical studies because of it. Even at that early date, he had had a bad conscience, he said, and was always waiting for one of his professors to give him a dressing-down sooner or later. But because of his influence at that time, they had merely flattered him and behaved obsequiously towards him, even going so far as to give him an "A" in his examination, despite his miserable knowledge of his subject. That this had harmed his personal development and had instilled in him a certain contempt for human beings was, he said, more than obvious to him. In my opinion, he had been one of the most decent people in the higher echelons of the Nazi party. In the late fifties, I met him again in Hamburg, where he was running a doctor's practice after studying under Professor Kunstmann to catch up on the material he had missed. As if to atone for what he had done, he took on Jewish patients in particular and soon gained their trust.

I sometimes reflected on the role of the "figures of authority" who had behaved in such a servile and demeaning way in the early part of Scheel's life history when I observed the same behavior on the part of the authorities towards the rebellious students of the late sixties. They, too, longed in vain for someone to put an end to their psychoterror but, as far as both the politicians and also many professors were concerned, they only came upon a

* Head of an administrative district in the Third Reich. *Translator's note.*

soft, soggy mass. *This*, and not the follies of the younger generation, is the cause of the alarming decline of the German university.

I was particularly moved by my meeting with the generals in Neu Ulm. I was greeted by General Reinhard, the most senior officer in the camp. Because I was very critical of the role the generals had played in the Third Reich (Goerdeler had, of course, supplied us with depressing information in this respect), I spared them nothing. I tried, however, to avoid sounding self-righteous and above all to let them sense my sympathy for the often hopeless conflicts in which they had found themselves. In this way I endeavored not to block their willingness to listen. They were a quiet group of people who listened to me thoughtfully and receptively. When I once mentioned the key word "Versailles" in my speech, an incident took place. The supervising American officer interrupted me and reproached me for moving onto a forbidden political level. Only after a lively internal discussion was I allowed to continue.

Afterwards, the generals took me to their quarters, where bunkbeds had been erected along the walls. Because there were no lockers, they had hung their uniforms in piles on the few hooks available. The red stripes that signified the rank of general could be clearly discerned peeping out from the tops of these piles. I was asked to sit down on a stool, in front of which another stool was then placed to serve as a table. A can had to play the role of a cup, into which a coffeelike drink was poured. A broken piece of dry biscuit took the place of the pastries that normally accompany coffeetime. The generals insisted that I sat down, while they stood crowded tightly around me.

I had difficulty in holding back my tears. There could hardly be a more moving allegory for the fall and decline of my country. They then told me about the harassment to which they had been subjected. Despite the winter cold, the camp authorities had insisted on removing the doors. This was justified by the commanding officer "on account of the danger of earthquakes." Nobody was able to talk him out of this. It was fortunate that the generals were allowed to have a number of young adjutants with them. The generals themselves were pretty helpless when it came to coping with the primitive conditions in the camp, because they were so used to being waited upon. They were thus greatly indebted to the resourcefulness and skill of their helpers, an example of which was the manufacture of the most essential household utensils from cans. We then had a long conversation about the guilt question. Their distance from the profession they had pursued up until then allowed them to perceive many things that had been pushed into the background or suppressed in the stress of having to make daily decisions, especially during the desperate final stages of the war.

I also learned, however, that they had been cruelly, often sadistically maltreated, especially those interned in the camps for members of the SS. The Allies' "crusade" against National Socialism was in danger here of completely losing its credibility, so that even those who were beginning to turn away from the false spell of the Nazi regime were succumbing to the temptation of renazification. The methods of reeducation and denazification the Allies employed were for the most part disastrous for the inner development of our nation. Expressed in simplified but unexaggerated terms, these methods seemed to be as follows: all those who formally belonged to a Nazi organization were first of all removed from their jobs, with the exception of those who showed a positive attitude toward the Allies. The same applied to all those whose job titles ended with "official:" school official, court official, government official, and so on. They were regarded without further ado as being loyal to the system and classified as Nazis. To be rehabilitated and allowed to work again, these people had to supply a certificate from persons untainted by a Nazi past testifying that they were innocent, that they had assisted endangered Jews, had made statements of opposition to the regime, or had evinced similar nonconformist virtues. Through this frankly perverse method of denazification a disastrous psychological effect was produced: it succeeded in nipping in the bud any vestiges of remorse and sorrow over his failure that the individual might have had. Instead, it provoked the autosuggestion: actually I did in fact behave quite bravely, I even played a heroic role in resisting the Nazis. What a noble portrait gazes out at me from my denazification certificate! There thus arose an "incapacity to mourn." Any pastor or astute contemporary commentator following the history of this inner development, anybody wishing the confused and remorseful people living in this time of transition to put the past behind them and start anew, could only cover his head in despair at these follies.

Whenever I witnessed this, and particularly after I had visited an internment camp, I came away frustrated at the shortsightedness of the Allies. Although some people were acting from a sense of masochistic pleasure, and others were only performing routine actions because it was expected of them, many people were genuinely locked in a constant struggle to come to terms with the past. I was tormented by the fact that everything that was happening in the camps usually blocked this process, and yet this was all hushed up and made a taboo subject by the authorities. Had we not already kept silent long enough in the Third Reich? Were we now once again to make ourselves guilty through not speaking out? Ought I not to shout from the rooftops what *I* had just experienced? But *how* was I to do this?

The Good Friday Sermon of 1947

The pressure my conscience was exerting on me intensified to such an extent that I decided I would have to speak out without mincing my words in a sermon I was to preach on Good Friday in the Church of St. Mark at Stuttgart. I intended to make a public statement on how the spiritual recovery of our nation was now being prevented by our having a guilt thrust upon us which was not ours. Apart from my Bible, Liesel also packed my toothbrush and pajamas because she reckoned with my being detained by the occupying power. Although she was worried, she did not stand in my way; she never did. Under the heading of "The Passion without Grace," I took as my text Jesus' saying, "Woe to the world for temptations to sin! For it is necessary that temptations come, but woe to the man by whom the temptation comes!" (Matthew 18:7). Later in the sermon, I described what I had come to know from my camp visits, and continued as follows:

> All of us must one day face the Last Judgement—that is, all of us who helped by our silence and complicity to release the hound of hell, *and* also those who now allow it to continue to rampage, despite their claim to come in the name of Christianity. In view of the coming Last Judgement I proclaim: *this is an injustice, this is a temptation to sin.* Not only the prisoners' bodies, but also their souls are in danger of dying, and the glowing wick of their faith is growing ever weaker.
>
> I think of the many refugees who are dying in the ice cold cattle trucks in which they are being transported, and who perish more mercilessly than cattle in an abattoir.
>
> I think of the prisoners-of-war and the many thousands that have been allowed to die of starvation by those who came in the name of humanity. In the name of Jesus Christ I demand from them the souls of our youth, our youth which no longer believe because they see nothing worth believing in. But there is at least one thing they should believe, namely that there is a community of Jesus that places itself *before* the souls of those who have been entrusted to it and proclaims to the world what is happening here in the name of Christianity and human rights.
>
> I see how in the name of denazification it is not the guilty that are punished and not justice that is helped to victory, but injustice and arbitrariness. I see

how the tormented nation (in a *new* surge of madness and bitterness) invokes the names of its former rulers and begins to wonder in grief-stricken scorn whether they had not been *right* when they had prophesied nothing but hate and destruction, whether they had not been the nation's true friends *after all* when they had called upon it to fight until final victory had been won or the nation itself had perished.

What has happened among us in the name of denazification is not only unjust, it is murder of the soul and of faith. It has not only led to families standing despairingly before an *earthly* void, but has also caused the void of *eternity* to gape open before human beings, because it threatens to shatter their faith that a heavenly Father could have anything to do with this insane pandemonium.

I also think of what is happening in the east of our country, where inhumanity reigns. I think of the secret abduction of living human beings in the dead of night, of the robbery of all possibilities of economic existence, the dismantling of machines and the dismantling of the German intelligentsia.

Perhaps I might have remained silent about all this if those who are doing it, together with their German henchmen, had said that they had come in the name of vengeance. Then our young people would have seen just where lawlessness and godlessness and the awful law of response and retaliation lead. Then we would have to submit silently to God's dreadful rod.

But, of course, they did not say that they had come in the name of vengeance, but solemnly announced that they had come in the spirit of Christianity and humanity. At least our former rulers were honest enough not to use the image of the Crucified Christ but the "blond beast" as their emblem. For this reason we, as a community of Jesus, must stand before the desecrated image of Our Lord, as some of us also at least tried to do in the Third Reich. We must *also* stand before the youth of our nation whose disappointed faith in the justice of the victors is destroying their faith in the Christianity in whose name the victors claimed to have come. And whoever has heard the voices that whisper in secret, whoever has traveled by night in the darkened trains where people converse without fear of recognition, that person knows that on top of all this there is the danger of a *large-scale renazification* taking the place of the denazification we have all been hoping for.

An English reporter wrote in the newspaper *Neue Zeitung* that the most distressing statement he had heard on his journey through Germany was the imploring cry of a young student, "For God's sake don't turn us into Nazis again!"

Someone has to stand up and shout this all out so that it may never again be said that the Church kept silent, that the Church was implicated in the murder of souls and through its silence had crucified Christ anew.

The effect of this sermon was indescribable. Outside, I was surrounded by a crowd of people, many were sobbing, many were worried for my safety, although this turned out to be completely unnecessary. In this respect we were all still living to some extent in the past, when speeches of this kind would have cost the speaker life and limb. Liesel had not needed to pack anything. Nobody laid so much as a finger upon me.

Scarcely had I arrived home when an army officer came to demand the manuscript from me. It was immediately translated and flown to General Clay, who was supposed to decide what was to happen to me. As I learned later, his answer was a simple "nothing." That *too* could be regarded as a way of dissociating oneself from my accusations.

The sermon was published in many foreign newspapers, including in the United States and England. The British publisher and author Victor Gollancz wrote me a letter expressing his approval of what I had said and assured me that he would do his best to circulate the sermon. His name was held in high regard by us. Although of Jewish origin, he publicly supported reconciliation with Germany and made a clear distinction between the Germans and the Nazis.

In Germany, including in the camps, the sermon was reduplicated countless times. A wealth of letters reached me from everywhere, several hundred in number. A small number of them thanked me for freeing their conscience, and enabling it to begin on a new path. A further small number of letters chided me for being an opportunist who was attempting to swim on the waves of a rising nationalism and who had betrayed his priestly office. The largest number of letters, however, thanked me in a way that gave me quite a shock. The people who had written them had not grasped my own moral dilemma and had overlooked my religious motives. They had merely heard aggressive statements against the Allies. The author Hans Grimm, who had specialized in books on the theme of "a nation without *Lebensraum*,"* wrote to me from Lippoldsberg, "You spoke as a brave German man. The liturgical section of your sermon was of no interest to me."

So the undertaking ended in some serious moral dilemmas. Had it been right that I for my part had now hardened the attitudes of many people again? But if one did not accept this danger, would it then still be possible to open one's mouth *at all*? A few people had indeed been helped by what I had said,

---

* Literally "living space." The Nazi doctrine that the German nation had insufficient space in which to live and therefore needed to expand into other territories (primarily eastwards, i.e. Poland, Russia). *Translator's note.*

however. And did not the New Testament saying also hold good here that there is more joy over the *one* sinner who repents than over ninety-nine righteous persons, *the* ninety-nine persons, that is, that make use of everything and anything in order to suck the poison of self-righteousness out of the Christian message? Once again I realized how dubious all human undertakings are, how dubious too the undertaking of theology is. It again became clear to me how little we know our own hearts and how little we can control the hearts of others, and that we consequently have to entrust everything to the judgement and grace of One who is higher than we.

All this depressed me more than the fits of rage and hatred that reached me from what had once been the Confessing Church. With a laugh that was not completely free of bitterness, I said to my friends, "I'm sitting between two stools—but under the protection of the Most High." I corresponded at length about the sermon with one of my main opponents, Hermann Diem, whom I greatly respected. This correspondence was published together with the sermon under the title of *Die Schuld der Andern* ('The Guilt of the Others') in a much-read and discussed booklet.

As a result of the mediation of the American military government I had been invited to visit the United States, a visit which was to include an extensive sightseeing program. After my long ghetto existence I was naturally very happy at this prospect.

Not long after Easter, however, I received a letter from the American military government regretfully informing me that my trip to America would have to be canceled for financial reasons. It did not call for much imagination to guess that this cancelation was connected with my Good Friday sermon. So I was all the more astonished when an American officer from the military government's staff visited me in Tübingen immediately afterwards in order to reveal the following to me: his conscience as a Christian, he said, compelled him to admit that the Americans had not told the truth. However, they had not been officially permitted to inform me of the true reason for the cancelation of the trip, namely the Good Friday sermon. He asked for my understanding that the army could not possibly have allowed me to travel to the United States. The sermon had circulated in the American press and would have resulted in reporters immediately pouncing on me in order to elicit further examples of dubious behavior on the part of the occupying power. He sked me to take their predicament into consideration. He, however, had found it unbearable to conceal the voice of his own conscience from a man who had allowed his conscience to speak. Whenever I was asked (during my later visits to the United States) about the behavior of the American occupying power, I always mentioned this officer. He remained for me a symbol of American Christendom, which I have since encountered in many other impressive figures.

The Founding of the Protestant Academy at Bad Boll

In the middle of the war, and stimulated by the forward-looking plans of our Freiburg resistance circle for the future peace, I had pondered on a project that I felt to be of great importance for the time *after* the downfall of National Socialism. I wanted to develop some of the things that had made a positive impression on me in our Lecturers' Academy in Kiel, such as, for example, cooperation between different faculties. Indeed, I wanted this cooperation not only to take the form of interfaculty discussions, but also to become a long-term relationship at conferences lasting days or even weeks. Could what had taken place at Kiel for *ideological* purposes not be employed in a *Christian* context to establish a completely new way of proclaiming the Gospel and create a community capable of exerting a formative influence on people?

I wrote a study on the feasibility of such an academy, which I submitted to the Württemberg church leadership in October 1942 and which was openly welcomed by Bishop Wurm. It was entitled, "Plan for a Protestant Academy." Its basic ideas were concentrated in three points.

First, the Church will be confronted with the task of filling the intellectual vacuum that will arise after the war. It is important for the renewal of the Christian message to show that the Gospel not only affects the human being's inner self but it is also relevant for *all* areas of life and culture. Only in this way will it become clear that the Gospel is directed at the *whole* person.

Second, to this end all the individual professions should be called together to conferences lasting several days and thereby gain experience of the nature of Christian community in a *vita communis*.

Third, the Christian character of the academy should find expression not only in the theological basis of what is offered but also in church services and meditations, the relevance of which to the theme of the conference must be clearly recognizable. This forms the basis of my aim to make the Gospel the foundation of a framework for helping people to deal with life's problems, a framework which although organized according to profession is nevertheless at the same time universal in scope. This framework could lead the Church's message out of the ghetto in which it is frequently observed to exist and, by considering factual questions central to those professions, clearly show the breadth of the Christian spectrum.

Of all the things I have thought up, this idea of a Protestant Academy certainly had the most far-reaching consequences. The first academy was founded in the first years after the war at Bad Boll and became the primordial cell for subsidiary foundations in the individual German states, and later also abroad (for example, in the United States and Japan). Very soon this idea was also taken up by the Catholics, who founded a number of analogous and sometimes impressive institutes.

It would nevertheless be presumptuous of me to do as some people occasionally did and describe myself as the "father of the Protestant Academies." I was far too inept in practical matters to bring such a plan to fruition. The great "doer" who succeeded in actually getting the academy of Bad Boll built and who was also the driving force behind the founding of other academies all over the world was Eberhard Müller. When I met him immediately after my appointment to my chair at Tübingen, it emerged that his thoughts were proceeding along similar lines to mine, and we set to work without delay. My contribution consisted above all in giving keynote speeches at the opening of the Bad Boll Academy and at the first conferences there and later at Hermannsburg (from which the academy in Loccum developed).

During my involvement with the academy I learned a lot about Eberhard Müller's skill at putting ideas into practice. He did not think very highly of enlisting church institutions for such projects, as I had naively done, but employed the strategy of setting up at *one* place a credible model that would encourage imitation. By means of his circumspection and vigor, he succeeded in getting the spa rooms at Bad Boll placed at his disposal and furnished them to suit our requirements. He also took advantage of the side effects of denazification, namely that primary and secondary school teachers as well as government officials and doctors were for the time being unemployed. By means of some impressive looking programs he had had printed (heaven knows how he got hold of the paper!), he called these people together to conferences that in the early days of the academy often lasted longer than a week. For these people the conferences meant not only receiving assistance in orienting themselves in their profession—especially since Müller knew how to acquire top-class speakers—but also receiving pastoral help, which gave them fresh heart.

Today, when I look back on those first days of the academy, it is not without some melancholy. Although its work did indeed flourish in later decades as far as outward appearances were concerned, it often succumbed all too willingly to the prevailing spirit of the age, and sometimes the conferences were determined more by new sociological and various other ideologies than by the Gospel. However, the basic idea that the Church should provide neutral ground for people and social groups that are often at loggerheads with each other—such as, for instance, unions and employers—and enable them to meet on a human level, continues to retain its promise.

Calls to Other Chairs

During this period, Ethelbert Stauffer, the dean of the theology faculty at Bonn, urgently asked me accept a professorship there. The reason behind this request was the worry that Karl Barth might return to his old domain and that a monocracy of his school could then come about. Consequently, attempts were being made to acquire some other colors for the faculty's palette. The corrective function expected of me was not able, however, to tempt me seriously away from my Tübingen job.

The decision was far more difficult, however, when I was offered a chair at Heidelberg. The letter I received from the ministry of education referred to my earlier work at Heidelberg and was written in an urgent and appreciative tone. Some of my closest theological friends were working in Heidelberg, such as Hans von Campenhausen, Martin Dibelius, Ludwig Hölscher, Edmund Schlink, Günter Bornkamm, and Gerhard Rosenkranz. Gerhard von Rad was also expected to join the faculty. That was a glittering battery of names which scarcely any other faculty in Germany could match. They all supported the ministry's offer with "love" letters. Schlink visited me in Tübingen in order to emphasize how much our mutual friends wished to have me in Heidelberg. I was pulled towards them with every fiber of my being. In Heidelberg, I would also find the academic cooperation I so painfully missed in Tübingen.

It was clear to me from the outset that I could not leave Tübingen without the blessing of my great benefactor, the Bishop of Württemberg. And once again he proved his noble, chivalrous cast of mind in his willingness to let me go. He also intimated, however, how difficult he would find my departure. Back in the days when he was the only person prepared to offer me a home in his church, he had reckoned with and hoped that I would one day in the future play a role in the training of his clergy. In the end, I could not overcome the feeling that this old man, who was so dear to me, might regard me as ungrateful, and so I declined the Heidelberg offer. My colleagues at Heidelberg understood my decision and even embarrassed me by awarding me an honorary doctorate and presenting me with a particularly ceremonial diploma. My decision to remain was also made easier by some indications that I had in fact put down deeper roots in Tübingen than I had realized: the university and the faculty, indeed even the French authorities—with whom I had reckoned least of all!—urged me to stay. The students organized a torchlight procession and declared to me their devotion with touching words.

A Kaleidoscope of Lecture Tours and Other Journeys

I have already mentioned that I was often away during my Tübingen years. Because of the obstacles arising from the contemporary situation, such trips certainly led to some overexertion on my part. At the same time, however, the new sense of freedom after the long period of ghetto existence was a delight that compensated for many difficulties. In view of the wealth of experiences I had during this period, I will content myself with describing a few highlights. These descriptions are above all intended to touch upon experiences that were of personal importance to me, and also to sketch some of the curious experiences I had.

In February 1946 I was asked to lead a church service to commemorate the opening of the Stuttgart College of Technology as well as the Academy of Art and the College of Music. The only building that came into consideration for this was the Catholic Church in König Street, which was to a certain extent available for use again. But even here the craftsmen still had to work right up until the last moment, so that we had to wait almost a full hour before we could enter. As a result, about five hundred students and professors together with various guests of honor were forced to stand in the square in front of the church, which was strewn with boulders and surrounded by large mountains of rubble. For lack of a sacristy, I put my cassock on in the middle of the group of professors. It was rather cold outside, and after we had been waiting for some time, I felt the call of nature. This was a call I wished to respond to before the service, especially since I felt that the removal of this need would assist the spontaneity of my sermon. So I called the verger over and asked him, "Is there anywhere here where I can spend a penny?" When he merely replied that he would have a look around for me, I realized that this was going to be rather difficult. I had already come to terms with this fact when I spotted the good man on a reconnaissance expedition, which consisted of peering behind all the mountains of rubble. When he was on the hill furthest away from us he put his hands to his mouth and shouted at the top of his voice, "Professor!" At this all hundred professors looked up at him and all five hundred students looked at the professors. Waving his arms to make clear that it was me he wanted, he cried, "I mean Professor Thielicke!" At this all the students and the hundred professors and guests of honor turned to look at me, while I, with a sense of foreboding, did all I could to get the distant scout to stop what I feared he was about to do. But it was too late. Again using his hands as a megaphone, he shouted in the same stentorian voice, "Is it big jobs or little jobs?" After that I had great difficulty steering the amused assembly back to liturgical matters.

During another lecture tour, one of the places at which I gave a lecture was Kassel, where I was very much looking forward to meeting Paeckelmann again, my old headmaster at Barmen grammar school. This teacher, whom we boys had once so idolized, was now in charge of a grammar school there. I immediately spotted his white hair in the midst of the crowd. His presence spurred me on and I sometimes had the feeling that I was speaking just for him. He invited me to go for a walk with him on the following morning. In a corner of my heart I harbored the expectation that this special and respected person from my youth would now express his joy that something quite reasonable had become of me. Instead I received a completely unexpected cold shower. "For whose sake were you getting so worked up in your sermon? What were you hoping to achieve by it?" he asked me with a curtness that was unusual for him. I bashfully replied that I was not doing it for any tactical reasons! If I had become a little high-spirited, I said, it was probably because I had been carried away by my "subject." Was I then not permitted to give way this? But this did not cut any ice with him. "What you call high spirits," he said, "is sometimes completely uncontrolled emotionality. The content, tone, and gestures of your speech can diverge so widely from the subject that your sermons are on the point of becoming unbearable. When you yesterday quoted Jesus' saying, 'Come to me, all who labor and are heavily laden,' you raised your fist in a threatening gesture and bellowed the saying out. That is completely inappropriate for this quiet and comforting invitation from Our Lord!"

I had already had to take a fair amount of criticism in my life, both justified and unjustified; but nobody had ever spoken to me in this way before. In a flash I realized that he was right; and because he meant well, I was also capable of accepting such criticism. The rapt attention of the crowded audience occasionally—and not only in Kassel!—sent me into a sort of euphoria. I had, without realizing it, been enjoying my rhetorical power. That was a diabolical temptation. I am still grateful today to my old teacher for not letting himself be impressed by my torrent of words. His criticism had the long-term effect of producing a heightened degree of self-control on my part. Since then I have not "let myself go" quite so easily when speaking (as far as I can judge).

A Visit to Barth's Studio

When I once had to give a series of lectures in the Ecumenical Institute at Château de Bossey near Geneva, I decided to make a detour to Basel and visit Karl Barth. I inquired first whether he would indeed welcome such a visit, for our relationship had after all been rather strained. He had of course read the press reports concerning my reply to his Tübingen lecture and naturally also knew of my Good Friday sermon, which he could not possibly have liked. And to cap it all, I had come out strongly against Niemöller in a lengthy newspaper article which I had simultaneously read out on various radio programs, including twice on Radio Beromünster. Above all I had criticized the negative effect of Niemöller's concept of collective guilt and also some of his slanderous statements about the German nation. This had caused storms of protest in the press and had prompted many abusive letters, but had also given rise to a flood of letters of approval. Since Niemöller was constantly referring to Barth, and moreover was close friends with him, my attack on Niemöller must doubtless have caused Barth some annoyance.

Much to my surprise, however, I was given a friendly welcome, invited to have a cup of black coffee, and despite all my attempts to leave, was constantly asked to stay. In all, I remained at his home in 25 Pilger Street for three-and-a-half hours. When I entered his study, I announced in military fashion, "Helmut Thielicke reporting for a dressing-down!" He declined to take advantage of this and assured me that he wanted to "remain like a bear in his cave" and just listen to my explanations of my behavior. First of all, however, he wished to inform me of all that he had said against me in order to "get things straight" and to give me the opportunity to reply. While he was doing this, it emerged that he had not only carefully read all my pronounce-ments, but had also questioned Tübingen students about me who were studying under him at Basel for a semester. Sometimes, he said, he had been angry with me, but then had thought to himself, especially after he had heard the students' reports, "Confound it! Thielicke is a man with a sense of humor," and someone with a sense of humor was always popular with him.

Referring to my statements on contemporary issues, he then asked me "Who gave you the right to pontificate on world affairs?" In his opinion, I was interfering in far too many things and was condescending in the manner in which I castigated people of merit and reputation like Niemöller. He too, Barth said, by no means took an uncritical attitude towards Niemöller and was often annoyed at the rashness and exaggerated aggressiveness of many of his formulations. "Perhaps you're still extremely young at heart," he said. And then with that mischievous smile that had so endeared him to us when we were students, he said, "You even occasionally indulge in youthful pranks. But now you're a professor and a doctor of theology. You ought now to begin to mature a little and to keep out of day-to-day struggles a little more. From now on, concentrate rather on developing a decent theology! That's what I'm doing."

We got onto the subject of our fundamental theological differences, dealing above all with the distinction between law and gospel and the Lutheran two kingdoms doctrine. This was then followed by a sharp and trenchant discussion. When the conversation turned to war, he confessed that he enjoyed playing with tin soldiers and could still reconstruct the battles of Königgrätz and Sedan down to the finest detail. In discussions about the Prussians (to whom he was certainly not favorably disposed) he occasionally bewildered his opponents by serving them up with his specialized knowledge of the history of war. He placated at a stroke a young German aristocrat in top boots who had called round to give him a telling-off, by asking him, "Wasn't one of your ancestors a general under Frederick William II?"

Barth's interest was particularly aroused when our conversations turned to persons who were important to him but whose development he disapproved of. One of these persons was Georg Merz, one of the cofounders of dialectical theology and former editor of the journal *Zwischen den Zeiten*, which in its heyday was a highly influential organ of the Barth school. "I just do not understand the path he has taken," he said sorrowfully. "Earlier, he was one of my most important people, but later unfortunately lacked a clear line in the struggle between Church and state. He is now a vehement Lutheran of the sort I dislike. Do *you* understand this?"

"I believe I do," I replied. "Merz is a magician when it comes to anecdotes. How often he used to enchant us all with his storytelling gifts! How vivid even great historical figures would become when he described their everyday lives! Now when one understands a man 'anecdotally,' that is, from below, from the perspective of his environment and chthonic roots, he then appears to be largely conditioned by his environment. When Merz is in the presence of Karl Barth, or in much earlier days also in that of Emil Brunner and Friedrich Gogarten, he is different from when he is living in the theological atmosphere of Neuendettelsau or working as a Lutheran dean in Würzburg. There is a touch of relativism about him and he may appear to be like a chameleon to some people. Such cases are not necessarily the result of weakness of character. That at any rate is how I explain the fact that Georg Merz once accompanied you on your daring attacks on a trite cultural protestantism, and yet now strolls with measured liturgical steps through the streets of Würzburg wearing a large black hat and a Lutheran frock coat." Barth laughed in agreement at this portrait of Merz and immediately repeated it to his assistant Charlotte von Kirschbaum when she looked in.

Everything that I felt was great and endearing about Karl Barth touched me during my visit in concentrated form, as it were. Despite finding much of his theology alien to me, despite the many critical things I have constantly written about it, I have nevertheless always received it eagerly right up to the present day. In contrast to the derivativeness and indirectness of many contemporary productions, I sensed an original tone in his works, a tone which constantly captivated me anew. In a later letter I wrote that, in contrast to the often "decayed countenance of theology," *his* theological thinking always showed "a freshly washed, laughing face, and one would not miss for the world even the freckles that the likes of us find fault with."

Since that afternoon in Basel, and all the more so since his lifelong theological companion Eduard Thurneysen deemed me worthy of his friendship and awoke Karl Barth's interest in my works on dogmatics and ethics, our relationship remained relaxed, and greetings repeatedly traveled back and forth between Hamburg and Basel.

Further Curious Events in the First Postwar Years

My visit to Karl Barth, which took place in the early part of my Tübingen period prior to the currency reform, was preceded by a trip to Switzerland in 1947. I put this in here because it is an interesting example of contemporary history. It shows the truly grotesque fuss and bother to which Germans were subjected in those days whenever they traveled abroad.

As early as 1946, my wife and I received an invitation from the Swiss

Church to come for a holiday, which in those days was a sensation. It took almost a whole year of red tape and alternately being given and then refused permission before the French were at last prepared to issue me with an exit visa. In the meantime, Liesel was expecting our daughter Elisabeth, which forced her to remain at home. Her mouth watered when I described the fantastic menus at my hotel in Heiligenschwendi.

Before I reached my holiday accommodation in the land of the Phaeacians, however, I still had to survive a small odyssey. Because of the overcrowded trains, it was a great adventure to set off on a journey with a rather cumbersome suitcase in those days. If the only way to get into a compartment was through the window, it sometimes happened that somebody would whip one's shoes off one's feet while one was getting in. For this reason, I got a student to accompany me as far as the border. He was a sportsman and was able to swing himself elegantly through the window. He then had me hand him my hulking great suitcase, and immediately pulled me in after it. He had to leave me when we reached Lörrach.

Because at that time hardly any Germans were allowed to cross the border, I suddenly found myself alone in the compartment with a friendly Swiss. He was obviously dying to know how it was possible for me to travel to Switzerland. I replied to his question by briefly explaining the whys and wherefores. He then immediately brought the conversation round to my money problems. The worthless reichsmark was not legal tender in Switzerland and could not be used. "How do you hope to get on over there with no money?" he asked, full of concern. "I'm going to be picked up in Basel; my friends have given me a firm promise to meet me," I replied. "But what will you do if they *don't* pick you up?" he continued. "But they *will* pick me up," I replied. The good man did not give up, however, and said that one ought always to be prepared for the worst; I ought at least to have some money for the telephone, otherwise I could end up standing around helplessly in the railway station. Having said this, he kindly forced a Swiss franc upon me, which he had divided up into ten centime coins so that I could use them for the telephone. I felt almost like a capitalist with all this money.

And look what happened! Mr. Jent, with whom I was later to become good friends, was *not* on the platform. Some stupid misunderstanding must have been behind this hitch. After anxiously waiting and keeping a look-out for some time, I tried to telephone my host, but in vain. After that, I dialed the names of members of the theology faculty that I knew. They were all on holiday. The awful thing was that on each occasion some helpful soul picked up the receiver so that my centimes rapidly dwindled and I eventually had only one left. After saying a quick prayer I dialed one more time and—lo and behold!—was answered by the son of the church historian, Ernst Staehelin, whose guest I had once been before the war. He collected me and took me to his parents' cultured house. When I wandered through the streets of Basel in the evenings and saw the full shop windows and let the stream of well-groomed and relaxed people pass me by, I was overwhelmed. At the same time, I thought sadly of the wretched conditions back home. Would our devastated cities ever again be rebuilt? Would we ever get out of the Balkanization of our once-so-cultured land? I can still remember that I did not sleep a wink during my first night in Switzerland because the contrast of images prevented me from settling down.

When I then traveled back to Germany after several wonderful, refreshing, high-calorie weeks that were interrupted only by invitations to visit the editorial offices of the *Zürcher Weltwoche* and to meet Emil Brunner, my student again collected me at the border. We had to break the journey somewhere, and ended up spending the night swapping stories in the study of a clergyman who had kindly taken us in. During our stay we drank the complete contents of one of my cans of Nescafé and threw it out of the window onto the street, which is something one should never do. Heaven's punishment overtook me immediately, for I had inadvertently picked up the full can, with which I was hoping to surprise Liesel, and kept the empty one. But the good luck I had at the border compensated for this misfortune. In those days, one was permitted to take only a hundred grams of tobacco into the country. I, however, had a kilogram in my wooden suitcase and thus awaited the customs examination with some anxiety. My fellow passengers in the coupé replied to the customs officer's question by declaring the permitted quantity of tobacco. Despite this, their luggage was searched with mistrustful meticulousness. My heart sank while this was going on; and when I was then asked whether I had anything to declare, I replied without any hope of getting away with it, "A kilogram of tobacco." "If only that were true," replied the customs officer with a laugh and let me off having my luggage searched. He even said goodbye to me in a friendly tone before going to the next compartment. "Is that really true? Have you really got a kilogram?" one of my fellow travelers asked in astonishment. "It certainly is," I replied. "One whole kilogram! Honesty as cunning—I can recommend it."

Another experience typical of that age happened to me when I had to give a lecture at the "Wittheit," a respected educational forum in the city of Bremen. That must have been around 1946. When after a tiring journey (my tour had already taken me to several towns) I left Bremen railway station, the first thing I saw was the lively bustle of the "Freimarkt," a very popular fair, rich in tradition. While I was enjoying this sight, I spotted a roller coaster. Roller coasters had always been a passion of mine and were something that I had had to do without for a good seven years. This was something I could not possibly allow myself to miss. I bought myself a card immediately and dragged my two suitcases to a car with the intention of taking them on the ride with me. In those days, it was extremely risky to let such possessions out of one's sight. Hardly had the boss of the business spotted me loading the suitcases when he rushed over and made clear in a most impolite manner his desire to fetch them down again. It "simply was not done," he said. Even my offer to pay double the fare made no impression upon him. The suitcases were extremely "hazardous to other passengers," he said; they could fly out and kill someone. But I remained obdurate, even when my fellow passengers gradually adopted a threatening attitude because of the delay. Because it had in the meantime become clear to the man that he was not going to make any headway with me, he finally reluctantly gave in and lashed up my suitcases, swearing profusely. The delightful ride could begin at last.

There is another reminiscence I would like to relate, namely, that of a lecture tour to Sweden, Norway, and Finland. Because I did not know whether and how my services would be paid for in Sweden, Liesel declined to accompany me to the paradise of a land untouched by war, despite the fact that she longed to see foreign climes. The thought of possibly living at the expense of foreign hosts as a "poor German" was unbearable to her. So she sadly remained behind. However, when I was in Sweden, I completely unexpectedly received fees that seemed fabulously high to me in those days. But I did not know what to do with the money. I was not allowed to take it with me and I was not allowed to take through customs the various beautiful things I had long been forced to do without. When I then received telegrams inviting me to speak to the faculties at Åbo and Helsinki, I decided to get rid of my money by at least booking a first-class cabin for the crossing. Then a new telegram arrived, informing me that a first-class place had already been paid for and that I would again receive a fee in Finland. For the first and only time in my life, I was at my wits' end because I had too much money. A cow with an overfull udder must have a similar feeling when nobody milks her.

On board the ship I then met a group of European students from various countries who were traveling economy class. I had a very nice conversation with them and suddenly had an idea of how I could get rid of my money. I invited them all to dinner and saw with pleasure how they pounced upon the sumptuous wealth of the smörgåsbord. Time and again I overheard expressions of astonishment that a German of all people was their host; after all, the students said, the Germans themselves had nothing. I did not, however, explain to them how this all hung together.

One of the most impressive journeys I made from Tübingen took me to the recently founded Free University of Berlin, where I was to hold a series of lectures lasting several weeks. We professors, who were given excellent accommodation in the university's guest house and met every evening for extremely lively conversations (I will in particular never forget my meeting with Paul Hindemith), were received with effusive gratitude by the rector and above all by the students and invited to many of their groups. There was no other place where the students regarded the new university as "their" affair as passionately as these did. They swarmed out all over the world and gathered books for the library in rucksacks and suitcases from second-hand bookshops and retired people. Precisely their commitment to this intellectual fortress of the isolated island that was Berlin played an essential role in their being granted a far greater right of participation in university affairs than was usual in the constitution of a university. The later student revolts started, of course, at the Free University, and exploded in an unprecedented intimidation of unpopular professors, in destructive mania and offensive graffiti. During these revolts I often had to think back to this period of "first love," when no one could have suspected how these student privileges would be so abused two decades later.

I held my lectures in cinemas and theaters, for there were not yet any normal lecture halls. Although the students had to travel long distances to their lectures, their intellectual hunger was so great that they everywhere flocked together in crowds and were constantly requesting additional talks in both small and large groups. Precisely their isolation and the constant threat to Berlin caused a sense of community to spring up between teachers and students that was unknown in the later period of affluent gluttony and in the overfilled universities and restricted entry we know today.

I was also received with effusive gratitude and found a receptive audience—like all visitors from the West—on my repeated visits to East Germany, where I preached and taught in Leipzig (in the Church of St. Thomas), Dresden, Cottbus, and other cities. Large numbers of people came, many approaching me about my books, which they knew from their captivity and were now reading together in all sorts of reading groups.

These trips came to an abrupt end when I undertook a theological analysis of Marxist-Leninist anthropology in my lectures in the early sixties at Leipzig and Jena. These lectures, I was told, met with great approval despite the many Marxists in the audience. On top of this, unequivocal agreement, often expressed in spirited terms, was loudly voiced in the ensuing discussions, during which the Marxists remained silent. After that, I was no longer allowed to set foot on East German territory (at least not until I had reached "retirement age," and even then was only once permitted to make a private visit). I was regarded as *persona non grata* and was subjected to disparaging and often slanderous polemical attacks in the press and on the radio, something that was later taken over by the leaflets of the extraparliamentary opposition. I was even granted the honor of being taken to task in a few books belonging to the corpus of official Communist literature. Parcels containing my books were constantly being intercepted by the censors, and either were sent back to the sender or simply disappeared. Despite this, adventurous methods were constantly being found to smuggle the books into the country.

Rector of Tübingen University and President of the Conference of Rectors

In 1951, the first volume of my *Theological Ethics* was published. The fact that I had managed to complete this first stage of what I had planned to be an extensive work despite all my other burdens gave me the inner freedom to respond positively to the inquiry about whether I would be willing to head the university. Nevertheless, I made clear from the outset that I was only prepared to interrupt my academic work for *one* year and would not consent to be elected for a second year. Quite a few people never found their way back to their desks after several years of this kind of managerial work, and afterwards often got bogged down in all sorts of honorary posts on various committees. Although my deanship already took up a good deal of my time, I did not shy away from assuming the rectorship for such a *limited* period.

The period leading up to my election was rather complicated and even delicate. It was not, in fact, my faculty's turn, but the turn of the science faculty to provide the rector. The honorable colleague they presented, however, was, for reasons that need play no role here, not very popular among the general academic staff and met with considerable resistance. I received numerous requests from the other faculties to stand as a rival candidate. This was an awkward situation because quarrels of this kind were quite unusual between faculties in Tübingen. My faculty, which was subjected to similar pressure, was unanimous in its willingness to present me as a candidate; I requested them to keep a low profile—as I myself also did—and to let things take their course. On February 15, 1951, the University Senate then elected me to the rectorship "out of turn" with an absolute majority in the first ballot. The defeated candidate's behavior was irreproachable and his loyalty, like that of his faculty, was unsurpassed during the whole year of my rectorship. I was very pleased to discover on this occasion how much both the university and the town had in the meantime become home to me.

I used the interval prior to assuming office to make inaugural visits to the leading personalities of the state, above all to politicians and men of industry and commerce. When Wilhelm Haspel, the president of Daimler-Benz, saw my ancient official car, he immediately presented me with a brand-new model for use in my post. I intimated to a few industrialists that I felt that it was important to establish a trust, which would make me independent of state and consequently taxpayers' money, and which would give me the freedom to make use of the money as I wished. These gentlemen were very sensitive to such hints and provided me with a great deal of such money. When I craftily hinted at the sum I had received from Mr. X or Mr. Y, the next person would want to splash out and if possible outdo his predecessors.

This fund came in very useful during my rectorship. I was able liberally to arrange meetings with students and colleagues, to put them at ease by giving them a meal, and thereby facilitate many negotiations that were in danger of becoming all too deadly serious. I was even able to come to the assistance of our glider pilots by helping them to buy an aircraft. As a sign of their gratitude, the pilots allowed our two elder boys together with their parents to sail through the skies. The boys were so taken with this that they themselves later became glider pilots.

Above all, however, these financial reserves enabled me to realize a special favorite idea of mine, which I will now describe.

In those days, provision for up-and-coming academics was not yet as generous as it is today. They came up out of the corps of assistants, of whom there were, however, only a very few. In contrast to today, where every professorship, even in the humanities, is endowed with at least one and usually several assistants, such an arrangement was in those days rather the exception than the rule. We had to eliminate this deficiency, I thought, by undertaking to support young academics. Because the state was over-stretched at that time, I kept a lookout for ways and means of hurrying things along on my own initiative. To this end, I arranged so-called university days throughout the state during my year as rector, and on each occasion took two renowned colleagues with me. My friend, the educationalist Hans Wenke, regularly took part. He possessed the special gift of being able to speak in a way that was intelligible to the general public.

The often rather small towns we visited as representatives of the state university and where we sought to bring the university closer to the people, felt honored by our presence and rewarded us with a good response. I got the mayor of each town to give me the names of the most important firms in the area and then invited their representatives to a reception. I had money, after all! At these receptions, I outlined my plan to them that both the business world and the towns should endow us with assistantships and lectureships in order to remedy the (graphically described!) crisis facing the rising generation of academics. As part of the plan, I introduced the idea of "sponsorships," which were also intended to establish closer contacts between the donors and the young academics they were sponsoring. I experienced the joy of being able to gain a considerable number of such sponsorships for the university. Once the beginning had been made in this way, the state government later took on increasing responsibility for this key problem facing the university.

The "enthronement" ceremony was a glittering event in accordance with the tradition of this ancient, nearly five-hundred-year-old alma mater. Two beadles wearing ceremonial dress and carrying the ancient sceptres of the university marched before the two columns of professors, whose gowns were the descendants of an ancient monastic habit. (In the name of "democracy," all this was later rather shabbily abolished.) Music accompanied this procession. The magnificent room did the rest to lend splendor to the occasion. Many friends had come from far and wide. I was especially moved by the fact that my elderly parents and Bishop Wurm were also present.

For my inaugural address I had chosen a socioethical subject that I felt would also be of relevance to the other disciplines, namely "Man and Work in the Technological Age, Industrial Rationalization as a Problem of Humanity." The chain of office that was placed around my neck had been worn by the kings of Württemberg whenever they had appeared as rector magnificus at ceremonial functions at the university. It was made of pure gold.

It was a *wonderful* post that I now had to occupy in my venerable office with its old furniture and paintings. The rectorship was also deeply rooted in the consciousness of the population. We were amused when even the butcher offered to deliver his meat personally to "His Magnificence's" door. Miss Becker, who came from Transylvania, worked in the outer office. She gave the "rector babies," as she affectionately called the first-year students, their first tips and, with a great air of secrecy, enlightened them as to the personal secrets of the university staff. She was also an affectionate Cerberus (there is such a thing, although I also would not have believed it prior to meeting her) who, with infallible instinct, was able to distinguish between unwelcome visitors, whom she ushered out relentlessly but with charming politeness, and people who had come about a serious matter. Having said this, there was admittedly one occasion on which her instinct failed her. This was when she not only let a confidence trickster in to see me but, because he had made a profound impression upon her, even recommended him to me in glowing terms. When the police appeared on the following day and made inquiries about him, she regarded it as a personal failure and was scarcely amenable to conversation for several days afterwards.

How varied this post was! When I later once again had to assume this office at Hamburg University, it was very much more down-to-earth in that quieter age and in the larger dimensions of that cosmopolitan city. At the end of my period in office I sang the praises of the rectorship in my speech summing up the year's results as follows: "The rector has to watch over the spirit of the university and at the same time be able to deal with an impoverished man wishing to sell his body to the anatomy department. He has to represent the university to the outside world—often in a ceremonial context—and at the same time has to look after our colleagues from the East who suddenly turn up penniless in his waiting room. To experience all this in major and minor decisions, to urge on the hesitant authorities, to guide the sometimes lively discussions in the various committees, to keep one's nerve as the troubles mount up and to talk politely to the other committee members, to be a paterfamilias to the personnel and a good friend to the students—all this goes to make up the burden but also the magic of this rich and lively post."

One of my officials, who among other things was responsible for drafting the rector's letters of condolence, assured me of his special loyalty right at the beginning of my rectorship. Although he was himself an atheist, he said, since his boss was now a theologian, he would use expressly *Christian* phraseology during my period of office. I was happy to do without this service, however, and wrote my letters of sympathy myself. I generally endeavored to give all my announcements a personal touch. I also sought to write my numerous speeches myself and not simply to read what somebody else had written for me; I tried not to bore my audience and also did my best to give the people a good laugh. This resulted in a great deal of work, but it was worth it. At the same time I resolved always to reveal myself in a unobtrusive way as a theologian when making my speeches.

I was unfortunately rather weak with regard to economic questions and had to rely on my advisers, above all on the loyal senior university official, Balbach. He and the others, however, soon discovered my weakness and were sometimes unable completely to suppress a certain feeling of superiority. Nevertheless, I once managed to impress them despite my lack of talent in this area. This came about as follows.

It was just not possible to obtain coal to heat the university and its many institutions for the winter of 1951–52. When my advisers conveyed this to me with great concern, I simply replied, "I'll arrange for a few goods wagons to bring some coal." This was naturally regarded as an expression of extreme unworldliness, as was clearly indicated by the embarrassed looks I received. A tactful attempt was then made to pass quickly over this to another subject. Shortly afterwards, however, the wagons arrived and the university was more snug and warm than it had been for years. Of course, I had to disclose my secret when my advisers turned up at my office full of remorse at having doubted me. The background to my success was that a year previously I had given a lecture to the management of the German coal-mining industry and had got to know the leading figures well. When I then informed them of my foolhardy promise and implored them not to make a fool of me, they sent a train loaded with coal to Tübingen without delay.

One of my most important official duties was to prepare the agenda for the monthly meetings of the University Senate and to act as chairman. The University Senate, which comprised all full and emeritus professors together with representatives of the nonprofessorial members of the university, was an assembly vested with considerable powers. I loved this institution, if only because it included most of the academic staff and thus brought its members into close contact with one another; each person got to know his colleagues from the other faculties. One of the many tasks of the Senate, and perhaps one of its most pleasant, consisted in submitting to the ministry the lists of names of people who were to be called to professorships. This took place after the faculties had forwarded their academic reasons for the planned appointment to the University Senate via the rector. The Senate for its part then appointed an examiner from its number who examined this list independently and possibly even demanded that it be handed back to the faculty for revision. On each occasion, the examiner had to come from another faculty, that is, from one unconnected with the subject for which the professor was to be appointed. By this means it was intended that two things should be achieved. On the one hand, it was intended that all egoism and the factionalism within the faculties concerned should be prevented or discovered in time, should the situation have already arisen; on the other hand, it was intended to find out on the basis of the published literature of the candidates whether they could also make themselves intelligible to an open-minded nonspecialist and thus be able to play a role in our general studies course. A beadle brought a suitcase full of documents to the examiner's home, which is what also happened to me when I had to report on the list of candidates for a professorship in law. And woe betide anyone who had been lazy and was not able to defend himself when cross-examined by the experts. Time and again the sparks would fly in these interviews! As a result of this policy, it could be said that the academic staff itself underwent a general studies course.

The worry of having to justify themselves before the forum of the University Senate certainly caused the faculties to exercise special care merely in the drawing up their lists of candidates. How much more honest and transparent this procedure was than the foolish modern custom of publicly advertising professorships so that people are forced to apply for them! I knew from the Scandinavian experience how much behind-the-scenes cheating and wire-pulling was associated with this procedure, and warned in vain against it. Set against modern procedure, the clear and honest appointments policy of Tübingen University Senate rises all the more impressively from my memory. I always enjoyed a relationship of trust with the Senate, and since objectivity was part of their code of honor, was never aware of any intrigues. In the many clashes that occurred with the minister of education, I could always rely on their loyalty.

I vividly remember a conference of the West German Pharmacist Association, which as host I was responsible for opening. My colleagues from this subject had informed me beforehand of the desperate condition of our pharmaceutical institute and had bewailed the embarrassment they were sure to suffer if any of the conference members wished to visit it. The primitiveness and obsolescence of the dilapidated building did indeed defy description. I was asked to take advantage of the presence of the state president and minister of finance at the pharmacists' conference and to describe the situation in my speech. But above all, I was asked to request urgent assistance. To many people's surprise, I took with me to the lectern a thick bundle of about two hundred sheets of paper and, after a few explanatory words on the pharmaceutical profession and its great benefit to mankind from time immemorial, spoke about how little resemblence the Tübingen Institute bore to this glorious tradition. I then gave as drastic a description as possible of the sights, sounds, and not to mention the smells of the conditions prevalent at the institute. As a result, I soon had the laughter on my side, while the government representatives accompanied my increasing eloquence with obvious apprehension. I then continued, "You see, ladies and gentlemen, what a long speech I have lying here before me." I then briefly held the manuscript aloft. "I will continue with my description of these dreadful details and of the many more prosperous institutes at other universities for as long as it takes the two gentlemen who decide such matters sitting in the front row to assure me by a nod of their heads that they will introduce radical changes and build a new institute for the university." While the hall shook with thunderous applause, the two gentlemen whispered to each other and then nodded at me, both laughing and with some relief. So I no longer needed to go any further with my mock manuscript but was only required to report to the audience the nodding that had resulted. It was now the turn of the two government representatives to receive the applause that was due to them. Work began on the construction of the new institute immediately afterwards.

I made a very special effort to establish contacts with the students, for whom the rector was as a rule a very distant figure. I was pleased that they often described me as the "students' rector" during my year of office. I always reserved the whole of every Wednesday exclusively for the students who wished to see me and for meetings with the student committee. Apart from very special "state" visits, nobody else was admitted to see me on that day. My young visitors came not only to discuss their course marks, conflicts with professors, and so on; many were simply seeking kindly advice and support from me. In this way I learned about many problems of university life that would have otherwise remained concealed from me. I was often able to intervene in a helpful way.

Besides this, I also regularly held "rector's discussion evenings." At these I gave a brief, introductory speech on a topical subject, and then threw it open for discussion. A particularly topical problem at that time was the question of whether a reestablishment of student fraternities was desirable and, if so, what form this should take. I had reason to fear that there was a danger of a stupid and reactionary resumption of superseded traditions as far as fencing and codes of conduct were concerned. All sorts of clashes kept on occurring during the discussion, because I advocated a very firm line on this issue. Mind you, I have to admit to the credit of the Tübingen fraternities that they were always prepared to discuss matters and were also usually quite reasonable whenever I had to summon them to me on any given occasion. These evenings were well attended and were regarded as useful by all parties.

The highlight of the academic year were the great balls—above all the winter ball—which the rector was responsible for arranging. I also made use of our magnificient botanical garden and organized an additional ball for the summer because I believed that there could never be enough of such festivities if the "abstraction" that institutions like the university create were to be counteracted and a greater closeness between human beings brought about. The winter ball took place on the university's own premises. The table for the several hundred guests was laid in the beautiful and splendidly spacious corridors of the main building; the hospital kitchens provided the banquet. We had enough musicians and performers of our own, so we were able to provide everything ourselves. Miss Becker was concerned above all that the building should be totally illuminated, so that there were no dim corners for cuddling and necking. The senior university officer warned me about putting poppy seed rolls on the table because the crumbs could easily find their way under the dentures of the elderly ladies and gentlemen present. So everyday I learned something new. After all the preparations, I fell ill shortly before the ball, so that my wife had to attend the evening alone, albeit under Eduard Spranger's chivalrous protection.

One day, the student committee turned up at my office to present me with their plan to revive the fine old custom of student torchlight processions. I was immediately as keen as mustard on the idea and asked them whom they had chosen for this most splendid of all academic honors. There then came the stunning reply, "That's precisely what we don't know. That's why we had the idea of asking *you* if you could suggest anybody."

I was both happy at and shaken by this question. When I later, in 1962, had to address the West German Parliament in commemoration of June 17,* I recounted this story as an example of the inner condition of German youth. In earlier generations, I said, students were filled with enthusiasm for a teacher, a statesman, or an artist and gave expression to their admiration in a torchlight procession. Now, however, it was the other way round. Young

---

* On June 17, 1953, there was an uprising in the German Democratic Republic against the Communist regime. The government called in the Red Army, which then brutally crushed the rebellion. The West German government later declared June 17 "German Unity Day." Since reunification in 1990 it has been replaced by October 3. *Translator's note.*

people now sensed their potential and capacity for enthusiasm and wished to admire something. But they did not know in which direction they should steer their enthusiasm. So they came to their elders with the question: Tell us *what* we can get enthusiastic about. (When I later read John Osborne's play "Look Back in Anger," I was reminded of this scene in my office: "Oh heavens, how I long for a little ordinary human enthusiasm. Just enthusiasm—that's all. I want to hear a warm, thrilling voice cry out Hallelujah! . . . Oh, brother, it's such a long time since I was with anyone who got enthusiastic about anything.")

I reflected for a moment. Then I had a bright idea that saved the situation, and suggested "Aunt Emily" to them for their planned torchlight procession. This old lady ran a very popular, indeed famous, student pub. She always let her young gentlemen buy on tick until they were able to earn their own living. Night after night, her pub was full of students singing and debating. She sat hunched up in the midst of them, while the students waited on the customers. She also sometimes intervened personally in the discussions and "rebuked the boys and instructed the girls." During the worst period of the famine, she fetched all sorts of nourishing things for her students from the country in a little handcart that she pulled herself. She was not afraid of rudely showing a prominent figure the door if he came at an inconvenient time, including once even a general in uniform. She had little sense of respect, but she was very fond of young people, who passionately returned her love. Once, on her birthday, she even received a festschrift, to which even Spranger had made a contribution. When her equally loved, utterly obese pug dog with the wonderful name of "Asta"* died, it was mentioned in several newspapers.

The idea of holding a torchlight procession in Aunt Emily's honor electrified my young people from the student committee, and they set to work on the preparations with gusto. When the appointed night arrived the whole of Tübingen was out and about, and filled the market square when the torchlight procession approached the town hall. Freshly crimped and unaccustomedly attired in an evening dress, Aunt Emilie sat in a beautiful, old-fashioned coach and greatly enjoyed the ovations that were heaped upon her. The philosopher Theodor Häring, author of that cheerful book entitled *Der Mond braust durch das Neckartal* (The Moon Races Through the Neckar Valley), and I myself held a speech in her honor surrounded by the light of the torches. Time and again we were interrupted by the crowd's cheers of

---

* "Asta" is a "wonderful name" because it is the German for "student committee." *Translator's note.*

approval. When her pub was later supposed to make way for a new development, I spoke up in her defense to the authorities and issued her with a letter of protection written on high quality deckle-edged paper and stamped with the seal of the rector. I was told that she had this letter framed and that it continued to hang in the pub long after her death.

Of the more serious official duties the rector had to perform, I can still remember the funeral of the former German crown prince at Hohenzollern Castle. The coffin, which was draped with the Prussian flag, was carried to the grave accompanied by the tones of the Hohenfriedberg March. As Crown Princess Cecilia, who was wearing the Order of the Prussian Eagle, went before us, I sensed that a belated epilogue in German history had come to an end. The Crown Prince was indeed a controversial and perhaps shady figure, despite his impressive appearance. During the funeral, however, this all sank before the pathos of history, as one of its epochs came to a conclusion.

Even on this tragic day, Aristophanes provided for a theatrical prelude. Whenever the rector appeared anywhere in his robes of office, etiquette required him to have an escort. Before I was able to begin looking around for a colleague I could invite to accompany me, the emeritus head of the gynecological clinic, August Mayer, got in touch with me and asked if he could act as my escort. "I've lost count of all the queens and princesses I've delivered!" this famous gynecologist said, who in his career had been summoned to numerous stately homes. "I would meet a lot of them again at Hohenzollern Castle!" So I gladly agreed to take him with me. On the way to the castle, there was a very loud rattling sound inside my car every time we drove over cobblestones. The puzzle was quickly solved. Mayer had placed a large cylindrical box on the floor that was literally filled to the brim with the medals he had received each time he had delivered a royal personage. He took out a few glittering treasures and told me at which noble birth they had been conferred upon him. Because it was rather difficult for me to scale Hohenzollern Castle in a gown, I had been given special permission to drive my car into the castle courtyard. It was while we were getting out that our little mishap occurred. Mr. Mayer knocked the box of medals over with his gown, scattering all his treasures across the cobbles. We certainly presented a far from dignified sight as we endeavored, half under the car and in very formal dress, to gather them up as quickly as possible.

The authority that the rectorship radiated in those days became clear to me once when I visited the university riding stables. I occasionally used to turn up at the stables because I wanted to take up riding again, a sport I had pursued (with very mediocre success!) in earlier days, in order to give myself a change from desk work. When I went to see the aristocratic head of stables, he asked me when I had last ridden. Since that had been quite a long time ago, he advised me to do a few exercises on the practice ground in order to brush up on my skills before I went for a ride in the country. This is indeed what I did. Because I was his boss, however, this aristocratic and shy man felt so inhibited that the corrections he called out to me were far too delicately expressed and merely hinted at what I was doing wrong. I first had to translate them into cruder cavalry terms before I was able to understand them. What would his request "Would Your Magnificence please move the posterior a little further forwards!" have sounded like in this more earthy language?

Every rector of a German university has experienced the human mania for titles. Many a company director, for instance, let me know via one of his leading employees how pleased he would be to receive an honorary doctorate on reaching an important birthday. He would also, I was often told, most certainly show his gratitude for such an honor. Sometimes I replied that it was impossible to bribe me for less than a million. Above all, however, I drew his attention—now with more serious words—to the fact that this title was awarded by the university exclusively for *academic* merit. If the individual in question were a really significant personality, then we could in such cases award the title of "honorary senator." But as a rule this title did not interest the petitioners very much. I was malicious enough to suspect that it was primarily the wives of these prominent figures who were not keen on this title because they very much wanted to be addressed as "Doctor" (in Southern Germany it is still often the custom to address as "Doctor" the wife of a man who possesses a doctorate).

I still have up to the present day in my file of anecdotes a similar request for a title I received from a lady. She wrote to me, saying that because her name (Meier, Müller, or Schulze) was so common, it was a great handicap in her career as a journalist and writer. In this respect her mother had had a very much easier time of it, she said, because her husband had had a doctorate. This memory had given her the idea of inquiring whether the university might not be prepared to award her on the occasion of her forthcoming sixtieth birthday an honorary doctorate in recognition of her life's work. She enclosed a list of the articles that had originated from her pen. They were innocuous reports on local events. At the conclusion of her letter, she added that, if contrary to expectations I saw no possibility of conferring this honor upon her, I should "not make use of her request."

On reading this letter I could feel my pen itching and urging me to compose a little gibe to dampen this lady's ambition a little. I replied to her that she had unfortunately sent her letter to the wrong person because the conferment of doctorates was decided by the faculties, the rector merely having to sign the diplomas. At the end of her letter, I continued, she had requested me in the event of a negative reply "not to make any use" of her wish. I then concluded with the words, "I shall, however, exceed my authorized powers and hereby appoint you to an honorary doctorate—on condition that you *too* do not make any use of it."

I myself had so much fun with this that I decided to let a few colleagues share in the joke. So I sent the deans a copy—without naming names, of course. They also enjoyed the joke—apart from the lawyers. Their head came quite dumbfounded into my room and informed me with horror that I had awarded a degree and was therefore guilty of overstepping my authority. "A title which cannot be used is surely not a title at all," I replied to him. "The most the lady can do is to step up to her bedroom mirror in her nightgown and say to herself: 'Good night, Doctor!' You surely can't have anything against that, can you?" But the man did not have the slightest sense of humor and even less of a sense of paradox. So he left me, shaking his head and in complete bafflement.

If I had hoped to bid farewell to all administrative work after a year and be able to devote myself exclusively to my professorship again, I was to see myself disappointed. Although I stuck to my decision not to place myself at the university's disposal for a second year, the conference of rectors elected me to be its president. This was a *nobile officium* that one could not turn down. In contrast to the rectorship, however, it took up a more modest amount of time so that I was at least able to hold my seminars again, albeit with a few cancellations. Nevertheless, I never settled into this office as well as I had in my beloved rectorship. In a comprehensive field of activity such as this, which encompassed all the universities, colleges of technology, and other seats of learning, close human contact occurred much less frequently than in our alma mater, where it was still possible to keep a general overview. To make matters worse, the head of my office in Göttingen was seriously ill and despite all his efforts was only able to fulfill his duties to a limited degree. Nor did the work itself exercise the fascination that managing a single university had exerted upon me. I had to prepare the rector's conferences with their often dry subjects, organize the motions, form an opinion on them, and then steer the negotiations in the direction I felt was desirable.

During my period of office we were unanimous in emphasizing the need to combat those traditions of the fraternities that had become sterile, above all certain forms of fencing duels and the concept of honor that lay behind them. After all that we had been through, this concept of honor seemed anachronistic and misguided. This policy constantly led to the individual universities becoming embroiled in legal clashes with the fraternities. As a result, the president had to make many journeys in order to give encouragement to the rectors and senates and to keep them at it. In addition, there were innumerable press interviews and conferences as well as all sorts of official and social duties. I found it very painful having to sacrifice most of my real work to this presidency. The contrast between my managerlike mobility and the work for my seminars, which I was at least partially able to keep up and which required peace and composure, was agonizing for me. It was more in keeping with my nature to do just *one* thing at a time—and to do it properly.

I sought to counteract the dryness of the conference material by always having the agenda of the plenary session begin with a seminar paper on a fundamental issue that pointed beyond the immediate topic of discussion. I either gave it myself or invited others to do it. In the process, I gained the impression that many people found this conspectus of what was fundamentally important to be beneficial. During all these specialist debates, I also endeavored to enhance the status of the human element, sometimes by means of evening parties at which talking shop was frowned upon, or sometimes by means of a few ideas that, although probably noted with some surprise, were, I felt, very gladly accepted.

Thus I was probably the only president who ever got the rectors' conference to sing together. This took place when the conference was held at Tübingen and the state government invited the assembled rectors to an evening festivity in the magnificent royal castle at Bebenhausen. I had secretly had the text of the planned song duplicated and placed on the chairs. After the state president, Gebhard Müller, had made his welcoming speech, I rose to make a brief reply and thanked him in particular for being a loyal supporter of his state university. I expressed my hope that all my colleagues had a similarly pleasant "overlord" and requested them to begin singing the hymn "Praise him with words so fine . . ." in homage to the state president, "Württemberg's beloved ruler." I had reckoned with there being a moment of amazement at this unusual item on the agenda, and indeed only a few timid voices began to sing at first. But then I must say, to the credit of my adversary, Sauer, the minister of education and the arts, that it was he who joined in with the harmony and that as a result a cheerful male-voice choir could be heard by the third verse at the latest. He certainly made an important contribution in enabling this evening to develop into an elated, relaxed get-together, which was enriched by all sorts of impromptu speeches.

Another scene I remember with pleasure involved John J. McCloy, the former American high commissioner and later president of the World Bank. When it was time for him to leave Germany, I had to present him with a certificate of honor from all the West German universities in gratitude for all that he had done. A rector from each of the German states came to Bonn to attend this ceremony. Representing Baden-Württemberg was the rector of Freiburg University, Johannes B. Vincke, a Catholic theologian of whom we were all very fond. Vincke was an extremely commanding figure. He had impressive, striking features and always wore clerical dress. He stood out at our conferences by virtue of the pleasant fact that his contributions were extremely brief and yet invariably hit the nail on the head and were always seasoned with humor.

After the ceremony at the university, I invited Mr. and Mrs. McCloy and my fellow rectors to lunch in Königshof hotel at Bonn. It was a glorious summer's day, and we wended our way by foot to the hotel. Mrs. McCloy was an extremely affectionate lady of alluring charms and youthful appearance. In those days, she stood out because of her American makeup, which lent her a very unmiddle-class touch, as it were, for the average view in those days. She quickly ascertained that Vincke was by far the most handsome and certainly the most dignified figure amongst the German rectors. So she linked arms with him in that nice, informal manner common to her countrymen, and in her lively manner sought to move him to conversation. In the process, she kept on patting his arm. It was truly a feast for eyes to see the two of them. Vincke, unaccustomed to such female proximity, was rigid with embarrassment and, standing bolt upright, exuded an air of unapproachability in the hope of escaping from a situation that he perhaps felt to be overly familiar and that a priest had to be on his guard against. But that was probably not the only reason that drove him to make gestures dissociating himself from his companion, for he had to watch with horror how the people of Bonn that he and Mrs. McCloy met on their way to the hotel kept nudging each other to draw each other's attention to this sight of a young lady of unusually worldly appearance clinging to the arm of an unusually dignified priest and giving open expression to her affection for him. The stiffer and more rigid Vincke became, the more touchingly and "affectionately" Mrs. McCloy strove to overcome what she took to be his shyness. It was a magnificent encounter of German and American mentality. When we were then by ourselves at table,

Vincke's inhibitions quickly vanished, once again allowing grace and dignity to unite in beautiful harmony in his person. It was a merry feast, especially since we were genuinely fond of our guest of honor because of his many merits and his often proven friendship with the Germans.

The university certainly made a mistake when it asked me in the final stages of my Tübingen period to represent it on the town council and to look after the cultural interests of the city in particular. There was, however, precious little mention of educational and cultural matters at council meetings. They were mostly concerned with the "subterranean" side of Tübingen, namely, with the town's sewerage system, the maintenance of the drains and other problems concerning the supply of water and the removal of waste. I have to admit to my shame that up until then I had been totally unaware of these "underworld" dimensions of this poetical town, dimensions that lay far below the level of Hölderlin, Hegel, and Uhland, because I had all-too-exclusively (and all-too-unworldly!) lived in the "superstructure." Because the town council had at its disposal enough well-informed and hard-working experts on this subject, which also included looking after kindergartens, schools, and public conveniences, I was in fact merely a useless encumbrance. So I occupied my time by secretly reading under the table various pamphlets that were of greater interest to me. I really did this quite discreetly so as not to make a bad impression on the press and not to set a bad example to the school children and their teachers that regularly filled the public gallery.

Now, one day I had only been listening with half an ear to a discussion on a segment of the sewerage system for newly constructed scientific institutes and, if I remember rightly, for the biochemistry institute as well. A slide show on this subject unleashed a lively argument, during which I once again switched off and read. This time the punishment for my inattentiveness followed swiftly, for I suddenly heard my name being called, followed by the mayor's request that as the university's representative I should express my opinion on this matter for once. (Had he spotted what I was doing and wanted to put me in an awkward situation?) Everybody looked at me, including the schoolchildren and their teachers. I became terribly embarrassed, for I did not have a clue what the subject of discussion was. But how could I have possibly admitted this! I simply *had* to say something—but what? I then rose and announced in a thought-provoking and weighty manner: "Ladies and gentlemen! That Professor Butenandt has accepted a chair in Munich and is leaving Tübingen is cause for alarm. I have nothing more to say on this subject."

This statement, which was simply the product of my embarrassment, was of course, utter nonsense and had nothing to do with the subject under discussion. But because I had quite a good reputation in Tübingen, everyone was full of consternation and reflected on what I had said for a moment. They obviously thought that some deeper meaning that they had not yet comprehended must lie behind my statement, and naturally did not wish to reveal what they believed to be their stupidity. A few even nodded meaningfully. So my tactical retreat had worked.

On the following day, my fraudulent and nonsensical statement was reported together with my name in block capitals in the newspaper. The names of those who had been honestly slaving away on the sewerage problem and discussing the issue sensibly remained unmentioned, however. This embarrassed me greatly and I realized with consternation how unjust public opinion can often be and how extensively it can distort the truth. I was later to experience this in much more drastic forms.

In 1954, I bid adieu to this fruitful phase of my life, because I had accepted a chair at Hamburg. I have remained there ever since and will probably live in this Hanseatic city to the end of my days.

It was hard for me to leave Tübingen, as it was also for Liesel and the children. On such occasions one realizes how deeply the roots of one's own existence have sunk themselves into the soil of the place where one had been working until then. Once again, the people—both great and small—made no attempt to hide their love for us. The students could scarcely grasp the fact that I was leaving the theological stronghold of Tübingen with its hordes of students for the "empty lowland plains of North Germany." There I would not only not find a theology faculty but would first have to found one and thus have to begin at rock-bottom. How could anyone, they asked me in a variety of different ways, move from the banks of the Neckar to the Elbe, from a temple of the muses to a sober business establishment! But there was no going back; Hamburg University had reminded me of my duty. Tasks were involved for the successful resolution of which I was, in their opinion, indispensable.

More than twenty-five years later, I gave a guest lecture in Tübingen for the first time since leaving. All my faculty colleagues, the beadles, and the cleaning women had long since gone. I only knew my new colleagues from their publications. I had great difficulty in finding my way around the one-way streets, which were overflowing with traffic. Immediately after my arrival, the editorial staff of the *Tübinger Chronik* took me to their office and, in an extremely merry atmosphere, inquired about the many legends that had grown up around me. They then reported on this reunion in their newspaper for two days. I was given such a friendly reception by the faculty that it was almost as if I were still a member.

And then something almost eerie occurred, something that shook me. I was just entering the corridor between the main lecture hall and the ceremonial hall where the people were crowding, because it had just been announced that we would have to move to the larger hall. The audience was now hurrying from the main lecture hall to the familiar hall where I had once held my *dies* lectures and received the rector's chain of office. I rubbed my eyes; it was exactly like the old days. The students were rushing from one hall to the other, there was the same jostling that had sometimes occurred in earlier days, and yet it was *not* exactly the same as it had been then: there was a new generation, there were new faces. What had once been was long gone and yet at the same time it was vividly present. I too, of course, had become another person. But somewhere there was a firm foundation in the flow of time, a riverbed which maintained its identity in the midst of all change. I have always sought after this permanence.

My First Decade in Hamburg

1954–1964

URING THE VARIOUS LECTURES I had given in Hamburg since the end of the war, and even during the preliminary negotiations on founding a theology faculty there, I never suspected that Hamburg would one day be the city in which we would settle down for good.

On the grounds of wishing to become a "full university," the university had repeatedly appealed to the Senate and City Parliament to comply with its wish to have a theology faculty. There was, in fact, unanimous agreement on setting up a theology faculty, something that usually only happened when the "harbor" was the subject of discussion. (I was informed of this by a beaming Senator Landahl, the politician responsible and one of the most enthusiastic supporters of this plan.)

But how does one go about founding a theology faculty? There had been an ecclesiastical college in Hamburg for almost ten years, which sought to fulfill the tasks of a theology faculty as far as its limited possibilities permitted. There were a few eminent theologians on its teaching staff, such as Walter Freytag, the professor of mission studies who was world famous in the ecumenical movement, and Kurt Dietrich Schmidt, the renowned church historian who had been driven from his chair at Kiel by the Nazis. As an autonomous, self-administrating institution, it was the university's academic policy to choose its own professors. It was therefore not possible simply to take over the ecclesiastical college. For this reason, the University Senate set up an appointments committee to take charge on the faculty's behalf of all the functions concerning the appointment of staff. The committee was composed of members of various academic committees as well as several theology professors from other universities, including myself.

This appointments committee initially received a number of prominent and blatant refusals, which eventually led to apprehensiveness and discouragement at Hamburg. It was, after all, not an easy decision for professors in exalted positions to leave established faculties where everything was handed to them on a plate and to entrust themselves to an experiment with so many imponderables.

During this period of depression, the appointments committee informed me that I myself would now have to accept a post, despite the fact that I was a member of this self-same committee. When I made clear my objections to this, referring to my work at Tübingen and expressing my fear that the suspicion might arise that I had had a hand in my own appointment, they informed me, "If you turn the post down, the appointments committee will resign and inform the authorities that it is not possible to set up a theology faculty."

This confronted me with the necessity of having to make a very painful decision. Could I accept the responsibility for preventing the establishment of a theology faculty in this city and in this intellectual sphere? While I was being torn first one way and then the other by this problem, I went for a drive in my car through the city with my friend Hans Joachim Kraus, whom the university wished to appoint to the Old Testament chair and who, like me, was faced with the necessity of making a decision. During our conversation, we had not been paying attention to the road and had lost our bearings. We stopped and beckoned to a trash collector on the other side of the road, who then asked us with a smile, "Have you gone and got lost?" He was very friendly and gave us a first-class description of the area, which enabled us quickly to find the right road again. As with *one* voice we both said, "Hey, if the ordinary people here are so nice, then we *will* come to Hamburg!" It was this that gave the last push, so to speak, to our increasing willingness to move to Hamburg. It seemed almost like a sign from heaven! Immediately afterwards I was elected to be the first dean of the new faculty.

This first impression of Hamburg was later confirmed. I have always had a good relationship with ordinary people. Postmen, porters, and workmen—in their own way they were "gentlemen," self-conscious, polite, and never familiar or crude. In the course of the years, I came to enjoy a relationship of trust with some of them.

During this period, I was constantly traveling between Tübingen and Hamburg in a sleeping car. In this, my last summer semester at Tübingen, the Neckar seemed more beautiful than ever, and both students and colleagues showed their devotion to me in ways that I found very moving. Even Aunt Emily and her pug dog "Asta" paid me a farewell visit. My last sermon in the Church of St. Mark caused many tears to flow, and I myself was also close to tears. When I finally approached my car, several managers from Mercedes were standing around it and said, "We're not going to let you drive to Hamburg with these tires." So I then rolled northwards on a new set of tires.

My car was full right up to the roof with all the things I would need during my first period in Hamburg while I was a grass widower, namely bedding, suits, underwear, and quite a few books. Only *one* of my Swabian students traveled north with me: Hartmut Jetter, later professor of education and today member of the Württemberg church leadership. It was his job to ascertain how promising the recent foundation of the Hamburg theology faculty had been, then a few others might perhaps want to follow him later. And that is indeed what happened. Not long afterwards, I was to find myself eating pea soup once a week after my lecture at Dammtor Railway Station with my Swabian students; another time it was to be with my American students, who were likewise soon to come to Hamburg.

When the two of us were not far from Hamburg, I stopped on the freeway to telephone my two assistants, Hans Schmidt and Jochen Rothert (both of whom were later to become theology professors) to inform them that we would soon be arriving. They greeted us in front of the entrance to our institute with the news that the liner *Italia* was in the harbor and could be visited for a mark. We inlanders did not know that the *Italia* was an old tub; we were just electrified at the thought of seeing a "ship," which was a new phenomenon for us. So we drove straight to the harbor. As a result of this decision our life in Hamburg was to begin with an adventure. For we had no idea that the harbor was surrounded by customs barriers and that, because my car was fully loaded, we would have very great difficulties when we came to leave. When the customs officer then asked me what goods I had to declare, the four of us kept on and on at him for all we were worth in an attempt to explain the situation to him. That I was a newly appointed professor arriving with his basic possessions made no impression upon him, because he presumably did not even know—which would have been impossible in Tübingen—that Hamburg had a university. The fact that we had immediately visited the *Italia* on arriving in Hamburg, this ancient hulk that was soon to be scrapped, seemed to him to be merely an unconvincing pretext for a highly suspicious smuggling operation. Because of our "honest faces," however, he eventually let us go, albeit with a bewildered shake of his head, for, as he informed us, he had never experienced anything like it in all the long years he had been working there.

We then drove to our institute in 1 Alsterglacis, a former dental clinic even more decrepit than the *Italia*. It stood on a corner in the middle of the busy city traffic. It is now many years since it was pulled down. I found it right and fitting that we did not set up shop in a secluded idyll, but were very close to the "gateway to the world."

The office that was placed at my disposal as dean, which was also the faculty's conference room, was situated in a small towerlike construction with glazed windows all the way round. It looked onto the traffic, the railway, and the streetcars, and also let in a colossal amount of noise. Later, my office was situated in a primitive, windowless bathroom, but I did not mind this. Indeed, it gave me considerable Christian pleasure to receive various prominent Hamburg personalities there and see their displeased looks.

The life and soul of the whole establishment, the comforter and coffee maker of frightened examination candidates as well as an untiring support to us all was Miss Dohrmann, the only secretary we had in those days. She was a kind and humorous person who was undaunted by the shortages of the early days (pencils, paper clips, and other basic things) and even made light of them.

The Planning and Realization of the New Faculty

It was not exactly inspiring to hear my colleagues tell me, "So far we have only ninety books and are expecting approximately ninety students." But this was soon to change. As early as the first few semesters the number of students grew to several hundred. The fact that there were many trainee teachers among them who were also studying other subjects often made our seminars especially stimulating. The library expanded almost like an avalanche. We plundered second-hand bookshops and the estates of deceased persons; since we had quite a large book budget, we were able to help ourselves to books in a big way. (Only a few semesters had passed when our "hovel" was closed, indeed, we came close to having the police force us to close it. Because of the vast number of books it was in danger of collapsing.)

We were supported by undreamed-of goodwill on all sides. Newspapers were constantly publishing articles about us, there were many interviews, and all the reports were in agreement that the university was now a "full" university, an opinion which we were unable to hear without a certain enigmatic smile.

During the negotiations on my appointment, the university authorities had granted us permission to invite visiting professors from other universities each semester to supplement our own academic staff. As a result, two brilliant names immediately graced the opening semester, namely the systematic theologian Paul Tillich, who rushed over from the United States and who also later often worked in our department (in 1958 he received the Hanseatic Goethe Prize), and the Heidelberg church historian Hans von Campenhausen. In addition to this, we were allowed to appoint people to give lectures in special fields. At first there were only single chairs in each subject, but these were later doubled for most disciplines.

It was of great significance for the foundation of the faculty and the first phase of its construction that my old friend and comrade from Tübingen, Hans Wenke, was now the senator responsible for university affairs at Hamburg. We had always been in agreement on higher educational policy, and Wenke did everything to ensure that the launching and first sea trials of our ship were trouble-free, as did also his predecessor and successor Landahl. The two rectors with whom we had to deal at the beginning, namely the jurist Eduard Bötticher and the geographer Albert Korb, also did everything in their power to help us to integrate into the university. I was particularly pleased at the tact with which Bötticher supported me during the preliminary talks on the foundation of the faculty, when we were often concerned with delicate discussions concerning members of what until then had been the ecclesiastical college.

Even in the very early days of the faculty, when our professorial staff was still an embryo—a provisional "rump parliament," so to speak—we discovered to our joy that we were in agreement on all of our basic objectives. With the same unanimity we also determined the criteria for regulating any further additions to our personnel. Apart from requiring the person that was to be appointed to be highly qualified in his field, we thought it important for each of us to preach once or even several times each semester. We wanted our students to witness a personal demonstration by their teachers of how all theology develops from and leads back to the preaching of the Gospel. From the very beginning we met once a month at each other's homes for intensive theological work. The purpose of this was to prevent us from becoming too individualistic and to help us to grow together into a community of teachers. In this way, I wanted to make positive use of certain deficiencies I had experienced at Tübingen.

We felt it was equally important to fulfil the expectations that the other disciplines had of us and that were paraphrased by the rather peculiar concept of the "full" university. We wanted to integrate ourselves into the whole of the university and to enter into a lively and permanent dialogue with the other faculties.

So, for instance, we held *dies* lectures in Tübingen style for listeners from all faculties. We also repeatedly let *all* the theological disciplines have a chance to speak by holding series of joint lectures lasting a whole semester, to which different speakers were invited (mind you, these were only introduced some time later). The success of these attempts even encouraged us to have some of these series of lectures published in book form. The lectures were well received in this form, too. Our joint preparation for these lectures also helped us to grow closer together, both as a faculty and as human beings. We became close friends, and for the first ten years were able to secure a majority on the issues that came before us without needing to take a vote. From the perspective of modern practice, this must seem like an unreal dream.

As well as lecturing on my own special subject, I regularly gave lectures for audiences from all faculties from the first semester onwards. As had been the case in Tübingen, these too met with general acclaim. Among the first themes I treated was a series on anthropology ("What is Man?") and on tragedy ("Guilt and Fate"); subjects, then, that were immediately recognizable as cutting across the disciplines, and as a consequence were also attended by colleagues and students from the whole university. Parallel to our general lectures, the Protestant Academy, under the unforgettable leadership of Gerhard Günther, offered similar interfaculty lectures at the university. These were very well attended, especially by the educated public of the city. During all the years that Günther was one of Hamburg's cultural focal points, we theologians enjoyed a working relationship with him that was both productive and mutually complementary.

We further agreed to confront all the academic staff of our university with theological questions. We sought to do this by inviting once a semester all the professors to an all-day symposium at a charming venue in the country, where we put forward subjects for discussion that were of relevance to several different faculties. One of us gave the opening paper, which was followed by a paper from a nontheological colleague. The focal point of our first interfaculty get-together was, if I remember rightly, the concept of "guilt" as understood theologically and juristically. This led to an extremely lively meeting, especially with the jurists, with whom we also maintained close contacts in other respects. Occasionally I even held joint seminars with them, at which colleagues, assistants, and students from both faculties worked closely together for a whole semester.

Later, the problem of guilt was once again the focal point of these symposia when Konrad Lorenz's book *On Aggression* was published and the author took part in our meeting. I will never forget this first encounter with him. The famous name had attracted a considerable contingent from the whole of the academic staff. In contrast to the many pictures showing him "in the wild," with his gray geese and other creatures, he appeared at our meeting wearing—rather unusually for him—correct civilian dress. Dressed in this manner and with his handsome, expressive features, he cut a dignified figure, until he suddenly began to run around the lectern uttering bestial cries in order to make clear the signals animals use to communicate. I can still see the shocked expressions of some retired privy councillors gazing in utter astonishment at this transformation, which was unprecedented in the academic world. The debate we had with him was of an unusually high level because here he was able to display his great powers of reflection, which at that time were still largely unappreciated by the general public. Later, however, when his book *Behind the Mirror* was published, these powers became the object of general admiration.

I may add at this point that I met Konrad Lorenz a second time, when Liesel and I were invited to Brühl Castle on the occasion of the Queen of England's first visit to Germany, and had the good fortune to sit at the same table as the Lorenzes. He stood together with a few other people on a slightly raised balustrade, from which we had a view of the many guests from the whole of the Federal Republic. From this vantage point we were able to conduct behavioral studies of West German "high society." This caused us such amusement that we often slightly overstepped the bounds of what was acceptable in polite society. It is only with some difficulty that I refrain from recounting the vanity we exposed and mimicked.

One day each semester was declared a *dies academicus* for our discipline. This day was kept free of specialist lectures, and a professor was invited from the other faculties—a jurist, sociologist, medic, or scientist—to come and discuss a topic from his own field of research with us. Lively discussions often took place at these meetings and our students followed our colloquia closely, especially when there was an argument between the professors. They themselves also participated by asking questions and raising objections. Thus I remember a fierce debate with our eloquent and witty psychiatrist, Bürger-Prinz, on Kierkegaard, whom he wished to interpret merely as a "pathological case," as a man with an unresolved Oedipus complex. We accepted that psychopathic traits of this kind were not to be denied, but asked him in reply whether it were not possible that precisely such a

pathological mind might possess a sense for existential enigmas that so-
called normal people lack; and whether it were not conceivable that many
things simply imperceptible to robust, healthy people might be able to
penetrate the extremely thin walls of such a hypersensitive person's soul. I do
not know whether we managed to bespatter his table of exclusively psychi-
atric categories with a few troublesome ink blots.

I believe, however, that I may have discovered a few traces of our disruptive and unsettling attack in Bürger-Prinz's autobiography, for there he writes
that many psychopathic traits seem to be unique to *creative* people, and that
they may therefore be of constitutive significance for such people's creativity.
He came across this fact, he writes, through an observation that caused him
great confusion; namely, if he succeeded in healing creative people of their
psychological suffering, they frequently lost their artistic capacity and became "normal" in a sterile sense.

I for my part undertook yet another attempt to prevent our students from
living in a theological ivory tower and to keep a window open to the outside
world, namely by reviving the fine institution of my Tübingen *Open Evenings*.
Mind you, because of the distances involved in Hamburg, it was possible
only on rare occasions to allow them to take place at our remote suburban
home. But then a welcome solution presented itself: one of the oil companies
at whose cultural events I often spoke offered me the use of their premises in
the center of the city for the Open Evenings. And that was not all. To cap their
generosity, they also provided huge plates of sandwiches and exquisite
drinks. If the discussions I had had with students in Tübingen had once been
so well frequented primarily because of the sandwich I had given each of
them during the famine, it may well be that attendance at the Hamburg Open
Evenings was prompted more by this delicious buffet than by the intellectual
stimulation on offer. However, since this stimulation stemmed not from me
but from the guests I invited, I may still sing the praises of the intellectual
repast that was offered.

My predilection for biographical literature—there are whole shelves full
of biographies in my library!—inspired me with the idea of inviting outstanding personalities in the public eye, such as politicians, industrial
magnates, actors, artists, and scholars, to my Open Evenings and getting
them to talk about their lives. Hardly any of those I invited refused my
invitation. They obviously enjoyed having the opportunity of presenting their
life's journey to young people for once. In this way, the students were directly
confronted with professional problems that were quite alien to them and
became acquainted with the various conflicts that can arise in life—often

more vividly and graphically than would have been possible by literary means.

Sometimes subjects were also treated that touched on hotly disputed, fundamental theological issues from the perspective of another discipline. The high point of such discussions were the three evenings on which our famous neurologist Rudolf Janzen discussed the subject "brain and personality." He also brought along his assistants and a few selected students to these evenings. The discussion touched on the most sensitive points of the theological question of truth.

There is one other evening that I have never forgotten. Dürrenmatt's play *The Visit* was being staged at the Hamburg Playhouse, directed by Ulrich Erfurth, with Elisabeth Flickenschildt in the leading role. Since this play is full to bursting with theological problems, I invited the director and actors for a discussion at one of my Open Evenings. Following my prompting, most of the students had seen the performance. At the end of the discussion, which was conducted with passion on both sides, Mrs. Flickenschildt said that only now had her eyes been opened to the significance of what she had been acting in and that she regretted that she and her colleagues had not spoken to the theologians *before* the performance. I firmly contradicted this. "We would have only disturbed the naturalness of your acting with such reflections," I said. I pointed out to our guests that according to his stage directions, Dürrenmatt wanted his tragicomedy to be acted "superficially," and that he would have been displeased if the actors had carried the play's profundity before them as if on a tray. Naive members of the audience should also be able to enjoy themselves; the profundity below the surface would become apparent to more perceptive theatergoers quite of its own accord.

In the course of this discussion, I recalled what Goethe had said about his *Faust*: "As long as the audience derives pleasure from the spectacle, the higher meaning will at the same time not elude the initiated." That evening I succeeded in impressing on the actors and students one of my favorite ideas, namely that theological questions are also present in the background of wholly "worldly" viewpoints.

Dramatic and Comical Incidents at the Opening Ceremony

But back now to those early days in Hamburg when we were beginning to realize our plans. The ceremonies that took place at the official opening (1954) of the faculty commenced with a church service in which the mayor and senate, rector and deans, bishops and clergy all took part wearing their ceremonial robes. The sermon was given by the future Bishop of Hamburg, Volkmar Herntrich, who succeeded in striking the right tone—which was not at all easy!—at this solemn assembly. He spoke as a preacher, without indulging in any embarrassing clerical remarks.

A few days later, the solemn state opening took place at the city council's ceremonial hall, where the senate had invited its guests. Here, too, the external setting was ceremonial: the liveried beadles with their buckled shoes, the imposing rooms with their tasteful, "legitimate" splendor, the sight of the colorful robes of German and foreign academic dignitaries, including a Russian metropolitan. With their clear and beautiful voices, the boys' choir of the Church of St. Michael lent a moving touch to the dignity of the hour. The mayor, Kurt Sieveking, held an extremely intellectual speech, partly in Latin, that was overflowing in equal part with grace and dignity. I believe a little pride could be detected amongst the assembled guests that a head of government—a pupil of Johanneum Grammar School—was able to find words of unforgettable significance that outlived the moment in which they were spoken. He was fervently involved in the cause with which all theological work is concerned.

It was then my turn to speak, and I gave a speech on the question, "What is truth? Theology within the scientific system." In this speech, I endeavored to clarify the tension that exists between the secular and rational understanding of the truth on the one hand, and the theological understanding of the truth on the other. However, I also attempted to show the interdependence of these two conceptions of the truth. The concluding passage of the speech perhaps conveys an impression of what I wanted to say to the representatives of state, university, and church:

> The presence of a theology faculty means a permanent inquiry into the ultimate presuppositions of our knowledge. And since the essential core of knowledge is not a truth that is intellectually "valid," but a truth that one "is," this inquiry is ultimately directed at the very person researching into the truth and thus at his personal existence. The passage in the New Testament, "Only he who *is* of the truth hears my voice," addresses the mystery that when all is said and done, the truth is not an object of knowledge but a condition of my own self.
>
> If the theology faculty is perhaps something like the conscience of the university, then the voice of this conscience calls upon us to seek the truth not

only forwards, that is, in the possible objects of our knowledge, but also backwards, namely in the truth of our being.

Perhaps this is in order that the theology faculty should be a thorn in the flesh of the university. But one would do better to say that it is a piece of gauze in the wound of our existence—in a wound that has been dealt to us by a mysterious spear, namely the spear of being which calls to us and which craves *alētheia*, unveiling. This wound should never heal over prematurely. The smooth skins of people who have completed their search for the truth and whose wounds have now healed can be deceptive. The university should never complete its search—not only with regard to its advance in knowledge, but also with regard to the revisions to which the people engaged in the advancement of knowledge subject themselves. For this reason that gauze in the wound, and for this reason the theology faculty, may possibly be of service to the university. And in this sense we as servants, and as fellow thinkers in the service of knowledge wish with God's grace to be good companions."

This eventful day concluded with a banquet in the imperial hall of the city council, during which many lively after-dinner speeches and toasts flew back and forth. The end was in fact rather abrupt, for in the meantime, Emperor Haile Selassie had arrived on a visit. And even as we were leaving, numerous workers were busily rearranging the town hall so that the representative of the "oldest empire in the world" could be received with the appropriate dignity.

I played a prank on one of our most dignified guests at the banquet, the Primate of the Bavarian State Church and the then head of the German Lutherans, D. Hans Meiser. This imposing, white-haired prince of the Church was personally a modest man, but stylized his episcopal office with such a constant display of dignity that it provoked my love of mockery (despite all the sincere respect I did indeed have for him). This mode of behavior was something he shared with many of his fellow bishops—for example, with Hanns Lilje, the head of the Hanoverian Church, and Abbot Johannes of Loccum, who was a virtuoso in the episcopal art of expressing commonplaces in such a way that they sounded like a sermon.

Before the ceremony, I had invited Bishop Meiser to lunch at the Hamburg ratskeller. Conversation soon ran into difficulties, however, because even there he insisted on eating his lunch in a rather stiff and wooden episcopal manner. Eventually I sprang the question on him, "Do you know, your Grace, that you once won first prize in a beauty contest between the German bishops?"

I can still see him staring at me in amazement at the fact that I could associate him, the exalted one, with a catwalk. He was just about to put a fork laden with peas into his mouth, which was already open to receive the food. At my remark his mouth stayed open and the peas rolled back onto his plate. I myself continued with my meal and eagerly awaited his reaction. Finally it came: "Why first prize?" he asked. Aha, I thought, so he is interested in the beauty contest; even a person like him would rather be the most handsome than the most unprepossessing. "Well, it was because of your beautiful white hair," I informed him. "When relaxing together after some taxing meetings they had had, your Bavarian clergy sang a song in its praise. By the way, the text ended with the verse, 'Bishop Lilje, as you all know, strives in vain his hair to grow' " (he was bald, you see).

I could see that this dignified man was struggling to appear to be above such childish nonsense. But it was as if a thousand-watt lamp had been switched on inside him and was shining through the skin on his face. Try as he might, his efforts to deaden the gleam by force ended in failure. I, at any rate, felt it to be agreeably human that even *he* was still susceptible to petty vanities and human weaknesses.

This brief comedy, incidentally, had a second act, in which I was once again able to poke my needle into this weakness of episcopal dignity. A few moments later, Meiser seized his right hand with visible alarm. "My episcopal ring is gone," he groaned, "This is awful! It was given to me by the city of Augsburg at the time of the Augustana Jubilee." I comforted him by saying that the ring was sure to be found again. I then signaled to the waiter and asked him to get someone to look for it. It was not long before he brought the ring to us on a silver tray. "Where was it then?" I whispered to him, already suspecting the answer. "In the bathroom!" was his reply, which even though it too had merely been whispered, did not go unnoticed by the bishop. It was bad enough that he had just been associated with a catwalk, but he was now even being mentioned in connection with the bathroom! I felt obliged to help him out of his embarrassment. "But that's all quite natural," I said to him. "Normal bishops, I have heard, just take their chain off on the toilet. But a Bavarian bishop also removes his ring!"

I was rewarded with a smile. Could this episode have been a spiritual lesson to him? All this happened quite on the margin of the historic event of the opening of the theology faculty.

Nest-building in Wellingsbüttel

I have already mentioned that we enjoyed the special kindness of the Hamburg authorities. This kindness was also manifested in the fact that the university consultant accompanied me and some housing experts in two cars on a search for a suitable house. I fell in love at first sight with what we then found: a homely, solidly constructed, 1936 clinker-built house in Wellingsbüttel. We later built an extension so as to have the space to invite large numbers of guests and above all to gather colleagues and students around us for regular social events during the semester. That Wellingsbüttel had been a wood and hunting ground a few decades earlier is still revealed today by the magnificent, ancient stock of trees in our large garden. For the children, the garden was a paradise, and they were each given a flowerbed to look after by themselves, whereas I myself had to mow the lawn and clear away the leaves in fall. The queen of the garden is a hundred-year-old beech tree, which we named the "Tillich tree." There was of course a special reason for this.

Tillich was often a guest at our home whenever he was a visiting professor in Hamburg. He was very keen on Liesel's cooking. She also always had his favorite wine ready. He made such ample use of this that a few students, whom we always invited for her own and Tillich's pleasure, had to escort him to his hotel right up to his room. At one of these evenings we discussed the question of whether *angels* were a serious theological subject. (In contrast to today, I at that time had no real appreciation for this issue.) Tillich thought that angels were something like "powers of being" and had an ontological meaning similar to that of the Greek gods. Now, I did not understand this at all and asked him, "Can you imagine Pallas Athena as a Christmas angel?" He denied this with a laugh and admitted that his comparison had indeed been rather inappropriate. "But in the grove of Delphi I really did behold the gods and I see them *now* in the branches of your magnificent beech," he said. At that moment the tree was suffused with the glow of the evening sun, and I could understand why the tree enchanted him. Nevertheless, I gave voice to my suspicion that the two bottles of wine might also perhaps have played a role in his inspiration, which, in the well-being brought about by this exhilarating evening, he also admitted.

The next day, the faculty held a little party in his honor, at which I had to make an after-dinner speech. During my speech I recounted the story about the angels and the beech tree and concluded my toast with the sentence,

"When Tillich had lost his grip on himself, he was gripped by powers of being." So relaxed were we in our dealings with each other in those days.

The day we moved into our new house was rather dramatic. That morning my family had arrived from Tübingen in a sleeping car. The Student Christian Society had prepared a festive breakfast. Afterwards I went to work while Liesel waited at home for the furniture lorry to arrive in order to begin arranging the house immediately. When, that evening, I returned to our new home full of excitement, everybody was shaking at the knees because Rainer, who was only five years old, had suddenly disappeared. His mother grew extremely agitated because a wood began right next to the house, in which he could have got lost (the putative wood soon turned out to be a tiny little thicket), and the Alster was not far away. The things that could have happened there! In short, the whole maneuver of moving into the new house was halted, and all the moving men went in search of the lost child.

When he just could not be found, somebody made their way to the police station—and, lo and behold, there sat little Rainer, enjoying the cocoa the policemen had kindly given him and shooting his mouth off. He was extremely reluctant to be separated from "uncle policeman." The police were very relieved when we arrived because they did not know what to make of Rainer's statements. He kept on giving Garden Street (our former Tübingen address) as his address, but there was no such street in Wellingsbüttel. Only when the overjoyed mother questioned her newly found son did everything become clear. Because he had felt rather lost in the chaos of moving home, Rainer had taken his moneybox and set off to visit Aunt Bechtle, the friendly proprietor of a café near our apartment in Tübingen. Because he had slept on the train, he was unaware of the distance he had traveled and did not realize that he was now in a different city. When he failed to find the café he thought was nearby, and everything was so completely different and strange, he stood freezing and crying in the easterly wind until a compassionate soul took pity on the child and brought him to the police.

On the following morning I allowed the children—indeed, I even went so far as to ask them!—to rollick about and to make as much noise as they were able to for an hour. We were after all now living in our own house and thus no longer needed to show consideration for any other occupants. That it was their father himself who was the initiator of this excess of noise, suddenly gave them a new lease of life. And *that* was precisely what I wished to achieve.

Nevertheless, the children had not yet completely accepted the new nest. When a little more law and order had returned, they overcame their homesickness for Tübingen and their friends. The different school conditions in the German states also contributed to make it difficult for my two eldest children to settle down. In Württemberg, children attended grammar school after four years at elementary school; in Hamburg, on the other hand, it was after six years. The consequence was that although the oldest child, Wolfram, was able to go to Johanneum Grammar School, Berthold was moved back down to the elementary school. His separation from his elder brother hit him hard, and Wolfram too had first to get used to the long train journeys and to the necessity of getting up early. One evening, Liesel confessed to me that she had sat on the sofa with her arms wrapped tightly around the sobbing children and had tried in vain to comfort them. They had been particularly indignant at being laughed at because of their Swabian dialect.

Berthold's homesickness increased to such a degree that he hardly ate at all, until my loyal colleague and friend Jochen Rochert invited him for a ride in his car and showed him the attractions of Hamburg: the harbor, the Elbe, the great ocean steamers, and the beautiful Alster. My assistants touchingly looked after the children in other ways as well, playing with them and telling them stories in the evenings, so that they gradually came to feel at home. And when the children began to bring their new friends home, Tübingen increasingly faded into a distant memory.

Despite the constant stress of school marks and examination results, our family life was cheerful and contented. This was entirely thanks to Liesel, for I myself, as I confess to my shame, was, as ever, absorbed in my profession, and for the most part played no role in bringing up the children. Every day she would read to them for an hour. Apart from fairy tales and children's stories, she also read larger books to them. Dickens' *David Copperfield* and *Oliver Twist*, Defoe's *Robinson Crusoe* and Swift's *Gulliver's Travels* are examples of those strange works that are able to fascinate children and adults alike and to become companions their whole life long. Carlo Schmid once told me that he was constantly returning to these books and could not get over his astonishment at the compactness of their philosophical substance, the way in which knowledge of life and society was portrayed in simple, narrative form, and the fact that such books could even interest a child that was completely ignorant of the background to the story.

When the children were bigger, I also read a little to them myself—a rare event!—and I was once so foolhardy as to choose a book that had been important to me in my youth, namely *Der Wanderer zwischen beiden Welten* (Traveler Between both Worlds) by Walter Flex. But they were not at all interested in this book. Its tone was too effusive and the language too plerophoric for them. I also read them a few of my old school essays, conceitedly expecting their praise, but these too only aroused their derisive laughter. The intensity of this laughter was only once surpassed: when I played to them the records of the speeches I had made in English. After just a few revolutions, I had to turn the record player off. Mind you, this time I was happy to join in with their laughter. Only Ernst von Wildenbruch's novella *Das edle Blut* (Noble Blood) was able to get under their skin, as it had once done mine.

Almost every day, even when my professional life was at its most hectic, I always found an hour to read nonspecialist books, even if I was never able to attain Liesel's wide reading in the area of belles lettres. Above all, I was constantly reading Goethe and Fontane, not to mention Joseph Conrad. Despite my repeated attempts, Joyce and Musil, on the other hand, always remained alien to me. I could, and can, positively imbibe first-class prose with esthetic relish. Indeed, such literature plays an important role in helping me to recover from the strain that so much modern theological literature inflicts upon my literary sensibilities, especially through that hideous "substantivitis" that is a sign of inertia and is hostile to all narrative forms of literature. (Since the Bible—and particularly the Old Testament and the Gospels—is storybook, this theological style also reveals an embarrassing lack of understanding of the Bible.)

Two authors who help me to combat the esthetic pain that specialist theological literature causes me are Ernst Jünger and Gerhard Nebel. Over the years I became particularly good friends with Nebel, which was a source of great joy to me. He repeatedly confessed that my books had helped him to find his way back to the Christian faith and that this was the reason he had sought to come into contact with me. For me it was fascinating to see this great authority on mythology and Greek civilization discovering the Gospel in its entirety. At the same time I was dismayed at how little known he was among his contemporaries and at the material poverty in which he was forced to live as a freelance writer.

Above all, however, I was, and am, as I have already mentioned, an insatiable devourer of biographies. I was fascinated by the question of how other earthly wayfarers experienced their joys on this planet and how they coped with their problems and worries. So many very different spirits coexist happily in my mind: I love Rilke and the *Wandsbeker Bote*, Wilhelm Busch *and* Winston Churchill (whose complete works I have read, some of them several times), Georges Bernanos, C.S. Forester, and Dorothy Sayers.

The wealth of experience that has accumulated in bringing up the elder children helps the parents to observe the youngest child's awakening and developing character with increased awareness. In this respect, Rainer, the last of our swarm of children, was a particularly rewarding object of study. He was constantly providing for excitement and agitation. I have already described one example. Things had also been no different in Tübingen. Shortly before our departure for Hamburg, we had paid a visit to Tübingen's little zoo, where Rainer had got into the monkey cage to stroke the animal and had promptly been bitten. His mother, who was not present when this happened, still remembers today the fright she received when she found my note: "Rainer bitten by monkey. Taken him to hospital."

After we had settled in Wellingsbüttel, it very soon became clear that this six-year-old boy had developed an embryonic philosophy of nature. A visitor had given me a box of particularly fine cigars, which had then mysteriously vanished. Even when the family had swarmed out to search for them, they were nowhere to be found. When I had long since overcome my grief at the loss, the puzzle was solved. While Liesel was raking the rose garden, she found some half-decayed cigars buried in the soil. I immediately suspected what lay behind this and had a word with Rainer. With a secretive and knowing smile, he revealed to me, "You were actually only supposed to learn about this later, when the cigar tree had grown!" He had watched his mother planting flower bulbs in the earth and this had given him the idea of planting a few cigar trees for his father. Since I smoked so much, homegrown produce of this kind would save us some expense, he thought, especially since we still had to pay off the mortgage for the house. Naturally, we could only praise him for his good intentions. He did not suspect that by his experiment he had put the teaching of the Soviet botanist T. D. Lysenko on the "transmission of acquired properties" to a severe test. When I was describing Lysenko's theory to my students, they were quite amused when I mentioned Rainer's refutation of this theory and pointed out that the Soviets were also eventually sure to see through this ideologically based theory (which was indeed what happened). That economic considerations also played a significant role in prompting the little man to conduct this experiment was indicated by his later development: he became a tax consultant.

Rainer's financial talents were also revealed in another way. He often helped with cashing-up and stock-taking at a neighboring shop, and the owner was astonished to see such mathematical genius and flair for organization in such a small boy. On the other hand, he was not exactly a star in dictation during his first years at school. When I told him that his teacher had informed me that he was one of the weakest in the class, he replied, "But of the weakest I'm the strongest." He was soon so well known in Wellingsbüttel that I myself had to be content with the role of being "Rainer's father."

Even in her early childhood, Elisabeth, our second youngest child, was an insatiable reader. Even novels that her parents had got out for themselves to read were not safe from her clutches, and the same applied to newspapers and magazines. She liked to blurt out questions on what she had been reading at the most unsuitable moments. Thus she once asked her mother in the middle of a ladies' coffee klatsch: "Mother, what actually is 'male impotence'?" She was generally of a tender disposition and was full of pity whenever she saw a crippled child or a "negro with sad eyes." At the same time she was a very thoughtful child and was not only emotionally moved by much of the suffering in the world, but also reflected on it and later made it the subject of sociological study. After leaving university, her great gift for languages—she is now a qualified translator in French, English, and Italian and is also competent in other languages—enabled her to take part in a research project on the language problems of immigrant workers, especially the Turks. To this end she lived as a worker among them for a while.

Because she was such a sensitive child, we were sometimes worried whether she would be able to cope with the harshness of life. Today we marvel at how independent she is and how she has traveled the world on her own initiative without making use of the prostheses of a tourist company.

Berthold was the most restless of the three brothers, especially during adolescence. He had a sharp and extremely critical mind, which made it impossible for him to overlook the weaknesses of his fellow human beings. When he was still a young lad he used to shake his head at my inadequate knowledge of human nature and often complained to his mother that his father had once again failed to see through this or that "loser." I later frequently had to admit that he had been right. As his confirmation approached and he did not get on either with the pastor who was teaching him or with the other members of the class, Berthold's problems mounted. Expecting me to blow my top because I was a theologian, he one day disclosed to me that he would *not* let himself be confirmed. To his astonishment, I took this quite calmly and even told him that he might well be behaving correctly in refusing to be confirmed, for confirmation was a question of conscience and if his conscience forbade him to go through with it, then he *ought* not to be confirmed.

When I then inquired into the problems his conscience was giving him, he cited two reasons. First, his confirmation classes had not moved him in the slightest. Second and above all, he found it offensive that "the others" were only taking part because it was tradition and in order to receive presents. It was all, he said, a hollow sham and he did not wish to be seen in such company.

I declared myself to be in agreement with his decision not to be confirmed and made only two demands of him: *first*, that he himself—and not via his father!—should inform the pastor of his decision; and *second*, that I myself should give him lessons for a year, after which he should then freely decide whether he would like to be confirmed somewhere else.

Berthold agreed to both demands. The pastor treated him very kindly and generously, even giving him tobacco for his pipe and speaking to him "man to man." When he returned, all he said was, "He didn't get around me." I then taught him myself and, a year later, my former assistant and friend, Quest, who at that time was a pastor in Lower Saxony, confirmed him with his complete consent. Because of Berthold's tendency to oppose everything, our life together did not always pass without conflicts. He now has a career in social education, we get on well, and some time ago he placed his first book in my hands after passing his doctoral examination with flying colors.

Even as a child, Wolfram, our eldest boy, was a person of almost fanatical honesty. It must have been while we were still in Tübingen that he went on a school outing with his class in the morning and the teacher asked the children to write a report on "My Day Out" as homework. In the afternoon, he sat down to do this work, chewing his fountain pen rather helplessly because he was at a loss where to begin. When his mother suggested to him, "Just simply write as your first sentence, 'Today we went on a school outing,' " he refused because it was a "lie," "For," he said, "when I hand in my exercise book tomorrow, it will no longer be 'today' but 'yesterday'!"

Although bizarre excesses of this kind abated with age, he always remained the paragon of an honesty that was in no way fanatical but was and is constantly sustained by an endearing humor, even when he was compelled to expose the weaknesses of his fellow human beings. Although he wanted to be an engineer and did indeed become one, he constantly emphasized that machines alone were not enough for him and that his career had first and foremost to bring him into contact with people. He then chose his profession accordingly.

During his adolescence, Wolfram was a dreamer, equally at home and at school, and as a result was almost invariably "miles away." That naturally had an effect on his school reports and prompted us to ask a lady psychiatrist who had specialized in the problems of adolescence for advice and assistance (which one should never do except in extreme cases). Her diagnosis was that Wolfram's intelligence quotient led her to expect that he would certainly never graduate from grammar school; at the best, she said, he might possibly graduate from a secondary modern school. When we then reported this to a paediatrician friend of ours, he laughed at us and said, "You only have to look this boy in the face to know that there is something special in him—something that will first have to struggle its way slowly up out of his present dreaminess." This fortifying statement saved us from making the foolish decision to have him moved back down to the elementary school. No less a person than the great educationalist Martin Hahn (the founder of Salem and Gordonstoun, the boarding school of the British princes in Scotland), whom I met at a reception, secured a place at Luisenlund, the prestigious private school in Holstein, for Wolfram. There he blossomed and went on to gain a reasonable pass in his graduation examination. We found this school so satisfactory that we also sent Berthold there.

For the mother of the household, these first years in Hamburg were extremely busy, nor were they in other respects easy. She was unable to pursue many inclinations and interests because she was kept completely occupied with housekeeping, bringing the children up, school marks, and guests. She only participated indirectly in outside life, through what I reported to her. Fortunately, the modern feminist urge for self-realization had not yet broken out, although she was and is not the type of person who is susceptible to such collective infections of the soul. She willingly made the self-sacrifice of taking these years of renunciation upon herself, well aware of the joys that also bloomed for her during this period. Perhaps she suspected that she herself grew and developed through what seemed at first—as Goethe's Orphic and elemental words make clear—to "lead her away" from herself, to alienate her from herself. Later, when the children had left home and the family was enlarged by the extremely welcome arrival of daughters-in-law and a horde of grandchildren, she too was able to return to herself. One cannot wish for self-discovery and self-realization directly, they are only to be had indirectly through the process of losing oneself. This too was something Goethe knew—to say nothing of the New Testament.

In the Pulpit of the Church of St. Michael

The nest that Liesel prepared for the children and me was the calming influence in the hustle and bustle of my professional life, however turbulent things might have been at home in the family. Liesel was and is in all things much calmer than I am. She does not have my fatal tendency to make the moment absolute, but sees it as a member of a chain of developments which are constantly overtaking it and inasmuch making it relative. As a result, she radiates a calmness that others also sense and that has led to all sorts of people coming to her for advice and assistance with regard to their personal problems.

In addition to my work at the university, I very soon had a second and very demanding field of activity, namely *preaching*. I have already indicated that I see preaching as indissolubly linked with being a teacher of theology and have also given my reasons for holding this view. So I immediately tried to find a pulpit in Hamburg and was pleased when Reverend Drechsler placed at my disposal the pulpit in the magnificent medieval Church of St. James, with its world-famous Arp-Schnitger organ. The great attention the press had paid to the foundation of our faculty certainly played a role in prompting the people of Hamburg to flock to the Church of St. James from the very first time I began my series of sermons on the parables of Jesus. When no less a person than the well-known journalist Edith Oppens then wrote a newspaper article on the (allegedly) "modern sermon experience," many churchgoers had to be turned away, especially since only the south nave was available because of repair work.

As a result, the old and venerable Bishop Simon Schöffel, who remained a fatherly friend to me until his death, offered me the pulpit of the Great Church of St. Michael, nicknamed "Michel" by the people of Hamburg. When I had a look around this magnificent light-filled church and stood alone beneath its huge dome, I felt a little nervous, but my worries soon proved to be unfounded. I was grateful that the congregation, who came from all parts of the city and the surrounding countryside, remained loyal to me to the end of my regular preaching activity and beyond. To avoid poaching on the preserves of my colleagues, I soon transferred my monthly sermons from Sunday mornings to five o'clock on Saturday afternoons. During my series on the first eleven chapters of Genesis, I had to hold each of the services twice and was thus compelled to repeat them on Sunday mornings.

The large number of people attending the Michel sermons led to a lively response in the press, culminating in 1955 with a lead article in the magazine *Der Spiegel*. Since this article reported the facts and was almost free of the malice usual in such cases, I feel I may quote some of the reporter's observations, although, of course, they are only concerned with the external aspect of the sermons.

"Whenever he preaches—usually once a month—in Hamburg's largest church, the "Michel," the almost three thousand seats begin to fill as early as an hour before the service is due to begin. A traffic policeman with a white cap and white sleeves stands in front of the door. He has to be stationed there each Sunday that Thielicke preaches, in order to direct the cars driving up and stopping in front of the portal. Anybody arriving just half an hour before the service begins can give up all hope of still getting a seat . . .

Yet he neither puts on a spectacle for his congregation nor offers them ecstasies. He bears no resemblance whatsoever to the Catholic worker-priest Leppich, that "market crier of God" who stands on a crate or a machine and hauls the industrial workers over the coals with a harsh voice and bold jargon. He certainly bears no resemblance to the American evangelist Billy Graham, who sweating with zeal and with businesslike staccato calls upon his hundred thousand listeners in sport arenas and parade grounds to reflect on their lives.

Thielicke does not regard himself as God's public relations manager. He preaches his message neither on the street nor on soccer fields. He preaches in the church on Sunday mornings before properly dressed people. He wears a cassock and that gleaming white, medieval ruff which is the traditional dress of Hamburg pastors. He speaks clearly and in a cultured manner.

He speaks before people who read newspapers about what they have read in those newspapers. He uses current events—in politics and the economy—to comment on the biblical passage that is the reading for the day. He knows the newsreels, he knows the language of the common man, he knows the West Germans. He knows about this world and employs this knowledge to talk to his audience about the next world.

Thielicke's audience presents without doubt a reliable cross-section of the population of a big city. It is in fact not only habitual Christians who come to him. On the contrary, on the rows of benches installed throughout the "Michel" and in the curved baroque gallery sit expensively dressed ladies, gentlemen with broad-rimmed executive spectacles, students and minor civil servants as well as those people from nearby St. Pauli—girls, sailors, tramps—who in the evenings either produce the entertainment on the Reeperbahn, consume it, or eke out their existence from its garbage.

The church knows that it stands or falls with the sermon and it is worried that the day of the sermon could be over. Thielicke is striving successfully to prove that the day of the sermon is not over. But he also knows that a complete renunciation of the traditional customs of the Christian church service—for instance, in the style of Billy Graham's mass evangelizations—will be of little use to the church in the long term. He sticks to the conventional, middle-class form of the Sunday service.

This tall, bronzed man stands in the protruding pulpit surrounded on all sides by his congregation, which has filled every seat and free space in the huge church. But he has none of the affectations of a fanatic. He knows that it is the exaggerated clerical tone of many clergymen that has brought the sermon into disrepute, and he guards against falling into this tone. He speaks in a matter-of-fact way with the well-practiced, rhetorical care of the modern university lecturer. . . ."

Before I add a few remarks to the picture this report has painted on the *inner* dimension of my new task, I would very much like to let the reader share in the enjoyment I experienced as a result of that article in *Der Spiegel*.

Of all weeks, it was published while a German-speaking theological congress was taking place in Berlin, in which I also had to participate. I could imagine that my colleagues had in the meantime become acquainted with the article and would have very mixed feelings about it. The picture of my face on the cover of the magazine beamed at me from every kiosk, and at the welcoming reception on the first evening of the conference I saw the magazine peeping out of many people's bags. All sorts of cheerful dialogues arose as a result of the article.

When I entered the hotel's breakfast room on the following morning, which was reserved exclusively for people attending the theological conference, I spotted that there was a seat free at a table occupied by two gentlemen. I knew one of them—it was my friend Gerhard Rosenkranz from Tübingen. He introduced me to the other man, a colleague from Switzerland. Usually when people are introduced in this way they say something or the other, especially if they know each other through their publications. He, however, said nothing, and enjoyed the egg he was having for breakfast with such abandon that I too had no opportunity to say anything. I assumed that he had simply not understood my name. At last he was finished. When the babble of voices chanced to cease for a few seconds—it is said of such moments that an angel is passing through the room—he spoke his first words very audibly and with a Swiss German accent in the ensuing silence. "We've got a droll man among us today!" he said. Everyone turned round and someone asked, "What do you mean?"

He then replied, "Haven't you read his description in *Der Spiegel*, then: 'tall and bronzed?' He won't ever be able to show his face in Switzerland again, people will roar with laughter at him!"

The effect of this was indescribable. These serious gentlemen giggled like a school class that had gone wild. For they had realized straightaway that he meant me and yet had no idea that I was sitting opposite him. Someone asked sanctimoniously, "Whom do you actually mean?"

"Thielicke!" he replied.

When there was another outburst of laughter at this, he appeared to be surprised but was also obviously enjoying it, for he was a rather dull man and certainly not blessed with successes in the social sphere. But these Germans, he seemed to think, appeared to be an appreciative audience and to laugh at the slightest thing. He now really got into the swing of things and launched the next of his inflamatory remarks. "What a conceited dandy!" he said. When the wave of delight this caused had subsided a little, he pulled one last arrow from his quiver: "What a pompous ass!" Breakfast time now positively turned into a paroxysm of unbridled merriment.

Unfortunately, at that very moment, the bus driver came to call us for the journey to the conference venue. I had to disappear for a moment to fetch my suitcase. When I returned, my Swiss colleague had gone, but the euphoria of the others, who were now beginning to leave, had not yet subsided. My friend Rosenkranz told me that after my departure our Swiss friend had asked him, "Who actually was that nice gentleman?" (He presumably found me nice because I had given free rein to my amusement.) When Rosenkranz then revealed my identity to him, he ran away horrified.

At that moment, I realized how unfair we had been in letting him run straight into such an embarrassing situation. I resolved to seek him out at the conference and to make clear to him that I had taken no offense and that despite everything we ought to have a good laugh *together* at this bizarre constellation of circumstances. Scarcely had I entered a hall in search of him, however, when I saw a cloud of dust in some part of the room as someone rushed at high speed for the exit. He too was obviously keeping a lookout for me in order to beat a hasty retreat whenever and wherever I appeared. But then despite everything, providence (which, I presume, was responsible) *did* bring us together, in fact it was in the gentlemen's toilet. There a person needs a few seconds before he can run away. And in those few seconds I was able to put him at ease. We then parted as good friends.

I have included this episode here as a brief marginal note to my description of the Michel sermons. Although preaching was a task that I undertook with joy and gratitude, it also carried a heavy burden of responsibility. When I saw the people gathered below me, above me, and around me in the great dome of the church, when I saw the little band of loyal churchgoing Christians and the much larger crowd of people who had only a peripheral relationship to the Church and who often had no spiritual home at all, I was, despite my happiness at the task, also oppressed by its immensity. The many letters and conversations in which my congregation expressed themselves revealed to me that people in a city as secularized as Hamburg were not so much longing for "salvation" as merely curious: they wanted to know how someone who looks like them and lives in the same way as they do exists as a Christian.

At soirées, when the conversation turned to religious matters, which often happened, I sometimes simply told "biblical stories." I did this because the questions were sometimes so elementary and true-to-life that one lost all interest in mere discussion and saw oneself compelled to preach the Gospel directly. I can remember a good example of this on the evening after the naming of a ship. We were all dressed in tails, standing together with champagne glasses in our hands in the foyer of a posh hotel. A well-known ship owner then approached me and, in front of the others, began to tell me about the death of his wife. "I can't make head or tail of the Bible," he said, "I prefer to read Homer or Hölderlin." (He was one of those highly cultured "royal businessmen" such as are frequently found in Hamburg). It had always saddened his wife that he did not share her faith—despite the close relationship they had otherwise enjoyed together. When she died, he said, one of her last statements had been, " 'If you knew what it meant to have a savior on one's last journey, then you too would make this journey.' Can you imagine what she meant by that?" Everyone looked at me expectantly. What a question to be asked when one is in so-called high society with a champagne glass in one's hand! All one can do is offer up a quick prayer to heaven that one can clearly bear witness to one's subject without adopting the wrong tone. I cannot think of another city where the people ask questions and hold conversations in such a blunt, realistic, and direct manner, regardless of whether the subject is problems at the stock exchange or the eternal questions. That is what I love about the people of Hamburg. And because they are prepared to discuss these eternal questions and never talk around them in a roundabout way, they also give the preacher the freedom and the inclination to address them from the pulpit in blunt language.

All my joy at preaching was admittedly overshadowed by the consciousness that I was not doing nearly enough for my congregation, and I felt a sense of guilt because of this. I stepped down from the pulpit and went back to pursuing my other work; but the people should have been gathered together, I ought to have personally taken care of them and given them the opportunity to talk things out. But I had neither enough energy nor sufficient time to do this. I learned above all from the letters I received that many people lacked the most primitive material prerequisites for faith. They did not and do not know how to use the Bible and to locate a passage in it, indeed they did not even know where to buy a Bible. The fact that I was unable adequately to look after precisely that which I had set in motion with my sermons came to weigh heavily on my conscience. Simply to point these people to a conventional parish that perhaps had little sympathy for their problems was not always the correct solution.

One day, two philology students came to me and asked if they could discuss questions of faith with me. They came from respectable social-democratic families, which—in accordance with the early anticlericalism of the working class in the nineteenth century—had broken with the Church. These two young people had had no religious instruction whatsoever; as far as religion was concerned, they were an absolute *tabula rasa*. They had never seen a church from inside before—at least not "at work"—but somebody had now prompted them to visit the Michel. They had been impressed by the crowd of worshipers, but above all by the powerful singing and the way everybody said the Lord's Prayer together, which was also unknown to them. We then talked to each other for a whole evening. I answered their questions as well as I could, told them stories from the Gospel, and also told them about some of my own religious experiences. After a few further evenings, I gave them my book on the Lord's Prayer, which contained a series of sermons that I had given in Stuttgart during the bombing. They thanked me for the book in almost gushing terms and then told me the following story which, although hard to believe, nonetheless reveals something typical of our age, albeit in an extreme form.

When the two of them had understood at least a few fragments of the Lord's Prayer they had heard spoken in unison in Church, they were bent on knowing the complete text. However, because everybody seemed to know it and to recite it from memory, they were embarrassed to admit their ignorance and ask someone for the text. So they betook themselves to the state library to search for the Lord's Prayer there, but were unable to find it. (Where, after all, were they supposed to look?) After that, they tried the theology faculty library, again without success. They found the whole business increasingly mysterious *until* they finally remembered that Sunday church services were broadcast on the radio and it was possible that the Lord's Prayer might occur during them. So they sat down in front of the loudspeaker with a shorthand pad. "And so we finally got hold of the text of the Lord's Prayer," they said, concluding their story.

We then had regular meetings to discuss religious questions whenever I was able to find time. One day they then informed me of their wish to be baptized into the Christian Church, preferably in a church service at the Michel, which was where they had first come into contact with the Christian faith. I naturally agreed to this with surprise and gratitude. But then they suddenly stopped coming for several months. One day, one of them finally turned up and told me what had happened. Before the date we had arranged for the baptism, they had suddenly realized that they had only come to know Christianity through me. In order to make their own judgement, however, they felt they absolutely had to become acquainted with the Catholic "variant" as well. So they went to a Jesuit college in Hamburg that specialized in missionary work to our secularized city. There they were looked after by a priest who had unlimited time for them and were given a sort of "intensive course" in religion. The influence of this course led them to join the Catholic Church. The young man was rather inhibited when he told me this because he was afraid I would react indignantly. But I was pleased that they had found a home for their young faith in this way. And if this joy was not completely devoid of sadness, then it was only because I had failed to care for them with sufficient intensity. I had to prepare my lectures, seminars, sermons, and many other things; I did not have as much time as the Catholic priest who was able to devote himself fulltime to this task. And yet I was tormented by the question of whether I had struck the right balance in my work. Should not everything else have taken second place?

Of all my duties, the preparation necessary for my Michel sermons required the most time. I regarded, and regard, the sermon as the greatest intellectual achievement that can be demanded of a theologian—and this was all the more the case with the congregation with which I had to deal. Preaching a sermon involved a large number of different activities. In the first place, I had to make a precise interpretation of the text and translate it into a form accessible to the congregation. Then it was a case of showing the relevance of the text to the questions, problems, and situations that arise in people's lives. (This is probably what the *Spiegel* reporter was referring to when he spoke of the role that newspapers played in my sermons.) I also had to avoid getting bogged down in an abstract train of thought. Such abstraction is possible and appropriate in a lecture, but in a sermon it is necessary to speak graphically, vividly, and to employ the narrative form. In this way ordinary people were able to follow the sermon and yet educated people also did not go away empty-handed. The aim of the sermon, after all, is to *create* something living and set it in motion. Consequently, it should be directed not only at the intellect, but must at the same time also be aimed at the conscience, will, and imagination. It is addressed to the *whole* person! Corresponding to the complexity of this goal are the wealth of reflections in which one is absorbed before one makes one's way to the pulpit.

The extremely pluralistic composition of my audience forced me to still further reflections. The different levels of education and social background necessitated an inquiry into that aspect of human nature that is common to *all* human beings, that center of their being in which—each in his own different way—human beings are moved by fear and hope, by their finitude, by ambition, desires, the search for meaning, by the burden of guilt and torment of conscience. My goal—and I strived to attain it at least partially— had to be above all to ensure that everyone could say afterwards (because he had been personally touched in this center of his being, "I was the subject of this sermon, he meant me."

In order to find associations with the text for my sermon and so to illustrate it with images, stories, and a human touch, I constantly kept an eye open during my varied reading for anything I could use in the pulpit. I started various collections in files and card indexes in order to have suitable quotations and other material at hand. If this material then nevertheless failed to hit the mark, I could at least comfort myself with the fact that I had done all that I could.

I did not, by the way, keep to the prescribed *readings*, that is, to the texts stipulated for use in church sermons. At best these prescribed texts have *one* useful function, namely, they safeguard the preacher from misusing the text by preventing him from choosing a text simply as a motto for his pet ideas. Preachers who do this quickly preach themselves dry. Their only achieve- ment is to cause deadly boredom—probably not only to the audience but also to themselves—by their constant rummaging through the remnants of a crop that has long since been completely harvested. A prescribed text is certainly the best protection against the law of inertia taking effect in this way. It is also possible for the preacher himself to build a defensive wall against this temptation. This can be done in the following way.

I forced myself to give series of sermons oriented towards a sequence of biblical texts or a single subject. This is how the aforementioned series on the Lord's Prayer, the parables, the biblical creation story, the pastoral conversations of Jesus, the creed, and many others came about. I also gave openly "didactic" sermons, which were a sort of catechism lesson for adults, in which I explained, for instance, the theological significance of histori- cocritical textual research and allowed the congregation to take a look into the workshop of academic theology. This principle of preaching series of sermons proved to be fruitful for both sides. It was fruitful for the preacher because it subjected him to a salutary constraint and safeguarded him against arbitrarily choosing texts on his own authority. It was fruitful for the audience because their interest was sustained by the continuity and development of a particular subject or train of thought, as a result of which they always looked forward eagerly to the next sermon.

The fact that I brought current events into play in my sermons should not be taken to mean that I had been talking politics in the pulpit. In my opinion, there are two *types of degenerate sermon*, both of which, although very different in themselves, are today having a ruinous effect on the life of the church service.

The first of these decadent forms is the transformation of the sermon into a set political speech proclaiming a particular political position as *the* Christian position. In my experience, this mostly gains the upper hand among people whose spiritual substance is too diluted for them to give a rousing proclamation of the Gospel. They are then forced to give their sermons a *political* shot in the arm to lend their dead spirituality the appearance of life. But this form of sermon has no permanence. People very soon wonder why it should need the circuitous route of the pulpit to get this political message across and whether they could not get the same thing cheaper and *without* the Christian paraphernalia simply by going *straight* to a political meeting.

The second type of degenerate sermon is a certain ritualism that suppresses or at least obscures the personal faith of the individual through the excessive use of time-honored phrases and traditional *musica sacra*.

This brief look into the "theological laboratory" has not yet touched on what goes on inside the preacher. This remains hidden to outside eyes. I can only give the following hint at where one should look for an answer. Whoever sees so many eyes directed towards him is in great danger. He may believe that they are directed towards "him," whereas he is in fact only the ambassador of another. In the sacristy of the Church of St. Michael there is a little altar where the preacher prepares himself to approach the pulpit and arms himself against the temptations that threaten him. This is all that I wish to say about this matter.

In a clear allusion to my Michel sermons, a weekly periodical published a comparison between a preacher who attracted very large congregations and another preacher somewhere in Schleswig-Holstein who each week waited to see if anyone else would come to his services apart from his wife and the verger. The author then posed the question of who had precedence in the Kingdom of God: the "successful" or the "loyal" preacher. I do not believe that this is a genuine alternative. But ever since then I have always given thought at the little altar to those fellow clergymen of mine who are loyal although they see no sign of their seeds bearing fruit.

It is now appropriate to follow these weighty issues concerning my profession with one of those curious interludes that have come to form part of the style of this autobiography.

Hamburg's secularism could sometimes manifest itself in some amusing forms. The people of Hamburg possessed hardly any religious vocabulary and were thus unable to find the appropriate words to express their gratitude for a sermon. When I think of how the Swabian pietists used to express their thanks, this verbal deficiency strikes me all the more. Thus, for instance, when the Swabians wish to express their grateful approval of a sermon, they will say, "You were a trumpet of the Lord!" or "Hallelujah, Amen!" The inhabitants of Hamburg, however, mostly say, "Thanks for the 'nice' (or also 'lovely') sermon!" But the look on their faces and the tone of their voices often intimated very much more than was contained in their words—and this amply compensated for their verbal shortcomings. One of my Michel sermons got particularly under the skin of one member of the congregation; with tears in his eyes and visibly moved he said to my wife, "Your husband's tongue has got both feet firmly on the ground!" Some similar surprising remarks occurred when some radio reporters took up position in front of the Church of St. Michael, held their microphones under the noses of numerous members of the congregation and asked, "Why do you go to Thielicke at the Church of St. Michael?" I can still recall *one* of the answers. An old woman said with a lovely rolling "r," "I rrrequire Misterrr Thielicke's serrrmons for my physical well-being."

My sermons were published in book form, and over the years have been translated into twelve foreign languages, including Japanese and Afrikaans. So the question I have just posed as to whether that common level to which the Christian proclamation of the Gospel appeals actually exists in all human beings once again became topical for me and, indeed, in a sharpened form. If it does *not* exist, what could possibly be the point in people from different continents and races receiving the same message in their own language? This question also confronts us with the problem of how best to carry out missionary work.

It was for me a great blessing to have in the person of John W. Doberstein nothing less than a charismatic translator of my works for the English-speaking world. I was greatly saddened when this kind and splendid man, with whom I eventually came to enjoy a close friendship, died so young. Through immense effort he was able to transform German into Anglo-Saxon idioms and to "Americanize" the language in such a way that many readers and reviewers believed they had an American text before them. Bilingual readers have informed me that the style of the American edition is appreciably better than the German original—which is not exactly flattering for the author. The first book Doberstein translated was my collection of sermons on the parables; the other volumes quickly followed.

Thus it came about that I first became known in the Anglo-Saxon world only as a "preacher" because the English editions of my works on ethics and dogmatics were only published later. During my first visits to the United States, I was not exactly happy that my work was regarded exclusively from this one-sided perspective, and once mentioned this to a colleague at Princeton. He gave me a wise answer that experience later showed me to be correct. "Be pleased," he said, "that your first encounter with the Americans was as a preacher and not as an academic. If your theoretical works were the first to be published, a conflict of opinion would arise immediately. The prejudices that would then develop among a minority of people would not assist the acceptance of your theology. Through your sermons, however, a sort of spiritual trust is developing among large sections of the population. As a result, people will later also take a much less inhibited attitude towards your theology."

Indeed, as a result of my sermons, even the fundamentalists (a large, strict group which radically rejects historicocritical research on the Bible) did not shun me from the outset. They saw that I was concerned with the interpretation of biblical texts. The liberals thought: he speaks in a "modern" style, therefore he is one of us. The Baptists thought: he has edited and written a commentary on the homiletics of our "sacred" Spurgeon, therefore he is on our side. The Lutherans thought: the Church of St. Michael, where he gives these sermons, is on our denominational territory. So wherever I went in the United States, all the denominations and schools of thought listened to me with an astonishing openness.

Wherever I went on my journeys I came across people with whom the printed word had forged links. Once on a sea voyage we made a detour to a Zulu university in South Africa. There the captain rummaged about in the library's card index and handed me a whole pile of cards with the English titles of my books. Mind you, the personal appearance of the author—to compare my insignificant case with that of the great apostle Paul—often caused severe disappointment; above all because my English was quite poor as I had only been trained in the classical languages. Foreign readers are not at all prepared for this. For the most part they naively assume that the author speaks the same excellent English that is written in his books. As a rule it usually takes them a while to understand what I immediately point out to them (and even in English), namely, "My books speak better English than their author." After I had given my first lecture in English at Chicago, a gentleman approached me and happily informed me (also in English, of course), "I always thought German was a very difficult language; but I understood at least two sentences of your lecture!"

I had another experience with language in Japan. My large academic works (the books on ethics and dogmatics) have not yet been translated into Japanese. (The translation of my anthropological work *Being Human-Becoming Human* is in preparation.) It is to be expected, however, that those who pursue academic theology in the narrower sense are capable of reading German works in the original. Since my lecture in Tokyo was to be translated simultaneously, I found it necessary to ask a rather skeptical question: If the audience could not understand a lecture given in German, I could hardly presuppose knowledge of my *Theological Ethics*—or could I? If this were so, I would have to restructure my lecture. I received an amazing answer to this: all the lecturers and students present were very familiar with the books, they had studied them in the original and discussed them in seminars, even if they were unable to speak German. Nevertheless, they must surely have, I said to myself, some idea of what they had read sounded like! I would have very much liked to have learned more about this. Sometimes I asked my Japanese doctoral students to read a few sentences aloud to me in the way a Japanese who could not speak German would imagine them to sound. Although we had a close relationship, I *never* managed to persuade them to do this. Thus right up to the present day I still do not know what it sounds like.

Some of the Italian translations are published by markedly Catholic publishing houses. If I am not very much mistaken, our Catholic "stepbrothers" are more receptive to my work than my own denomination. But there is bound to be some friction when the books of a Protestant theologian come under Rome's direct and powerful influence! This friction was mild, however, and manifested itself, for example, in the publisher's request to be allowed occasionally to include the footnote "Here Thielicke is mistaken!"

There was, however, much ecumenical common ground between us, and the footnotes, I was assured, were only concerned with nuances. In the case of one of these books I was even granted the honor of an episcopal "imprimatur."

Hamburg Personalities and Episodes

Not least among the influential personalities in Hamburg are the head doormen of large hotels and important business concerns. One of them got in contact with me while I was still living in Tübingen. He unintentionally provided me with an impression of the relaxed and yet serious manner in which the "worldlings" of Hamburg treat theologians, clerics, and other "pious" people. When I came to Hamburg, so he told me, I absolutely had to put a stop to the mischief-making of the most wicked clique that existed in those parts. He meant people in the advertizing profession(!). For some reason or another he had a particular aversion to them. I answered him with a noncommittal "Yes, yes, I suppose so."

Hardly had I arrived in Hamburg when I was surprised to receive an invitation printed on deckle-edged paper to a discussion that I myself was supposed to conduct at such-and-such a place with leading figures from the advertizing business. As the initiator of this discussion the invitation was signed by that very same doorman. The man obviously had no idea of how one goes about arranging such an event, and particularly that the people concerned have to be informed beforehand and their consent obtained.

I was now in an awkward situation and had to take part whether I wanted to or not. My head doorman was standing at the entrance in a black sport coat and wearing rimless spectacles. He looked as dignified as a member of a papal consistory. The other gentlemen had already gathered in the conference room and were sitting in a large semicircle. In front of them stood a chair that was obviously intended for me. We looked at each other rather distrustfully and nobody was quite sure what was now supposed to happen. Eventually, the head doorman held a brief welcoming speech in which he announced that I would now hold a talk "for the reason announced(!)." At that moment I realized that I *too* had not behaved very cleverly and had missed the opportunity of discussing the necessary arrangements with him. This was something I should have done at the latest on entering the building. Now I had no other choice but to do my best to remove my head from the noose.

So I said to the gentlemen present that I had not come to teach them but would first like to hear and learn something from *them*. If only by virtue of their profession, advertizing men are never at a loss for words, and thus one of them responded to my demonstration of modesty and immediately took the floor. "Professor," he said, "I don't know if you are aware that you and we pursue a similar trade: you sell religion [I was almost speechless at this!] and we sell margarine. We are both equally concerned with finding a buyer for our products. And in this respect the Church can learn something from us margarine people! Above all one must not speak over people's heads. If we were to extol our margarine with details about vitamins and calories, we would have just as little success with our customers as you would if you were to deal with high-falutin dogmas and eccentric formulae. In advertizing one must always take the intellectually weakest partner as one's guide. In our case, that is the German housewife. That's why we don't torment her with chemical details about our product. Instead, we serve her up with a poster of a little child biting with relish into a slice of bread and margarine and write underneath, 'Oh Mummy, that tastes good!' That is what the German house-wife understands, and that is how I obtain my success. And listen, you ought to do the same with religion!"

These were tones of a kind that I had never heard in Swabia. The man was polite, but quite without inhibitions when faced with a profession that was foreign to him. It did not even seem strange to him to measure everything—from religion to margarine—with the same economic and psychological yardstick. He at any rate left nothing to be desired as far as directness was concerned. Because of his profession he felt himself to be a connoisseur of human nature, and since preachers also had to deal with people, he was convinced that they could take a leaf out of his book and benefit from his professional knowledge. The crazy thing was that there was at least a trace, a "mustard seed" of truth in his daring comparison.

So that was how the "worldlings" of Hamburg talked to people like us! One had to be prepared for everything. That is why this meeting acquired great significance for me. From then on the question of "How do I impart the truth to my worldlings?" occupied me even more. I crossed the threshold into completely new considerations on how the proclamation of the Gospel and pastoral care should be undertaken in an area of extreme secularization.

After this refreshing cold shower in the secular worldview, I also became acquainted with more sublime forms of Hamburg's worldliness. I was very soon invited to speak at Hamburg's famous Overseas Club—and was later even more often their guest. After the speaker had given his lecture, it was customary for him to dine there. At this club I very quickly came into contact with those who have "the say" in Hamburg: city leaders and senators, businessmen and bankers, ship owners and artists. Several of the big businessmen were famous patrons who had endowed their home town with important cultural institutions. One of them offered prizes for services to society, literature, art, nature conservation, poetry in dialect and many other things. The prize money came close or even surpassed that of the Nobel prize. The noble side of the Hanseatic businessmen was revealed in these prizes. They were aware of the obligation imposed by great wealth. Many of these so-called money-grubbers—what a misjudgment this is!—lived personally very modestly and invested large parts of their fortune in serving the general public.

I was just as amazed at the intellectual charm, at the sophistication of the after-dinner speeches, the welcoming speeches, and the speeches of thanks on such occasions, which were like nothing I had experienced in any other town. The considerable intellectual power and culture these businessmen had at their disposal was also manifested in the level of conversation at the Overseas Club. A ship owner who was a friend of mine collected French impressionists; an insurance broker's hobby was to translate the Odes of Horace; another was an expert on Eastern Asian religions. Correspondingly, the homes to which we were invited were highly cultured. They were always furnished with a wealth of priceless furniture and works of art that had been accumulated over many years. These were not there to show off, however, and delighted the guest just as much as the warmth of the company and—for all their observance of form and style—the frankness of conversation did.

I have avoided naming names because the selection would be too delicate and would also be of no interest to the reader living far from Hamburg. There is *one* person, however, whom I must mention, because we had a close relationship with her, namely Liselotte von Rantzau, the "boss" of the German-African shipping line. We were often guests at her magnificent estates at Trittau, Austria, Cape Town, or Mombassa in East Africa, but above all at her residence on the River Elbe, the "White House," which contains one of the most priceless porcelain collections in Europe. Whenever we entered this house, which was illuminated only by candles, we always felt as if we had entered into a fairytale world. For me, Liselotte von Rantzau is a woman worthy of admiration. She rules over her empire singlehandedly and is constantly traveling to negotiations with industrialists and statesmen all over the world. She may indeed be something of an iron lady in her business dealings, but all who meet her are impressed by her grace and kindness, care and humanity. I have sailed on many of her ships and the crew have often told me of all she does for the families of the officers and crew to compensate them for the long absence of their fathers and husbands. Above all, she played an important role in making us feel at home in Hamburg. I will describe later how she alone of all the people of influence came to my aid during the student revolt.

There were some impressive figures at the university too. In those days— until the student revolt and the subsequent disfiguring reorganization of the university brought this all to an end—the academic staff were constantly meeting for parties and social gatherings. Here the different faculties used to meet, and human friendships were struck up that continued outside these gatherings. Especially among my very old colleagues there was a whole string of famous characters at these meetings, such as the great neurologist Max Nonne, for instance, who had invented shock therapy during the First World War. I met Nonne for the first time when the rector gave a banquet for all the professors after the opening of our faculty. He was then already over ninety. At my table, my colleagues told me some of the anecdotes that had grown up around him. Although he was now rather hard of hearing, they said, one still had to be wary of his quick and sharp tongue. In the course of the evening I went to his table with my younger colleague Hans-Joachim Kraus and said, "May we introduce ourselves as members of the youngest faculty at Hamburg, Mr. Nonne?" He put his hand to his ear and had probably only understood something about "young" or "youth." At any rate, he asked my friend Kraus, "Is that so? And in which semester are you, young man?" Kraus was so surprised at this that he let slip, "I'm no longer a student, I'm a professor!" Old Nonne immediately apologized and said, "Please forgive me, colleague. I can no longer distinguish between anything that lies between puberty and forty!" Soon afterwards, we saw that the venerable president of the City Parliament, Adolph Schönfelder, who was also about eighty and likewise the subject of many anecdotes, was making a beeline for Nonne. A few of us quickly rushed over to them to hear what two such ancient men had to say to each other, expecting to hear some words of wisdom. The only thing we overheard, however, was old Nonne's question, "Can you still put your trousers on by yourself? I can!"

When I was asked during my first years at Hamburg to take the chair of the nonpartisan Society for Economic and Social Policy, yet another aspect of this multifaceted city was revealed to me. As chairman, I was responsible for looking after the large conference center at Rissen, where we also later liked to hold our interfaculty conferences. Here we organized discussions between industrialists, trade unions, and the generals of the newly formed West German armed forces. Many firms also made use of this beautiful house, which was set in a park, for their training courses. Since the meetings there did not take place in a bureaucratic ivory tower but in a cultured and convivial atmosphere, even heated specialist discussions always remained within the bounds of agreeable and civilized behavior. The main credit for this goes not to me, however, but to the heads of studies who worked at Rissen House full-time.

My portrayal of the people of Hamburg with whom I had, and have, to deal would be very inadequate if I did not also include the so-called ordinary people in this picture gallery, especially the manual workers. These workers are proud of their status and ability and yet, even when one has developed an almost friendly relationship with them, never take crude liberties. We have never noticed any of the Nordic coolness and distance I had been warned about in Tübingen. I can still see our children gathered around the old, wise bricklayer to listen to his stories. When he built our fireplace, he told us that he had also walled up all his love in this place of contentment and human conversation.

And then there were the female toilet attendants in Hamburg! One often met some truly eccentric characters among them. They were self-assured women who were committed to their profession, not least because at quiet moments it made them into mother confessors for many people. I would now like to paint a little portrait of such a woman; this portrait at the same time gives an indication of the milieu around the Michel.

One day, when I entered the study of one of the Michel pastors, I found him reading a postcard while shaking his head and muttering to himself, "What am I supposed to do now?" The events leading up to his receiving the postcard were as follows. At the landing stage in St. Pauli there was a ladies toilet, the attendant of which was a loyal member of the Michel congregation. For some reason this toilet had been torn down, whereupon the woman had rushed in despair to her pastor and poured her heart out to him. "My whole reason for living has gone," she said, "I lived for my toilets!" She had a Lutheran work ethic—in the midst of the realm of the sewer—and thus showed that she had understood the reformer exactly. The pastor now attempted to comfort her, as indeed his position required of him. At the same time, however, he wanted to prove himself to be a man of action and thus did everything in his power to restore to the woman her reason for living. He thus lobbied the relevant authorities right up to the senate in his fight to get this useful institution reestablished. He accepted the ridicule and forbearing smiles he received when people showed their surprise that a pastor should extend his pastoral work to such areas. And lo and behold, his efforts paid off. A new and better ladies toilet was built close to the old site. The woman was overjoyed and was able to continue to follow her vocation.

So the pastor now held the ominous postcard in his hand and let me read it: "Dear Reverend, I invite you to the opening of the new business at 8 o'clock Monday morning. With many thanks, yours. . . ." Her pastor was not quite sure how he should best do justice to this invitation. Did she expect him to flush the toilet for the first time? We agreed that the best course of action would be for his wife to appear on Monday morning with a bunch of flowers.

I have already told a few stories about the students with whom I spent most of my time, such as their assistance in setting up the faculty and their attendance at the Open Evenings we arranged both at home and outside. But there were also gatherings that fell outside my usual routine. I only wish to mention one of these here, because it meant a great deal to all our lives. We had heard that the barracks at Wentorf, a village not far from Hamburg, were completely full of refugees and their families from Poland, Czechoslovakia, Rumania and other countries. We had also heard that they often had to wait there in extremely wretched conditions for months and that they were increasingly falling prey to despair and hopelessness. I thus deliberated with my students whether it was not our duty to come to the assistance of these people when the winter semester of 1957–1958 was over.

Our offer of help was accepted with delight by the camp authorities. So I set off with twenty male and female students and spent three weeks there. We stayed at a youth hostel and chartered an omnibus to take us to the barracks each morning and to fetch us again in the evening.

At the camp we split up into separate groups and spent the whole day visiting the many halls of the large barracks complex. There we talked to the people, inquired about their difficulties, and did everything in our power to help. Each family had partitioned off its "own territory" with curtains. They slept on military bunkbeds. There was also a great muddle of clothes and various household utensils everywhere because of the lack of cupboards. Worst of all, there was insufficient freedom of movement for the children and adolescents. Many people could hardly speak any German and consequently were helpless when it came to dealing with the authorities. They were very intimidated by the numerous forms they had to fill out. So they were very happy when we took care of the paperwork in particular and accompanied them to the relevant authorities. The very fact that somebody was prepared to look after them was in itself of comfort to them. In the evenings I said prayers in the camp church and our students sang with them. We sensed how much calmer they became.

Every day one or other of the families was "filtered out" in order to be settled in some north German town and reintegrated into normal life. Each evening we sang hymns in the corridors of the barracks and each family about to leave the camp on the following day was allowed to choose a song. This was nearly always "So take my hands." At first there were some of us who recoiled at this. This hymn offended their sense of liturgical style. But then they saw how moved these people were, who after losing their homes and possessions and suffering an unsettled fate as refugees now stood on the eve of a change of fortune. They saw their tears and this gained the upper-hand over any questions of taste.

Every afternoon I got together with my people for about two hours to speak to them about all the misery they had witnessed during the day and to advise them on solutions to the problems that had arisen.

During such discussions, the question arose as to how we could free the young people from their apathy, tension, and increasing mindlessness. We decided to organize evening dances in the hope that this would help to relax them. After some initial inhibitions, this too was rewarded with the nicest success. The young people began to laugh again, to come out of their shells and strike up relations with each other. For the children we set up a daily Punch and Judy show, for which we first had to make the puppets. During our bus journeys to the camp, we used to give thought to the course of the drama we were about to perform, which gave us great enjoyment. These shows even provided me with the following theological experience.

During these shows I always had to play the devil, and the puppet I was in charge of had flaming red hair. The students named what I did with this puppet "Thielicke ethics." I had indeed resolved to carry out a "moral" task. I asked each of the parents about the children's particular vices and learned of all sorts of little sins: they refused to wash, they just threw their banana skins on the camp road, and so on. In order to get the children to behave a little more orderly, I did something that initially gave the adult members of the audience quite a shock: I introduced myself as the devil and announced that I wanted to teach the children a lot of bad things. The children immediately shouted me down. They did not want to have anything to do with the devil. I then advised them that they should under no circumstances wash their feet, for, I said, I loved the smell of unwashed children. I further encouraged them to throw their banana skins on the street wherever possible, because I loved to hear the squeals people made when they slipped on one. The children were so outraged at this diabolical advice that I could scarcely hear my own voice above the cries of protest that kept bursting forth. I was in the end so hoarse that I had to seek medical treatment.

This little episode did indeed contain a theological point. The biblical fall was only able to come about because the serpent had preserved its anonymity and thus appeared to Eve to be a serious conversational partner with whom she could discuss the subject "God." If the serpent had *revealed* itself in its satanic role, Eve would have recoiled and certainly not have taken any notice of its evil attacks. I had reckoned on these connections becoming clear when I openly revealed myself as the devil and only then launched my despicable advice. A devil who shows his cards immediately arouses protest and resistance. That was why my educational successes were so stunning. From then on, the children willingly let themselves be washed and litter visibly decreased. Many parents surreptitiously whispered their thanks to me.

I concluded each evening by telling my male students a story in the dormitory, much like when one gives children a goodnight treat. My female students were rather envious that this was denied to them. Every now and again we caught them listening at the door, where they had been attracted by the men's laughter. Despite all the hardships, it was a splendid and fulfilling time. Even many years later many an old Wentorfer confessed to me that this intensive course in humanity and spirituality had given him something for the rest of his life. This was also the case with me.

Since I have just been talking about my students, I must mention another ritual which was repeated every three years when I gave my lecture on the history of theology. The history of theology was my favorite course of lectures—as I believe it also was for my audience—because it was not only concerned with tracing great theological and philosophical conceptions, but also with graphically portraying and visualizing the characters of great thinkers. To this end I was not afraid to make use of drastic methods of illustration.

I had dug up a Catholic priest from the baroque period, Michael von Jung, who had been a highly eccentric Swabian character of the first order. At funerals he did not preach sermons but sang songs to lute accompaniment in front of each grave. The text of these songs described the life and death of the deceased in the style of a street ballad. The people flocked from far and wide to witness this truly unusual form of Christian preaching. However, the bishop felt that this form of funeral oration was inappropriate and wished to prevent it. The king, however, was so taken with it that he awarded Jung a high decoration that admitted him to the ranks of the aristocracy. For his part, the priest was so immensely happy at the honor that had been bestowed upon him that on the following Sunday he had the organist play a military march in celebration. He then marched through the church in time to the music and sprinkled the congregation with holy water in exact time to the rhythm of the march.

A collection of particularly odd street ballads has been preserved, including songs about a youth who danced himself to death, a man who hanged himself while stealing pigs, and many others. (I later published them as a paperback with Herder publishing house.) Whenever I was due to lecture on the Baroque and Enlightenment eras, I always found a member of my audience who was prepared to get dressed up as Michael von Jung and recite a few of these songs in the lecture. On each occasion, the cloakroom attendants and porters were invited to attend, so that the lecture became great fun. Above all, this unorthodox approach enabled the practical moral applications of the lecture to stick in people's minds. Indeed, passages from the songs sometimes became standard quotations which continued to circulate throughout the semester. Thus the edifying conclusion of the ballad of the young man who suffered a heart attack through excessive dancing, once became the motto of a faculty ball.

Wise men also dance, it's true,
But their movements are not hasty;
They dance with use of reason too,
And therefore only briefly.

Major Journeys in the 1950s

A S A RULE, it is precisely the first impressions we receive on traveling to a foreign country that are the strongest and for that reason the most informative. Habit has not yet deadened one's awareness of everyday events. For this reason I would like to devote special consideration to my first encounter with the United States, while only giving a brief summary of my many later journeys to North America, South America, and Canada.

My First Journey to the United States, Spring 1956

My first invitation to visit the United States as a visiting professor came from Drew University in Madison, New Jersey. For me, America began with the little drink we had in New York Harbor with the friends who had visited us on board the *Göttingen*. On leaving the ship, I kissed the hand of an elderly lady with whom we had spent many hours together through fair weather and foul, at delicious dinners, and in swapping stories in the smoking room in the evenings. This good motherly woman from old Europe looked like a pale splotch in the midst of the colorful faces and even more colorful hats belonging to all her female friends in her age group. This kiss on the hand was a little signal. Her colorful female friends watched this little Old World ceremony with a sort of melancholy amusement. The Americans are familiar with such encounters but do not themselves practice them, a fact that sometimes causes paradoxes in their behavior. Thus one of the old ladies called to me with that wonderful American spontaneity that so charmingly upsets the orderly manners of the European: "Professor, kiss my hand too!"

I later discovered that this harmless scene had been a typical example of American behavior. The Americans' impromptu life style imposes little restraint on their moods. It permits them to be informal at meals and often even to keep their chewing gum in their mouths during prayers at church. Nevertheless, this style contains an element of longing for the correct way of doing things. This longing is revealed, for instance, in the Americans' slightly ironical love of the splendor of European royal weddings, and perhaps the same motive—among others!—betrays itself in the ecclesiastical sphere in the growing tendency towards liturgical forms. The ahistorical person occasionally seems to feel the cold and to long to be clothed in history. Sure, the future has already begun. One sits in the high-speed train of a still cheerful belief in progress on a seat facing the direction in which the train is traveling. But occasionally one changes to the seat opposite and looks back into the countryside that has already been covered. The human being is a creature that is coming from somewhere.

This yearning for history was to strike me even more often in later years. It was touching how our friends showed us the former battlefields of the American Revolution, how they took us around the neo-Gothic churches, to which one as European initially reacts purely esthetically and precisely for that reason incorrectly and unfairly. In all of this the debate with the past, indeed the *seizing* of the past was manifested. There is nothing that it is not possible to make. Why then should it not also be possible to make the past? This often violent act of visualizing the past may be determined by a certain sentimentality: the emigrants would like to have a piece of England or a piece of Germany in their midst. By attempting to make the country of origin present in this way, they are seeking their "father," seeking their own ancestry, the connection with what is permanently present. They know that they have to take charge of themselves out of the past.

That is why the category of taste, if it becomes an exclusive criterion, is so inappropriate here. We theologians ought perhaps to say: the neo-Gothic cathedrals should be interpreted not esthetically, but existentially. Thus one can only love the Americans' neo-Gothic style when one loves the Americans themselves.

By seeing how human beings live in a country with relatively little history, by ascertaining that there actually exists a sort of "punctual existence" in the moment, two things become clear. First, it becomes clear that it is indeed possible for the human being to live in such a way—although the *character indelebilis* (the indestructable character) of the historical entity keeps betraying itself in that painful and devoted fishing for history I have just described. And second, the freight that we Europeans drag around with us in history, in the forms and prejudices that have evolved over centuries, becomes clear. Normally we do not notice all this. We are too close to it; it is, as it were, a piece of us. We are, so to speak, covered with history and believe that it is our skin, that it is a piece of our very selves.

Only when we are in the United States, where apartments and furnishings are only rarely inherited, where people are moving in and out of homes in constant succession and where property is repeatedly alienated, does one realize that the human being is not deeply rooted in the traditions that have developed and the property he possesses. Rather, one becomes aware that this can all be taken away from the human being and *yet* he still is something. Of all places, it was in the wealthy United States of America that I realized what the human being is *in puris naturalibus* (in his natural state). And American forwardness, which we Europeans initially find slightly shocking but then so pleasant, is certainly much more than mere manners.

On a university campus like that at Drew (or for that matter, anywhere else in the United States) students and professors live together. Not since my student days have I lived on such intimate terms with students as I did in those weeks. They looked through my window, and even when I was in my pajamas, one or the other would come in for a discussion. I found it pleasant that there was no false feeling of distance towards me, which is something that can so easily turn into an inhuman respect. And yet I never experienced any crude familiarity but invariably only an often touching friendliness. A distinction was certainly made in age and status between the teachers and the students despite all reports to the contrary, but this all had a more sublime effect that it does with us, not destructive but rather agreeable.

The virtually complete omission of the ceremonies of greeting a person when one meets him and bidding him farewell when one leaves was constantly providing me with food for thought. Not only do people not shake hands, no, they even do not always say hello. It frequently happens that one suddenly finds oneself in a conversation with another person without the preamble of having exchanged greetings. And, especially when it was a good conversation, one is astonished to see the other person disappear without saying goodbye just as suddenly as he had arrived. At first I was shocked by this custom of suddenly striking up a conversation and then abruptly departing. I thought I had done something wrong.

This way of encountering another person is certainly more than a merely meaningless form. We Europeans put everything that we feel for or against the other person into the way in which we greet him and bid him farewell. If our conversation has perhaps been rather impersonal and lacking in discernible communication, then we make up for it with a suitable facial expression and handshake when we leave. Or we do the opposite and confirm the breakdown in communication by saying goodbye in a stiff and cold way. In the United States, on the other hand, standard greetings and farewells are unstressed and indifferent. As long as people are in each other's company, warmheartedness reigns and each person is completely there for the other; yet one may perhaps not even accompany the other person to the door.

What is the reason for this? I have spoken to many clever Americans about this. One historical explanation I was given I found rather too simple. This pointed out that life was extraordinarily hard during the pioneer period. When people parted in those days, it was uncertain whether they would ever see each other again. For this reason, so the explanation goes, people forced themselves to be unsentimental when they said goodbye. The other person simply "passed on." The same phenomenon can also be observed in the United States with regard to death; to a certain extent death is respectfully passed over and made a taboo subject. Here too the same euphemistic circumscription is employed: "he has passed on."

Precisely this parallel between saying goodbye and death pushed me towards another explanation. In the history of ideas it can be easily demonstrated that the less individualistic a society is, the less stress is placed upon the death of the individual. Before a sense of individuality awoke among the Teutons, death was regarded as a relatively trivial act. The hero killed in battle was preserved in the well-being and honor of the tribe. And because death did not bring anyone's individuality to an end, but caused it to merge in the supraindividual, the sting which prompted the belief in a personal immortality was also absent.

And now I think: Could the lack of emphasis on death as well as the strange way Americans greet and take leave of each other not be connected with a tendency to reduce everything to a common denominator that has eroded people's individuality? Is it not possible that this tendency, which can be observed in every country, has merely become evident in a particularly striking form in the United States? In America—as many people who love their country have told me—it is dangerous to be "different." One only wears white shoes from such and such a day onwards and only stops wearing them on such and such a day. Whoever goes directly by the weather instead of by what his neighbors are doing and makes his white shoes a matter of individual decision, creates a bad impression.

One thing at least is certain. To the extent in which individuality becomes indistinct, the encounter of individualities loses some of its specific gravity. The more concrete and unique the other person is, the more the encounter with him becomes an event. The more he is merely a general archetype, however, the easier it is to replace him and turn to someone else. The manner in which Americans greet each other indicates that no event is taking place. Hello Dick! Hello Jack! Dick and Jack are, to put it pointedly, two expressions of the same kind of human being. Oh, how it is good that the creature "man" exists in such variety and takes away our dreaded loneliness!

All of this is again, of course, only partially valid. How many Americans of the highest originality I have come to know, how many have revealed distinct and unmistakable personalities! And on the other hand, how many insubstantial shadows wander specter-like around old Europe! Life is full of contradictions. One puts forward some interpretation or other, and the very next moment is almost forced to retract it.

The extent to which *psychoanalysis* had become both the secular religion and the subject of conversation at parties was astonishing. Even church pastoral care is largely content not only to cooperate with the psychotherapists and to train the clergy in psychology, but even to let psychoanalytical subjects infiltrate sermons. Thus it can happen that a sermon might almost have "Healing one's inferiority complex" as its subject.

Neal, a young Lutheran pastor from New York, told me that there were many young people in his parish who had never left the city. They had not the slightest idea of what the countryside looked like and knew practically no meadows, trees, or woods. The landscape of their lives consisted of the shimmering neon signs within the rather narrow confines of their district of the city. And although they lived in a cosmopolitan city, they had an unimaginably narrow horizon. In the fascinating city of New York with its skyscrapers and fabulous bridges and tunnels, with its bewildering variety of people, with its Negro, Chinese, and Jewish quarters—in this city, as was generally the case in the United States, asphalt and primeval world met.

I would like to cite an example to illustrate this. We were in the cinema watching a western. I had expected the audience to consist of adolescents, such as can be seen at such films in Germany. But this was not at all the case. All the age groups were there and probably also representatives from all the different professions. I was particularly astonished at the large contingent of "serious" people present. We immediately had a debate about this, of course. A young Swiss professor, Markus Barth, who had already lived in the country for some years, was of the opinion that the Americans were a young nation and had what they call a "yearning for history." This yearning, however, wanted more than just history, it also wanted myth. Since the Americans did not possess the necessary prehistory for this, they elevated the pioneer period to mythical status. "You will," he said, "be able to observe the same basic mythical characters time and again in the western. On the one hand, there is the representative of the good principle, who is threatened somewhere by an evil adversary. It is necessary to recognize this evil one as early as possible. And then one has to fight him." The story also always has the same happy ending. The good man—or, if one wishes to formulate the mythical message in clearcut terms, the good power—triumphs. "The mythical structure," Barth continued, "is also apparent in the fact that the category of contemporaneity can be clearly observed. The audience does not experience what takes place in these films as a piece of the past but identifies with it. Each person grows into the role of the good man: his *own* life is threatened by the adversary, he himself now hears both the demand to play a combative role in the plan of life, and the promise that as a champion of the good he will ultimately triumph."

Professor Barth immediately provided a second example of this phenomenon. "You can observe exactly the same mythical process at work in certain cases of what we intellectuals initially feel to be kitsch, such as, for example, the fuss in the press about the marriage of Prince Rainier of Monaco to his Grace. Virtually all the newspaper columns are almost bursting at the seams with this story. This is by no means unique to the United States, of course, but is especially prevalent here. A local newspaper recently conducted an interesting survey among its readers inquiring whether the editorship should continue to print all the trivial details about Grace's favorite dog, the lace borders on her nightgown, and her make-up secrets. I can best summarize the pretty unanimous reply to this survey by quoting the reply given by a young girl, 'Please continue to inform us of all the exact details,' she said. 'Then we'll be better able to put ourselves in Grace's position and know what to do in the same situation.' In the same situation! That's it exactly. Here the basic mythical features have once again become apparent: one enters into a contemporaneous relationship with certain events and identifies oneself with the leading figures. One becomes a little more compassionate towards people," Barth concluded, "when one sees this little piece of primeval world suddenly emerge where the purely esthetic perspective believes it sees only kitsch. In this instance, of course, it is kitsch. But this concept does not encompass all of what is manifested here."

Elderly Americans constantly made a depressing impression upon me. I can still see the large hall of a hotel on the coast before me. Old ladies were sitting there with wrinkled faces that were not just made up but, frankly, plastered with cosmetics. To me they seemed like masks, consumed with boredom. They stared straight ahead, or looked with unseeing eyes through the gaps in the sun-blinds onto a street where nothing ever happened, or sat for hours in front of the television. A few of them played patience. The same was true of the old people with whom I lived in a house together for a few days. None of them ever read a book, at the most they might occasionally read a magazine. And always that unseeing stare and always television as a desperate protection against drowning in boredom. Some friends confirmed the correctness of this impression to me.

What is the origin of this despairing attitude to old age? One of the reasons is certainly not least the fact that people's exclusive dependence upon the car kills any real attachment to the countryside. One can indeed wander all over nature and get to know it inside out, but despite this never actually experience it. When Moltke retired he was asked what there was now left for him to do, since he had always been such an active man. He replied: I shall watch a tree grow. How many elderly Americans could give a similar answer? (This question could, of course, also be directed at many elderly Europeans.)

The life that is determined exclusively by external influences prompts a sham vitality on the part of the individual. However, when contact with the outside world becomes weaker as the individual's receptivity for impressions decreases and he is forced to have a life of his own, the pseudocharacter of his vitality inevitably becomes apparent. The friendly manners in America only inadequately disguise the fact that elderly people are often regarded as a burden. "But we don't have elderly people like in Europe," a clever woman once said to me with whom I had been discussing this problem and whose memory had perhaps caused her to idealize the Old World too much. "Such a thing as the serenity of old age is here rather the exception," she said. Alongside this, there is also a sociological side to the problem of aging. This takes the form of an idolization of youth. After the loss of youth, life is regarded as a decline and people live in fear of this. That is why people basically do not have a positive attitude towards aging and do their utmost to conserve their youth.

One day I received a wonderful lesson in *democracy*. On the campus a student took me to lunch in the refectory. On the way there we cut across the lawn, because a straight line is the shortest route between two points. I drew my companion's attention to the fact that such behavior was not allowed at home in Germany and that set paths had to be used. As I said this I had a rather self-righteous feeling of superiority, such as "tidy" people have toward the "untidy." The student asked, "Really, then how do such paths come about in your country?" Without knowing what he was driving at in asking this strange question, I said to him truthfully, "The architect includes them in his plans. Of course, in drawing up his plans he gives thought to the most suitable routes for the paths." He then replied, "We do things differently. Either someone just walks across the lawn once by chance. Then it doesn't matter. Or, on the other hand, people keep taking the same route across. Then they wear a track in the grass and the lawn is ruined. If possible, the track is then converted into a proper path, because people want to cross the lawn just at that spot."

It is worth reflecting on the American relationship to authority. In the little university town where I was staying, a famous student choir was making a guest appearance. The conductor dominated the event—not only in directing the choir but also in organizing the whole evening and speaking the introductory words between the pieces. He was the sustaining and motivating force of the concert. He had authority.

On the following day I saw him in the refectory where he was standing in line to fetch his meal just like everybody else. He then had difficulty finding a seat because he had arrived last, before eventually finding one in the middle of his team. They had arrived earlier than he had, and had already sat down and begun their meal. People paid no *more* attention to him than to any other of their comrades. The same phenomenon appeared a few days later in the concert hall, where works by Mozart were being played and sung. After her song recital, a young but already quite well-known singer came down from the podium and, still in her soloist wardrobe, sat down with her family among the "crowd." On taking her place in the stalls, she immediately ceased to stand out as a soloist. Like everybody else she was part of the audience, and we were probably the only people to peep furtively over at her. I was in a good position to draw comparisons with conditions in Germany, because I had once experienced in Bonn how Elly Ney had come down from the podium in order to watch the last part of the concert from the stalls. This caused quite a disturbance among the audience, who reacted by secretly peeping at her, whispering, and expressing their admiration! It was really quite different in this small American town.

The distinguishing feature is exclusively the *function*—in this case singing and conducting—and not, or at least not to the same degree, the person who performs the function. One almost seems to keep a close watch that the "soloist" function that distinguishes a person from his fellows is not transferred as a mark of distinction to the person himself. On the contrary, after he has performed his function, it is made clear to him by deliberate indifference or casual directness that his role is now finished and that he is back in the ranks of general equality. The function does not become a predicate of honor for the person who performs it, but simply signifies the service he provides to the community. The community tolerates this service, indeed it takes it for granted. When benefiting from the function, the community honors the function but not the bearer of the function, for example, the artist. Thus the person is not defined by his function. A very strict separation takes place between what a person is and what he does.

A special sense of community arises from all this, which one immediately notices. But it is not a community in our sense. It often lacks depth, if I may permit myself to make such generalizations. This lack of depth manifests itself in the constant repetition of routine, colloquial phrases such as "How are you?" "Let me know if I can do anything for you!" "Come and visit me!" "I'm very pleased to meet you." And of what phonetic variation, of what cooing wonders is the word *very* capable! Community is a highly dialectical reciprocal relationship, it is full of tensions between individuals and overcomes these tensions by establishing relations between individuals. However, because this tension decreases according to the degree in which everything is reduced to the same general level, it is easy for a superficial babble—again in extreme cases—to come about.

This has both its positive and its negative sides. The individual is always immediately involved and in the thick of things. People such as, for example, those sitting next to him at church or the students in the refectory, speak openly to him. They are touchingly ready to help and are receptive to their fellow human beings. Nevertheless, they think of the individual as less than a person; he could at any time be exchanged for someone else to whom they would be just as kind. The individual is a human particle that files past on the conveyor belt of daily intercourse and whose place is immediately taken by other particles of the same species. The negative side of this form of community is already intimated in what I have just said. This negative aspect is that communication frequently remains superficial. It is not easy to get onto an important subject of discussion with the famous Everyman and to break through the routine pattern of normal conversation. One can occasionally philosophize with a Swabian gas station attendant. Whether it can be taken for granted that he will polish the windshield till it shines like his American colleague, is not quite so certain.

We Europeans lack this general openness that makes life so pleasant especially for the newcomer in the United States. In Europe there either exists a deeper communication in the form of friendship or comradeship, or there is no communication whatsoever, in which case a defensive wall is even often erected. That is why friends move closer together in the refectory, that is why there are student communities that cut themselves off from others, and that is why exclusive circles exist within society. In the United States, on the other hand, everyone approaches everyone else and is open-minded about the other person, unless he turns out to be a "nasty character." This willingness to trust another person in advance impressed me greatly.

Goethe once said that one can only understand what one loves. In this sense I must have understood one or two things about the Americans. But one does not love rightly—at least not as a Christian—if love makes one blind. Real love makes one alert and thus also critical. This love does not *distance itself*, however, but includes the other's failings in its love. I like the Americans just as they are.

Amusing and Serious Episodes in Scotland

In the mid-1950s I was given an honorary doctorate by the University of Glasgow. So I set off for Scotland to take part in the solemn ceremony at which I, together with a few other people, was to be awarded this honor. This all took place during the period when I still spoke hardly a word of English. Consequently I awaited this ceremony with some trepidation and with sealed lips, for I had at least enough experience of life to know that the chances of an embarrassing situation increase in proportion to the degree of solemnity. I was well aware that the curse of ridiculousness is always close at hand on such occasions. And it was indeed precisely this law to which I was to fall victim, albeit in muted form and perhaps more in *my* eyes than in those of the audience. At any rate, I was depressed by the sins of my youth in having failed to study foreign languages.

The university had informed me that a reception committee would be waiting for me at the airport and would escort me to the home of the dean of the theology faculty, whose guest I was to be during my days in Glasgow. But when I landed at the little airport, no one was there. Assuming that they had been delayed, I wandered up and down over and over again past the counters on the creaking wooden floor for almost two hours with my hopes fading all the time. The stewardesses behind the counters naturally noticed my lonely wandering. It also did not escape my attention that they sometimes looked over at me with surprise and whispered to each other. I could have asked them for assistance, of course, but I was embarrassed to reveal my ignorance of the English language. When I was finally at my wits' end, I walked up to a large picture of the Queen of Great Britain in her crown jewels, wrung my hands and said out loud, "Elizabeth, you can't help me, either!" This worked like a signal and prompted two stewardesses to rush over to me and say, "Can we help you?" I now simply pulled out the solemn official invitation from the university and let the ladies read it. Their faces did not show the slightest trace of scornfulness. On the contrary, they fell over themselves in their readiness to help, ordered me an enormous taxi and, with a friendly wave goodbye, sent me on an extremely long journey. Not having any British money on me, however, I expected soon to be confronted with new complications.

When I arrived at the house of my host, Dean Henderson, it was still very obvious that he was worried at my mysterious nonappearance. Then everything was quickly resolved, and I once again ascertained that I positively attract strange interconnections of fate. Up until that time, the flight path from Hamburg to Glasgow had gone via London. My aircraft, however, had been one of the first to fly direct to Glasgow but had landed at another airport. The gentlemen had not known that, and thus had been waiting for me at the wrong place.

The award ceremony was an exceedingly dignified occasion for us doctors designate. The hall was filled with the splendor radiated by holders of high office: bishops and senior judges with their chains and colorful gowns, and the academic staff in their traditional dress. The three people who were to be awarded doctorates were called up one by one and, standing on a platform facing the audience, had to let the eulogies wash over them. We then knelt down to receive the doctoral hood from the incredibly dignified-looking chancellor.

So after my name had been called, I stood all alone on my raised platform in my scarlet Glasgow gown and looked down at all the splendor that lay before me. A short time prior to this the Dean had whispered to me that it was customary for there to be two jokes in each eulogy. It did not matter, he said, if I did not understand them; I only needed to join in the laughter when the others laughed. So I stood there and understood nothing. Suddenly the audience roared with laughter; a few even slapped themselves on the knee. This caused me extreme embarrassment. Had my eulogist perhaps said something ironical about the Scots, English, or Germans? If that were the case, then I ought only to join in with a "meaningful" smile. If, however, he had couched the praise it was his duty to bestow upon me in a witty form and the assembly had also found this amusing and even applauded, then I for my part ought on no account join in with their approving laughter but had rather endeavor to smile in a modestly defensive way. But I could only mimic these nuances if I *understood* what the Dean had said. But this was exactly what I had not done! So I was in a state of nervous embarrassment and could not think of any better course of action than to endeavor to force as neutral and general a grin as possible which could be interpreted in different ways. It then came as a great relief when my tribulations were brought to an end by my kneeling to receive the doctorate.

This special day concluded with a ball at which the students wore their national dress and gave displays of wild and partly virtuoso Scottish dances, and we all tripped the light fantastic in our regalia. I have never before or since experienced a celebration of such colorful emotion. The Scots have a wonderful way of divesting gowns, regalia, and robes of their solemnity, of taking away all their formal affectations and incorporating them into the compass of their lives.

Later on, when I was a little more proficient in English, I visited Scotland on many other occasions to give lectures and sermons. The most impressive of these journeys took place in 1965 when the City of Edinburgh invited me to open their great annual festival of opera, concerts, and theater with a church service in the magnificent Cathedral of St. Giles. It is best if I immediately insert this later Scotland experience here. On this trip, too, an episode of an exceptional kind took place during the outward journey. After we had landed and while we were still in the aircraft, an elderly lady approached me and asked, "Excuse me, aren't you Friedrich Luft, the critic?" After my negative reply, she apologized. I politely refused to accept her apology, saying, "You don't need to apologize, Madam. It was an honor for me to have been mistaken for Luft by you!"—When sometime later I had finished my sermon and was removing my clerical vestments, this very same lady suddenly rushed into the sacristy. "How foolish I have been," she said, "I *do* know you. I know you from your sermons in the Michel. But I had never seen you in civilian dress before and only had the feeling, 'You know that gentleman!' "

Before the church service began, the clans of Scotland marched into the church to the sounds of the overture from the "Meistersingers." There was a vast procession of people wearing their national dress and carrying flags and various scepters. During this procession I had to stand in front of the gate with the court chaplain of the cathedral; we had to make a slight bow to each of the groups. Again, this too took place—as always in Scotland—with a complete lack of stiffness. Now and then I even noticed the slightly amused, perhaps self-ironical wink of a standard-bearer or dignitary that seemed to say: Aren't we just dandy?

On the stroke of three, after the national anthem had died away, the church service proper began, which, despite the enchanting blaze of color and the sometimes bewitching sounds, touched one in the core of one's being. Because of my wretched English, my pulse understandably beat faster in the midst of all this splendor. But everything went quite well, even if a newspaper did write with justification, "The elderly preacher had some trouble with the English language."

All the other duties associated with my actual task likewise allowed us to enjoy our stay in Scotland. We were guests of the Lord Provost of Edinburgh and had a huge Daimler with chauffeur and escort at our disposal. So we were mobile and took in all the impressions that were showered upon us by Scotland's scenery and history. Our greatest experience, however, was an evening with Radio Moscow's orchestra and the young pianist Nikolai Petrov at Usher Hall. After Shostakovitch's Fifth Symphony, the audience erupted into thunderous applause. Although the musicians kept on being called back, they did not seem to be prepared for an encore, and as a result were forced to make some rather helpless gestures of capitulation. Eventually, when the incessant waves of applause meant that something had to happen, the pianist once again took his seat at the grand piano, said "Bach chorale," and then played the chorale from the St. Matthew Passion: "Before Thee I yield my all; My all I open full to Thee." We were moved and deeply stirred by the significance of this, coming as it did from *this* musician in the context of *this* orchestra. This impression has remained with me right up to the present day. Perhaps we Germans were more profoundly moved by this than the Scots.

Sea Voyage to the Far East, 1958

When I was on sabbatical for a semester in 1958 the Hamburg-American shipping line had invited me to travel to Eastern Asia aboard their beautiful ship *The Braunschweig*. This journey took me to Pinang (Malaysia), Hong Kong, the two Chinese ports of Shanghai and Hsingkang, and above all to Japan, where I interrupted my journey until the return of the ship, held a lecture in Tokyo, and conducted long conversations with the academic staff of the universities and above all with a great Zen master. On the return journey I visited the Philippines and Colombo. At many places the German diplomatic representatives had gathered together fairly large groups of people to whom I spoke and through whom I obtained important information about each country and its people. In Shanghai, where we were tied up at the harbor for thirteen days, the crew were able to make shore visits every day. I, on the other hand, was not allowed to leave the ship. Various signs indicated that the authorities had received politically unfavorable information about my person. All the same, I was at least allowed to receive visitors from Shanghai on board, although they were incredibly strictly checked and searched by the harbor police. The police even carried out spot checks on Mozart and Beethoven records in order to satisfy themselves that they did not contain any secret messages.

I will now content myself with relating two experiences from the *Japanese* section of the journey because these are perhaps a little special. Although Japan has to a large extent emancipated itself from its Buddhist traditions and is characterized by the secularism common to all industrial societies, it has nevertheless *indirectly* preserved some of the religious content of its tradition by carefully guarding the ceremonial forms that have been handed down. Thus, for instance, respect for the other person and consequently the religious anthropology upon which this respect was once based are betrayed in the forms of Japanese politeness. I myself experienced an example of this consideration for one's fellow man and its ritualization in the ceremonial of politeness in the following episode.

A theoretical physicist from the university, Tadasu Suzuki, who had translated the first of my books to be published in Japan (the one on nihilism), had been assigned to me as my assistant and escort. He now faithfully followed me on all my journeys like a shadow. Since I am not very good at finding my way around in strange cities, and moreover was unable to read the Japanese script, I was very grateful for his constant presence, especially since he was such a stimulating conversationalist.

Now when the professors of Kyoto invited me to a discussion evening, Suzuki informed me full of despair that he would not be able to escort me around Kyoto because he could not cancel his lectures. He would certainly still accompany me on the train journey to Kyoto, he said, but would then have to take the next train back to Tokyo only an hour later. A German-speaking colleague in Kyoto by the name of Ito had, however, given him his firm promise that he would take over his responsibilities and look after me. During the journey he kept on assuring me again and again that only a higher power prevented him from continuing to discharge his duties towards me. Each time he apologized with a low bow.

Apart from my new helper, Professor Ito, some other gentlemen were waiting for us on the platform, including Theodor Jäckel, the missionary to

East Asia whom I knew from earlier days and who spoke fluent Japanese. Since our friend Suzuki had to return shortly afterwards, we stood chatting on the platform until his departure, during which time trains were constantly arriving and departing. During these arrivals and departures, I was captivated by the many scenes of greeting and leave-taking with their innumerable bows. It was clear from the lowness and number of these bows that no one wanted to be outdone by his partner. Then suddenly Tadasu Suzuki asked whether I would not after all agree to allow him to stay with me in Kyoto until the following day. He said that he had changed his mind and that it would give him immense pleasure if he could remain in our company.

Although I had great difficulty comprehending this about-turn and informed him that I on no account wished to hinder him from fulfilling his duties in Tokyo, I naturally expressed my joy at his decision to stay. On the way to the hotel I then told Jäckel how incomprehensible Suzuki's behavior seemed to me, since he had kept on expressing his painful regret at not being able to stay and giving me his reasons for having to return to Tokyo immediately. "There is a very simple explanation for this," he replied, "Just as his train was departing [I had not noticed that it was *his* train!], you were telling an anecdote. He was too polite to interrupt you. So he missed his train."

The second experience that occupies a special place in my memories of this journey is my *religious discussion with a Zen Buddhist*, to which I was accompanied by my crew. The external circumstances under which this discussion took place were rather dramatic because typhoon Grace was approaching Kyoto. In the afternoon the radio began to play serious music and kept broadcasting reports on the devastation that the whirlwind was leaving in its wake. Towards evening the inhabitants were then requested to leave the shops and to secure their houses. I will never forget the storm that broke over us shortly afterwards. Our discussion took place on the morning of the day on which the typhoon struck. Although the typhoon had not yet arrived, it was already being heralded by many smaller storms.

A great—perhaps the greatest—master and researcher of Zen Buddhism invited me to his temple for a discussion. He was called S. Hisamatsu but wrote under the nom de plume of Hoseki. Three Japanese professors, Theodor Jäckel, and my Swiss host accompanied me. Professor Ito undertook the task of translating. I wrote up what took place at our meeting immediately afterward and include here an extensively abridged excerpt from my notes.

The wild rain has fortunately eased off temporarily upon entering the temple grounds. After passing through several courtyards, covered corridors, and finally crossing well-tended carpets of moss in a garden overgrown with dense bushes, we reach the small, extremely secluded residence of the Zen master. Can this garden be intended as a botanical watch-fire to shield and protect the contemplation of the master? That I employ the image of the watch-fire may be because the typhoon's vanguard is already driving into the bushes, bending them apart and knocking them together, and making them look like tongues of fire.

A woman stands waiting on the little terrace. Because we are neither now nor later introduced to her, I take her to be a servant. But one of my colleagues tells me later that she was in fact the master's wife. When we have drawn closer to the terrace, she falls to her knees and bows right down to the ground as each of us passes by. She then gets us to sit down in a circle on woven mats in a very simple, beautiful room—though it does not contain a single piece of furniture. Trees and bushes nestle closely against the house, so that as long as the walls are drawn up we initially feel as if we are sitting in a little glade. The storm shakes the bamboo blinds that indicate the boundaries of the room. We would certainly hardly be able to sit here in a wind of this strength if the dense bushes did not protect us.

Scarcely have we sat ourselves down when the head of the household enters and an extremely solemn and elaborate greeting ceremony begins. My companions bow with particular reverence, that is, particularly low and often in front of the master. In his great modesty—which is certainly not *only* the form but also the expression of his being—he himself seems to refuse the reverence shown to him by bowing even lower and repeatedly prostrating himself on the floor. It is strange: usually I have only found this reverence that people show for each other "interesting"; here, however, I find it moving. One senses that the form is here filled up to the brim with what it is supposed to express.

Eventually we sit down again. The master, in his simple gray robe, has taken a seat in the middle at the rear of the room. During the general conversation that opens our discussion, I am relieved to discover that the talk is very general and conventional and deals with the weather and my journey. During our discussion, I am able to observe him. He is a man of between sixty and seventy, delicate, with lively and honest facial expressions. And he conducts his conversations in exactly the same way as he looks. He does not make a show of his wisdom by giving a lecture, but conducts the discussion in the tone of a simple chat, even when we come to speak about the most profound issues. In this way he quickly puts his visitors at ease.

As a small gift, I present him with the English translation of my book *Between God and Satan*, in which, according to Japanese custom, I have placed my visiting card. He touchingly expresses his thanks with several bows and places the book and the card one after the other against his forehead. This juxtaposition of particularly pronounced ceremonial form and a light, natural flow of dialogue makes a very strong impression upon me in a formal respect.

After this overture, Hoseki signals to his wife with a little bell that the tea ceremony can begin. This initially takes place in silence. Whenever Mrs. Hoseki serves tea to one of the guests, both of them bow right down to the ground. This is not a discussion that is dictated by the minute hand on the clock, nor one in which one seeks to get to the point as quickly as possible. Here the disposition that makes a good discussion possible is first judiciously prepared. Here communication is first established in order to create a readiness to receive the subject for discussion. The tea ceremony is supposed to be an exercise that cultivates the "manners of the soul." As a rule we Westerners feel it to be objective to consider objects from a distance and thus ignore the person; here it is the other way round: here the object is tied to the person. That is why the person has to undergo training before he is allowed to encounter the object. I suspect, however, that this is no longer the case with business discussions in Japan. But here at the house of the Zen master, traditional knowledge is still alive and in force.

The master has granted me the honor of using his cup for the tea ceremony. He tells me that he also takes his cup with him on his journeys, which surprises me, for it is without doubt three or four times heavier than normal tea cups. It has thick sides, a completely asymmetrical shape, and because of its almost grotesque ungainliness is a little displeasing to the eye.

Perhaps Hoseki notices my slight astonishment when telling me that this is his tea cup. He then explains to me that Zen Buddhism loves asymmetry, even in the ground plans of its temples. It shatters, so to speak, the harmony of the forms and gives them almost a hint of inadequacy, in order to prevent the form from becoming a goal in itself by virtue of its perfection. The form should always be only a way and a bridge to a reality, it must retain the inessentiality of the mere symbol, it should only be a servant and must always restrain itself.

For a moment the thought occurs to me that Bertolt Brecht might have intended something similar with his so-called estrangement effect. Why was he so passionately opposed to perfection and virtuosity on the part of the actor, why did he dislike the singers having trained concert voices and chose—as was the case, for instance, with the *Three-Penny Opera* and his songs in general—actors who had gravel in their voices? He feared that the perfect form would have too smooth an effect on the petit bourgeois character in the stalls. Perfection could cause such a person to content himself with the esthetic and not to progress beyond the external form. As a result, such perfection could help the bourgeois individual to avoid getting involved with and committing himself to the real issue. That is why the listener has to be scandalized by asymmetry. It is precisely this that is *here* the estrangement effect. And does not Kierkegaard also intend something similar with his concept of offense? He wants to prevent the Gospel from becoming too neat, too harmoniously edifying; he wishes to prevent the listener from evading its demand and contradiction; to prevent him from merely fishing for self-affirmation and thus to prevent him from behaving esthetically and not ethically.

Time and again in the ensuing discussion I am able to recognize these strange formal parallels between Zen Buddhism and phenomena drawn from *our* intellectual world. And as long as the conversation is concerned with these formal similarities, much of what Hoseki says seems very familiar to me. I also tell him this, and he appears to be pleased at a good many of the details I relate to him.

It would be a pity, however, if we were to get bogged down in formal analogies. So referring to his explanation of the tea cup, I ask: "So the asymmetry of form is intended to ensure that this form does not become a goal in itself but serves merely as a helpful signpost? But doesn't everything now depend on describing the goal towards which this signpost points?"

"Yes," he replies, "everything does indeed depend on the content of this form, and in defining it the difference in our positions will perhaps also become discernible. I would reply to your question thus: the shattered, imperfect form points towards the path of perfection."

I tell him that I am very well aware of how little Zen Buddhism values definitions and that it regards them as a somewhat crude attempt to capture in rational statements that which is inexpressible and can only be experienced in contemplation; I know that such definitions force a superficial form upon the truth and thereby distort it. I am thus, I tell him, in a rather awkward position: a discussion moves in the medium of words, and if I am to be able to gain anything from him, then this can only come about if I ask him to attempt to express the inexpressible in words. I apologize for expecting of him something that he must regard as inappropriate. It is as if I were demanding a Beethoven symphony to be freed from its tone language and described in words instead.

I have the impression that the master is grateful for the understanding I show for his difficulty. Perhaps this is the reason why he for his part now accommodates me by providing a philosophically formulated statement: "Perfection consists in recognizing the *One in the all and the all in the One*." This, he says, is the true Zen principle. Here the distance between subject and object, the inward and the outward is overcome.

I now ask him cautiously whether he can tell me how he evaluates the significance of the human self in all this, and whether the Zen principle does not mean an *identity* of subject and object, self and outside world. "Does," I ask him bluntly, "the self still actually retain its personal autonomy so that it stands in genuine and distinct *opposition* to the world it encounters—or does this distance, this autonomous being and thus in the final instance also its ethical quality, remain beyond its powers? Does the self not dissipate into the world, so to speak, in order to become one of the anonymous elements that make up the world?" One of the others rushes to my aid and employs the brief conceptual formula: Zen Buddhism is clearly concerned with an identification and no longer a confrontation of the self with reality.

I appreciate the master's not losing his patience in the face of the Western conceptual language we have been using. Although he is familiar with this language, it must appear to him to be a watered-down abstraction that has lost its substance. On the contrary, far from losing his patience he attempts to accommodate us by employing our own concepts. He says that the concepts of identification and confrontation are not really appropriate for what he means, for it is not at all a question of an identification of self and reality: "It is rather a question of discovering myself in my primal relationship to my surroundings. I must thus become aware that from the very beginning I myself have been created as part of this reality and that consequently I can only deal with the reality I encounter—with a horse I am riding, a bow with which I am shooting, a tree I am felling or beneath which I am lying—*when* I have discovered my primeval *union* with it. Thus the Zen principle of *One in all and all in One* does not mean that all distances between subject and object, inward and outward, thought and being disappear and the self is submerged in a universal primeval mush. Rather, this principle means that I discover myself in my cosmic place as a link in the chain of being and thus in a fraternal relationship to all forms of reality. It is precisely in this knowledge of what is related to me, in my knowledge of the unity of the whole in which I exist, that I know how to treat, recognize, meet, and handle existence. I do not first *create* my own world as the Western activist and man of action perhaps wishes to do, along the lines of: here I am and over there is the *world* upon which I must act. Rather, I discover the world as something to which I am related, to which I am assigned, and of which I am a part from the outset. In the case of that abstract identity of the inward and the outward which you have just mentioned, all action, all decision, and thus also all responsibility would indeed cease. But, as I said, I do not at all mean this type of identity. I am concerned rather with discovering a form of human existence which, precisely because of its primal union with reality, is reconstructed so as to be near and related to the material world and exactly for that reason also able to *treat* the world correctly."

For me it is a gripping moment in our discussion to find ourselves confronted with this dissatisfaction with conceptual language. This man, who calmly fans himself during his speech, has not only a different *form* from us but also draws

upon different *sources* of thought than we do. He exists in a different sphere. He
has received both his knowledge and his personality from sources of contemplation that are alien to us. We are far from being in a position to adopt a
specific standpoint towards him or to begin making a "critical appreciation" of
his position. We must initially simply stand firm and seek to understand. When
I speak of "we" here, I do not mean the Japanese who are present, for whom
this is all, of course, very familiar, but us two European Christians, my friend
Jäckel and me.

As if Hoseki has noticed our hesitation and our secret efforts to comprehend
him, he continues with his train of thought and seeks to clarify what he means
by employing a few classical symbols from Zen Buddhism. I was already
familiar with these symbols through my philosophy teacher Eugen Herrigel
(whose book *Zen in the Art of Archery* is held in high regard here). The first
model that Hoseki employs is that of the *rider*. In this situation and coming
from this man, this model acquires a completely new vividness for me. This
model is as follows.

The perfect rider forms a unity with his horse. Only for this reason can he be
at all perfect. And only for this reason can he "handle" the horse. Precisely
because he has become one with it, he has a relationship of authority to this
piece of reality that is called "horse." The principle of *One in all and all in One*
when applied to this case thus means, "There is no rider on the saddle and no
horse beneath the saddle." One can only express the unity involved here by
means of negations. These negations, however, do not stem from describing an
objective void but from indicating the void that exists in relation to the
relationships familiar to us in our everyday lives.

Hoseki elucidates the same point with the example of the *art of archery*. It
is well know that the archer who emerges from the Zen spiritual exercise is
able to hit the exact center of his target from approximately sixty meters and
is then capable of shooting a second, third and fourth arrow into the first.
This achievement is due not to a masterly training but is a mystical art in
which "It" looses off the arrow and guides it to the target, while the archer is
merely employed as an instrument in this process. That the archer can be
such an instrument, however, is again based on hidden relationships that
produce a state of oneness: the archer is one with the bow, the arrow is one
with the target, the bow is one with the arrow. Contemplation leads to a
mystical insight into the primal interrelation of all the ontic elements, which
makes it possible for archer, arrow and target to become one because they
already *are* one. The incredible accuracy of the mystically trained archer
therefore stems—contrary to all Western modes of thought—not from an
aggressive *confrontation* with the target, which one forces oneself to hit;
rather this achievement comes from the archer's *fusion* with the target, a

fusion which is nothing other than the *comprehension* and visualization of an already *given* unity of being.

"I must thus give myself up as an independent factor standing over against the target," the master says, "I must become a *formless self*." This term *formless self* is constantly recurring in his explanations. It is one of his standard concepts.

I then ask again whether this concept of a *formless self* can really allow genuine encounters to occur between man and man, man and animal, and man and thing. Can this renunciation of the self still permit a "historical" community to exist which is not a mere collective but consists of *individual persons*, together with their conflicts, cooperation, and mutual respect for each other? Is there not rather a danger that the formless self could result in something like ahistoricity? In response to these questions, Hoseki replies:

"Perhaps you are still laboring a little under the prejudice that the archer example is intended to express a hidden atemporal and ahistorical identity, that is, a contourless monotony. It is important here to convince you that I mean something rather different. It is not a matter of positing a monotony that might shatter tension-filled encounters or not even let them arise; the issue is rather that of experiencing a communicative relationship in which all the ontic elements—that is, both myself and the outside world—cohere. It is precisely on this basis that encounter and confrontation with as well as contact and use of the material world become possible."

Various concepts from the West's intellectual history occur to me that are possibly analogous with what he means. I point these out to him and ask him whether he sees any relation between these intellectual endeavors and his own position. Thus I mention an idea from Wilhelm Dilthey's hermeneutics that one can only understand that which is "already contained in the depth of the interpretation." There is thus a given community between a *text* we would like to understand and the norms, questions, and criteria of the *person* who wants to understand it. In the same way, there is a preestablished harmony between the structure of the world and the structure of the reason that understands the world. "If the eye were not so sun-like, it could not perceive the sun. . . ." This statement of Goethe's would also seem to indicate that there is a preceding unity of the inward and the outward, and that it is only this that makes it possible to understand anything.

Hoseki does indeed acknowledge this to be a parallel and seems to be pleased at discovering a concept related to his own position. He also has a sympathy for certain Platonist ideas that point in the same direction. In particular he approves of the fact that the philosophical exercise Plato puts forward as the means of achieving contemplation (theoria) of the Ideas bases all epistemological processes on the presupposition that a preexistent relationship exists between the knower and the known. Consequently, all knowledge is based on recollection (anamnesis) and the diversity of the individual things in the world is also founded on a unity of the Ideas.

But perhaps there are other, still more obvious associations triggered off by the Zen concept of unity, so I throw Hegel's philosophy of identity into the debate—that is, his concept that the world is rational and noetic and that the human being is precisely for that reason (since the world mind is an expression of *his* mind) able to understand it.

The master listens to all this with interest and repeatedly replies in the affirmative when I ask whether he feels himself to be understood here and whether he acknowledges that there is a similarity of intentions between Hegel and himself. Sometimes his affirmations are accompanied by a slight touch of enthusiasm. Nevertheless, I am not quite certain to what degree this is due to his politeness, and whether he does not secretly think to himself now and again: I have seen the sun, and this man here (together with his European authorities and intellectual heroes) only sees the shadows on the wall of Plato's cave; he only knows the conceptual outlines of Ideas that *I* have encountered *in person*. I do not know whether he is perhaps thinking this. If he is, he is too tactful to let it show.

Our dialogue has indeed reached a strange point. When I look over the stages through which it has progressed so far, I still do not feel the theological problem of *paganism* to be at all acute. For up until now we have only been concerned with the question of how I "appropriate" reality and am myself "assigned" to it. We have thus been concerned with epistemology, or better with an exercise in epistemology, and consequently with a neutral, formal problem or, as we theologians like to say, with an *adiaphoron*.

The actual *theological* problem seems to me to lie elsewhere, namely with the question that I now ask the Zen master: "How is the being that is perceived and grasped—that being, then, to which the principle of the *One in all and the all in One* applies—how is this being understood as a whole? That is, how do you understand it with regard to its foundations, meaning, and goal? Where does it come from and where is it going to? Instead of posing this question from the objective perspective, I could also ask it from the point of view of the *subject*. Then the problem would be: What do you understand by *formless self*? Is it autonomous? Is it guilty? Is it redeemed? I am not asking you for a reply to these details, but merely wish to give you an indication of the direction in which my question is moving."

Hoseki: "I believe it would be useful to pose this question in terms of the second variant you have put forward, that is, in terms of the formless self. The formless self should not be understood as an exercise in subtraction that works out, so to speak, as zero. For the formless self is not a void; rather, formlessness is intended only to mean that the self is no longer *defined* from outside and thus is not *established* by something else. The point is rather that the self is emancipated from everything and thus is free."

It suddenly occurs to me that the concepts of formless self and freedom offer a quite different and much better chance of bringing about an encounter between Christianity and Buddhism and of allowing their contents to collide in a way that transcends all formal analogies. I mention Luther's words concerning the freedom of the Christian and ask Hoseki whether he is acquainted with this doctrine of freedom. If not, I ask whether he might allow me to give him a brief outline of it and then to request him to say something about it from his own standpoint.

He gives me to understand that this does indeed interest him, and so I briefly sketch the essential points. The freedom of the Christian means that the believer is no longer subservient to anyone or anything and that despite his involvement in the world (as a person who suffers, loves, works, dies, and so on) he "can have as if he did not have" (1 Cor. 7:29f). He is thus no longer determined: neither by mammon and a false need for security, nor by his finitude and the anxiety this causes him; neither by the spell of his physical urges nor by the spell of the mind and its ability to compose philosophies which are no longer intended to question the individual but merely to confirm him in his position.

The Paulinist statement about "having as if one did not have" seems to make a particular impression on the master. He even emphasizes it and would like to adopt it as an expression of his basic position. I believe I know why he wishes to understand this statement as an expression of his own thinking: although Buddha advocates that we detach ourselves from outward things, he does not mean that we should withdraw from them and cease actively using them. On the contrary, it is precisely the inwardly detached person who receives the freedom to act on the world without becoming a slave to it. Characteristically, Buddha's knowledge of a new possibility of being-in-the-world was not granted to him during the period when he was attempting forcibly to obtain enlightenment and redemption by undergoing the severest mortifications of the flesh and eating calf dung. Rather, this knowledge was granted to him when he had discovered the *hopelessness of the ascetic way*, when he began to eat again and even accepted invitations to exquisite dinners. "To have as if one did not have": in this phrase both participation in and distance from the world are expressed.

However, when the master alludes to these connections and, so to speak, picks up Paul's saying like a precious stone in order to let it sparkle in the light of various Buddhist ideas, I feel compelled to point out an objection to him: "The *opposite of freedom*, namely that which we have just this moment described as the state of being determined, appears in Christian terminology under the label of *slavery*. In this slavery I stand under the dictatorship of fear, anxiety, guilt, and false hope. Now the opposite of this enslavement, however, should not be described simply in negative terms as mere liberation from slavery, but in positive terms as childhood, as a state of being accepted by my Father. And it is Jesus Christ who makes peace between the Father and me. Freedom is thus not the opposite of being bound but is a new form of bondage."

I now give him a very simple account of the parable of the prodigal son, who went off to a foreign country to be free of his father and hoped to come to himself in the wilds of a strange land. Because he only had a negative understanding of freedom—as *freedom from something*—he did not gain freedom but fell under the spell of new powers, namely, the dictatorship of his physical urges, his need for admiration, and finally his loneliness and home-sickness beside the pig's trough. Only when he returned home did he discover that he could only find himself when he found his father, for it is his nature, of course, to be a "child." The secret of our journey through life does not consist in our first being children under a father's authority and then becoming autonomous adults; rather, according to the Christian understanding of exis-tence, our journey should be that of progressing from being immature children to becoming mature sons—and please note that I said *sons*! I apologize for having had to speak for so long, but Hoseki asks me to continue. I am grateful to him for this. Our discussion has certainly long since crossed the boundaries of mere disputation. We can now only "address" each other.

So I go on to tell him (we can admittedly only touch upon the subject in this discussion) that in my opinion the problem is as follows: if I have freedom only in passing through the void (but is that not expressed too superficially, have I not oversimplified his position?), then the question immediately arises whether this does not mean that I win my freedom by means of my own powers. Do I myself take the initiative through an act of self-obliteration, through training myself to be impassive, or through undergoing a masterly spiritual exercise in dying away from the world? The Christian, too, knows something of the truth that freedom is only won through dying, through *mortificatio sui* (Luther). But here it is precisely a matter—despite all the apparent parallels in modes of thought and concepts!—of dying with Christ, of being graciously brought into his death and resurrection. "Thus although you are concerned," I say to the master in objection, "with acts that are directed against the *natural* self, it seems to me that you are not dealing with a gracious gift, but on the contrary with a sort of *self-creation* on the part of the human being. That is, you are advocating a sublime form of self-assertion by means of which the human being wills to gain his higher self. By virtue of its negative structure the concept of the *formless self* would then only disguise the fact that an enormous accentuation of the self is present here. For somebody who reckons with God, such an accentuation may come to mean *You shall be like God* and conse-quently could entail the usurpation of divine privileges. If I have understood the crucial point that separates us correctly, then I would formulate it as follows: everything depends on the power through which the human being becomes a self, that is, achieves *authentic existence*. Does this process of becoming oneself occur by some means of self-assertion whereby the human being wrests himself loose from the force that determines him or from the clutches of the void? If so, even if this takes the form of training oneself to obliterate the self, it still remains a form of self-assertion. Or, on the other hand, does this process of becoming a self occur when someone tells me that he accepts, loves, judges, and puts new heart into me, and that this Someone is Almighty God and that this Almighty God is my Father in Christ? One could also formulate the relation on which everything depends in the following way: Do I define myself on the basis of my fundamental relationship with the world that I wish to overcome, or, on the other hand, do I define myself on the basis of my relationship with the person who has overcome the world on my behalf and who now accepts me and draws me into his victory over the world?

The master has a wonderful capacity to listen and I do not have the impression that this is merely polite patience. Although I have now and then lapsed into a monologue (and yet here in particular I would have preferred to have listened and learned than to have spoken myself), since we have arrived at the crux of the discussion, I comfort myself with the fact that Hoseki himself keeps on asking questions and encouraging me to make objections and to express my position, indeed he almost compels me to do so. But perhaps there is also a more profound reason for the course this discussion has taken, namely that the Gospel lives from the *Word* and seeks the Word, whereas the Zen Buddhist flees from the Word and stays in quite different regions. Thus, within a discussion that has to make use of the idiom of language we both occupy a different place.

The discussion has been going on for a long time. The rain and the storm have grown stronger, and the paper walls have been pulled shut. The mood in the little room has become even more concentrated. Only for brief moments do I remember what is going on outside, otherwise we are all absorbed in our topic. I am scarcely conscious even of the pain in my legs caused by sitting crosslegged.

I have resolved to put another question to the master that Romano Guardini once raised in a lecture. Guardini argued that the Eastern peoples, particularly those who base their lives on Buddhism, would probably cope better with the world of technology than the secularized Westerners, for the people of the West, he said, have largely lost their inner substance. They are thus helpless to resist external control and would for that reason—repeating the fate of Goethe's sorcerer's apprentice—be seduced by technology. The lives of Eastern peoples, on the other hand, are to a greater extent steered by internal control, and in this respect they would respond to the phenomenon of technology with greater composure and distance. And, as I added to my little lecture, even though I know that such wisdom and introspection as he, Hoseki, represents is an exception and that secularization is also rife in Japan, I nevertheless find Guardini's thesis convincing. The consequences of Japan's ancient traditions are clearly evident to the visitor in the greater peace and many ceremonial forms of serenity that exist there.

The master is pleased that I mention Guardini, and we are both delighted at possessing a mutual acquaintance in him. The master then very modestly and cautiously states his approval of Guardini's conjecture. His words, which are obviously intended to avoid injuring the Western spirit, make clear where he believes the main dangers of our inner situation to lie.

Our discussion touches on a few further subjects of fundamental importance which I must pass over here. One could constantly sense the powerful aura of this man, who certainly did not live merely from the intellect alone and whose training in life focused on quite different dimensions of his personality. Despite the considerable concentration demanded by the discussion, he always sustained a mood of relaxed kindness, which stood in charming contrast to his home's intensification, as it were, of Japanese ceremonial. He knew how to impart a human atmosphere to our meeting. In appearance he seemed strangely sexless. He could also have been a wise old woman.

This man and the high rank he held—reinforced by the reverence showed to him above all by my Japanese companions—helped me understand very clearly what Albert Schweitzer had meant when he had rejected half-educated people as missionaries and had regarded only men of high theological and cultural standing as suitable for the missionary profession—especially in the domain of the high religions of the East. It would certainly have an absurd and fatuous effect if the only idea somebody had with regard to this ancient culture was to diagnose it as "benighted paganism" and, without any feeling for its greatness, pass immediately over to an attack aimed at converting it to Christianity. That would be like a mouse gnawing away at Mont Blanc. (But does this inferior type of missionary still at all exist nowadays? Or does it perhaps only have currency in the imaginations of its opponents?)

This certainly does not mean that I would like to get rid of the concept of paganism and especially not that of conversion! Nor does it mean that I would like to understand paganism and conversion as merely relative terms. (Rather, I believe that in Buddhism the unredeemed state occurs in its ultimate sublimation.) The concept of paganism should not be used as cheaply and self-confidently as was perhaps once the case at many a missionary coffee circle (of a style that is now past, thank God!). The word *paganism* can never be a fixed, sweeping statement but at the most can only signify the final result to which a diagnosis leads. I am pleased that it is in particular my European missionary friends in Japan who are men of high standing. Their self-criticism and skepticism, which their faith helps them constantly to overcome, won my admiration and trust.

Finally, the master then shows us around his temple. We stop in front of a bell which in earlier days once hung in a Christian church and goes back to the activity of the Jesuit missionary Franz Xaver in the sixteenth century. The Church of Jesus Christ will exist until the Day of Judgment. But individual churches can pass away. The Gospel's cloudburst of which Luther spoke can drift past. I seize the clapper hanging next to the bell, look inquiringly at the master, and when he gives me his permission, strike the bell a few times. Its high-pitched tone rings through the temple. Centuries before it had called a Christian congregation to worship.

At the solemn farewell ceremony, Hoseki presents me with a fan on which he has painted the word *void* in ornamental Japanese characters, and reminds me of some of the stages of our discussion. With this he gives me a roll of Japanese paper which he has likewise inscribed with his own hand. Professor Ito translates and interprets the characters as follows: "Through great doubt—and thus again through confrontation with the void!—to great questions and knowledge."

Although I was only able to include a fragment of my extensive discussion here and nevertheless had to ask quite a lot of the reader, I did not believe that I should pass over this important period in my life. Perhaps this will also give a little insight into the sort of intellectual work with which we theologians are concerned.

In Southern Africa, 1959

I undertook my first journey to South Africa in 1959, where I was to work above all within the framework of the Christian Academy there. Its founder and head was Dr. Bofinger, a theologically trained young Swabian of enormous energy who had studied under me at Tübingen. Liesel and I were later often his guest in Washington, D.C., where he worked as a pastor to the German community there until his death in 1983.

This academy had set itself the goal of bringing together, under the heading of theological and cultural cooperation, leading representatives from sections of the white population, namely the Boers (Afrikaners), the Germans, and the English, all of whom lived alongside each other with very little contact. I experienced lectures and discussions of a standard there—especially in the south west and even sometimes "in the middle of the bush" where the farmers met—that would do credit to the top conferences of our academies in Germany. Thus I have never forgotten the lecture given by a German specialist from Pretoria on Hugo von Hofmannsthal. Besides my work for the academy, I also gave lectures in Johannesburg, Pretoria, Stellenbosch, and Capetown.

To acclimatize myself, I spent the first days of my tour in Johannesburg, where such effusive hospitality awaited me that I repeatedly had to change my quarters because numerous families insisted on inviting me to their homes. The lush, late fall vegetation glowing with color, the refined architecture of the houses, the social events, the hordes of black servants—all this seemed like a fairytale to me, even if the dark background to the racial problem was already becoming apparent. The black population of this great city had been freed from the discipline of the native tribal units and now lived in oppressive social conditions. As early as my first visit to South Africa they already formed an explosive, unpredictable mass of people, and later vented their rage in what were often bloody revolts. I was warned not to walk the streets alone at night. Bars had been fitted to all ground-floor windows for security reasons; despite this, I was told that I should keep valuables far away from the window because thieves at night knew how to circumvent the bars with long fishing rods.

I shall mention only a few highlights and important episodes of my eventful journey and the duties it involved. One of these highlights was the very first leg of the journey in Capetown. If I had to name the three most beautiful cities in the world that I know, Capetown would quite certainly be among them, along with Hong Kong and Hamburg. The road to the Cape is for me without doubt the "dream road of the world." It also lost none of its magic on my later visits.

Following my evening lecture in the German church, which the German ambassador Dr. Granow and the Secretary of State for Apartheid Affairs Dr. Eisele had also said they would attend, there was to be a reception in a palatial villa, where a discussion of my lecture was planned. The news that the government's apartheid minister would be present electrified me. (It turned out, by the way, that he was the son of a missionary.) At last I was going to get a genuine representative of this despicable racism in my sights! Ever since I had begun to consider the apartheid question, a certain excess pressure of rage had for a long time been building up within me, and was now pressing to be vented.

The crowd of invited guests now gathered on the terrace of the house, where the lights of the city gleamed up at us. It was an "ambrosian night." At first everything began as if the evening were simply a cocktail party with everybody indulging in cheerful small talk. My thoughts were elsewhere, however, because I was mentally couching my lance and waiting for the discussion to begin.

Then I was at last asked to begin the discussion. I began rather passionately, describing the symptoms of apartheid I had been shocked to notice (separate park benches, separate box offices at the cinema, even racial segregation in church and so on), inveighing vehemently against certain Boer Calvinist attempts to justify this racism with sham biblical support, and condemning the state guilty of this sin against humanity. During my lively speech, on which I secretly congratulated myself(!), I kept an eye on Dr. Eisele. Although he listened to me attentively, he seemed completely unmoved by my speech and not at all to suffer from the thrusts of my oratorical lance. The other guests naturally also kept surreptitiously looking over at him—how would he react?

He then replied to me with a lengthy monologue. If I thought, he said, that I had surprised him with new critical ideas, then I was thoroughly mistaken. He then outlined the enormous complexity of the problem and also made clear that solutions could be only expected in the long term. Every word he spoke revealed the burden of responsibility he carried, his great gravity, and also his human warmheartedness. He did not dispute that there had been and (unfortunately) still was racial defamation of the kind I had mentioned. He assured us, however, that it was the government's goal for the future to work for an amicable separation of the races by cultivating a more *geographically* oriented racial segregation and a certain degree of self-administration and cultural autonomy for the natives. The government had already begun to pursue this goal. During his speech he indicated the difficulties that even this intention contained. But on the other hand, he said, what other alternatives were there? Should the authorities perhaps mix the races or introduce total democratic *equality*? But then there was the white minority to be considered, to whom the country owed its cultural and economic development—a development incidentally that enticed black workers from neighboring countries because there was nowhere else where they could earn as much and have as high a standard of living as in South Africa. Furthermore, he said, the whites had not taken the country away from the native inhabitants by conquest, but had entered a virtually empty space when they first began to settle the land.

The speech at least showed me that there were many more psychological, economic, and political problems involved than I had previously taken into consideration, an omission that was due to the terrible simplification of information provided by our press and propaganda. I was completely cured of any arrogance towards this country, which had been struggling with the most difficult of all conceivable problems—the racial problem—especially since Dr. Eisele himself seemed to suffer from the burden of immeasurable aporia.

In the following semester I devoted several Open Evenings to considering the apartheid problem. I invited both South African and native students to each of these meetings, in order to avoid making the questions too easy for ourselves and to answer for our deliberations before the very people affected. And here too I noticed more clearly at each meeting how thoughtful my people were becoming and how the cheerful proclamation of seemingly self-evident postulates increasingly declined. It again became clear to me how cheaply principles are to be had when one lives at a comfortable distance from a problem. Ethical issues only reveal the burden involved in making real decisions when one goes into detail and deals with concrete problems. (This also applies today to the problems of nuclear armament, which are cloaked in a haze of slogans and crass generalizations.) For me this experience was a welcome confirmation of the methodological principles upon which I have based my work in theological ethics.

I later visited South Africa on several other occasions and was able to observe that at least something was being done, albeit very *slowly,* to overcome racial discrimination. I received the most intense impression of the severity of the problem on my last journey (1981), when I had the good fortune to have a discussion lasting several hours with Dr. X, one of the most important leaders of the black opposition. Dr. Eickhoff, the German ambassador, and a man who was particularly open to the country's problems, stressed Dr. X's reliability, intelligence, and controlled energy. This man, who had been educated in Europe and had originally been a historian, had spent ten years in prison. Despite this, he was not embittered and had lost none of the objectivity with which he sought to do justice to the complexity of the problems facing his country. He gave Liesel and me an insight above all into how apartheid affected individual families and the seething mentality of the younger generation. His historical education enabled him to explain the South African situation to us by drawing many analogies with European history. An example of this occurred when I pointed out that in all the countries from which the white colonial masters had withdrawn, the black tribes had waged war among themselves and had often brought about chaotic conditions. I then added the deliberately provocative question as to whether black Africa in all its diversity was at all capable of establishing a Pax

Africana. He replied by referring to the "tribal" wars of European history. The unity towards which Europe was now heading at full steam had, he said, also required several centuries. In exactly the same way Africa was involved in long-term processes that demanded patience. He at any rate did not think much of economic sanctions, which various zealots were calling for in West Germany.

Of all the effects of apartheid, I found those in the *ecclesiastical* sphere the most unbearable, especially when Boer Reformed theologians dared to proclaim that white rule and the enslavement of the blacks was a sort of creative order that could be justified biblically. In my discussions with such people I opposed them in the strongest possible terms, nor did I scorn employing vicious irony against them. I even *once* had the opportunity of personally expressing opposition in symbolic form. This occurred as follows.

During my stay in the southwest, I spent a day travelling with a few young missionaries in a lorry to the *Herero Reserve*. The long journey was filled with intense conversations. Some of my companions traveled with me together in the cab. Every twenty miles the crew changed, so that I was able to talk to all of them. What men they were! Their vocation, their theological passion, and their alert self-criticism preserved them from ever acting merely routinely or becoming too sure of themselves. In these conversations I learned to understand what it means to be a missionary.

The main topic of conversation was the great break with Christianity that had come to pass some time ago within the Herero tribe. This painful event was regarded as a sort of a provocation by the young missionaries. It was a model case which prompted them to think through for themselves many of the dubious aspects of the history of Christian missionary work. They were certainly full of respect for previous generations of missionaries, who— separated from their children, endangered by malaria, living in the most primitive conditions and in a mostly hostile environment—had confronted black and white magic and sought to win the people over to their liberating good news. But the mistake they had made, and one that we only recognized in retrospect, was that they had not taken into account the ethnic and religious presuppositions under which primitive African tribes lived. As a result of these presuppositions, the Christian understanding of God often went down differently than the missionaries had intended. God was simply integrated into the given religious schema and thereby merely became one pagan god among many. The pre-Christian powers and ideas also lived on in the form of ancestor worship, which continued to exist beneath the surface.

Thus Christianity frequently did not lead to a profound inner rejection of the old gods, but remained a sort of external imposition that could be shaken off again. It was often felt to be merely an imported product, especially when it appeared in association with European colonialism.

This young generation of missionaries was aware that their message had to be expressed in a new and different way and that they had above all to endeavor to tune into those deeper conceptual levels of the African tribes. To that end, comprehensive analyses and new efforts were necessary. We discussed all this on this journey.

In the middle of the bush we then met the Hereros. We paid a visit on the self-assured and extremely imposing chief in his hut before calling on the elders of the badly decimated Christian community here. These elders had loyally withstood the great breakaway movement from Christianity and the return to pagan gods and ancestor worship. In order to call together all the Herero Christians in the surrounding area as quickly as possible, the bush drum was used, which in this case consisted of pieces of railway track that one rang like a bell until the signal was taken up in the distance by similar pieces of equipment. In addition to this, messengers were also sent out. About two hours later, I was able to give an open-air sermon to the people, who had rushed over in their colorful tribal dress. An old colonial army officer translated the sermon for them at a terrific speed. After the sermon we celebrated communion together, knelt with each other in the sand, ate the same bread, and drank from the same chalice. There suddenly existed something like a primitive Christian community, and apartheid had become an unreal specter that had been banned to distant climes. Afterwards we visited a few of the Hereros' huts and enjoyed the hospitality of the beaming inhabitants. Through the miracle of faith we had become brothers and neighbors.

During my stay in South Africa I spent a very merry evening at the German embassy. During the many courses of the lavish dinner an amusing episode came to light. The ambassador had only recently been transferred from Kuala Lumpur (Malaysia) to the Union. When I myself had visited Kuala Lumpur—scarcely nine months previously—a tropical cloudburst had caused my escort and me to flee to the embassy for shelter. Shortly beforehand my escort, who was a young businessman resident there, had said to me: "The ambassador's not here; the senior first secretary's a good friend of mine, but he's not here either. And the only person left, the Malaysian servant, answers to me." So we indulged in a bit of scrounging and let ourselves be served up with the most splendid things in somebody else's house. Although a gentleman certainly ought on no account to do such a thing, the euphoria of the moment removed all our inhibitions. Now back in Capetown I said innocently to the ambassador that I felt extremely at ease in the German embassy. Indeed, everything seemed so very familiar to me that I had the impression that I had already once been there. Indeed, I felt almost at home. This seemed rather odd to my host and he asked me a few probing questions. In the process, this silly prank in Malaysia suddenly came out. It was only the ambassador's sense of humor that prevented me from sinking under the table with embarrassment. He even said, "After I returned I noticed that some wine bottles and cigars were missing. Now the mystery has been solved." I have always been found out whenever I have done something wrong—and in this case in another continent three-quarters of a year later! Schiller's theory of a moral world order is obviously correct!

When on the same evening I expressed my concern about whether I would be met at Windhoek on the following day, the ambassador said to me, "Don't worry! Provost Höflich [translated as Polite] and Consul-General König [King] will be at the airport." Because of the many names whirling around my head I wanted to make a written note of this. "Come now," said Dr. Granow, "all you need to do is to remember the proverb 'punctuality is the politeness of kings!'" The outcome of this was that when I arrived at Windhoek I inquired at the information desk, "Is Provost Punctual here yet?" So confused was I by the many impressions I was receiving.

During my stay in the southwest there was a long catastrophic drought that was endangering livestock. So the farmers embarked on a long trek with their black herdsmen to lead their herds to watering places, which, however, were also becoming scarcer. I was asked to hold a church service at such an assembly point for the rather dejected and exhausted farmers. I was delighted to do this. What better text was there for this service than the twenty-third psalm, "He makes me lie down in green pastures. . . ." In this borderline situation, people's readiness to listen was heightened.

After journeys all over Namibia, after many speeches, and after listening to many people and holding numerous discussions, I fell into a state of extreme exhaustion and urgently needed a week to recuperate. I had the great good fortune to be invited by one of the most important farmers in Namibia—Mr. von Bach, who also played a significant political role in Windhoek—to his farm Kamanjah in the northwest of the country. Von Bach took me there in a twelve-hour car drive over dusty and extremely bumpy roads. He lived with his family in a grand country house, which despite being in the middle of an arid steppe was surrounded by an area bursting and blooming with vegetation. A huge windmill that pumped the water up out of the ground had brought about this botanical miracle.

When we sat with the family by the light of a kerosene lamp on the terrace, telling stories or philosophizing, when one or other of the black servants was called over and the biblical names "Isaiah!" or "Obadiah!" or "Jonathan" rang out into the night, the enchantment was complete. On one such evening, Mrs. von Bach told me a story about some elephants. This story made such an impression upon me that I would like to devote some space to it here.

A few years earlier, a family of elephants led by a bull elephant had appeared in front of the house each day to still their thirst at the huge reservoir. In the process, the mighty animals trampled on many of the green areas that had been so laboriously planted. When all attempts to chase the intruders away proved to be fruitless, Mr. von Bach got authorization, which was not at all easy to obtain, to shoot the bull. He was then given an exact description of the spot on the elephant's head for which he had to aim. The animal would then drop dead after fifty or a hundred paces. The shot then followed from the terrace on which we were sitting. The bull bellowed and staggered away, while the herd beat a hasty retreat. Two of his companions immediately turned back again, however, pressed themselves tightly to his right and left, and in this way sought to support him. "They actually overcame their shock and came to his assistance," my hostess added. After a short distance, the bull collapsed and the others moved off. In the evening they returned once again and circled the dead bull for half the night, as if they were mourning. When they then finally departed, the black servants got down to disemboweling the animal. "Did the herd stay away from then on?" I asked. "Yes—that is to say, they came back once more on one of the following days. They stopped in front of the reservoir with lowered trunks but did not drink. After they had remained like that for quite a while, they toddled off and have never returned."

I would not have bought this story about the elephants and their seemingly human mourning rituals so easily from another person. But no doubts could be raised about a story told by these people. Mr. von Bach was visibly moved by the memory of this event. "Never again will I shoot an elephant," he said and got up.

I could only marvel at the level of culture present at this farm and at the neighboring German farms we visited. I was also impressed by the magnificent libraries, where I was able to bury myself in a book. Adalbert Stifter occupied a privileged place in one of these libraries and I noticed how pleased the owner was to enjoy an exchange of ideas on his favorite author. I was also constantly coming across well-stocked record collections, and scarcely an evening went by without our listening to classical chamber music. In these barren wastes the heart and senses were tuned to the highest sensibility. It was here that I first realized how dulled our senses have become through our engorgement with civilization. I have never forgotten these people and their fate, especially when I later heard of the radical political changes taking place in Namibia. I thought then and still think now of the many hints I detected of a secret fear at how events in this country, which had been their home for generations, would continue to develop. At that time there still seemed to exist something like a patriarchal balance, almost a sort of bond of loyalty between black and white on these farms. And yet now and then a muffled rumble could be heard. People sensed that they were living on a volcano.

My Encounter with Konrad Adenauer and Other Rhineland Impressions

I have only been able to give a brief sketch of the wealth of experiences I had on my journey to the Far East and my first journey to Africa. Accounts of my lecture tours in West Germany and other European countries must of necessity take second place to these journeys. Nevertheless, there are two experiences that I had in Germany that I would like to single out for special consideration.

One day in 1957 I was visited by Kai-Uwe von Hassel, who at that time was minister president of Schleswig-Holstein. He had come to ask me on Konrad Adenauer's behalf whether I would be prepared to give a lecture on the ethical problem of nuclear weapons at the national conference of the Christian Democratic Union in Hamburg. This request had been preceded by a declaration by leading theoretical physicists on the dangers of nuclear weapons.

I told Mr. von Hassel politely but firmly that I would have to decline this invitation because I wanted to keep my position as a theologian free of any public involvement in party politics. He replied that "the old gentleman in Bonn" would simply not accept my refusal since he had absolutely set his mind on having me make this speech. He would quite certainly get in touch with me. A few hours later, a call came through from the Federal Chancellery with an urgent invitation to visit Konrad Adenauer for a personal conversation. I accepted with the firm intention of keeping to my refusal but I was sufficiently curious to take advantage of this opportunity of meeting the great old man in person. In the meantime, Adenauer had also put pressure on Eugen Gerstenmaier—the then President of the West German Parliament—because he knew that we were friends. Gerstenmaier then also telephoned me and invited me to stay at his house during my trip to Bonn.

When I arrived at Gerstenmaier's home, he was of the opinion that I could give the lecture without worrying and would by no means be branded as being party political, as long as I was able to express myself completely independently. "Incidentally, the old man will do his utmost to talk you round. Watch out! He'll employ emotional tactics against you for he thinks that theologians are men of feeling. I don't know *what* sort of emotional tactics he will use, but *that* he will do so is something that I can guarantee."

When I visited Palais Schaumburg* the following morning, I was impressed by the peacefulness there, which could not have been further removed from the bustle and stress one usual encounters in official buildings. I had scarcely entered the Chancellor's waiting room when he was already on his way to meet me with outstretched arms. He then erupted into speech. "Professor," he said in his Rhineland accent, "You surely don't want to leave an old man like me in the lurch!"

I immediately recalled Gerstenmaier's prophecy. Adenauer did indeed receive me with great emotion, and in fact did this so movingly that I had to summon all my strength of character not to give in immediately on the threshold of his study. Scarcely were we inside his room when he asked me to tell him openly of all my reservations. I began with my main reservation, namely that in order to avoid appearing attached to a political party (if only because of my post!) I had to be allowed to make clear criticisms of the CDU as well, even if I had nothing at all against them. But, of course, I said, he himself could not possibly wish this, especially not in an election year.

To this he replied, "You can be as critical as you want. I give you complete freedom—if you will only give the speech. What *other* conditions do you have?"

---

* The then residence of the German Chancellor. *Translator's note.*

I then told him that nobody would be permitted to have a look at my manuscript before the lecture and propose possible alterations.

"Granted," he said, "anything else?"

I replied, "Many speeches are made at party conferences. One is then jammed between other people and urged to be brief. I cannot, however, rush at such a subject. It requires the audience to think and follow a line of argument, and I must therefore have unlimited time. Although I feel that such a demand is unseemly, it is indispensable for the sake of the subject."

He again replied, "Granted. You can speak for as long as you want. Was that all?"

Yes, that was all. No other objection occurred to me. The old gentleman had actually overcome me with his generosity. I thus agreed to give the lecture after all my conditions had been fulfilled. Thinking that a Chancellor had a lot to do, I got up to take my leave. But he stopped me, saying, "I've set aside an hour for you. So we can now have a good talk." Alluding to the ethical subject of my lecture, he then said—with that gift for trivial generalizations that was typical of him (and once again in Rhineland slang)—"I'm also in favor of ethical behavior in politics!"

That provoked me to tease him a little. "But Chancellor," I said, "don't politicians sometimes have to tell lies?"

"I never tell lies in my family!" was his prompt reply.

I now made a big mistake that is unfortunately typical of people in my profession. I began to "lecture." "What does lying and telling untruths actually mean, then? When a mother wishes to explain the facts of life to her little child, surely she cannot simply confront him with the sum total of all the biological facts? She will perhaps resort instead to a fairy-tale and tell a story about an angel placing the mother's still tiny little child beneath her heart until it is big enough to leave its shelter in the mother's body. This, of course, would not be a 'scientific truth,' but would it for that reason be a lie?"

Before I was able to get round to the political moral of this example, I realized that Adenauer had obviously switched off. I therefore broke off my speech as quickly as possible. Scarcely had I fallen silent when he immediately awoke from his self-immersion and said, "I think what you have just said about sex education is really very interesting!" I probably looked at him with some bafflement because the subject of sex education was, of course, not a goal in itself but was only intended to illustrate the *real* subject, namely the ethical question of truth. But Adenauer continued unwaveringly, "I must confess to you that I never had anything to do with my children's sex education; I left that to my wife."

"Why did you do that?" I interjected. His amazing answer was, "I was scared that I might go too far!"

So I am able to boast of having spoken to Adenauer on a subject that is probably unique in the many volumes of his conversations that have been published. I am sure that not even de Gaulle or Queen Elizabeth learned anything on this subject from him.

My lecture took place and despite the unreasonable demands I had made on the party assembly it was met with "loud applause" (as it was put in the minutes of the party conference). Even the President of the European Movement, the Frenchman Robert Schumann, shook my hand and spoke to me in the warmest terms.

Although it was not at all in accordance with the program, Adenauer asked to speak immediately after I had finished giving my paper. (The Chancellor had the right to speak at any time and straightaway). It was music to my ears when he thanked me for my lecture in almost effusive terms and, as it were, presented me with a verbal bunch of flowers. It was only when I read the transcript of his address at a greater distance from the event that I noticed the thorns in his beautiful bouquet. With masterly improvization he had extracted virtually all my criticisms with one hand, while stroking my cheek with the other. Above all he had suppressed to the point of nonexistence my qualified agreement with the physicists' proclamation on nuclear weapons. Outwardly and publicly, however, he declared his support for me. And when I entered the hall on the following day as a member of the audience, he even climbed down to me and firmly shook my hand.

I experienced Adenauer's incredible skill at handling people all the more vividly at an evening banquet in the City Council's Imperial Hall. After the meal he fetched me from my table and took me to a distant corner where there were two thrones for royal guests. I could positively feel the gaze of the guests burning into my back as they watched what was happening with astonishment. When we arrived in the corner, he took out of his inside breast pocket a typewritten document of about a page in length that was stamped: "Top secret. For the Chancellor's eyes only." "You can see," he commented, "that this is very secret. It is an indication of my trust that I am showing it to you. In gratitude for your beautiful speech." I can no longer remember what the document was about. But while I was glancing at the page, I could sense the breath of the Hegelian world spirit and I felt uplifted at being a participant in this secret knowledge. On one of the following days, however, all the document's contents were reported in the newspaper. But Adenauer had won my heart the moment he had shown me the document. This old connoisseur of human nature knew how to handle ordinary citizens. We normally sit *before* the stage on which the world drama is being played and go pale with pride and happiness when we are—apparently!—granted a brief glimpse *behind* the scenes. Some might perhaps see traces of a certain degree of contempt for people in this psychological game that Adenauer played on the naive and inexperienced. This is, of course, a danger to which all great men of this world are subject. In Adenauer's case, however, I see it to be rather his sense of humor that was at work. Why, he must have thought, should I begrudge people this harmless edification and myself such enjoyment?

He was a master, this Adenauer, and had the intensity and aura of a figure of authority.

As far as the other great men in Bonn are concerned, I had besides Gerstenmaier an especially good relationship both in person and by letter with Theodor Heuss during his last years as president and later during his retirement at his "little" house in Doggenburg, Stuttgart. We first met at Tübingen when he was awarded an honorary doctorate by my faculty. As was the custom in those days, we waited for him at the entrance in our ceremonial robes. When he arrived he immediately took me to one side and whispered, "Mr. Thielicke—for God's sake, what do I have to do now? I've got no sense of ceremony whatsoever!"

Besides letters, we later also exchanged our publications. This was a source of great enrichment to me. I admired Heuss' broad intellectual horizons and his powers of association, which enabled him to bring the most diverse sorts of things in relationship with each other. Yet his charming wit always put one at ease. At the same time his self-irony created a human closeness and allowed one to forget one's reserve towards the head of state. But woe betide anyone who was prompted by Heuss' relaxed conduct to adopt the wrong tone with him! He certainly attached importance to dignity and although, if need be, he was prepared to allow it to retire into the background in the presence of grace and charm, he would never permit it to be treated with irreverence.

Heuss described our various encounters in his *Tagebuchbriefe* (Notes from My Diary) and even made a few observations on my possible political future, which I today find strangely moving. He often invited me for a chat, especially when he was in Hamburg. Indeed, he occasionally even invited me to early morning breakfasts—and always delighted me with his intellectual charm.

On reaching the age of seventy, the gift he requested from the state was that the usual custom of appointing people on official suggestion be waived and a few people of his choice be awarded an honor. It was not the honor that was important to me—people in Hamburg in any case react with considerable reservation toward this sort of thing. What pleased me was rather that this honor was an indication of this man's friendship toward me.

The fifth decade of this century concluded with a long lecture tour through various Rhineland towns, during which I spoke to very many people. Although this meant a great deal to me, it would only bore the reader if I were to list all my experiences. I would just like to mention a single encounter, although I can no longer remember in which Rhineland city it took place.

In this city, so I was told, a very relaxed and truly ecumenical relationship existed between Protestant and Catholic clergy. They even met to eat and drink together in a cheerful and convivial atmosphere. In 1959 the holy cloak of Trier was put on exhibition. This cloak plays an important role in the following story. During the car journey to my lecture, my companion told me about what had taken place at a meeting eight days previously.

At an advanced hour, when spirits were already pretty high, a Protestant participant in this lively group of people said to his Catholic neighbor, "Colleague, the holy cloak of Trier is not genuine!" "Why's that, then?" said the priest, "After all, the Holy Father himself blessed it!" "No, it is not genuine," replied the Protestant, "I once felt around the collar and found a shop label!"

Things of this sort were possible without giving rise to any bad feeling. At the party after my lecture, in which the same group of people were taking part, our Catholic friend had thought of an answer; I was a witness of his riposte. This time it was the Catholic who initiated the exchange. Raising his glass he said, "Colleague, the holy cloak is genuine!" "No," the other interrupted, "I felt behind the collar and. . . ." "That doesn't matter!" the Catholic interrupted. "I once put my hand in the pocket and what did I find there? An invitation to the Wedding of Cana!"

It was now the turn of the aggressor of the previous week to fall silent.

The Turbulent 1960s

THE NEW DECADE BEGAN with an invitation to hold a series of guest lectures in Salonica. Since Liesel had just recovered from a serious illness and was still in need of a rest, the doctor suggested that a sea voyage would be the best follow-up cure. At the same time, he also maintained that this would be a very pleasant way to visit Greece. We did indeed find a Swedish freighter to take us there—a journey that lasted three weeks and was interrupted by various shore visits. As the only guests on board, we were pampered by the captain and officers as if the journey had only been taking place for our sake. In other respects too this voyage was like an unreal dream.

This dream began straightaway with our first three-day stopover, when we visited London. When we entered the ship's breakfast room, we were received by a lady whose job it was to show us the sights of London, and also by a liveried chauffeur who revealed himself to be the driver of a fabulous Daimler. He too was to be at our disposal for the days we spent in London. We had no idea how we came to receive this honor. It was only when we were invited to a formal lunch that we learned to whom we owed this unexpected reception. A short time previously, I had given a talk to the Hamburg Commercial Oil Association and, during the meal that followed, had told the head of one of these oil companies how much I was looking forward to our voyage. This had prompted him, without my knowledge, to inform his British parent company. The result of this was that the top managers of the firm were now gathered around the dinner table and invited us to their homes. So our days in London were very eventful, especially since I also preached in two German churches.

346

Some Greek Impressions

After various intermediate stops which I cannot deal with here, we at last arrived in Greece, the land of my dreams. For a classicist it is a moment of unparalleled fulfillment finally to come face to face with what has dominated one's thoughts from youth onwards. It is a joy to experience at first hand what one learned during the study of ancient languages and read in books at school, to stand in person before the ancient temples or to relive the battle at Thermopylae. But I will not relate here what others have described more beautifully and vividly, but will content myself with describing the insignificant but, for all that, special things I encountered against the exalted backdrop of the Greek spirit. The unique light that shines over the Hellenic world not only conjures up the gods of Mount Olympus but also transfigures the miniatures and arabesques of life.

When we landed at Piraeus, there was once again a surprise waiting for us. In the middle of a small deputation from Athens University a young Greek bearing a surname that was well known far beyond the borders of Greece, also stepped up to us. He had studied under me during my Tübingen period for a few semesters, but I had since lost touch with him. In Tübingen he had led an elegant existence on independent means—even his study of theology, including his doctorate, had only been pursued as a hobby. He was the owner of one of the largest hotels in Salonica and knew all the religious and secular celebrities in Greece. He now placed himself together with his car at our disposal and delighted us with a lovingly prepared itinerary. He was, of course, not content to wait for us *in front* of the barrier at the harbor. On the contrary, the cerberuses shrank back from him and, together with a few Athenian professors, he came straight onto the ship. While we were making our way to customs I confided to him that I was worried that I would not be able to get the ample supply of cigarettes I had in my suitcase past the customs authorities intact—as far as cigarettes are concerned, Greece is a deprived area. "One moment," he said and disappeared into the customs office. Immediately afterwards he returned with the chief customs officer, who not only painted magical signs of protection on our luggage, but even carried it personally past the trouble spots. Without this young Greek's help it would not have been possible to fill our days so completely and yet still to structure them so restfully. In him we had the best of all possible couriers, full of ideas and empathy. Only he could hit on the daring idea of invading fashionable private houses as late as midnight, only he knew enchanting restaurants and secluded villages untouched by tourism, whose charm he revealed to us.

In our hotel we discovered an invitation from Queen Friederike to visit her at the Royal Family's summer palace. It later emerged that we owed this new surprise to Prince Ernst-August of Hanover, who had once been Liesel's dinner partner. He had read about our journey in the newspaper and had suggested to his royal sister that she give us this audience. The ladies of the embassy taught Liesel the court curtsy and apprised her of other questions concerning court etiquette, which was still taken very seriously (for example, ladies had to wear a hat and gloves that went right up to the elbow).

We passed the saluting castle guard in their picturesque uniforms and landed in the hands of the Lord Chamberlain, who was wearing a monocle and was covered in medals. Some pages then took us to the chief master of ceremonies, who finally conducted us to Her Majesty's chambers. After Liesel's curtsey we took a seat next to a very warm fire, and a lively conversation immediately developed. The somewhat disjointed manner of Queen Friederike's questions reminded me of her grandfather Wilhelm II, about whom I possessed a copious collection of monographs and thus knew a great deal. I will describe our conversation, which I noted down immediately after the audience, in direct speech and in the question and answer form in which it took place.

Queen Friederike: What are you doing in Greece? [This seemed a rather blunt question to me so I answered just as curtly.]
I: I'm giving some lectures in Salonica.
Queen Friederike: What on?
I: My subject is "Historicism and Existentialism".
Queen Friederike: Existentialism? What's that then? Oh, aren't those the people with the hideous velvet trousers? [After this remark I attempted to explain briefly the meaning of the word *existentialism* to my discussion partner—not a very simple didactic undertaking.]
Queen Friederike: I myself am primarily interested in theoretical physics. [The embassy had already drawn my attention to this hobby of hers. It is also mentioned in detail in her memoirs, which were published some time later.] But, of course, as a theologian you won't know anything about this. You just concern yourself with your dogmas.
I: I believe that is not quite the case, Your Majesty!
Queen Friederike: Oh, really? You know then that modern physics is of great ideological and philosophical significance? I have had many conversations

about this with leading physicists in America. But, of course, that can hardly be of any interest to you. [This dressing-down—at least that is what I felt it to be—annoyed me, and I had difficulty suppressing a rather sharp riposte. When one constantly has to say "Your Majesty," however, it has a calming effect on any animosity that might be trying to break out.]

I: What strange ideas Your Majesty has about theologians! But, of course, I cannot know how the world is reflected in the royal heart.

After that she fell silent for a moment and seemed rather taken aback. By her standards this little dose of irony may have affected her like a soft blow. But then she laughed out loud and was from then on considerably more courteous. Lengthy phases of the conversation were then given up to this and that, including the Greek Orthodox clergy, whose intellectual horizons were, in her opinion, indeed restricted to dogma and liturgy.

Suddenly, like a bolt out of the blue and with no connection with the subjects we had been discussing up until then, she turned to a completely different question.

Queen Friederike: Do you believe in hell?

I (once again imitating her bluntness): Yes.

Queen Friederike (turning to my wife): You too?

Liesel (endeavoring to support her husband): Yes, me too; as long as Your Majesty isn't thinking of people roasting in a fire in the way we are in front of this fireplace. [Queen Friederike laughed and led us to a place further away from the fire. At least Liesel had managed to achieve that.]

Queen Friederike: My husband and I do not believe in hell. [There was then a long discussion about this subject, which I can pass over here. Some of the Queen's remarks seemed to indicate that this question had already preoccupied her family for decades.]

Queen Friederike: When my son [the then crown prince and later King Constantine] was about eight years old, he once sat next to the British ambassador at a state banquet and asked him, "Does Your Excellency believe in hell." When the ambassador replied that he did, Constantine said, "I don't, nor do mum and dad." The ambassador then sought to justify his standpoint with children's language: "But, Little Prince, where are the bad people to go if there's no hell?" Prince Constantine replied, "Bad people *also* go to heaven, but with sad hearts."

I: Your Majesty, that is a beautiful and truly remarkable description of hell.

This little story enabled me to understand this royal lady better than did many of her otherwise rather explosive statements.

Rector of Hamburg University

When the academic staff of Hamburg University elected me in 1960 to be
their rector, I was once again only prepared to assume this post for *one* year. I
did not look forward to this year of office with the same excited sense of
adventure which had filled me nine years previously with my Tübingen
rectorship. I now knew, after all, a little of what the leadership of a university
entailed, even though Hamburg was on a completely different scale. Apart
from the usual official and social functions of representing the university to
the outside world, the main focus of my work consisted in chairing the
various committees dealing with the continuation or completion of a wealth
of building projects—for example, with the "Philosopher's Tower," in which
our faculty was also later accommodated. Here I was constantly able to reap
what I had not sown. My predecessors—especially Karl Schiller, the future
West German minister for economic and financial affairs and a man of great
administrative skills and energy—had already driven these building projects forward at a brisk pace. In those days, our finances had not yet run up
against those bottlenecks that were later so painfully to hinder our freedom of
action. This side of my duties led to a particular occupational burden: I had
to rush from one topping-out ceremony to the next, consume knuckle of pork
with sauerkraut and the obligatory schnapps early in the afternoon, and yet
still retain control over the more sublime thoughts appropriate to an inauguration. This was the "asceticism" that was demanded of *me* during this
period!

Of the external duties that my official position called upon me to fulfill,
one of the most important was membership of the Academic Advisory
Council to the Thyssen Foundation, which was founded in 1960. I took part in
this council's meetings until 1982 and received a wealth of stimuli from the
collaboration of all the faculties in deciding which projects to sponsor. For
me the best thing about this council was being able regularly to meet old
friends, especially Adolf Butenandt, Helmut Schelsky, and Wolfgang
Schadewaldt, whose magnificent specialty embraced classical philology and
the influence of the ancient world right up to Goethe and Schiller. After the
conclusion of the Cologne meeting, Schadewaldt and I retired to a quiet
corner of our hotel and talked until the departure of our trains, where he
derived great pleasure in telling me his whole life story.

My most important assistant at the helm of the university was its extremely
capable and loyal syndic, Dr. Richard Münzner. This copilot of mine pos-

sessed a far greater knowledge of the ship's course than the captain. He not only had an overall view of the manifold branches of the university's entire structure, but also of its intellectual foundations, so that he was much more than just a legal adviser. Furthermore, he also possessed psychoanalytical and psychotherapeutic abilities in dealing with such complicated people as professors and students. He also had an instinctive sense of academic style. I used to like to nickname him "the university as such." As a result of the later student revolt, he was removed from office and shunted off to the sidelines in a disgraceful way that showed nothing but contempt for his services.

I arranged many things in the same way as I had back in Tübingen and also set up "rector's discussion evenings" again, which were just as well received by my colleagues as they were by the students. Nevertheless, the huge organism that was Hamburg University did not allow the same degree of personal communication that had been possible at Tübingen. In the public mind, the university servants receded into the background behind the famous names. Precisely by virtue of my office, however, I knew of their loyalty, and long afterwards was to experience it anew when the great student unrest descended upon us.

Whenever there was any trouble and I had to take vigorous action, it seemed and still seems to be part of my destiny that the cleansing storm I initiated usually brought about a positive effect afterwards. This was the case, for example, when the magazine *Konkret* launched an intolerable attack—I can no longer remember on whom or what—and I banned its distribution and sale within the university. I was then visited by the editor of the magazine, Ulrike Meinhof, who wished to call me to account and to protest at the ban. After a long conversation that also ventured into some very fundamental areas, she reacted with astonishing understanding and even asked me to tell also her editorial staff what I had disclosed to *her*. I then invited the entire editorship of *Konkret* for coffee and likewise met with a good response. I even (astonishing in the light of what we know today) allowed this magazine to publish an interview with me.

The stylistically perfect thank you letter that Ulrike Meinhof wrote to me afterwards stands in an almost inconceivable contrast to the gutter and anal terminology that she later employed. I was constantly haunted by my encounter with this highly talented woman when I later followed her diabolical fall. Despite all the horror hanging oppressively over her terrorist career, I have never been able to share the loathing that most contemporaries felt towards her. I was very profoundly moved by the entanglement into which her ethical motives had led her. She wanted to intervene and change a structural situation in our society that filled her with despair. When her prophecies of doom in newspaper columns proved to be fruitless, she believed she had to resort to direct action. In doing so, however, she got bogged down in acts of destruction that eventually culminated in her own demolition. My pity for this woman always outweighed my rage at the horrific acts she committed. I look back on my meeting with her as one of the high points of my Hamburg rectorship.

During my year of office, I not only had dealings with the gigantic complex of clinics at Eppendorf on a professional level, but also as a patient. The special risk of pulmonary embolism to which I was subject had once again—in the midst of my rectorial duties—threatened my life and forced me to undergo hospital treatment for a few weeks. In human terms, one of the good consequences of my stay was that I gained the friendship of some doctors who were to enrich my life until their deaths.

Above all I enjoyed the friendship of the cardiologist Ernst Gadermann. He was a man of vigorous, elemental force who had been awarded the Knight's Cross as a fighter pilot in the Second World War. He was also a cheerful boozer and a thoughtful conversationalist. From the very first moment I met him in my desolate condition, I had the feeling: this is a good chap—he himself liked to use the term "buddy"—who is there for you day and night and will never leave you in the lurch. I shall describe later how he fulfilled this expectation. He was also a man of the finest artistic taste and was a great collector of paintings.

I once became very angry with him in a conversation. He was friends with a leading journalist and publisher whose newspaper had published what I considered to be a disgraceful article. (I no longer know what it was about.) I reproached him for having such a person as his friend and told him that it was impossible for him to be associated with two such antagonistic "buddies." He replied that I should kindly tell this to the other "buddy" myself. "I'll never manage to get him in my sights," I replied. "Yes, you will. He happens to be here and I'll bring him over straightaway," he said and disappeared. Immediately afterwards he pushed the journalist through the door and then withdrew. In doing so, he had played a nasty trick on me. Tubes were hanging out of the famous man's mouth and nostrils. He was only able to mumble and smirked to himself because he had noticed my horror and felt safe from being on the receiving end of a severe telling-off. The wrath bottled up inside me could not possibly vent itself in these circumstances and I could not think of anything better than to wish him a "speedy recovery." Even his "thank you" was only an inarticulate grunt.

The well-known Eppendorf surgeon Ludwig Zukschwerdt and his wife also became our friends, especially since we were next-door neighbors. I have met few doctors who possessed such an all-embracing diagnostic perspective and, leaving aside his own discipline, such a command of internal medicine and neurology as he did. When I later held the funeral oration in his honor at the Church of St. James, I made mention of the unique and absolute concentration with which he treated each of his patients. I was once lying in his surgery ready for examination when outside the door I heard him furiously hurling a colossal barrage of abuse at an assistant who had "botched" things up. I not only felt sorry for the poor chap but was even myself rather afraid of this wrathful Jupiter. But when he came in, he changed in a flash. Indeed, he came close to embracing me and announced with beaming euphoria what joy it was for him to see me again. All the while the red blotches of rage still stood out clearly on his skin. This radical adjustment to the person with whom he had to deal at that precise moment was typical of him. Whenever we had difficulties with our children, we sent them to him. His presence also did them good; they would have gone through fire and water for him.

I had a similarly close relationship with Otto Lindenschmidt, the head surgeon of Barmbek Hospital, and not only because he lived in the same street as us. He was both a highly cultured man and a particularly gifted teacher. There was nobody who was able to explain medical interrelations as he could. As a convinced Christian he was also receptive to questions that were on the borderline between medicine and theology. During his final period of suffering, I was able to accompany him as a friend and pastor until shortly before his death. These friendships with doctors were very helpful to me in the following years and decades when I often had to speak on borderline questions in medicine at medical conferences and needed the advice of my friends.

Because of his heavy workload, the head of the university was granted the privilege of not having to wait whenever he appeared as a patient at Eppendorf. When I once turned up to be x-rayed, the head of the clinic was already waiting at the gate for me and welcomed me as "Your Magnificence." After I had removed my jacket, he addressed me as "colleague," and as soon as I was stripped to the waist, he called me Mr. Thielicke. I found this extremely tactful and also replied with the appropriate gratitude. All the same, he wanted to pay a special tribute to me by carrying out the x-ray himself without the assistance of the operating staff. But as head of the clinic, he seemed to be rather out of practice in this elementary area. At any rate, there was a strange hissing, humming, and flashing, and all that could be seen on the plate were two suspenders. After that he called his experienced ladies back in.

Speech on June 17, 1962, to the Bundestag

It was an important event in my life when I was invited by the West German Ministry of the Interior to give a speech on June 17, 1962, to the Bundestag. I was pleased at having this opportunity of being for once able to express in criticism and in an as helpful continuation of the general debate as possible some of the things I had been itching to say for a long time. My lecture had one central theme: I posed the deliberately exaggerated question of whether we in the West were not suffering from a loss of inner substance, indeed whether we still had any authority at all with our degenerate concept of freedom to set ourselves up as a guide for the Eastern bloc countries. With this in mind, I criticized the abstractness of our understanding of democracy, which seemed to have hardly any room for a concept like "Fatherland" any more. For the term *Fatherland* had become colorless, hollow, and formalistic, and was also devoid of symbols. The justified struggle against National Socialism should not lead us to throw the baby out with the bath water and banish the nation *itself* from our consciousness.

For all that, I was stimulated not least by the methodological aspect of my task, namely as a Christian to give a "secular speech" without lapsing into a sermonic style, and to bring to birth Socratically in my audience an inquiry into the foundations—themselves not expressed—of the conception conveyed in the speech. The comments I received afterwards from Protestant clergy ranged from the remark that I had denied Christ, to a bishop's statement that although God had not been mentioned in the speech, he had been present behind every word.

The scale of the general response to my speech surprised me. Scarcely had I left the platform of the Bundestag when the first telegrams began to arrive, and afterwards I received more than a thousand letters. (The speech had been broadcast on radio and television.) Of these letters, I was especially strengthened by the comments of Theodor Heuss and Eduard Spranger. The apostolic nuncio, Archbishop Konrad Bafile, sent me a copy of *L'Osservatore Romano*, in which the speech had been printed. It was published in many daily papers as well.

This mass of letters was a treasure trove for investigating the inner state of the German people. In these letters all the various professions and age-groups had expressed their thoughts on the basic questions of our political and personal life: the history of the German nation, coping and not coping with the recent past, and the concept of nationhood and its symbols. At the time I deliberated on whether these letters, which because of their sponta-neity were especially powerful, should not be systematically analyzed. The industrialist Otto A. Friedrich, who once had a look at the "linen baskets" full of mail at my home, then arranged for a sociologist to edit them statis-tically and published a book on them with Rainer Wunderlich Publishers: E. Othmer, *Deutschland—Demokratie oder Vaterland. Die Rede an die Deu-tschen von Helmut Thielicke und eine Analyse ihrer Wirkung* (Germany—Democracy or Fatherland: Helmut Thielicke's Speech to the Germans and an Analysis of Its Effect.)

Apart from a few exceptions, the reaction to the speech was astonishingly positive. I had expected something rather different. Even with the negative responses, humor was not lacking. One person wrote, "How good it is that there is another Thielicke living in the same town as that horrible theo-logian." You can imagine what Christian pleasure I had in disclosing my identity to the writer of this letter. He was then very rueful, however, and confessed that he had been taken in by a false newspaper report about me in the light of which I had seemed "horrible" to him.

During those years—and right up to the present day—I also had to give many lectures in other similarly "secular" forums. I found this a stimulat-ing experience above all because in such cases I had as my audience people whose philosophy of life had not "filtered" them out in advance. When giving such lectures I was constantly observing anew how very receptive precisely this kind of audience is to the fundamentals of the Christian message and how they have no desire whatsoever for any clever tactical accommodation to their position. Precisely for this reason it de-pressed me that it was only partially possible to get these people to come to a "normal" church. In a post-Christian society it is not only *offense* that stands between the message and the recipient but above all *prejudice*. This prejudice, however, is even more dangerous than the *skandalon* because it does not arise *as a reaction* to the message but from the very outset keeps people out of earshot of the message. I myself endeavor to bridge this gulf by seeking to show the relevance of the Gospel to a general problem and to bring out the new and surprising light this sheds on the subject in question. Thus when I once spoke to leading representatives of the German auto-mobile industry I attempted to portray the relationship between law and

Gospel with reference the excessive number of road signs we have on our roads.

Pages from a Sketchbook: North America

Of the almost yearly trips I made to the United States over a period of approximately one-and-a-half decades, I only wish to give a more detailed account here of my five-month visiting professorship in 1962, especially since I am forced to pass over my later visits. Before I left Germany I gave a speech in the glass-roofed court of Munich University to commemorate the twentieth anniversary of the martyrdom of the brother and sister Hans and Sophie Scholl. My thoughtful preoccupation with the story of these young students, who had sacrificed their lives in the struggle against tyranny, my recollection of the macabre greatness of the period we had endured together, and not least the room in which I spoke, which was heavily laden with memories, were moving experiences for me.

Shortly afterwards, I left for New York on board the Hapag ship *Heidelberg*, where I was cocooned in their famous hospitality and surrounded by stimulating traveling companions. I was accompanied on this journey by my American secretary, Darrell Guder. Darrell had studied under me at Hamburg and had lived with us for a few months in order to subject me to a rigorous intensive course in English and to prepare the translation of the manuscripts of my lectures. Besides that, his task was to organize geographically the wealth of invitations I had received from the states of New York, Texas, New Jersey, California, Pennsylvania, Illinois, Georgia, Minnesota, South Dakota, Ohio, Massachusetts, Indiana, and Washington, D.C. He was also to correspond with the organizers, coordinate dates, accompany me on the journey itself, and act as my translator during the discussions. I could not have wished for a better and cleverer assistant. We were eventually so well attuned to each other that whenever I said half a sentence in German in a discussion, he would then break in with the English translation. He would raise his voice when I raised mine, repeat my gestures, and almost became my alter ego. It was priceless to observe the audience while this was going on. Their eyes clicked from one to the other of us like spectators at a ping-pong match. His skill as an interpreter was so perfect that I sometimes forgot that I was in a country where a foreign language is spoken. In the process I, at any rate, learned so much English that—to the delight of the audience—I occasionally interrupted him with a "stop" and corrected a word in his translation.

I had also learned by heart a wealth of well-translated English jokes, which the Americans love, of course, and with which it was my custom to begin my speeches. Above all, self-ironical references to my "poor English" were a good prophylaxis for the disappointment that people felt when they discovered that the author of books written in such brilliant English was in person such an incompetent stammerer. When I assured them in their own language that I myself loved the English language but that it did not return my love, then they accepted without complaint many phonetic barbarisms from me. I was eventually even able once to permit myself to extemporize; thus I informed them at the beginning of a lecture: "Last night I dreamed in English (at this they already began to laugh!), but unfortunately I can't tell you about my dream because I didn't understand it."

From New York, we went on a seven-hour flight to Los Angeles. We cruised at a height of thirteen thousand meters as if on a magic carpet, passed over mountainous clouds, broad plains, mountains, deserts, and rivers, all the while stimulated by champagne and good conversation, during which the sun never set. The unreal beauty of this flight, which seemed almost to outstrip the course of the sun, was something that I had never before or since experienced.

We spent our first days in America at the home of Darrell's parents in Hollywood. Of all places, it was here, through meeting the many guests that populated this house, that I realized for the first time what significance the *Church* has in American life. All these different people—artists, film actors, theologians, students of all faculties—were molded by the Presbyterian parish of Darrell's parents. Besides church services, lay theology courses and Sunday school, the Church also offered musical evenings, theater performances, and many other social activities. People were constantly coming *from* or going *to* the church. It was an intellectual and spiritual home that brought about friendship and even marriages.

One of the reasons for this is surely the fact that American hymns have not been affected by the liturgical purism that is so prevalent in Europe. Although this purism allows our church services to convey the exalted feeling that we possess only original and stylistically correct hymns, it also frequently paralyzes them. The verve of American hymns could positively lift people from the pews (if they were not already standing). When I later spoke in the neighboring mountains to six hundred and fifty students at the Forest

Home holiday camp for a week, their singing was so powerful and charming that I was no longer able to hear an operatic tenor standing next to me, although the veins on his neck had swollen to thick blue lines.

I have occasionally spoken to cultured church musicians about this, because I was surprised that they—I am thinking especially of an eminent Bach expert—played religious "songs" at some event or other without the slightest trace of snobbery and were themselves carried away by the enthusiasm of the singers. They had great difficulty in understanding the reason for my surprise. "Why shouldn't we?" one of them replied. "We want to have Christ with us in *every* mood. We are, after all, not always 'sacral' but also robustly 'worldly' and lively. Are we in such cases to do without Christ and borrow words and sounds only from those who do not know him?" While they were saying this I was reminded of the Middle Ages, where no distinction was made between spiritual and secular songs. *For us Europeans*, on the other hand, the world is split up into two dimensions that, although we are constantly striving to glue them together theologically, nevertheless remain "existentially" separate. The Americans certainly sometimes have the inferior theology—a rule which is incidently swarming with exceptions—but what we are fishing around for in hopeless reflections is in many instances inherent in still unbroken form in the unreflective way they lead their lives.

I once witnessed a masked ball at Forest Home that involved wearing bizarre headdresses. There were gigantic turbans, someone was wearing the tower of Babel on his head, and I saw a huge variety of fool's caps. Despite the fantastic turnout, grace before the meal was not omitted. Everybody bowed their heads to pray, despite the huge constructions perched on top of them, and all sorts of bells rang and chimed. On seeing this, my so-called sense of style nearly caused me to burst out laughing and spoiled for me the moment of prayer. The Americans, however, did not want to exclude God even from their fancy dress party.

In the great First Presbyterian Church of Hollywood I then dared to hold my first sermon in English. Before the sermon I was standing next to a pillar with terrible stage fright and looking like a picture of misery, when a lady wearing an entire flowerbed on her head noticed my nervousness and sought give me some encouragement. I can still hear her beautiful words of comfort, "Have fun in the pulpit!" That did me more good than a whole litany of blessings. When I then entered the pulpit and saw an entire flowerbed of ladies' hats below me, I felt I had been transferred to a botanical garden. Indeed, I suffered a little from the idea that I ought first to take out a watering can and water the congregation from the pulpit. This rather frivolous idea did, however, help me to shake off my stage fright.

My meeting with Billy Graham, who was at that time holding his huge evangelization crusades in Los Angeles stadium, was of great importance to me. I at first had reservations about accepting his invitation to sit next to him on the balustrade. When I then did indeed do so on the insistence of my friends, I kept my eyes wide open critically. As the people came forward in their thousands to confess their faith, however, I was aware only of calm meditation on the part of his crew and detected no expressions of triumph. His message was good solid stuff. His warmhearted, unpretentious humanity made a great impression on me. Afterwards I wrote him a thank you letter in which I confessed that whenever I had previously been asked for my opinion of him I had said that I felt that many essential elements were lacking in his proclamation of the Gospel; he advocated an individualistic doctrine of salvation, and even this took place only in relation to the initial stages of faith. Although I had now personally experienced his message, I did not feel compelled to revise the objective side of this criticism, but I had resolved to modify the question in which I raised my criticism; it now ran: "What is lacking in my and the conventional Christian proclamation of the Gospel that makes Billy Graham necessary?" I found the answer he gave me extremely significant. I was, he said, completely right in my criticism. What he was doing was certainly the most dubious form of evangelization. But what other alternative did he have if the flocks that had no shepherds would not otherwise be served? This answer gave him credibility in my eyes and convinced me of his spiritual substance.

The best part of my work was, as I mentioned earlier, the time I spent at Forest Home in August. Forest Home was ninety minutes by car from Los Angeles and located at an altitude of sixteen hundred meters in the mountains. It was my base for the whole month.

Forest Home is an interdenominational conference center with an Indian village. Here young people live entirely in the style of the native Americans and devote themselves to the study of Indian folklore. One of the chiefs there was a genuine young Indian of regal stature and behavior, a Winnitou redivivus, who knew how to enthrall us above all with his dancing. The weeks I spent with the students were of great human and spiritual intensity, and it was very painful for me to have to tear myself away from them when the time came for me to leave.

It was in Forest Home that I heard my best sermon—from a policeman of all people. I was in a particular hurry to get to a church service and I forgot to stop at a red light. As a result, I got lumbered with a policeman on my tail. But then a lorry came between us. The policeman signaled the truck driver to stop and shouted at him to let him pass because he had to give a traffic offender a ticket. But the truck driver—a student who knew me—shouted back that he could not do that, for the person in the car was a preacher and was in a hurry. At this, the policeman pronounced a judgment that was worthy of King Solomon. "Well," he said, "then tell that gentleman that he should not only observe the commandments of God but also the laws of this country." It is really nice when the police are more at home in the heavenly Jerusalem than on the barrack square.

In the magnificent city of San Francisco I was invited by my "employer" there, the Pacific Lutheran Seminary, to plant a tree in their grove of honor. There was already a Dibelius and a Lilje tree to remind people of Germany. These two predecessors of mine, however, had not had a particularly lucky touch. The one tree had become rather withered and the other had shot out excessively widthways. Any reader who wishes to do so may himself guess which fate befell which tree. During my address I quoted the famous Arabic dictum that a man's life has only reached fulfillment when he has built a home, fathered a son, and planted a tree. The latter had eluded me until that day.

At the Divinity School at Chicago University I had to give thirty lectures on the anthropology of the sexes. I used as my manuscript a translation made by Dr. Doberstein from my *Theological Ethics*, which at that time had not yet been published in the United States and only later appeared in its several volumes. I had to do a colossal amount of work so as to be able to serve the material up to my audience—for the most part older doctoral students—in a reasonably intelligible English.

Of the church services I held in Chicago, I shall in particular never forget the sermon I gave to a negro congregation. At first there was some concern about letting me preach there because it was feared that the congregation might not be able to understand me. But the congregation responded enthusiastically, kept on interrupting me with loud cries such as "Yes, Lord!," "Hallelujah," "Amen!" and many other acclamations. That stimulated me so much that I was carried away as if on the crest on a wave and, in a sort of pentecostal miracle, the English language was suddenly transformed into a willing instrument in my hands. The ecstasy of the congregation was constantly being given fresh impetus by adult, youth, and children's choirs. The solemn, formal, and ceremonial character of the service's external structure stood in strange contrast to this wild passion of spiritual excitement: stewardesses with sashes and white gloves showed each churchgoer to his seat with ritually stylized gestures and moved with slow yet dance-like steps through the aisles. When I asked the black pastor about these antitheses, he explained to me, "I had to incorporate these subdued forms into the service because they form a counterbalance to the enthusiasm of the congregation. If I were to lose this control there would be no holding them!"

My lectures were held at the same time two days a week. As soon as I had given the last one, I was off to the airport and we flew out to other universities in the country. As a result, my time was more than fully occupied and I sometimes had to contend with severe states of exhaustion. I shall pass over all these excursions and mention only the "Dahlberg Lectures," which I had to hold in Rochester, and my first encounter with Princeton, which in later years became something like my home university in America. The theological seminary, with its high standards, English flair, and cultured hospitality, was always an especially favorite academic abode of mine.

During the months I spent in Chicago I was profoundly shaken by the murder of John F. Kennedy in Dallas, where I had a short time previously held some guest lectures. I was just doing some shopping in the city when I observed groups of people staring as if spellbound at the neon writing on a press building. At first there was only mention of an assassination attempt. I then heard radio reports coming from a parked taxi, walked with the others up to the car, and now listened to reports of a catastrophe coming in quick succession and relaying ever more serious news, until the death of the president was confirmed. Minute by minute, a universal shock spread through the groups of whispering people, as if a large, dark-winged bird was hovering over us.

I now found myself in a difficult position. It was Friday, and on the coming Sunday I was supposed to lead the church service at Harvard University and to give a few lectures in the days following. Harvard had been Kennedy's university, and as early as the following day the press was publishing news that Harvard was being considered as the place for Kennedy's funeral. But even leaving this aside, I felt that it was now inappropriate for a German to lead the service at Harvard. So I telephoned to ask to be released from my task. But it was insisted that I come. Merely for linguistic reasons it was impossible for me to prepare a new sermon appropriate to the situation. So I kept to my text about the sinking of St. Peter, and thought of the discovery I had made during the aerial bombardment of the war that a time of catastrophe does not require a special text; the eternal Word is equally present at all times. So, after saying a few sentences on the terrible event, I interpreted my text as usual. Rarely have I spoken to such a severely shaken congregation. More than two thousand students and professors dressed in black filled the spacious room shoulder to shoulder and spilled a long way out onto the street. Probably for the sake of the guest the choir sang passages from Pachelbel's chorales in German. That was particularly moving at this moment.

Since all lectures had been canceled for the following days but the academic staff would still have liked to have had a discussion evening with me, a substantial number of Harvard professors assembled on Sunday evening. I admired the self-discipline with which they were prepared in these agitated days to conduct a polished debate on Luther's doctrine of the two kingdoms, that is, the doctrine of the relationship of the worldly kingdom to the kingdom of God. At this discussion I had to argue above all with Anglican theologians. In between times we were constantly sitting in front of the television during that weekend. The commercials that were otherwise so dominant in the United States were totally banned. Only programs on Kennedy were shown, especially his interviews from the last years. I was forced to reflect that I had previously met scarcely a single Kennedy supporter in academic circles. In contrast to his elevation to mythical status, such as I had observed back home especially among the German youth, the Americans regarded him soberly and with greater critical distance.

Kennedy's successor Johnson was much more popular. His museum of remembrance—a collection of fabulous kitsch—and ranch were places of pilgrimage to which large hordes of pilgrims flocked daily. The average American was obviously more easily able to identify with Johnson's simpler intellectual constitution and character. Somebody once said to me, "For us Johnson is like an old, well-worn shoe that does not give us corns."

Of my many later trips to the United States, I shall only give a few snapshots, as it were, describing above all outstanding human encounters. The chronological order is of no importance here.

Approximately twelve years after Kennedy's murder, I made the personal acquaintance of another American president, namely Jimmy Carter. Mrs. Carter and her sister-in-law, who both knew my books, had read of my lectures in Washington in the newspaper and invited me to the White House. During the lively discussion on theological and youth issues that immediately ensued, they both gave us the impression of being extremely clever, pleasant, and lovable women. When after a good hour we made a move to depart, Mrs. Carter said, "But now Jimmy wants to see you!" At first I had not rightly understood what she had said and was surprised when she then immediately led us into the open in order—as I only gradually realized—to take us to the president's famous oval office. I knew from the newspaper how many foreign dignitaries Carter had to receive that day. I was therefore amazed at the concentration, cheerfulness, and relaxation with which he conducted his discussion with us.

In the evening the German ambassador von Staden and his wife gave us dinner at his residence. Mr. von Staden spoke of our reception in the White House as a "sensation" because American presidents had an incredibly busy engagement diary, and private individuals were usually hardly ever admitted to an audience. The ambassador had also invited many other guests, above all journalists, in order to offer us as many opportunities for obtaining information as possible. Incidentally, during the table talk astonishingly critical words were spoken about the president and the host was virtually the only person to defend him and emphasize his good side. Among the reservations harbored against him I remember above all the objection that Carter was completely lacking in ideas and moreover had no experience in foreign affairs (which a president is already supposed to have *before* assuming office!) He was, it was said, also undiplomatic in his dealings with the allies, whom he intimidated and alienated from the United States. The only good thing about him, they argued, was that he was the first "devout" president for many years and did not feign religiousness for merely opportunistic reasons. This alone, however, could not attest to his competence for this office.

When we returned to Hamburg, our reception by President Carter was followed by a sequel. A few newspapers had learned of our visit to the White House from the Washington press and wanted to know further details. I refused to oblige, however, because it had, after all, been a private conversation and I felt that it would be tactless towards the Carter family to shout this from the rooftops. A well-known popular daily was incensed at my refusal and the next day published a photo montage showing me in conversation with Carter. Beneath this there was a record of our alleged discussion that, because of the many quotation marks, gave the impression that it was a literal transcript. Yet it was all just sheer invention from start to finish. The reporter had given free rein to his imagination and simply imagined what the American president would probably have said to a German theologian. My protest at this more than frivolous behavior led to the amazing answer that I only had myself to blame since I had refused to give the newspaper an interview. This made me all the more determined to refuse any request for an interview from this newspaper in the future.

For several years I gave guest lectures at the Medical Center in Houston, Texas. The theological institute that had been incorporated into the Center was run by my former doctoral student Kenneth Vaux. My lectures were often followed by colloquia with the professors, which brought me into contact with leading clinicians, including the famous heart surgeon Michael DeBakey. Liesel and I were not only invited to his home (where we were guests of his charming wife, who came from Hamburg), but were also permitted to view an open-heart operation. What fascinated us the most about this was the incredibly well thought out and organized system with which the large team of participants involved in the operation worked together and used the extremely impressive apparatus. This "classic" system, this teamwork, could almost be described as elegant and was reminiscent of an orchestra. It was probably this systematization that prevented us lay spectators from suffering any shock at what we witnessed and which allowed us to follow this spectacle and the way it was managed in breathless suspense.

Houston also provided me with other important meetings. Following a sermon I had given in the Presbyterian Church, one of the city's fifteen hundred (!) churches, a meal was given at which probably the most famous man in the United States at that time was also present, namely Judge Leon Jaworski, the man who had ultimately brought about the fall of President Nixon. In those days he was known to every child, for the Watergate trial was for many weeks broadcast daily on television. I had imagined him to be a hard prosecuter type of person, but to my surprise I now encountered a kind, thoughtful, and highly cultured gentleman. We immediately got into a lively conversation about the Nuremberg trials, in which he had taken part. As we were talking, I discovered an astonishing fact: during the investigations, Nixon had dismissed the previous examining magistrate presiding over the Watergate proceedings and appointed Jaworski in his place. He did this in the mistaken belief that he would find in Jaworski a sympathizer and a supporter of his interests, since they had been friends for years. Jaworski now found himself confronted with a conflict between the expectations Nixon placed in him and his duty to be neutral and objective. In his torment he asked the pastor of his Presbyterian parish and a few elders for advice. They discussed the issue thoroughly, prayed for clarity together, and became absolutely convinced that Jaworski had to take up this task. He thereby became a sort of role model in the eyes of American youth because, despite his earlier friendship with Nixon—which was common knowledge—he resolved to be relentlessly just. Even if Nixon himself was bitterly disappointed by this, the Americans at any rate heaved a sigh of relief that such an unimpeachable character still existed in that corrupt age.

I was once invited by the astronauts, doctors, and physicists of the neighboring *space center* for a meal, which was to be followed by a discussion on the ethical and philosophical problems associated with space travel. I was impressed by the seriousness with which they devoted themselves to questions that went beyond the merely technological and computable. I am ashamed to admit that I had rather expected them to be robots and apparatchiks. Instead, I found thoughtful people moved by the question of "meaning." John Glenn, the first American astronaut in space and to orbit the earth, was unable to come, but visited me the following day. He had heard how the evening had gone and now wished to have a personal conversation with me. I knew what personal, intellectual, and psychological criteria were decisive for the selection of astronauts. Among these is not only a high level of intellectual and technical ability, but also equilibrium of character, composure, and courage—quite apart from the physical requirements. Only the gift of an overly powerful *imagination* is (for obvious reasons!) unwelcome. I was not able to ascertain whether John Glenn had this desired shortcoming. In all other respects, however, he seemed to me to fulfill these criteria perfectly. After this pleasant meeting, I said to the people standing round about, "We have just seen a completely 'healthy' human being." I did not know of a better word to describe the impression I had of him. One of the reasons that I formulated it in such a way was probably the fact that I had that morning been shown around the intensive care units of the clinic for internal medicine and around other sections. John Glenn's flawless appearance now caused me to forget for a moment that there can never be perfect human beings and why this is so.

My lectures in the northwestern state of Washington, where I had been invited by the Pacific Lutheran University, fell quite outside my usual trips to the United States. My duties, however, were above all to speak at a fairly large theology conference that was taking place high up in the mountains of this probably the most beautiful of American states, at Holden Village, near Chelan.

We had to leave the car behind while we were still a long way off from our destination and travel a good hour by boat. We then climbed up incredible winding roads in a rickety omnibus until we suddenly found ourselves in a fabulously beautiful mountain village, which—completely un-American— was clothed in a mantle of well-tended flower arrangements (with no plastic imitations!). The village consisted of the abandoned houses of a redundant copper mine that the church had acquired and had had former drug addicts convert to a homely leisure center.

So there, together with two colleagues, I gave my lectures as well as a sermon. Since my books were well-known to everyone taking part—even my works on dogmatics and ethics—there were many penetrating, factual discussions in the midst of this agreeable human atmosphere.

Communion services here were very joyous occasions. Everybody shook hands, many people embraced each other. The services were community celebrations that were devoid of any liturgical stiffness. The relaxed and happy mood of the people was constantly venting itself in powerful singing. In the evenings, we sat around a huge fireplace above which galleries had even been built in order to include the village's inhabitants. There the daily workload was discussed, but I also had to tell a story each evening.

Holden Village was a human oasis surrounded by huge rocks and primeval wilderness. Liesel and I almost had to force ourselves to remember that we were in the United States. There was no television and no radio, not even a telephone. In the afternoons one went "hiking," a new word for rambling and climbing. It was here that I became acquainted with the first traces of a development that was then beginning to unfold in the United States. It had as its motto Rousseau's cry of "Back to nature!" One abandoned the car and put on one's walking boots. In some universities the students made their own slippers, spun yarn, sewed, knitted, crocheted, and also grew organic vegetables. It was a countermovement to technological civilization and the artificial world it had created. That people also wished to escape from the spell of civilization's rationality could be seen alone from the fact that Hermann Hesse was being read everywhere and being published in almost fabulous numbers.

I would like to conclude this series of snapshots with a few portraits of my American friends, especially my former undergraduates and doctoral students, whom I met again in many places where they themselves were now researching and teaching. I wish to take Professor Edward Schroeder in St. Louis (Missouri) as a representative of these many people. As a professor of the Missouri Lutheran Seminary, he had been driven from his chair—and with him several of his colleagues, a few of them likewise my pupils—by the radically "super-Lutheran" President of the Missouri Synod. This had happened because on the basis of the education he had received in Germany, Schroeder denied the doctrine of the verbal or literal inspiration of Holy Scripture. (Incidentally, in advocating this, he was in line with Luther's own understanding of the Bible.) After his dismissal, Schroeder opened his own seminary, the "Seminex" (seminary in exile). Devout Christians who were deeply rooted in theology fell victim to this "super-Lutheran" fanatic.

A few hundred students followed their professors into exile, where they were then just about able to manage. For the students, incidentally, this was a leap into uncertainty, for it meant losing their synodal home and nobody could guarantee that they would ever be employed by a parish. So this procession into exile was a confession of faith that was paid for with sacrifices. I wanted to declare my public support for this courageous band of people, and for that reason gave some lectures in the Seminex.

Pages from a Sketchbook: Latin America

After the summer semester of 1965, Liesel and I flew at the invitation of universities, seminaries, and churches to Latin America.

Our route led us from Rio de Janeiro, where we were greeted by extremely hot sunny days, to the coolness of high-lying São Paulo, where I (Liesel had remained with friends in Rio) enjoyed a condensed version of old German culture at the home of Bromberg the industrialist. In his library there were first editions of my favorite authors, Raabe, Fontane, and Stifter. At the Protestant Academy in São Paulo, I gave lectures to a public from widely differing educational backgrounds. During a discussion on some ethical subject I was surprised by the question, "Up to what level is bribery ethically permissible?" Please note, the question was not *whether* bribery was allowed but to *what degree* it was allowed. In countries such as Brazil, the fact itself was taken for granted as a universal custom. Can the reader imagine my embarrassment? However, I did not want to let my embarrassment show and simply said like a shot "ten percent," at which I received lively applause. Only later did I reflect that I myself did not know what I had meant by this ten percent. Did I mean a percentage of the ticket we expected to receive from a traffic policeman that would be enough to placate him and allow us to escape from the fine—or what? I was never very good at arithmetic. I was only clear about my intentions. I had wanted to say the following.

If bribery is part of the general way of life, it loses its exceptional and clandestine character and can thus acquire a certain legitimacy. It is then only its excesses that become questionable. Consequently, the custom itself has to be limited and tolerated only within these limitations. It was obviously this principle that the audience had applauded and not so much my rather bizarre percentage.

Afterwards, I visited the flood area of Porto Alegre and São Leopoldo; from there I traveled on to Argentina. In Buenos Aires I lectured at various universities. The highlight was a three-day discussion with ethics professors of different provenance—with Jesuits, Marxists and Jews—in José C. Paz; our different backgrounds provided a source of friction that caused the sparks to fly.

From there I flew to Chile, where I had some particularly intensive contacts with Catholic theology in Santiago. I lectured at the faculty of Catholic theology and at the Benedictine abbey there.

A day in Lima (Peru) was completely devoted to archaeology, for which I had a wonderfully well-informed guide in our friend Dr. Sellschopp. My strongest impression was of the archaic monument of the sun pyramid, which towered gigantically on an artificial mountain situated between desert, ocean, the Andes, and a fertile valley. Idols of terrifying cruelty and strangeness threatened to spellbind the observer. Even today, so I am told, young, pretty girls are occasionally sacrificed to the rain god in the interior, and the police never find out.

The last stage of my journey was a visit to Mexico City. At the Lutheran Seminary there I had to fulfill an exceedingly densely packed but extremely lively schedule of work in the form of lectures, discussions, and numerous personal conversations. It was probably Mexico City's altitude, as well as the time difference and my arrival in the middle of the night that caused my utter overexhaustion to break out right at the beginning of my visit. This expressed itself in a grotesque form during a reception that was followed by dinner in my honor given by Steinle the surgeon in his spacious house.

From 8:00 P.M. to 10:00 P.M. we at first stood about until we were fit to drop. As a guest I was always surrounded by groups of people, who spoke to me partly in German, partly in Spanish, in the latter case, of course, with the assistance of a translator. So I always had to be politely attentive. I finally dragged myself, already affected by a slight dizziness, to the table, where I was placed next to the extremely kind hostess. It was then that it happened. I had imperceptibly dozed off and my head had fallen into my soup plate. I was rudely awakened by the hot soup and I can still see the many horrified faces gazing at me in complete silence. Mrs. Steinle then saved the situation with a witty remark.

The geographical focal point of the tour was the theological seminary in São Leopoldo (Brazil). I lectured for three weeks on the "mirror mountain" and in the evenings discussed theological and political problems with the students over maté tea. My reunion there with Harding Meyer, who had once studied for his doctorate under me and now taught systematic theology on the "mirror mountain," was of particular joy to me. Apart from these human contacts, my time in Brazil was darkened by constant storms breaking over us, by rain and gales, thunder and lightning. Nowhere have I ever felt the cold as much as I did in the sunny land of Brazil, a land which does not care for heating. Flooded land lay all around us for miles and miles. Sometimes we visited the people who had been driven from their homes by the flood in their depressingly primitive emergency accommodation.

In the immediate vicinity I was able to observe how a new saint was "constructed." A certain Father Reuss of the neighboring Jesuit university was honored after his death as a saint and intercessor. Every day there were announcements in the newspaper expressing thanks for his miracles and deliverances. Even a cathedral had been erected in his honor and was constantly being visited by swarms of pilgrims. From a popular biography, I rather gained the impression that he had been a psychopath who had inflicted absurd self-tortures upon himself while he had been alive and had every day rattled off innumerable Lord's Prayers and Ave Marias like a prayer wheel. A stand selling sacraments also sold little pieces of his habit, which were supposed to bring about miraculous cures when touched. When I conjectured that the Father's robe would, if all of this had been genuine, have had to have been a hundred meters long, I was told the following: "Of course. These textiles originate from somewhere else, but they have been allowed to touch his robe and through this contact his power has passed to them." At the cathedral I also met a Father from Bavaria, who told me that he had lived with Father Reuss for thirty years. To my question whether he had noticed anything of Reuss' holiness while he was alive, he gave the astonishing reply, "Not at all! But since he has been dead, the Savior grants him every favor!" It was only with difficulty that I was able to suppress my displeasure that the educated Jesuits (at whose center I had likewise given a lecture) tolerated this fantastic cult that had grown up around one of their members. Although they smiled with a certain superior air when I spoke to them about this, they appeared to find this dualism of sublime theology and primitive, magical, popular devotion quite all right.

Magic, which was here covered with a thin veneer of Christianity, still lives on in elemental and immediate form in Brazil's widespread spiritism and syncretistic cults, in macumba and other forms of magic. By means of special contacts open to me I was able to attend several of these esoteric cultic events that were hidden from normal tourists. At these events I always found two altars: a Christian altar and an African pagan altar. The latter was adorned with the grotesque faces of gods, demons, and other symbols of those things that burst out frighteningly from the background of the world. The cult congregation was a colorful mixture of all age groups, classes, and races.

There were blacks and whites, intellectual academics with large horn-rimmed spectacles, and ordinary people. The outbursts of ecstasy that took place at these events were of unimaginable passion. People went into wild convulsions, some stood on their heads and flailed about with their legs, others uttered piercing cries. The obviously highly respected cult heroine, an old woman with an impressive face who must certainly have weighed more than two hundred pounds, once did a high jump that seemed to defy the law of gravity. The rhythm of the jungle drums, which went on for hours, and the colorful movement of the scenes haunted me for a long time afterwards. The pagan origin of this cultic event was covered only by the thinnest veneer and, as the new cult of saints showed me, here and there even broke out in the sacraments of the Catholic church.

There are historical reasons for this syncretism. The law stipulated that only baptized Christians were permitted to enter the country. When they arrived, the black slaves had received a sort of mass baptismal sprinkling with an aspergill in order to transform the new arrivals into Christians without delay. This did not drive away the African gods, however; they at best coughed and sneezed but continued their rule undisturbed.

The greatest adventure of the trip was without doubt when Pastor Lützow took Liesel and me from São Leopoldo deep into the interior to Tres des Maio. This involved a car journey through the red, rain-drenched mud of the sierra. Only a few believed us to be capable of overcoming the clayey, slippery desert of mud and the distance of approximately 650 kilometers in our little Volkswagen Beetle. We were constantly getting stuck, had five punctures, and several times spun the car round a full 360 degrees. But when we finally made it through all the emptiness and darkness, in which we sometimes felt as forlorn as astronauts, and at last reached our destination after eighteen hours on the road, our joy was all the greater. On our arrival we were greeted by the dignitaries of this deserted region and after the church service, which I led, several cows were roasted on a spit. From there we traveled to even greater wastelands and visited Pastor Schwantes in Tenente Portela. There he had set up a boarding school and a hospital on the Indian reservation with funds he had arduously acquired through begging. I admired the pioneering deeds of this man. He was a cultured and educated theologian who selflessly served the Indians in this empty wasteland.

Politically I was interested above all in the position of Latin America in the East-West conflict. In this respect I was often filled with concern at the South Americans' strong Yankeephobia (hatred of North Americans). It seemed to me almost as if they had decided against the West from the outset. For this reason I looked into this problem in some detail and would now like to indicate the most important results yielded by my observations.

The core of their resentment is their reaction to the specifically American form of anti-Communism. Everywhere social revolutionary tendencies appear in the Latin American states—tendencies that are more than understandable—the Americans immediately see Communist motives at work. This diagnosis presents itself *first* because of the certain formal analogy that exists between *all* types of social revolutionary tendencies and thus also with their Communist variants, and *second* because of the almost neurotic character of this American form of anti-Communism, which in its incapacity to differentiate acts at least as simplistically as Communism itself. In exactly the same way as Communism it sees everything in black and white terms and as a result is only capable of making sweeping judgments; it is neurotic because "seeing red" is virtually a complex, which is something that is obviously difficult to overcome with realistic considerations and rational arguments.

On the other hand, I was told unanimously by all the people I talked to in the Latin American countries I visited that their passion for social reform was originally unambiguously nonideological, and I am convinced that this self-assessment is correct. To the outside observer this impression was marred only by the fact that the Communists naturally exploited these tendencies and attempted to use them as grist for their mill. But one must distinguish very precisely here between what is substance and what is only a phenomenon of peripheral importance. The movements in Latin America are *not* naturally Communist.

Admittedly, the connection of the nonideological, social reforming strand with the ideological strand in this complex state of affairs is further complicated by yet another factor, that is, the neurotically simplistic and false diagnosis made by American anti-Communism additionally has a destructive effect in an *active* sense. What this means in simplified terms is that the Americans say: you are Communists (or at least in danger of becoming Communists). From this they then deduce the following two consequences.

Either they withdraw and dissociate themselves from that particular country. The result of abandoning people in this way is that these people then make friends—especially since they need help and support—with those powers who are prepared to receive them, namely Moscow and Beijing. I have always felt it to be a dreadful and tragic blindness on the part of

American policy that it ignores that it is precisely *this* form of anti-Communism that stimulates and consolidates Communism. I have had the validity of this assessment confirmed in innumerable conversations, a fact which indicates that I am here describing a general mood. Fidel Castro was often cited to me as a model case for the consequences of American policy. Since Castro was mentioned by people from the most diverse geographical areas, completely independent of each other, this constituted a particularly impressive consensus of opinion.

Or—and this is the other consequence—the Americans seek to protect themselves against this ideologically unstable continent by seizing it economically or even politically or by holding it under military control. In doing so, they cause the South Americans to feel threatened by imperialism and to suffer from a sense of national incapacitation. Thus, whereas the first consequence I mentioned produces a *Communist* reaction—by bringing about dependence on Communist powers—the second consequence provokes a *nationalistic* reaction. In this way Communism and nationalism have become the two most menacing emotions on this continent and both join forces to form a universal and extremely militant anti-American resentment.

I ought again to emphasize that all this is not my own personal interpretation. I am only reporting how the people to whom I talked, who varied in geography, nationality, and profession, interpreted the situation. I would also like to add that numerous North Americans living in Latin America to whom I spoke also shared this interpretation—often in a mood of melancholy and despair.

When I look back on this trip, it fills me with profound joy to know that Christian pioneers are at work on this continent, and I am very pleased at the way they are carrying out their mission. They not only preach the Gospel but also teach the way to culture. They teach farming and cattle breeding, reading and writing, and also build schools and hospitals. We often complain with justification that our foreign aid suffers from a lack of helpers and that nobody is grateful when they receive merely material gifts. Here, however, there are people who are working hard and who have made great sacrifices. Yet we constantly leave them without material help and thus on their own. The Federal Republic of Germany has left visible traces everywhere, we have bridgeheads of sympathy towards us at our disposal— yet we (and our politicians) are strangely unaware of this continent, of all places. My thoughts often go out to these courageous people who serve in isolation.

The "Workhouse" in Mustin

Between my great journeys, term work in Hamburg naturally continued as usual. In the vacations, apart from the two-week holidays I took each year, I went into seclusion and worked on my books. When I had no distractions, was unobtainable by telephone, and for the most part did not even bother to open my mail, a monk was almost a profligate in comparison with me. I certainly did not feel such times to be periods of renunciation, however. To be able to concentrate undisturbed is a real pleasure for me. It is astonishing how much one can reap when one devotes the whole day to just a single subject. Since our house was frequented by many of the children's friends and there are, moreover, certain stages in adolescence when happiness in life consists of playing loud, wall-shaking music, I built myself a little thatched-roof cottage in the beautiful duchy of Lauenburg. There, in the village of Mustin, close to the border with the German Democratic Republic, I was able to get the cloistered peace I required. To the front and rear of the house were some lakes, which I jumped into several times each day during the summer months. Because it was not supposed to be a summerhouse but a workhouse for writing books, it was possible to build it away from the road on a nature reserve. The quiet there was so complete that the only sound to be heard was the blood roaring in one's ears. Not even an airplane was to be heard in this part of the world, except when the Federal Border Guard picked me up to take me to a lecture, which happened from time to time.

I spent the evenings reading relaxing literature, or at the homes of a few friends, who allowed me to participate in the troubles, worries, and joys of the village. Among the joys was the annual shooting contest, where the unusual but much to be recommended combination of buttermilk and schnapps gladdened the heart. Incidentally, the proclamation of the new "champion" was taken incredibly seriously; there were parades with flags and the men marched in old Prussian goose-step with their faces frozen into stony masks. The comprehensive view possible in this little world also enabled me to perceive the nonsense of German educational policy. The little village school was closed (as is also happening everywhere else), making it necessary for the children to be taken each morning by bus to the bloated mass school at the center of this rural catchment area. With the departure of the teacher one of the village's cultural centers vanished, leaving only the pastor behind all on his own. Soon there were also no longer any shops and scarcely any craftsmen. The reparceling of agricultural land caused the small farmers to disappear, who were then forced to work as roadmenders or do similar jobs.

So it was in this village that I completed the *Theological Ethics* and later the three volumes of the *Evangelical Faith* together with my anthropological work *Being Human—Becoming Human*, as well as smaller works and lectures. Now and again Liesel came to see that everything was all right. She was horrified that I had made do for the whole week with just a cup, a plate, a knife, and a fork.

Call to a Chair at Munich

My peaceful work on my books was abruptly interrupted in 1964 when I was confronted with a difficult decision. I had to decide whether to respond to a call to take up a chair at the University of Munich.

This call was naturally very tempting. Together with Karl Rahner, who was to represent the Catholic position, I was supposed to assume Romano Guardini's chair and, in the philosophy faculty, become professor of Philosophy of Religion and Christian Philosophy. It would certainly have been an opportunity to have had far-reaching influence, for it was intended that this professorship should cut across faculty divisions. To represent general studies full-time at the largest university in Germany—that was really appealing. The other, almost even greater task that would have been entrusted to me was to initiate the foundation of a faculty of Protestant Theology at Munich. I do not need to say what opportunities were contained in such a project, especially in this city and at this university. The Munich task tempted me even more when the University, the Church, the Ministry of Education, and many personal friends called on me to accept the post with an urgency and in such warm terms that my reservations initially melted way. I was especially touched by the unreserved openness with which, of all people, the Catholic faculty received me and by how hard they worked for the foundation of a faculty of Protestant theology.

In this regard I had an experience that portrays what is probably a unique symptom of the changed relationship between the two denominations. One of my biggest worries consisted in the question of what would happen to my pupils studying for their doctorate or habilitation under me, especially those from abroad. Could I look after them as a one-man band? In addition to this, there was also the problem that I would, of course, have only been able to award the doctorate in philosophy but not—at least not until the foundation of the faculty—the doctorate in theology.

It is true that Erlangen very generously offered me a permanent visiting professorship, which would have solved a few difficulties of this kind. But, and this was just the point, it would not have solved all of them. Merely the journeys back and forth between Munich and Erlangen would have meant an additional burden. The dean of the Catholic faculty in Munich, Michael Schmaus, found an astonishing solution to these problems with my doctoral students, which deserves to be recorded as a sign of the times. He asked Cardinal Döpfner of Munich to allow my pupils to gain the doctorate in theology with the help of his—that is, the Catholic!—faculty. Of course, this would have only been possible—and it was precisely this possibility that he sought to open—if the Tridentine oath of confession, which was binding for Catholic theologians studying for the doctorate, was dropped.

The Cardinal was "full of enthusiasm" and willing to agree to Schmaus' suggestion, but because of the radical character of such a decision, did not feel he was competent to make it alone. He therefore consulted the pro-prefect of the Roman congregation, Cardinal Alfredo Ottoviani, a man who had a reputation for extreme "conservatism." It was thus all the more astonishing that he likewise gave his consent. Sometimes I thought that it was worth going to Munich just in order to create a doctorate in theology that had come about in such a manner. I, at any rate, took cognizance of this degree of openness with gratitude and some embarrassment.

In the end, however, there were two reasons that prompted me to back away from Munich. *The first reason* was my concern at the organizational tasks awaiting me, which would have taken years to complete. I had, of course, already experienced the trials and tribulations associated with founding a faculty at Hamburg. And I had also, after all, already devoted a few years to administrative work during my Tübingen and Hamburg rector-ships. Although I had learned a great deal from these and do not regret them, they had nevertheless led me away from my real work. I still believed that I occasionally had a few good ideas and my files were full of outlines for books and articles. Was I now to suppress all this in order to become a manager again—even if it were for a great task?

The *other* reason was that I felt very much at home in Hamburg. How would I be able to live without my dearly beloved faculty? Would I not become a "soloist" and theologically impoverished without its strengthening and corrective support, without the security of my circle of good friends? Furthermore, I thought of the great congregation at the Church of St.

Michael, with whom I had now enjoyed a relationship of mutual loyalty for ten years (already). Could I abandon them? And how many friends I had been granted in Hamburg! How I depended on their cultured conviviality and conversation, which was never merely empty palaver! I simply could not bring myself to bid farewell to all this—or to the town itself with the Alster and Elbe, with the sea nearby, and with its spirit of generosity. I have often wondered whether I ought not to relinquish everything to which I had become so attached. But I could not—there were, after all, also deeper ties associated with my office and my message. And how clearly the people of Hamburg also told me that I should stay! I would have had to have had a heart of stone to ignore this.

Although I remained in Hamburg, the call to Munich had a positive effect. During the negotiations with the Munich Ministry of Education, I was able to get them to commit themselves to enlarge the university so as to incorporate a faculty of Protestant theology. Despite my refusal to accept the post, both Ministry and University were then generous enough to nominate me as a member of the appointments committee for the new faculty to be established. So I was able to contribute to building up its academic staff. From the way in which the new faculty made its presence felt, it was clear that we had not made a bad selection.

The Student Revolt in University and Church

ON NOVEMBER 9, 1967, one of the saddest phases in my life began in the main lecturing hall of Hamburg University. What is more, it began during what was supposed to be the "ceremonial" change of rectors. It was here, in a paroxysm of wild incidents, that the student revolt broke out. This depressing phenomenon not only darkened the following years but also shook the structures of the German university to the foundations. The cowardice of politicians and professors permitted an almost perverse and paralyzing form of "democratization" to take place; this cowardice allowed people to have a say on matters for which they were not responsible, gave rise to a scandalous increase in titles—how meaningless the word "professor" has since become!—and made possible the creation of rival groups whose competition let to mutual paralysis. This revolt constituted a historical caesura marking the beginning of the decline of the German university. I was able to observe the loss of prestige of this once so respected institution all over the world.

The Disturbances at the University

That procession on November 9, 1967, was the last time academic staff ever wore gowns. It was accompanied by the loud din of the students, which drowned out the music. Without our being able to read the inscription, a banner was unfurled in front of us with the now famous text, "Under the gowns lies the dust of a thousand years." By using a telephoto lens, the eagerly filming television crew brought this banner so close to the professors entering the hall that it created the impression that the people carrying it had been part of the procession and that the banner had been tolerated by the professors wearing the gowns. Television continued to play a destructive role in the period that followed. Television reporters were always at the scene of any trouble, having been alerted in good time by the students, and did not content themselves with the task of merely registering the events, but played an active and provocative role in stimulating these events. This very soon prompted me to write an extremely polemical and satirical article against these evil television practices in *Christ und Welt* (Christian and World), which the editor-in-chief described as a "direct hit." He induced the newspaper editors at any rate to take part in a special conference. They did not, however, exactly show any "active" repentance for how they had behaved.

The rest of this academic ceremony continued in the same depressing vein. The new rector's speech was constantly interrupted by yelling and shouting. People were smoking, couples were lying in each other's arms, and balloons were rising into the air, and while all this was going on press photographers and cameramen were storming up and down the aisles. The rector was completely helpless in this pandemonium; even then, however, he did not break off his speech but, bowed over his manuscript, read his text to the bitter end. I had given some thought to a suitable remark for our processional exit and now yelled it at the top of my voice into this seething crowd, which was interspersed with frightened citizens and dignitaries: "You had the opportunity to prove yourselves to be mature partners. Instead all we got to see were adolescent tantrums. See to it in the future that we can take you seriously and not be constantly forced to interpret you psychoanalytically." In the *Student Committee Info* it was then reported that I had described the students as "adolescent riff-raff."

This awful morning marked the start of several years of disturbances, during which offices and seminars were occupied, the walls daubed with red slogans—"Smash the state, power to the soviets"—and many professors terrorized by mass disruptions and organized protest yelling. One of the main victims of this unrest was my colleague and friend Hans Wenke, with whom I had been friends since our time in Tübingen together. He had come to Hamburg as a school senator and had later founded the University of Bochum. Radical students set up a stall distributing defamatory literature and leaflets against him right next to his office so that the walk to his room was like running the gauntlet. At the instigation of Oberlercher, the spokesman of the group and whom Wenke's doctor blamed for his death, Wenke's lectures in the main lecture hall were constantly being violently interrupted by hundreds of intruders. Four times he stood at his lectern facing the seething crowd. He was unable to begin his lecture and each time he had to leave the hall to the accompaniment of scornful shouts and physical harassment until, after a courageous battle, he gave up. In general, professors are constitutionally not especially well equipped for such incidents. I could well imagine what Wenke and his steadfast wife had to endure.

When nobody stood by him—not even anyone from his own faculty, not even that colleague of his in the philosophy faculty who over the years had been extolled as Praeceptor Germaniae (Teacher of Germany) and at that time was still an influential figure—I resolved to come to his aid publicly by pointedly canceling my lecture. I announced my decision by circulating leaflets headed "Instead of a lecture" and had people spread my intention by word of mouth. As expected, in the second main lecture hall I met besides my usual audience a crowd of well-known ringleaders—Oberlercher was again there—who had got wind of the lecture on time. Since this "lecture" was what prompted the later disturbances in my church services at the Michel, I would like to include a few sections from it here.

I am not going to give a lecture today but am going to make a statement and then leave this hall. If you wish to discuss what I am going to say, however, I am prepared to do so. But I refuse to give a lecture today. I am aware that my real audience does not deserve to be affected by this act of protest and the small remnant of humor and self-irony I still have enables me to see myself in the role of the pastor who scolds his congregation because other people are indulging in the sins of the carnival. I see no other possibility, however, of giving expression to my protest at how my colleague and friend Wenke has been treated. This is, I know, an impotent protest and will be swept away without having any effect in light of the collective neuroses that have broken out. . . .

It does not take long to describe the case itself. A student [Oberlercher], whose behavior had already repeatedly tried the nerves of the professors as well as those of his fellow students, wrote an article in *The Auditorium* attacking Professor Wenke. The concept of a bad upbringing is inadequate to describe the vulgar insolence of this article. It also goes beyond the vocabulary permitted in a democratic society. Furthermore, to my mind the article shows psychopathic tendencies. I do not wish to blame the author for these but to criticize the editorship of the organ that published such rubbish. . . .

Professor Wenke reacted to the article by saying to the author in his seminar, "After writing this article I do not understand why you still come to my seminars. Please leave the room!" Incidentally, he said "please." There is no question of Oberlercher's having been thrown out, as a Hamburg tabloid described it. That this disruptive student then did indeed leave the hall was the result of pressure from his fellow students, who induced him to leave in unanimous protest at his insults. . . .

It is indeed intolerable to be faced by a vulgar mud-slinger in the audience when one wishes to pursue the serious work of collective thought. In a community for whose continued existence I am responsible—a responsibility I carry for the sake of my students!—I would certainly tolerate any critic, but never such a lout. I must confess that I for my part would probably not have been able to remain as polite and courteous to the degree in which Professor Wenke forced himself to be.

Certain people then dared to give my colleague an ultimatum: he should apologize, otherwise he would be given the opportunity to do so in his lecture. What a brutalization of common decency! People obviously no longer had any sense for the sort of hack they had supported and for the verbal excesses they had helped him to make. At the same time as this call for Wenke to apologize was made, Mr. O's group circulated a "supplementary" leaflet which spoke of "arse-lickers" for whom there was no place at the university. This leaflet also made clear that these people were prepared to resort to any falsehoods they felt to be necessary, for the anti-Wenke article was headed by a shocking, gross Nazi statement that Mr. Wenke was said to have written. In reality, however, this text was merely a quotation of a Nazi "decree" and was also described as such in Wenke's paper, in which he also gave an exact reference to where this passage was to be found. But this was not mentioned in that *Auditorium* article. As I said, falsehoods of this kind, which cannot possibly be explained away as mere oversights, were allowed to pass unreprimanded. . . .

You are now informed about the shameful events that allowed a German professor to be banned from entering his own lecture hall. The single ray of hope for me in all this is that there were obviously many people who remained rational during this expression of uncontrolled mass emotion and came to the support of their teacher. Such people also existed.

All this was done to a man who has spent his whole life helping young people and who, at the cost of almost destroying his health, has accomplished the great work of founding the University of Bochum. Probably nobody else could have completed this task in the way that he did. Only he had the vigor, the organizational ability, and the strategic awareness to achieve this. But even for this he has sometimes received little gratitude.

So much for the facts of the matter. I would now like to say something about the consequences resulting from it.

What makes me despair at the moment are not the wire-pullers of the *Sozialistischer Deutscher Studentenbund* (SDS) [German Student Socialist

Alliance] but the behavior of the vast majority of students. These students only protest in a very small way against the new oligarchy of functionaries—that is, against those functionaries whose main occupation has already long since moved from proper study to making the din they call university politics. I have been told that in another Hamburg faculty where a good working climate seems to prevail the students were calling to each other, "Let's go to Wenke's lecture in the main lecture hall, there's something going on there." Look, these people and others like them who swim with the tide make me despair. This should not be taken to mean that I regard it as illicit to go along and observe such scenes. But there is a difference between whether I wish to be a witness to an event and whether I go there just for a joke and, in my obsession with having fun, do not notice to what ignominy I have subjected myself and on whose bandwagon I have jumped.

Dear students, I am so depressed that I am now going to say something that I hope I will soon be able to retract. Never would I be happier to admit that I am wrong; I even long to do so. But first I will give voice to my despair. I believe that this nation of ours is beyond help. All I can say is "poor Germany!" I have been criminally guilty of nurturing illusions. I really believed that we had overcome Nazism and that a new Hitler—even one coming from a different political direction—was now unthinkable among us. And in all the countries that I have visited as a visiting professor I have testified to this in countless discussions. I now accuse myself of misleading people—albeit unwittingly. I now *no* longer believe that we are immune to a demagogical dictatorship. Nazism also began with intimidation and yelling back in those days. And back then the nation also went along with what was happening because "there was something going on." The nation was helplessly susceptible to anything that looked dynamic and promised the spectacle of public denunciations. . . .

The functionaries talk about shaping political ideas and awakening political maturity. But all that results from this is indoctrination and emotion, an awful dimming of consciousness that I would never have held to have been possible at a German university.

For this reason I do not know at the moment what I am still doing in a German lecture hall. Although I am grateful that all of us here are able to get on well with each other, this does not remove my despair. For the university is indivisible. . . .

On top of everything, it is not only the German university that is at stake, although this alone would be grave enough. It is also our nation and our political destiny that is at stake. These are weighty words, I know. . . . But in expressing them I am only following the stated intentions of those people I hold to be our undoing. We are all suffering from the university's distress—both professors and students!—and we would all like to overcome it together. These people, however, use the plight of the university as an opportunity and a springboard to destroy the established order as such through their anarchic subversion. . . .

I will continue my work and carry on doing theology, and in this respect my theology students constitute a salve on the wound I feel. But with regard to the university I have been cut to the quick. May this all still be graciously reversed by a higher hand. I have lost my faith in human beings.

This "lecture," which was also sent to every member of the academic staff, caused a considerable stir among the public. Many newspapers, as well as the media, published excerpts and endorsed or criticized it. Quite a few people were annoyed at my cry of "poor Germany" and showed their solidarity—even in those initial stages!—with the criticism and demands of the SDS. In the process I was occasionally portrayed as a sinister reactionary. Once again mountains of mail piled up at my home. The positive response to my lecture was considerably greater than the criticism and abuse. Many people felt it almost to be a "release" that someone had belled the then still so lovingly pampered cat that was "rebellious youth."

At any rate, the result of my "lecture" was that from then on the radicals' collective rage was turned above all against *me*.

When shortly afterwards I had to give a set speech at the North-West German Surgeons Congress that was taking place at Hamburg, my leftist opponents took up position carrying abusive banners in the foyer of the main lecture hall. A few surgeons' wives were not prepared to put up with this, however. Under the leadership of Mrs. Gabriele Zenker from Munich, they tore down the abusive slogans and trampled them underfoot. The people carrying the banners were so dumbfounded at this unusual deed that they let it take place without saying a word and without offering any resistance. During the banquet at the Hotel Atlantic that evening, the surgeons gave this courageous "street fighter" a standing ovation for her bravery. In the midst of all the melancholy there was once again cause for cheerfulness.

On repeated occasions in the following months, intruders saw to it that there was turmoil in my lectures and seminars as well. But I always coped with this, especially since I could rely on the support of my people. Only slowly did I notice that a group of students always accompanied me from my office to the lecture hall. When I inquired as to the whys and wherefores of this, I learned that they wished to protect me from being harrassed. The "chief" of this group was Heinrich Kuhfuss, the future pastor of the Church of St. Michael, a man who was respected even by the demimonde and underworld of St. Pauli. He was one of the most loyal of my supporters.

The Disturbances at the Church of St. Michael

Things were very much more difficult when rebellious students chose to make my services at the Church of St. Michael the target of their aggression. They were, of course, bent on having as massive an effect as possible, and since they could not have got a gathering of three thousand people off the ground by themselves, the congregation at the Church of St. Michael was just what they wanted. They could park themselves in such a crowd and turn the church service into one of their protest actions. At the university I was able to react fiercely and ironically to any harassment and was also often able to have the last laugh. But how ought I to behave in a church service where I would be wearing my cassock and standing in the pulpit? Here I was in a completely different role and was confronted by very much more delicate tasks.

The attack on the Michel service was sounded for the first time on January 13, 1968. As early as the previous December's services, however, there had been a few hints of what was to come, such as heckling during the sermon and an invasion of the sacristy where passages from Mao's *Little Red Book* were read out.

The signs of what was now in store for me increased during the first days of the New Year. My friend, Hans Jürgen Quest, the chief pastor of the Church of St. Michael, informed me that the SDS and other groups belonging to the extraparliamentary opposition had told him that the Hamburg Christmas services had only been spared protest rallies because everything was to be concentrated on the Thielicke evening in the Michel.

At the same time a delegation from the various opposition groups descended upon me at my apartment and categorically demanded that I agree to take part in a public discussion within the context of the church service. I refused this equally categorically but offered to have discussions with them in the parish rooms after the service. This did not appeal to these people at all, however, because only the "crowd" was important to them.

Even my old university friend Hans Martin Helbich, the general superintendent of Berlin, had heard of the threats against me and traveled to Hamburg to give me his support. But, if anything, he was in even *more* need of comfort than I was. He was quite distraught at the disturbances that had been taking place in the Kaiser Wilhelm Church of Remembrance at Berlin and suffered from his depressing isolation within the Berlin Church leadership. Not only had the Church Leadership left him without support, but they constantly promoted understanding for and loving toleration of the rebellious students, without this being acknowledged in the slightest by the students themselves. This course of action was supported especially by Bishop Scharf, who had been so courageous in the Third Reich. "I've now escaped the inferno for a few hours," Helbich said on greeting me. It shook me to see this once jovial fellow, who in earlier days had been positively bursting with vitality, so bowed, depressed, and without hope, especially since I was struggling with my own troubles.

On January 5 I received a telephone call from the police station responsible for the Michel telling me that they had been informed by their colleagues from the crime squad that large-scale disruptive action and the distribution of inflammatory leaflets was planned for my next church service. Chief of Police Sch. now wanted to know what I expected from the police. I had already arranged with Quest that they were under no circumstances to be allowed to take action within the Church. We would do everything in our power to cope with the situation ourselves and if absolutely necessary would prefer to stop the service. When I disclosed this to the policeman he seemed to be very relieved. That detectives would keep an eye outside on people visiting the church—many of the potential troublemakers were already known to him—was of course exclusively a police matter and was none of my concern, he said. He would in any case pass on my request to act with the utmost restraint.

Soon fresh news rolled in. Because of the large crowd of people in the church, which would be infiltrated by hundreds of troublemakers, the ministry responsible for internal affairs believed that the situation could intensify to such a degree that there was a danger of panic breaking out, which could have unforeseeable consequences. For this reason the head of this ministry, Senator Ruhnau, would take up position in one of the clergy houses and take command of any police operations that might be necessary.

I too had already thought of the possibility of an extreme escalation. If such an eventuality took place I, standing alone on the pulpit, would have to know how I should behave and what directives I should give. From my studies of Spurgeon I knew that he had been haunted by such a shocking experience until the end of his life. In the jam-packed confines of one of his church services, a few troublemakers had shouted "Fire!" In vain he tried from his pulpit to calm the crowd of people who were leaping to their feet in panic. But they could no longer be stopped. Seven people were trampled to death and many injured. I confess that this thought caused me great concern.

For this reason I had already agreed on few precautionary measures with the parish council, who loyally and unanimously supported me. Parish council members and reliable students were to guard the pulpit and altar microphones. A small guard was also planned for the organ so that we would not suddenly have the pleasure of hearing the "Internationale." These guards also remained steadfast when the attempt was indeed made to seize the altar microphone.

At the same time I asked for some advice (not—as was later said—for the help of his men) from the commander of the Second Army Officers School, Brigadier General Wulf, with whom I was good friends. Wulf, Quest, and I located the trouble spots in the Church. The general approved of the prophylaxis we had planned and announced with a smile that he himself would sit on the steps leading to the pulpit and act as a guardian angel for the pulpit and its microphone.

In the week leading up to January 13, the poster and leaflet campaign at the university and its institutions was stepped up. At the same time, huge inscriptions painted on wooden fences and walls with the demand to disrupt "Thielicke's Michel" positively shouted at the passers-by from all sides. As well as this, leaflets containing a blasphemous mimicking of the Lord's Prayer were circulated, which the uninvited guests were supposed to shout in unison when the congregation said the Lord's Prayer together (which is indeed what happened):

Our capital who art in the West,
Remunerative be thy investments,
Thy profit come,
Thy share prices rise
In Wall Street as it is in Europe.
Give us this day our daily turnover
And extend for us our loans,
As we give our creditors time to pay.
And lead us not into bankruptcy,
But deliver us from the unions.
For thine has been half the world, the

Power and the riches,
For two hundred years.
   Mammon.

I will pass over the many slanders made against my person in the leaflets that were circulated—except one perhaps (although it was one of the more innocuous). I was portrayed as a friend of the rich and said to have the dream car of a white "Jaguar" at my disposal. My students then put a model of this much sought-after but never attained car on my lectern, with which my grandsons very much enjoyed playing in later years.

There were, however, also heartening displays of support. The whole of my faculty resolved to take part in the church service and to make clear their loyalty towards me. Many people likewise assured me of their solidarity in letters, telegrams, and long-distance telephone calls, and touchingly sent me their regards.

I slept very badly during the nights leading up to January 13 because I was constantly going through every conceivable situation in my mind and considering how I should react. I was confident that I was serving as a witness to the Gospel, but I could not rid myself of the worry that my overtiredness might cause me to react in the wrong way. There was indeed a difference between whether I encountered the troublemakers casually in the lecture hall or whether I was standing in the pulpit, since I could not allow myself to adopt the wrong tone at a church service. I was moved when, on the morning of January 13, two of my Eppendorf doctors—naturally unsolicited and also quite independently of each other—brought me some medicine to help me relax.

At last Sunday evening arrived. Before I even entered the church, I had to run the gauntlet past groups with leaflets and a crossfire of hostile glares. When I stepped up to the altar to deliver the opening liturgy, I sensed a strange agitation in the crowd. People were also standing in all the aisles and there was constant movement in the congregation. Immediately in front of me, however, sat the whole of my faculty and the loyal parish council.

Outwardly everything was still calm. It was only when I entered the pulpit and had begun my sermon that the trouble then started. A particularly active student ringleader, Peter Schütt, got up and vociferously demanded an immediate discussion. This was accompanied by rapturous applause and chaotic shouts from his clique, while multiple "boos" and "nos" burst forth from the rows of the congregation. At the same time the air was pierced by shrill heckling. These were all routine clichés with which I had been familiar for a long time and which were intended to impress ignorant people. Among these ignorant people were also many newspaper writers, who in the following days could not praise the clichés enough as symptoms of an "inner seriousness" on the part of the troublemakers. And yet they only had three constantly recurring refrains: "You're making it too easy for yourself!" "You only ever talk about yourself!" and "Get to the point!"

When the noise got out of control and the congregation was threatening to take physical action against the noisemakers, I resorted to one of the measures I had prepared. I had had "extra hymns" printed on the reverse side of the hymn sheet handed out at each of my church services, which I intended to get people to sing if any trouble broke out. So I now asked the congregation to rise and sing the hymn "Great God, we praise you."

Everybody leaped to his feet and the powerful singing of the thousands of people present, combined with the sounds of the organ, whose organist pulled out all the stops, completely drowned the shouting. When the shouting began again immediately after the end of the hymn, I once again had the congregation stand up and sing the next song. I can still see how one parish council member, the valiant Sieverts, a master plumber and one of my most loyal supporters, covered the megaphone of a particularly obstreperous individual with his hat.

After this second hymn it at least became quiet enough for me to be able to finish my sermon. People had probably noticed the further supply of hymns I had had printed. Attempts to storm the pulpit and altar microphones were repulsed by my friends who were keeping guard. The "Our Capital" also failed to have an effect when the congregation said the Lord's Prayer together. It was only heard by those sitting and standing in the immediate vicinity. After the service had ended, Hans Jürgen Quest remained behind in the Church for a long time in order to calm the ringleaders and persuade them to leave. Visibly disappointed, they had remained in their places, smoking their cigarettes and behaving in other impertinent ways. Eventually, Quest's persistence met with success.

On the following evening the discussion I had announced took place in the parish hall. The main ringleaders did not turn up for this, however. They were not at all interested in having a factual discussion but only in the large crowd whose church service they had wished to distort into a propaganda event. Thus, apart from my friends and the many parishioners who sympathized with me, only second-rate representatives of the student revolt gathered there. I can only remember a *single* sentence of what was hurled at me in the stuffy, overfilled hall. I remember it because it caused me considerable astonishment: "How can anyone who has never done anything for his students talk about student matters!"

The incidents in the church service produced a lot of commotion in the press, the repercussions of which reached the Bundestag. Above all, an editor of the *Sonntagsblatt* (today: *Deutsches Allgemeines Sonntagsblatt*), a newspaper that Lilje had founded, began the legend that I had called for assistance from seventy German army officers whom I had appointed as "voluntary reserves." Even *Der Spiegel*, and in its wake many other media, spread similar stories. *Die Zeit* published a large caricature which showed a squad of soldiers in the gallery wearing steel helmets and training a machine gun on a man who had forced his way next to me in the pulpit. The satirical magazine *Pardon* published a whole side of cartoons portraying me as a pulpit demagogue surrounded by a band of soldiers bristling with weapons.

The mere idea of a clerical apostle of peace allowing his poor personage to be protected by armed troops seems to be irresistible to many a journalistic soul even up to the present day. It was no use whatsoever that documentary evidence exposed this to be pure fantasy. General Wulf himself has put on record that it was only in the context of a routine meeting of his teaching staff that he raised the question of whether and to what degree the army ought to intervene to exert a "calming" influence when there was imminent danger of an outbreak of panic. In the course of this discussion a variety of opinions had been voiced. He had at any rate, he said, asked nobody to undertake any protective duties in the Michel. Accordingly, after a question in the Bundestag from a representative of the Ministry of Defense, Secretary of State Eduard Adorno, General Wulf was certified as having behaved utterly correctly. Incidentally, the officers in question did in any case not have to be summoned to the church because many of them—as was also the case with the General himself—had for a long time regularly attended my Michel services. Even more bizarre rumors than those of the media were produced by the students' scandalmongering leaflets. There it was even said that each soldier participating in the service had been paid 15 DM, and further that I had organized bands of thugs armed with karate clubs whom I had recruited from youth groups.

The Painful Aftermath

All the excitement, the resulting sleeplessness, but above all the immense disappointment that terrorist methods I had wrongly believed to have been overcome were able to return with a vengeance and were feebly tolerated by the "establishment," had brought me to a dangerous state of exhaustion. Despite all my medication, my exhausted state resulted in the reactivation of my old tetany illness. Anyway, my doctors sent me to Eppendorf clinic, where I had to spend a few weeks. I implored them to help me to get back on my feet at least well enough for me to be able to hold my next Michel sermon on February 17. For the sake of my ministry I felt that it would be a catastrophe if I had to be withdrawn from circulation just at the moment when the struggle reached its climax. To the public this would have appeared to have been a capitulation, a capitulation that would have been confirmed by my alleged trepidation and supposed call for assistance from the armed forces. My doctors, who understood me and sympathized with my cause, promised me that they would do everything to enable me to stand in the pulpit again in February.

While the doctors supported me, I was subject to dangers and attacks from a quite different quarter, namely from my own people. On around January 25, the Hamburg synod met and dealt with the events in the Michel. I had actually expected something like a declaration of solidarity from them. But there was no question of that. On the contrary, malicious attacks were made on the putative role of the army officers without the people concerned being even superficially informed about the events. Above all, however, the synod took the decision to cancel my February service because they feared that the rioting could escalate still further. They wished instead to comply with the demands of the rebellious students for a "discussion service"—in the unworldly and moreover rather spineless expectation of thereby being able to appease them. It was decided that the Bishop of Hamburg should take the pulpit in my place. None of those in whom I had trusted protested against this. I felt myself to be on my own and left in the lurch. The result was that I was suddenly struck down by an attack of physical weakness.

The Bishop then visited me in hospital with the aim of forcing me to agree to the synod's decision. Naturally there was no way I was going to comply with this and I instead sought to make clear to the Bishop that we had to resist the young people for their own sakes. If the so-called authorities presented themselves to the students as slimy soft frogspawn, we would only strengthen them in their errors.

At the same time another churchman badgered my wife to arrange for my doctor, Ernst Gadermann, to detain me in the clinic beyond the critical date. She firmly rejected this in my name, but informed Gadermann of this impertinent demand. He too was outraged by this and said that, had he carried out this request, he would have done me an injustice that he could not defend either as a doctor or as my friend. In a language that left nothing to be desired as far as clarity was concerned, he expressed his contempt for these "capitulators" and declared his complete solidarity with me.

But I had not reckoned with the Michel parish council. They asked me whether I was really willing to give into the decision of the synod and to entrust the Michel pulpit to the Bishop for a "discussion service" on February 17. In reply I informed them that I was filled with indignation at this decision and was willing and prepared to hold the sermon even if I were still so run-down "that I had to be lowered onto the pulpit with block and tackle." On the next day or the day after Liesel, who had made a fantastic showing throughout this period and had defended me like a lioness in countless telephone conversations, then came bursting into the room with a broad smile on her face and said, "We've won!" In *Die Welt* a large headline could be read: "Thielicke Sermons as before." The parish council had resolutely and unanimously fought the Bishop and synod, had declared their support for me and decided that I should preach. Furthermore, a number of well-known personalities telephoned from all over Germany to strengthen me in the war that had been declared. From then on I made use of every waking minute to prepare myself for the sermon.

A few days before the date of the sermon I was discharged from hospital. Terrible reports again reached me, some even from a few of my former comrades-in-arms, who now made a last attempt to keep me from the pulpit. Large groups of school students from Hamburg, Pinneberg, and Bergedorf wanted, so it was said, to march "in huge columns" on the Michel. I should realize, one of my colleagues said, what responsibility I was taking upon myself in going ahead with the church service. But there were also good and sturdy friends who came and visited me, headed by Jochen Rothert. Rothert, a former assistant of mine and currently a professor, had come specially from Bonn to support me. I will always remember him for the way he took his leave of me on the evening before the sermon: "You will be attacked where you are at your strongest, namely in the proclamation of the Gospel, and not at some peripheral point. For this reason you'll be able to stand firm. Have complete confidence in your cause. May God protect you! See you tomorrow." Rothert was an extremely restrained man who hardly ever expressed his personal feelings. Consequently, to hear this statement from *his* mouth was a pick-me-up without equal. Of all my loyal supporters he was the most loyal and was always at hand whenever my family or I were in trouble. The hour I spent with him reminded me of Bonhoeffer's comforting hymn:

Wonderfully safeguarded by good powers,
We await with confidence whatever may come. . . .

Late in the afternoon of February 17, I entered the sacristy through a side entrance. There I looked through a window and noticed that people were already milling around long before the service was due to begin. While I was wondering what was happening outside, Bolzmann, a young member of the parish council, came to me and said, "I know the uncertainty you must be feeling here on your own. So I would like just to report that everything is quite different from last time. So far I haven't seen anyone from the SDS; they've all gone by bus to Berlin." I could have shouted for joy that I would now be able to hold my sermon without inhibition. And there was indeed not even a trace of a disturbance. We experienced a splendid hour. Afterwards the people surrounded me to express their gratitude and joy that the "enemy" had withdrawn. From then on even the subsequent discussions in the parish hall were—despite the wide diversity of opinion—serious and composed.

This day was a milestone in my life. I did indeed have to continue watching with sorrow and helplessness how the authorities cowardly tolerated the decline of the university to a conglomerate of competing interest groups and its infiltration by sterile structures. Together with my colleagues I suffered sometimes almost unbearable humiliations. Thus during the search for a replacement for my sister chair in systematic theology I not only had to put up with assistants taking part in the appointments commission, but also students and moreover—as representatives of the nonacademic personnel—secretaries. They all examined the names on the list of candidates and at the ballot each of their votes carried the same weight as ours.

From then on I was left in peace and was no longer molested. People seemed to respect the fact that I had not given in, whereas many colleagues who had courted the "leftists'" favor had scorn and derision heaped upon them by those they had wooed and were abused as a "liberal bastards" because of their "repressive tolerance."

On Board the *Transvaal* with Various Adversaries

The head of the German-African Shipping Line, Mrs. Liselotte von Rantzau, had invited Liesel and me to dinner. During our conversation with her and the other guests, the subject of the student rebellion very soon came to the fore, as was quite inevitable in those days. People complained that the extremists were not prepared to engage in discussion and illustrated this with various horror stories. The students, it was lamented, were not open to argument—especially not in individual conversations; their polemics amounted to nothing more than the violent, emotional production of noise, and they also only ever appeared as mass collectives.

Nonetheless, Liselotte von Rantzau urged insistently that an attempt should be made to engage the students in discussion and made a suggestion that I at first found incredible. "How about," she said, "if I place one of our Africa ships at your disposal for this purpose?" You could go on board with these people while the ship is being loaded at Bremen and then sail to Rotterdam as if you had all the time in the world. We'll take your cars with us so that you can all travel back without any problem." After my initial moment of shock I decided to agree to this and to undertake the attempt to engage the students in discussion. And in fact several of my chief opponents could not resist the temptation of taking part, and so together with two of my allies, Heinrich Kuhfuss and a student, I met up with them at Bremen harbor. Each person was given a single cabin, the bar was placed at our disposal and all the stewards were there just for us. I hoped that this luxury and the distance from events that the ship's atmosphere gave us would have a favorable influence on our discussions.

When we then sitting in the sunshine on the deck of the *Transvaal* for the first time and while the ship was being loaded, a clash took place between the two sides straightaway. One of the students made an aggressive, almost blasphemous remark that I could not possibly tolerate. I suggested returning home on the following day because I was not prepared to allow myself to be spoken to on this level. On saying this I turned on my heel and withdrew to my cabin. After some time had passed, one of my friends came to me and reported that the students were very embarrassed at what had happened and had given the culprit a piece of their mind in no uncertain terms. They had had intense discussions on how I could be placated and persuaded to continue the journey. Only around midnight, when they were sitting down-cast at the bar, did I mix with them and behave naturally towards them. They were very nice and open towards me and we told each other about our lives. This had a liberating effect. I was now again able to hope that things would develop favorably.

On the following morning one of the officers asked me to baptize his child. The child was already five years old, but because of her father's frequent absence from home, the baptism had been constantly postponed. At first I was rather hostile to this idea and made clear to him that baptism is more than merely a pious custom and means something rather different from just the sacral use of H_2O.

When it emerged that he was really serious about this and that the little girl was even able to tell me Bible stories—though this was not meant to be an examination!—I agreed to do it and asked my group whether they would like to join in the baptism. They were immediately and unanimously willing to do so. Scarcely had news of this got about when yet more crew members likewise wanted to have their children baptized! They thus telephoned around the country, but were no longer able to round up the children and their mothers quickly enough.

One of us sought to get hold of a cassock long enough for me. I did not have a suitable collar as I was only wearing a white pullover. But a cassock with a woolen polo neck—that was almost irresistible for my beloved lefties. They were able to tolerate me in these progressive textiles.

In a flash the dining saloon was transformed into a chapel, complete with font and altar. Apart from ourselves the congregation was made up of the crew together with the captain and his officers. The men's singing did not sound too bad, there was complete silence when the ancient biblical texts were read.

And now something like a pentecostal miracle occurred. This baptism had completely transformed our little company and had created a community out of us. We were suddenly friends, and were inexplicably happy. Only *one* of the lefties was disturbed by this. He was afraid of being "taken over" because he too had been seized by this new experience and believed he had to resist it. In his way he wanted to prove his character. We respected this and were sorry when he left us while we were still in Bremen. Some of the former ship's company are today good friends of mine and share the same views. One is an active member of my Faith Information Project Group.

Der Spiegel had heard of our adventurous journey and wanted to publish an article about it. It was a sign of the recently awakened sense of community that my companions asked me if I would agree to the requested interview. When I said no and told them that this was "our" trip and we would destroy what we had been granted if we shouted it from the rooftops, they turned down the editor's request. However, on the basis of the few hints that *Der Spiegel* had gathered from our negative replies, it nevertheless went ahead and published a story under the title of "Godly Cargo." The magazine had no information on anything essential, but the details concerning the register tonnage of the ship were correct (the magazine can always be relied on in such matters!). The concluding sentences were something like: "In

Rotterdam the godly cargo left the ship. Cattle were herded on board" (this too was correct).

The conversations on the ship allowed the garish scenes of the student revolt to file past us once again. I shall now give a broad and simplified outline of what I said on this matter.

The student revolt did not come like a bolt from the blue, but had been in the air for a long time. Apart from an unsuccessful educational policy there were other more deep-seated reasons for this. Young people need something to be enthusiastic about, they need goals. And for this the room for movement seemed alarmingly restricted. The great institutions—political parties, unions, churches, and many others—were to a certain extent fossilized and inflexible. Decisions were made upon which one had no influence. This produced mental states characterized by a Kafkaesque sense of imprison-ment. And the grand coalition in Bonn was certainly also unsuitable as a means of dismantling feelings of this kind. Furthermore, there had to be taken into consideration the tormenting contradiction that inevitably results from being subject to the demand to produce mature academic work and yet at the same time being merely one of an anonymous mass of students.

I also did not conceal what I found pleasing about the basic motive of the student protest. I was thinking here of the "humanistic" impetus that had led them to make their criticisms of society. People who had read Herbert Marcuse, for instance, rebelled against the affluent happiness of the masses and saw themselves—which was often overlooked—fighting on a different front from that of Marxism, which begins with social discontent. They opposed a false feeling of happiness, namely the euphoria of the lemures in the affluent society. They felt that the banality of the customary willingness to compromise, something that they believed they perceived in this affluent society, was a self-mutilation of human existence. Human existence had adapted itself to society; it no longer transcended the social structure but allowed itself to be absorbed by it.

I openly confessed that I regarded this point of criticism as absolutely correct. It even took up a motif that has been constantly emphasized by Christian cultural criticism—including the form that I myself have advo-cated. It was only tragic that the students simply diagnosed the symptoms of human failure without having the ultimate criteria at their disposal, that is, without knowing the faith on the basis of which the image of the human being has to be defined if it is to hold its own against the powers of the world and thus also against being integrated into society. Without this foundation of human existence, what alternative is there, I asked, than to flee into utopian dreams? The serious or ironical question as to the eventual and ultimate goal of one's social revolution can then hardly be answered by anything other than failure. The sociological gobbledegook that the students employed to express their views was in addition hardly suitable to equip other partners of the social structure with the political consciousness one needs for an effective social revolution. I had complete understanding for the fact that the student rebellion took tempestuous and demonstrative forms. After all, it was unfortunately true that although the authorities had patiently listened to the suggestions for reform that the students had been proposing for years, they hardly took any notice of them. That these suggestions—for example, on the degree of student participation in the decision-making process—frequently overshot the mark and thereby triggered off a defensive reaction on the part of the professors, was in keeping with the pendulum swing of history and, over and above that, with the especial tendency the Germans have toward extremes.

There were only two things in the course of events that I felt were tragic. *On the one hand*, the understandable attempt after years of ineffective negotiations to make the old lady that was the University get a move on for once had had some negative consequences. By now resorting to rather more aggressive methods to achieve their aims, the students had aroused emotions that had become detached from their original motives and had acquired an independent existence. When I saw hordes of students fooling around, blowing soap-bubbles, stage-managing groups of chanting demonstrators, hammering on the professors' doors, then it was hardly possible any more to speak of serious motives and objectives. Essentially they were here giving free rein to their pleasure at fooling about. They discovered that it was possible to disrupt large gatherings and respected institutions with a minimum expenditure of intellect and by merely being aggressive. It is extremely banal but that is really how it is. Five people are more effective at making a lot of noise than two thousand are at being quiet and attentive. This simple acoustic calculation exerted an obviously enormous fascination over numerous people who lacked self-control, and could develop into a state of intoxication. Intellectual work did not remotely exhaust, so to speak, the students' potential for vigorous action. In previous generations, some of this energy had been vented in student pranks. But where was one supposed to go with one's vitality nowadays, where humor is in short supply and where there are no mapped-out stylistic forms, or even communities in which it can discharge itself? The young Churchill went to India as a reporter, or to the Boers. But where was one supposed to go in West Germany?

It would not only be unfair but also far too superficial to diagnose student tomfoolery as an essential *cause* of the events that took place. Underlying these events were much more serious motives. It seemed appropriate to me, however, to understand the students' tomfoolery as a factor that was *also* at work within the very complex phenomena that led to the student revolt. I even found this thought rather conciliatory, for I wanted in spite of everything to discover at least some human—perhaps *all too human*—element in their behavior.

On the other hand, the rebels were considerably less enthusiastic when they suddenly came across understanding on the part of the professors, for in order to demonstrate and behave rebelliously, it is precisely *resistance* that is required. One could not annoy people determined to protest more than by taking away from them their cause for protest. This became clear to me through an experience I myself had (although I did not at all wish to annoy the students).

In early 1968, the students set up a "Critical University" (CU) with oppositional and supplementary lectures that were intended to show "established" learning with its "overspecialization" what's what. When a news service requested a statement from me on this, I said that I welcomed the undertaking and thought that it showed gratifying responsibility on the part of the students, and requested the university to place rooms at the CU's disposal. My understanding, however, was by no means greeted with joy by the students. In fact, they were hopping mad and described my reaction as an example of the Leninist strategy of the suffocating embrace. The whole thing was supposed to be a protest that they hoped would prompt a defensive reaction from the university. This defensive reaction was supposed to ignite the propagandistic sparks that would enable them to hurl a firebrand at the authorities. The students now believed that this plan would be spoiled and the CU degraded to a peripheral undertaking if it were to be welcomed by the authorities. That is why the only reaction to my support was a furious and offended article in the *Auditorium*.

How then was one actually supposed to behave as a professor? Clearly both alternatives open to us were wrong. It was wrong to oppose but also equally wrong to show understanding. No one was able to help me find a way out of these sterile alternatives. A very earnest student who was among the initiators of the CU and whom I asked about this, merely shrugged his shoulders with a smile.

Controversies Surrounding a Politicized Student Christian Society

I was dragged into a similar tumult for one last time when I published in 1974 a documentation on the desolate state of the Protestant Student Society in Hamburg and other universities. There were hardly any church services any more at the Society and the chapel had sunk to being a junk room. The agenda for the semester no longer indicated any interest in biblical work unless it was to subject a prophet to a strict examination from the standpoint of fashionable sociological issues. Instead, the society placed its rooms at the disposal of left-wing radicals. Indeed, they in general joined forces with the radicals, participating above all in constant demonstrations and disturbances. I was annoyed—and I was certainly not the *only* one—that the Church simply stood back and watched this dubious mutation of a Christian society and its troublemaking activities. Indeed, the Church even financed malicious tirades against itself with church taxes. Through its feeble tolerance, it only strengthened the young people's contempt of the so-called official Church still further. I simply could no longer tolerate such a public travesty of the Church and the intimidation of loyal members of the society. Above all, however, I felt that by its passive refusal to put a stop to their activities, the Church was wronging the members of the Student Christian Society themselves, for they were being driven into a state of permanent self-assertion.

Eventually, I decided to shout all this from the rooftops and so I denounced it in a document, which was taken up in a lively manner by the press. I thereby provoked an avalanche of the fiercest polemics—both in the press and in the form of leaflets—which was conducted in the rude tone customary in those years.

Nevertheless, I was concerned to avoid getting bogged down in mere criticism and in an appeal for "church discipline," for at the same time I also wished to promote understanding for the processes that had so disastrously been set in motion here. For this reason I sought to demonstrate that the initial motives behind the Society's transformation into a Marxist political collective were thoroughly Christian. It had been learned from Karl Marx—especially from the young, still clearly *humanistically* motivated Marx—that love for human beings means not only giving immediate help to the poor, the suffering, and the exploited—this, after all, might be treatment merely of the symptoms!—but also setting about to change the *systems* that allow such forms of misery to arise. Love, including Christian *agape*, should not only

bandage wounds but must also prevent wounds from being inflicted; prophylaxis is also one of its tasks. For centuries the Church's active love had
amounted to nothing more than caring for the poor and sick. It offered, as it
were, umbrellas to protect against the rigors of society's weather, whereas
Karl Marx sought to change the general weather situation itself and thereby
to make umbrellas more or less superfluous. When young Christians now
took up this agenda of a "systematic" transformation of the state of human
misery and pressed for changes in the structure of society, had they not
thereby in fact discovered new horizons of Christian *agape*? Did not *agape*
thus also have a *political* dimension in which it had to strive to achieve a
transformation on a large scale, that is, precisely in those structures which
constitute society? And had not Christianity previously overlooked *this*
dimension by expending its active love exclusively in diaconal work?

Thus I believed that utterly earnest elements worthy of consideration
could be discovered in the motives of these young people. Precisely for this
reason it seemed tragic and disastrous to me that they were exclusively fixed
on this idea of altering the structure of society. In the process, many people
were caught in the maelstrom of the Marxist program and thus eventually
forgot the original Christian motive that had prompted their actions. By
wanting to change the "schema" of this world, they eventually became
enslaved to it (compare Romans 12:2). Here a process was repeated that had
already come to pass with the French "worker priests." These priests had
wanted to prove their *agape* by showing their solidarity with industrial
workers. They made common cause with the workers, joined their
syndicates—including the Communist ones—but in doing so did not notice
that they were becoming more and more estranged from their priestly calling.
This *consequence*, but not the respectable motive of showing Christian solidarity from which it had proceeded, was eventually the reason for Rome
"whipping them back into line."

As great as my anger was at the gross blunders of the Student Christian
Society, it was far outweighed by my sorrow that a great impetus had so
wretchedly gone to waste and that, apart from a few plaintive cries, nothing
was to be heard on the part of the Church. At least my modest intervention
did in fact have some effect. Two special synods were convened in Hamburg,
which resolutely shook up the previous leadership of the society and set up a
completely new "University Christian Society" under the leadership of that
steadfast theologian, Dr. Uwe Böschemeyer (he had been both a doctoral
student under me and my assistant, and was also a member of our Faith
Information Project Group). That the society nevertheless eventually got

stuck in half-measures again is something that I do not need to say any more about here. What I have here only hinted at in a few lines fills a thick file in my archives and determined my work for many weeks.

Since this dramatic epoch in my life was a strain both on my intellect and my nerves, I sought—true to my constantly tried and tested remedy for life's problems—to free myself from this strain by writing down a concentrated analysis of what had sucked me into its whirlpool in this manner. Only in this way was I able to force myself to distance myself from events and thereby to achieve calmness. The book that resulted from this, which I wrote during my constant visits to my little lakeside house in the country at Mustin, was entitled *Kulturkritik der studentischen Rebellion* (The Student Rebellion's Cultural Criticism, (1969). Alone, this way of formulating the issue intimates that I was concerned not with portraying revolutionary phenomena but with their background in intellectual and social history. For this reason I analyzed above all the intellectual father of the movement, Herbert Marcuse. I criticized his anthropology, which basically is merely negative, and finally came to the theological diagnosis that the syndrome of utopian fixations in the younger generation was nothing less than a substitute for lost transcendence. The book triggered off fierce discussions both for and against, although these discussions were more fully expressed in the countless letters I received than in the press. At that time the newspapers were more concerned with sensational reports than with an analysis of the background to events.

Nor in other respects did my literary work cease in these years of unrest. First and foremost, I wrote the first and second volumes of my dogmatics, which I entitled *The Evangelical Faith*. In an age when theological thought was almost exclusively sociologically oriented and concerned with questions of emancipation, this investigation of the foundations of the Christian faith from the long-term perspective probably seemed like a meteoric, extraterrestrial, alien element to many people. For me, however, the intense concentration that such a wide-ranging systematic work demanded was an act by which I overcame the moment because it compelled me to think beyond the moment.

Into the Final Rounds

W HEN I READ in an autobiography the chapter describing the author's old age, I am usually overcome by a certain sense of boredom, even if the author himself was not at all bored in his later years but awaited the next day of his life with eager curiosity. But when one reads these chronicles of old age, the excitement is often missing. It is not difficult to guess the reason for this. Whatever takes place in the eighth or even ninth decade of an individual's life—even if he has remained bright and healthy!—consists mostly only of dotted continuations of a baseline that has already been drawn in the life he has lived up until then.

This certainly need not mean that an autobiography must inevitably end with a dull conclusion. On the contrary, new phases of one's life with completely new aspects can open up. These phases may stand out clearly from earlier emotional epochs and be transfigured by what Goethe describes as the "happy overview of the earth's hustle and bustle and its continuously circular and spiral-like repetition," and by "love and affection floating between two worlds. . . ." As Goethe rightly says, "What more could Grandpa want?"

In any autobiography, this "happy overview," as Goethe puts it, by which he means a sort of wisdom that comes with old age, is something that has already been projected back into the earlier decades of the author's life— Goethe's *Poetry and Truth* is the best evidence for this. Consequently, an individual's autobiography could actually be rounded off with a description of the beginning of his retirement. In this case, my account of the student revolt *would* form a fitting and dramatic finale and would not need to be followed by any epic conclusion, especially since this turbulent phase in my life led into my discharge from active service. Why, then, should I nevertheless still carry on with my story? Is the *loquacitas senilis* never to cease?

400

I am now indeed traveling through more peaceful waters. They are not, however, any less eventful. The only difference is that I now receive my impetus less often from outside. I no longer have to mark examination work or suffer the boredom of endless routine meetings. I only need to give lectures when I want to. Mind you, I *still* enjoy cultivating contacts with new generations of students and I take pleasure in the rich contrasts each change brings. I also believe that I still understand students. Do they also understand me? They at any rate seem to accept me, despite the considerable age difference, and enjoy coming to Open Evenings at our house. That in other respects there are differences in how we understand each other has a very banal but compelling reason: I myself, after all, was twenty once and still know what it is like. They, however, have not yet been seventy-five—that says everything!

It is one of the peculiarities of the biography that it proceeds, albeit on a smaller scale, in a similar way to the historian with his very much broader perspective. The people the historian describes—in the case of the biography it is the author himself—have each experienced their lives as unfinished moments and as something with an open, uncertain future. The person looking back on history and life in general, however, sees beyond those moments. He *knows*, after all, how things developed afterwards and therefore sees the past in the light of the conclusion or at least in the light of the continuing course of history. As a result, the past acquires a quality that is completely *different* from anything the actual moment of the experience could have had. It is now interpreted in the light of what followed later— perhaps even on the basis of what followed later. Anyone who looks back on his life is, of course, more knowledgeable than he was at the time of the events which he is now and here describing. "A person leaving the town hall," as the saying goes, "is cleverer than when he entered." That is why looking forward and looking back are intertwined with each other in a biography.

Perhaps the past is transfigured by this. (Could this also have happened with my retrospective look at how the university was in the old days? If so, this would then admittedly be *not* an indication of increased knowledge, but rather of a distorting nostalgia, which is something that I have self-critically endeavored to be on my guard against.) It may perhaps also come about that a decision we once made earlier in naive credulity turns out in retrospect to be disastrous. We at any rate cannot—and indeed *should* not—banish from our biographies the future we have in the meantime experienced since that past event that we now wish to describe.

The main focus of my work, however, has now been transferred to my desk. I am attempting to harvest and get into the barn all that I feel to be essential and have noted down in advance in my many papers. When one is old, one's contemporaries use especially those birthdays on which one reaches a round number as an opportunity to survey in speeches, in print, and even in television films what one has gathered into one's barn so far. For me, too, such days were occasions to pause and take stock. I asked myself in gratitude, sometimes also in self-criticism and sorrow, what yield had "emerged" from my work so far. But I would not like to let this retrospection degenerate into nostalgia, to let it become a veteran's fixation with the past, but would prefer to keep a lookout for the tasks that are to come and still *remain*. Although the fact that I have directed my gaze forward in this manner may reveal that I have retained a certain youthfulness, it is precisely here that I notice how much my view of the future has changed in comparison to that of a *young* person. The future now no longer lies before me like a broad landscape with mountain ranges and hills behind which new, boundless spaces open up. It has become rather a temporal symbol of our finitude, of our limited period of life; it is now the tense of death. Suddenly I begin to count my days from the end and wonder how much time remains for me to transport my harvest into the barns. It is the evening phase of the eleventh hour. I see myself at the countdown.

One of the essential things I wanted to preserve was a history of recent theology, which was one of my favorite lectures; and I am grateful that it was able to be published in 1983 as the imposing concluding volume of my *systematic theology*, which up until then had already reached seven volumes. It gave me a lot of pleasure to allow all the great theologians to file past me once again and to turn them into partners with whom we could discuss our modern problems. In literary terms, too, this task gave me special pleasure: I love alternating between theoretical analyses and vivid descriptions of the great figures of the past. At the same time the memory of the many genera- tions of students on whom I had sought to impress this material rose up within me.

So now I am entering the final rounds. Warned by the biographies of other old men, I do not wish to continue in the narrative style I have employed up until now but want to restrict myself to those events in which not only the past is summed up but which also have constantly opened up new perspec- tives for me!

It was precisely these perspectives that brought to mind Goethe's thought that something like a "repetition of life" comes about in old age, albeit on a higher level and with a mature understanding. In this sense my curiosity for life has remained and I retain it with the command: never begin to stop; never stop beginning!

Faith Information Project Group

Nevertheless there was one place where I did stop. After I had continued my Michel sermons for a year after the student disturbances had died away, I brought them to a conclusion, at least as a regular event. I believed that the time was now ripe to tackle *new* tasks and to pass my experiences in the pulpit onto younger men. I felt it was important to make clear to them what mattered about preaching the Gospel and to preserve them from many mistakes that I believed I had discovered in the preaching practice of the Church. My dream was to prompt young theologians, first, to continue on the path I had discerned and, second, to go on to do it better.

I was constantly thinking over this plan with two young collaborators: my assistant Siegfried Scharrer and an older student, Hinrich Westphal. Both had proved themselves in the preceding years of struggle to be loyal friends; Westphal had even written leaflets against the student revolt and distributed them on the street himself. Around the time of my sixtieth birthday we founded a preaching circle. The people I first invited to join this group were a number of my former students who had attracted my special attention by virtue of their possession of the appropriate gifts and their willingness to get involved. We gathered once a month in my house at Wellingsbüttel, and Liesel did her part to create a cozy, human atmosphere for our meetings.

At each meeting we dealt with one of the texts on which a sermon was due to be preached. During the first years I myself gave a meditation on the text and endeavored to stimulate lively discussions about it. In the process I discovered that each of us had a wealth of highly attractive issues on his mind. As a result, man himself in all his dimensions became our subject, as did also pastoral tasks, commentary on contemporary issues, psychotherapeutic problems, and also theological disputes. The people taking part were so enthusiastic that the pastors among them founded similar discussion groups in their own parishes and worked together with them on their Sunday sermons. In the process, they likewise experienced an exhilarating enlivening of their parish work as a consequence of their concentration on the central contents of the Gospel message. Because we plumbed the whole of human life during our discussions—"exploring the finite in all its dimensions"—we soon supplemented our circle with experts from other disciplines, especially psychotherapists and educationalists.

After a few years of this communal work, we decided (around 1971) also to give the larger public the benefit of what we had produced and to create a sort of "Catechism for Adults." Hamburg appeared to us to be the right place for this. We had had some really grotesque experiences of the lack of even the most elementary religious knowledge here. Hamburg seemed to us almost like a religious no-man's land, like a tabula rasa. So we endeavored to find a form of expressing the Gospel that could give the secularized people of this "Ninevah" a first introduction to the Christian message.

Our attempt to put this plan into action began with our organizing ten lecture evenings in the Church of St. Michael on the foundations of the Christian faith. So once again I entered my old pulpit, albeit now in a changed capacity. The generous supply of rooms enabled us to form ten discussion groups for conversations afterwards. Each of these groups was led by two of my fellow workers. This was all prepared with military precision, so that everything went like clockwork despite the large audience. I discussed the argumentation of each of my lectures with the discussion group leaders and prepared them for the questions the people taking part in the discussions would probably ask. During these evenings I went from group to group to help with any difficulties that might have arisen.

Evening after evening the Michel was filled by a large stream of visitors. The discussions were lively and profound. At the same time the colorful mixture of elderly, often pietistic Christians and many young seekers from "neopaganism" posed very great problems for us. Thus I well remember a dialogue between the two groups. A young man very movingly described his futile search for meaning and security and then with a sincere lack of inhibition requested that his discussion circle give him an answer to his problem before ten o'clock, because his train was due to leave at half past ten. A pious old man attempted to soothe him by replying that all the young man's problems would melt away into nothing if he let himself be washed in the blood of Jesus. The young man replied, "What's that supposed to mean? I don't understand a word." The old man now began to stutter badly. He and people like him suddenly seemed to realize that they had allowed routine Christian vocabulary to flow from their lips all too easily and with not enough thought about what they were saying. As a result they found themselves in difficulties when they attempted ad hoc to compensate for the intellectual clarity lacking in their statements. As a result of this, the devout, conventional Christians present gradually grew quieter and resorted more and more to listening attentively—which could only be to our advantage. Incidentally, I was constantly surprised at the consideration with which the generations treated each other and how seriously young and old took each other.

Our discussion evenings met with an astonishing response in the press and on television, which resulted in our receiving constant requests to repeat them in other towns. For ourselves, too, the Michel evenings had unexpected consequences. Although our work was an attempt to teach and proclaim the Gospel at the grass roots level, the last thing we wanted was to retreat into the ivory tower of mere dogma. We wanted rather to show—my young companions in particular insisted on this—that faith and action belong together, though not in the way that a widespread contemporary sickness wishes to suggest, namely that theology should be transformed into "practology." What mattered to us was rather to make as clear as possible that all Christian action has to be determined by the unequivocal priority of our *religious* motive. We also understood ourselves, after all, to be above all a *spiritual* community, to be a *militia Chrisi*.

So in the period following, we set a number of practical projects in motion. Thus we looked after adolescents who were at risk, especially drug addicts and rockers. For many years—as long as I was able to recruit students from my lectures and seminars—we visited a prison in Neuengamme each week, where the inmates had asked us to repeat the Michel course for them. (The television film about our work had prompted them to make this invitation.)

Here it was again above all Siegfried Scharrer and Hinrich Westphal who were in the forefront of this work. They prepared the prisoners for freedom and accompanied them in the initial period after their release, when they were especially at risk because, having been pent up for so long, their energy was now looking for an outlet. We even rented an apartment so as to be able to care for released prisoners in the first critical days until they had found accommodation and work. We also noticed that the prison personnel, who appeared to welcome our work, were astonishingly unprepared, indeed virtually helpless, with regard to many of the prisoners' inner concerns. For this reason we focused attention on this matter in particular. It was above all Scharrer who organized the discussion evenings with the prison officers, which they gladly took up. When Westphal had passed his examination, he was ordained in the prison—so much had it become "home" to him and to the rest of us. Many former inmates came to this ceremony, now as visitors, and augmented the musicians and choir, who added solemnity and dignity to the evening.

But that was not all. The constant call to continue our teaching on faith eventually induced us to undertake a fundamental reorganization of our work, even to change our name and to describe ourselves thenceforth as "Faith Information Project Group" (FIPG).

In the following years—right up until the present day—we wrote a series of *educational letters* on a numbers of self-enclosed subjects. To name but a few, these were: "Whoever believes, carries on thinking" (dogmatics), "Whoever believes, learns to live" (letters to young parents); "Whoever believes, has a future" (letters to the parents of confirmation candidates); "Time to talk to God" (letters on the Lord's Prayer). The number of copies that have since been sold now reaches into the millions. The letters have also been translated into several foreign languages (even Japanese). Whenever we completed a letter, it was published in book form. The correspondence that we— rather naively and unsuspectingly!—had stimulated in response to these letters, was initially so immense that it would almost have bowled us over if we had not looked around in good time for a larger number of people to help us to deal with it.

Our work together (as well as many a party), which has now already lasted one-and-a-half decades, has welded us together in a firm and close friendship, indeed we have almost become a small holy order. We are close to each other in both sorrow and joy. For Liesel and myself, this sense of community is one of the riches of our old age. We are so closely attached to each other that even those of us whose careers have taken them off to more distant geographical climes, spare neither time nor energy to join us every month.

Encounter with a Monastic Community

For many years I have enjoyed what one might call a spiritual correspondence—interspersed with numerous amusing anecdotes and descriptions of all kinds of human behavior—with Irmengard Katheder OSB, a nun of the Benedictine Abbey of St. Gabriel in Styria. She knew me from some of my books of sermons, which were occasionally read aloud during the lunchtime lesson at the convent. Each line of her letters reveals the contemplative depth in which she lives. At the same time, I am impressed by the supreme freedom with which she is able to write about the oddities of human nature—including both her own and those of her fellow nuns.

After having been repeatedly invited to visit the abbey, Liesel and I made use of our holiday on Liselotte von Rantzau's Austrian estate to spend a week there. The venerable convent of St. Gabriel stood on a mountain in solitary splendor. My stage fright at the strange atmosphere I had supposed I would encounter at such an isolated monastic community had already vanished when we entered. We were received with utter warmheartedness, indeed with overflowing joy. Even the magnificent countryside was often not able to tempt us away from conversations with these highly cultured, open, self-sufficient, and unutterably happy women. I spoke on many occasions to the nuns, who all left their cloisters in united procession to come and listen to me. I even held—which was very unusual!—a church service in the abbey and each day conducted numerous individual conversations.

When I saw the nuns all sitting before me in this way, I was uplifted when I looked into the faces assembled there. They all seemed to be unique characters—"God's handiwork" is what I once used to call them. There was no trace here of physiognomical fashion, imitation, or uniformity, although the different backgrounds from which they originated—some came from the aristocracy, others were scholars, others were simple workers in the Lord's vineyard—had been completely blurred. And I was particularly struck by the beauty of their old faces, which had been molded by the spirit!

The candor with which they spoke to me about their problems sometimes amazed me. A nearly ninety-year-old nun, who was versed in foreign languages, enormously well-read, and a first-rate painter and musician, once conveyed some of her highly original (how could it have been otherwise!) theological views to me and then asked, "Is that heretical?" To this I could only reply with a laugh, "And you ask this question of a heretic, of all people?" Even when she was over ninety she still continued to write me many letters, in which she expressed her opinion on recently published literature—Tilman Moser's *Gottesvergiftung* (God Poisoning), for instance— or reflected on the student rebellion.

These encounters made one thing clear to me, namely that it would be fanciful simply to hold that the boundaries between denominations no longer exist. However, I was much more impressed by the fellowship in *faith* as well as the fellowship in the *humanity* that has been molded by faith that I experienced here. Our theology limps behind what our faith already knows or at least senses, namely that we are sons and daughters that belong to the same parental home. These women were at any rate much closer to me spiritually and humanly than many theologians in my own camp. At such moments an intuition of what God knows about his children steals over me. If one has experienced this, once acquires composure and can look forward to the time when the mind is also able to express what the heart already knows.

The year 1978 concluded with a festive week in celebration of my seventieth birthday. For me the highlights were the profound and linguistically polished lecture Rainer Röhricht gave in my honor on "Contentment as a little praised virtue," together with the big birthday party my publisher friend Georg Siebeck laid on in the Hamburg Hotel Vier Jahreszeiten [Four Seasons]. There he presented me with the last volume of my dogmatics, namely the *Theology of Spirit*, which had just been published. The complete work, which now comprised three volumes, had been decorated in a particularly festive fashion for the occasion by the bookbindery Haute Couture. My project group surprised me with a literary gift published by Herder Publishers, namely a book entitled, *Christ-sein in Zukunft: Zeichen, Ziele und Vermutungen* (On Being a Christian in the Future: Signs, Goals and Conjectures.) In retrospect, an element of grief also clings to my memory of this day—it was the last visit I received from my friend Hans P. Schmidt from Frankfurt before he was killed in an accident with his youngest son. I will always treasure the memory of the words with which he extolled the happiness of our unique friendship, a friendship that had lasted many decades.

For me 1979 began with two television films by ARD* on channels one and three. The first film was the broadcast of a lengthy interview in which I was questioned about my life's work and beliefs. The other, for which Jürgen Möller and Günther Specovius had been responsible, showed everyday scenes from my work. For several weeks a television crew accompanied me almost everywhere I was working or was staying. When they insisted on filming a boat trip on "my" Lake Mustin, the producer, who had no idea of how to handle a rubber dinghy, knocked me over fully clothed into the wintry cold water. Probably the only reason that this did me no harm was that I laughed myself warm. It was only with difficulty that the press photographer also present was able to be dissuaded from publishing photographs of this grotesque scene in his magazine. He did, however, give me two impressive

---

* Abbreviation of *Arbeitsgemeinschaft der Rundfunkanstalten Deutschlands*, which is a German television company and literally means Association of German Broadcasting Corporations. *Translator's note.*

enlargements as a present and said that they very much reminded him of the story of the sinking St. Peter! During the filming I developed a close relationship with both recording crews, which led to many theological conversations. They were so interested in the "subject" being discussed that they even once said, "This scene will have to be repeated. We were so absorbed in what you were saying that we forgot to do our job."

I had the impression that they must have eventually amassed so much material that it would not be even remotely possible to show all of it despite the long broadcasting time they had at their disposal. When I spoke to them about this waste of time and material, they replied, "We're keeping it for your future obituary!" As if somebody had been eavesdropping on this, there were three reports of my alleged death in the following years.

Visiting Professorships in New Zealand and Australia

At the end of February 1979, Liesel and I embarked on a major lecture tour to New Zealand and Australia. It was the only continent which I had not yet "talked my way through." The well over thirty-hour flight first took us to Melbourne. Despite all the comforts we were permitted however, the journey was quite strenuous and we required a few days in a Melbourne hotel to recuperate and acclimatize. When we had set out, it had been icy winter in Germany. As early as the stopover in Singapore, however, and all the more so on our arrival in Melbourne, we met with a heat of more than thirty degrees celsius. Indeed, it was so hot that it positively bowled us over and almost took our breath away.

The first part of the journey took us to the paradise-land of New Zealand, in the first instance to Auckland. After my lectures at the Baptist seminary there and to the country's theologians in the Spurgeon Tabernacle, we went on a few excursions into the North Island's interior under the guidance of our friend and courier Kevin Yelverton. The strongest impression we had was our encounter with the Maoris, the native inhabitants of New Zealand. They invited us to their community house, which was almost bursting with mythological sculptures and pictures. The room radiated a strange fascination. The Maoris gave us a solemn ceremonial welcome consisting of antiphonal singing and various speeches. We did not understand the words, of course, but the wild gestures that accompanied these speeches led us to presume that they referred to some incredibly dramatic current event. Consequently, we felt obliged to adopt expressions of consternation and shock. Our translator was able to reassure us, however. These gestures, he said, were concerned merely with quite banal commonplaces that it was the custom to bring to a rhetorical boiling point in honor of and for the entertainment of their guests.

Although this minority culture with its ancient traditions is fostered in New Zealand, all forms of ghetto status are avoided. The Maoris, an intelligent and extremely sociable people, are integrated in every walk of life. Thus at the country's universities we kept on meeting well-liked Maori students, some of whom had considerable intelligence quotients. At university they as a rule first learn their own tribal language from the white linguists there. These languages have for the most part been submerged in the ocean of everyday English.

A two-day trip to Roturua—a patron of the arts had invited us there— shines with enchanting beauty in my memory. Everywhere there were bubbling geysers filling the air with sulphur vapors. Lakes, forests, and spacious, partly idyllic, then again monumental panoramas transported us into a fairytale land. When I once spontaneously exclaimed, "I'd like to stay here forever!" Kevin dismissed this with a smile, saying, "You simply wouldn't be able to put up with it. We are a country that lacks drama and exists in an ahistorical peace, if one disregards the horseracing by means of which a somewhat artificial excitement is created. Even the kiwi, our national bird, has forgotten how to fly during the last few centuries. Why should he make the effort to take to the skies when there lies on the earth all that he could wish for within range of his beak and moreover where there are no enemies to flee from?" New Zealand is (or at any rate was) something like a super-paradise. It is "super" because there were once not even any snakes there. At least that was the case until the land was settled by the white man; it was he who first brought most of the creatures—apart from the birds—into the country. Thus one lives here at the end of the world, indeed almost outside the world. When we inquired what developments had taken place in the hostilities between Vietnam and China, which we had been following with some concern before our departure, nobody knew anything about it—it was much too far away. The press only printed local news, above all sports news, and the financial section only dealt with a few problems connected with the declining wool exports. As a result, we sometimes felt as if we were in another world.

From Auckland we flew to the very English city of Dunedin on South Island, where I lectured at the ivy-covered university and at the Catholic

Holy Cross College. Here too I was occasionally stunned by the New Zeal-anders' unreal distance from the problems that dominate us Europeans. I no longer know at which discussion it was that I was asked whether the World Council of Churches could not see to it that the divided Germany was reunited! I was often struck dumb in New Zealand.

After our eventful and moving stay in New Zealand we then returned to the Australian mainland, which was where this tour's main field of activity lay. The initial impulse for this lecture tour had come from the Lutheran students in Adelaide, who very much wanted to have me at the celebrations of the twenty-fifth anniversary of their Student Christian Society. Since the costs of the journey, even if I waived all my fees, were considerable, larger student groups joined together in order to earn the necessary money by making and selling handicrafts. The pastor in charge, John Sabel—who was descended from the Sabellians of the third century, and who looked as if he had been chiseled from ancient stone—had publicized the purpose of my stay in the country. As a result there were so many invitations from universities, semi-naries, and churches of all denominations that I was not remotely able to accept all of them during my six-week stay. I had to restrict myself to the great cities and visited in succession Brisbane, Sydney, Melbourne, Adelaide, and—on the west coast—Perth.

In my memory the images of this busy and eventful period almost merge into other. They consist of confusing impressions of many meetings, magnifi-cent English university halls and churches, and the ceremonial processions of the academic staff. The last of these not only warmed my tradition-loving heart but, weighed down with ceremonial garb and in the midsummer heat, also warmed the body—in fact, too much! I recall the time I spent with the various student groups that had already been gathering for many years to discuss my books. I think back also to the few days' holiday we enjoyed at the spacious country residence of some Swiss friends and our trip to Kangaroo Island in the south, where we were taken on a rather exciting flight in a small private airplane.

I was surprised that, in this part of the world of all places, my books had been translated and avidly read for years. The tiresome language problems that dogged me on this tour were considerably alleviated by the presence of our friend Dr. Friedemann Hebart, who was also our nephew by marriage. Hebart had studied for his doctorate under Edmund Schlink at Heidelberg and is now a professor in Adelaide. He now accompanied us and was at pains to help with the many discussions, press conferences, and radio addresses (one of which was broadcast across the whole continent) that I had to give.

It was precisely these press conferences that provided me with an important experience. I discovered that not only Lutheran but all Christian denominations in Australia revolve almost exclusively in and around themselves. So-called public life, on the other hand, is completely secularized and streams past and over the churches unaffected. The daily press usually took virtually no notice of church events or theological literature. That it was different in my case and that the newspapers showed an interest in my activities had a rather strange reason that could not in any way delude me into thinking that it was simply that people were convinced of the importance of *my* work. The reason for the interest shown towards me was that it had been discovered from some obscure source that Jimmy Carter had received me in the White House. The aura of this important personage obviously sufficed to transfigure an insignificant contemporary such as myself. The reports of my statements that were then published and the questions I was asked in many interviews were, however, often so banal that only a sense of humor made it possible to tolerate them.

I was profoundly impressed by many of the clergymen I met during this tour. As representative of these I would like to mention a fairly young pastor whose congregation was scattered over more than two hundred miles of this vast country. In his isolation he was constantly having to struggle against his parish's many narrow-minded peculiarities, above all with the hyperorthodox errors that are bound to appear at such a great distance from the centers of civilization. He was always going to great lengths to obtain journals and books from Europe in order to keep in touch with current intellectual debate. On his long journeys overland he used to listen to lectures on cassettes and sought in this way to make best use of his time, because he was unable to read at the wheel.

To conclude I must tell another little anecdote, which illustrates the curiously hillbilly quality that can arise when people live at such "remoteness from the world." In many, though by no means all, of its forms, Lutheranism in particular is strangely rigid and fossilized. Only one or two days before my departure for Australia, some friends informed me in a roundabout way of a matter they seemed to find extremely embarrassing. They told me that although I could give lectures everywhere without impediment and would also be welcomed to preach in Anglican, Baptist, Methodist, and other pulpits, the Lutheran Church would only be prepared to place their pulpits at my disposal when a bishop appointed by the synod had convinced himself of the "purity" of my Lutheranism(!) in a conversation with me. It was now feared—not without reason—that this unreasonable policy might prompt me to call off the tour at the last moment. For the sake of the many people expecting me, they implored me to submit to this ridiculous formality. I was, however, much too curious about this grotesque plan to put up a fight against it.

The bishop appointed for this task even came to New Zealand to see me and asked to have a talk with me after one of my evening lectures. The organizers badgered me to be nice to the poor churchman for he was very frightened of me and showed symptoms of considerable nervousness. When I was then taken to an adjoining room to see him, I pretended to be completely ignorant of the purpose of his visit and asked him whether my wife might also be permitted to make his acquaintance and join our conversation. (I was concerned to have a witness.) He could not easily refuse this request and indeed even greeted it very chivalrously. When we were then sitting together, this extremely friendly man first beat about the bush, talked about the weather, and asked how my trip had been; he also mentioned the titles of some of my books. Eventually I seized the initiative and asked him to come out with what he wished to say.

He now talked around the subject a little and with a variety of main clauses, subordinate clauses, and parentheses said that he had been instructed by the synod to ask me a question. "I'm dying to hear it," I replied.

> *He:* I'm not quite sure how I should put it . . . (pause). I am supposed to ask you . . . whether you intend to say anything against the Lutheran Church.
>
> *I:* You said just now that you know my books. Do you have the impression that they are anti-Lutheran?
>
> *He:* No, certainly not!
>
> *I:* Do you then think that in Australia I would retract what I said in my books and assert the opposite?
>
> *He:* Oh no! How could I assume that!

And then with a broad smile and much relieved he said: "That will do for me. Thank you very much. I'll now tell the brothers that they can put their minds at ease."

In this without doubt unusual manner the doors to the Lutheran pulpits in Australia were opened to me! And a bishop was able to take his leave of me freed of a great psychological burden.

After he had bid us a warm farewell Liesel said, "It's a funny old world!"
Once again it became clear to us that the Lord above must occasionally have
a little chuckle at his strange ground personnel—probably not ironically as
we human beings with our dubious nature tend to do, but full of loving
kindness and forbearance.

Finale

M Y SEVENTY-FIFTH BIRTHDAY now lies behind me. The parish council of the old Church of St. James at Hamburg had expressed the wish that my birthday should be celebrated there. Almost three decades earlier I had first begun my preaching activity at Hamburg in this church.

The celebrations began in the late afternoon with Christmas music by candlelight in the spacious nave of the church. Lutz Mohaupt, the chief pastor of St. James, said a few kind words about his old teacher to the assembled congregation. I did not need to blush at these; they were intended only as an expression of his loyal and affectionate attachment to me.

Afterwards, the actual reception took place. A dinner was given for many invited guests in the south transept, which is separated from the rest of the church and is used for more general gatherings. My hosts had permitted only three speeches: one from the senator responsible for academic affairs, one from the bishop, and one from the spokesman of the theology faculty (now called "school of theology"). Incidentally, my Faith Information Project Group had arranged the program for the evening. Everything went off perfectly. The evening was playful and relaxed and acquired the character of an extemporization of a "higher order." Interspersed between the baroque musical entertainment were witty cabaret performances in words, songs, and pictures, which filled the beautiful gothic room with merriment and festive splendor. These soon welded the diverse company—which was made up of representatives of state, church, and university, many friends from earlier and later days and also, of course, my own family—into a laughing but also contemplative community. As a result, the evening ended with us all completely naturally and spontaneously singing a song together. For decades it had been the custom to conclude my Open Evenings with this song, namely "There is no more beautiful land at this time. . . ."

When the lights then went out—the television spotlights had already been extinguished a long time previously—and I looked one last time back at the venerable and now peaceful hall, I thought of some verses that Friedrich Petrenz had dedicated to an old friend on his birthday:

The footsteps die away. The last person has gone.
The big day draws to a close.
I am so awake I cannot sleep.
I know you are waiting to receive me, O God.

I bring you what the people brought me
in flowers, laurels, gratitude, and glory—
For, after all, it is all your own,
It was your praise alone of which everyone spoke.

This also applied to the mail I received on my birthday. When I read that some of what I had said, written or done had helped one or another person along in life, had perhaps even helped him to break through to a "new existence," then I gratefully understood myself as a tool—often enough as only a fragile, unsuspecting, constantly failing vessel—that another had employed. At the same time, this service I had given was a source of constant fulfillment to me. It far surpassed everything that I had to renounce and was a reward in itself. I experienced the truth of Albert Schweitzer's beautiful saying, "Happiness can only be multiplied when it is shared." When people's response to my work then reached me in condensed form, as it were, on important birthdays, I felt this to be a *donum superadditum* but understood that I could not possibly apply this gratitude to myself and keep it as my own. A human life has been worthwhile, I realized, if it has helped just a single fellow man or woman to find his or her way to the source of all life. Whenever I read something of this kind in the letter of somebody I did not know personally or had forgotten—sometimes expressed clumsily and very simply—then I could gladly have exchanged all the high-flown congratulations sent by prominent figures for it.

A considerable part of my life, insofar as I have pursued academic theology, taught at the university, and written books, was filled with my quest for the *truth*.

My profession involved the interpretation of ancient texts, which I sought to penetrate until I rediscovered in them my own questions about life and those of my generation. In this mirror I saw these questions—*sub specie aeternitatis*, so to speak—light up anew: "In your light we see the light." To many contemporaries it seemed and still seems grotesque to consult an ancient book, that is, the Bible, on where we have come from and where we are going, and with its help to fathom the purpose for which we have been created. Can we not send our probes into space? Are we not constantly on the hunt for the novel, for "innovations," if I may employ a magic word from the computer world? Is it thus not backward to take this other route when dealing with the fundamental truths of our lives? Is it not retrogressive to grope one's way towards the ancient places where God left his tracks, the places which he deemed worthy of his presence, and where he uttered his command "Let there be" in ever new variations?

In my long life I have seen so many truths claiming to be the "last word" come and go like nine-day wonders! How comical the gods of the day seem just a few hours later, how absurd they look from behind! Perhaps one has to grow as old as I now am to be no longer moved by the day's noise and fashion or to be unimpressed by the accompanying applause of the media. Perhaps one needs to be old to be prepared for even the most abnormal things. When one is old one always sees the seeds of destruction contained in the cries of jubilation at the latest innovative interpretations of, and solutions to, life. There are only very few gospels that endure. Both with the Nazis and later the student revolt, people like me who sought the truth in this ancient and eternally young book and wished to stick by it were constantly cursed as representatives of the past tense. I, on the other hand, felt myself through this ancient book to be already facing the future, namely that period in the future that would make clear the futility of the gods of the day and testify to the eternity of the one God. How foolish in contrast are the banal alternatives of "conservative" and "progressive," "reactionary" and "forward-looking," and even "right" and "left!" In this epilogue I would like to reveal to any young readers who have followed my biography up to this point the principles I have followed throughout my life with regard to the *truth*.

> I will not consider something to be good just because it is new and to be bad because it is old (even if it has perhaps proved its worth).

> It does not matter whether a truth is so old that it is coated with a patina or so new that it shines like fresh copper or so forward-looking that it is still only a bud or even a seed.

> I am only interested in whether a truth is true and why it is true. Therefore I will first inquire after the truth itself and avoid questions concerning its temporal qualities. I will permit myself neither a reactionary nor a progressive expectation of the nature of truth.

Whenever I encounter the truth in a novel and unexpected form, I will try to be
open to it.

On the other hand, whenever I discover the truth in something that has already
been established by tradition and perhaps goes back to archaic times, I will
greet it with deference.

In my encounter with the Gospel I must be prepared for two things: first, for an
eternal truth that has already carved its traces into millenia; and, second, for
new horizons that I may enter without fear.

Without fear? That is actually an understatement. I enter rather with the
"divine curiosity" of a person who has discovered the new and unknown not
only as something that is hidden but at the same time as something that is
secure. Even that which is new and unknown rests in the peace of those
hands that embrace the orient and the occident, the past and the future.

Precisely this is the curiosity of the believer: it means forging ahead and
not looking back. If the believer is not afraid of the mystery of the future, it is
not for any heroic reason, for he knows who ordains the future and who yet
does not allow the future to become our undoing. The believer knows who
sets the goals and guarantees them. In this knowledge the restlessness of all
our thoughts and quests abates.

What makes us anxious and curious is the question of along which
unknown paths we will be led to goals made known to us.

There is one last explanation that I owe the reader, namely the justification
for implying that we are mere guests or wayfarers on our beautiful planet. I
could well imagine that for those who have been following closely many
passages in my autobiography this bit of otherworldliness might seem a
baffling contradiction.

I was once invited to give a lecture and hold a discussion at the space
center in Houston, Texas. While there I experienced the rapture with which
the astronauts described the sight of our Earth from space: a green oasis of
life in the midst of the vast deserts of the cosmos.

Naturally I also know that this beautiful planet not only knows fragrant
summer meadows and sunny hillsides but also oceans of blood and tears, and
deep, dark valleys. To be sure, in my journey through life I was not spared
painful episodes, such as sickness, the torment of tyranny, and many other
things that I have described. The future also casts its dark shadows over us
and seems to do everything in its power to plunge us into anxiety. Young

people in particular are fearful when they think of what is to come; they, after all, have the longest future.

Why then do I still dare to extol the time we spend on this perilous and beautiful planet? Why am I glad of its hospitality (although I am by nature by no means an optimist)? Why do I look back with gratitude at this eventful three-quarters of a century? Whenever my gaze wishes to bore its way into the overcast future, there comes to my mind God's utterance after the Flood with which he had judged the world: "And it shall come to pass, when I bring a cloud over the earth, that the bow shall be seen in the cloud." This rainbow is intended to assure us of God's abiding concern for our welfare:

> While the earth remains,
> seedtime and harvest, cold and heat,
> summer and winter, day and night,
> I shall not cease.

Time and again I have caught sight of the seven colors of this rainbow glowing in my life—at least when I have ceased to stare monomaniacally into the darkness and raised my eyes to search for it. Indeed, I have encountered no darkness above which it does not shine and no valley, no matter how gloomy, which some of God's greetings have not reached.

Only because of this shining rainbow do I extol our time on this beautiful planet and face the future with confidence. Only on its account am I certain that nothing can separate us from Him who—according to an ancient symbol—holds our earth like a golden ball in his hand.

We are admittedly only guests on this beautiful planet, wayfarers on call and with sealed orders in which the day and hour of our departure are recorded. Our departure is certainly not easy: "I would have loved to have stayed longer, but the wagon's moving on. . . ." But as Christians we are certain that the lifespan allotted us is only the advent of a still greater fulfillment. The land to which we are called is a *terra incognita*—an unknown, even inconceivable land. There is only one voice that we will recognize there because it is already familiar to us here: the voice of the Good Shepherd.

Select List of Publications in English

Man in God's World, translated and edited by John W. Doberstein, New York: Harper & Row, 1963.

Nihilism: Its Origin and Nature—With a Christian Answer, translated by John W. Doberstein. Westport, Conn.: Greenwood, 1981.

Between God and Satan, translated by C.C. Barber. Edinburgh: Oliver and Boyd, 1958.

Theological Ethics, translated by William H. Lazareth, Philadelphia: Fortress Press, 1966–69. Volume I: *Foundations.*

    Part One: Christian Ethics in the Age of Secularism.

    Part Two: The Foundational Principles of Ethics.

    Part Three: Man's Relation to the World.

    Volume II: *Politics.*

    Part One: Political Ethics in the Modern World.

    Part Two: The Nature of the State.

    Part Three: Borderline Situations.

    Part Four: The Theological Debate on Church and State.

    Part Five: The Message of the Church to the World.

The Waiting Father: Sermons on the Parables of Jesus, translated by John W. Doberstein, New York: Harper & Row, 1959.

Encounter with Spurgeon, translated by John W. Doberstein, Philadelphia: Fortress Press, 1963.

How the World Began: Man in the First Chapters of the Bible, translated with an introduction by John W. Doberstein, Philadelphia: Muhlenberg, 1961.

The Ethics of Sex, translated by John W. Doberstein, New York: Harper & Row, 1964.

Faith, the Great Adventure, translated by David L. Schmidt, Philadelphia: Fortress Press, 1985.

The Freedom of the Christian Man: A Christian Confrontation with the Secular Gods, translated by John W. Doberstein, New York: Harper & Row, 1963.

The Hidden Question of God, translated by Geoffrey W. Bromiley, Grand Rapids, Mich.: Eerdmans, 1977.

Christ and the Meaning of Life: a Book of Sermons and Meditations, edited and translated by John W. Doberstein, New York: Harper & Row, 1962.

Our Heavenly Father: Sermons on the Lord's Prayer, translated with an introduction by John W. Doberstein, New York: Harper & Row, 1960.

The Silence of God, introduction and translation by Geoffrey W. Bromiley, Grand Rapids, Mich.: Eerdmans, 1962.

Life Can Begin Again: Sermons on the Sermon on the Mount, translated by John W. Doberstein, Philadelphia: Fortress Press, 1963.

Between Heaven and Earth: Conversations with American Christians, translated and edited by John W. Doberstein, Westport, Conn.: Greenwood, 1975, 1965.

I Believe: the Christian's Creed, translated by John W. Doberstein and H. George Anderson, Philadelphia: Fortress Press, 1968.

How to Believe Again, translated by H. George Anderson, Philadelphia: Fortress Press, 1972.

The Evangelical Faith, translated and edited by Geoffrey W. Bromiley, 3 vols., Grand Rapids, Mich.: Eerdmans, 1974–77.
   Volume One: *Prolegomena. The Relation of Theology to Modern Thought Forms.*
   Volume Two: *The Doctrine of God and of Christ.*
   Volume Three: *Theology of the Spirit.*

Modern Faith and Thought, translated by Geoffrey W. Bromiley, Grand Rapids, Mich.: Eerdmans, 1990.

Living with Death, translated by Geoffrey W. Bromiley, Grand Rapids, Mich.: Eerdmans, 1983.

Being Human—Becoming Human: an Essay in Christian Anthropology, translated by Geoffrey W. Bromiley, Garden City, N.Y.: Doubleday, 1984.

Being a Christian when the Chips Are Down, translated by H. George Anderson, Philadelphia: Fortress Press, 1979.

How Modern Should Theology Be? translated by H. George Anderson, Philadelphia: Fortress Press, 1969.